THE MIDDLE AGES

VOLUME I

THE MIDDLE AGES

VOLUME I

*Sources of
Medieval History*

FOURTH EDITION

BRIAN TIERNEY

Cornell University

ALFRED A. KNOPF 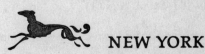 NEW YORK

THIS IS A BORZOI BOOK

PUBLISHED BY ALFRED A. KNOPF, INC.

Fourth Edition

9   8   7

Copyright © 1970, 1973, 1978, 1983 by Alfred A. Knopf,
Inc.

LIBRARY OF CONGRESS CATALOGING IN PUBLICATION DATA

Middle Ages (Knopf, 4th ed.)
    The Middle Ages.

    Contents: v. 1. Sources of medieval history.
    1. Middle Ages—History—Sources.   2. Middle
Ages—History—Addresses, essays, lectures.
I. Tierney, Brian.   II. Title.
D113.M49   1982   940.1   82-4632
ISBN 0-394-33062-5 (v. 1)

Manufactured in the United States of America

NOTE ON THE FOURTH EDITION

This new edition of *Sources of Medieval History* is similar to its predecessors in content and structure. In the early sections new material is included on the Anglo-Saxon church, the conversion of Germany, and the reign of Charlemagne. There are also new selections from Peter Abelard and from Dante. Additional material touching on the activities of medieval women and attitudes toward them is included in readings 21, 26, 47, 50, and 91. In the last part of the book some of the sources from the previous edition have been grouped with fresh readings to form two new chapters, "Fourteenth Century Calamities" and "Late Medieval People."

PREFACE

This two-volume collection of *Sources of Medieval History* and *Readings in Medieval History* is intended for use in college history courses. The collection was prepared to accompany *Western Europe in the Middle Ages, 300–1475*, by Brian Tierney and Sidney Painter, but it can be used equally well with any of the popular textbooks in the field.

The purpose of the work has helped to determine its form. In particular, the amount of introductory, narrative material has been deliberately kept to a minimum. It seemed more useful to present the widest possible variety of medieval *Sources* and modern *Readings* in these volumes rather than to reproduce routine information that any teacher can supply or that the student can find for himself in any standard textbook. Again, while every anthology must reflect to some degree the taste and judgment of its compiler, I have tried not to emphasize unduly my own idiosyncrasies in making the selections. The *Sources* and *Readings* illustrate topics in the mainstream of medieval history, topics that most instructors will want to discuss with their classes.

The *Sources* are drawn from many different kinds of medieval materials. The *Readings* include essays on social, economic, political, religious, and intellectual history. Some of these modern readings are controversial. One or two of them seem to me thoroughly wrongheaded. But they are all writings that my students have enjoyed reading and arguing over. In arranging them I have used a "problem-oriented" approach where this seemed appropriate. For example, the sections on "Spiritual and Temporal Power" and on "The Medieval State" present sharply conflicting views of modern historians on central problems of medieval history. Other sections are intended to illustrate diversity rather than disagreement — to show the various ways in which historians with different backgrounds and different interests will approach the same set of problems. One criterion that I have tried to keep constantly in mind is that of Johann Huizinga—"Unreadable history is no history at all."

CONTENTS

THE THIRTEENTH CENTURY

THE EARLY MIDDLE AGES

chapter

I

The Late Roman Empire

1. Ammianus Marcellinus: Faults of the Roman People

Ammianus Marcellinus (ca. 325–392) was the last major historian who adhered to the old Roman pagan religion. He wrote this account of manners and morals at Rome while living in the city during the last quarter of the fourth century.

And first, as I have often done, so far as space allowed, I shall give an account of the delinquencies of the nobles and then of the common people, condensing the events in a rapid digression. Some men, distinguished (as they think) by famous names, pride themselves beyond measure in being called Reburri, Flavonii, Pagonii, Gereones, and Dalii, along with Tarracii and Pherrasii, and many other equally fine-sounding indications of eminent ancestry. Others, resplendent in silken garments, as though they were to be led to death, or as if (to speak without any evil omen) they were bringing up the rear preceded by an army, are followed by a throng of slaves drawn up in troops, amid noise and confusion. When such men, each attended by fifty servants, have entered the vaulted rooms of a bath, they shout in threatening tones: "Where on earth are our attendants?" If they have learned that an unknown courtesan has suddenly appeared, or a woman who has been a common prostitute of the crowd in a country-town, or some old strumpet, they all strive to be first to rush to her, and caressing the

Reprinted by permission of the publishers and The Loeb Classical Library from Ammianus Marcellinus, *Rerum Gestarum Libri Qui Supersunt*, John C. Rolfe, trans. (Cambridge, Mass.: Harvard University Press, 1939), Vol. III, pp. 141-159.

new-comer, extol her with such disgraceful flattery as the Parthians do Samiramis, the Egyptians their Cleopatras, the Carians Artemisia, or the people of Palmyra Zenobia. And those who stoop to do such things are men in the time of whose forefathers a senator was punished with the censor's brand of infamy, if he had dared, while this was still considered unseemly, to kiss his wife in the presence of their own daughter.

Some of these men, when one begins to salute them breast to breast, like menacing bulls turn to one side their heads, where they should be kissed, and offer their flatterers their knees to kiss or their hands, thinking that quite enough to ensure them a happy life; and they believe that a stranger is given an abundance of all the duties of courtesy, even though the great men may perhaps be under obligation to him, if he is asked what hot baths or waters he uses, or at what house he has been put up.

And although they are so important and, in their own opinion, such cultivators of the virtues, if they learn that someone has announced that horses or chariots are coming from anywhere whatever, these same men hover over them, and ask questions about them, as anxiously as their ancestors looked up to the two sons of Tyndareus, when they filled everything with joy by announcing those famous victories of olden days.

Their houses are frequented by idle chatterboxes, who with various pretences of approval applaud every word of the man of loftier fortune, emulating the witty flatteries of the parasites in the comedies. For just as the parasites puff up boastful soldiers by attributing to them the sieges and battles against thousands of enemies, comparing them with the heroes of old, so these also, admiring the rows of columns hanging in the air with lofty façade, and the walls gleaming with the remarkable colours of precious stones, raise these noble men to the gods. Sometimes at their banquets the scales are even called for, in order to weigh the fish, birds, and dormice that are served, whose great size they commend again and again, as hitherto unexampled, often repeating it to the weariness of those present, especially when thirty secretaries stand near by, with pen-cases and small tablets, recording these same items, so that the only thing lacking seems to be a schoolmaster.

Some of them hate learning as they do poison, and read with attentive care only Juvenal and Marius Maximus, in their boundless idleness handling no other books than these, for what reason it is not for my humble mind to judge. Whereas, considering the greatness of their fame and of their parentage, they ought to pore over many and varied work; they ought to learn that Socrates, when condemned to death and thrown into prison, asked a musician, who was skilfully rendering a song of the lyric poet Stesichorus, that he might be taught to do this while there was still time. And when the musician asked of what use that could be to him, since he was to die on the following day, Socrates replied: "In order that I may know something more before I depart from life."

But a few among them are so strict in punishing offences, that if a slave is slow in bringing the hot water, they condemn him to suffer three hundred lashes; if he has intentionally killed a man, although many people insist that he be condemned to death, his master will merely cry out: "What should a worthless fellow do, notorious for wicked deeds? But if he dares to do anything else like that hereafter, he shall be punished."

But the height of refinement with these men at present is, that it is better for a stranger to kill any man's brother than to decline his invitation to dinner. For a senator thinks that he is suffering the loss of a rich property, if the man whom he has, after considerable weighing of pros and cons, invited once, fails to appear at his table.

Some of them, if they make a longish journey to visit their estates, or to hunt by the labours of others, think that they have equalled the marches of Alexander the Great or of Caesar; or if they have sailed in their gaily-painted boats from the Lake of Avernus to Puteoli, it is the adventure of the golden fleece, especially if they should dare it in the hot season. . . .

Some lie in wait for men of wealth, old or young, childless or unmarried, or even for those who have wives or children—for no distinction is observed in this respect—enticing them by wonderful trickeries to make their wills; and when they have set their last decisions in order and left some things to these men, to humour whom they have made their wills in their favour, they forthwith die; so that you would not think that the death was brought about by the working of the allotment of destiny, nor could an illness easily be proved by the testimony of witnesses; nor is the funeral of these men attended by any mourners.

Another, who attained some rank, moderate though it be, walking with neck puffed up, looks askance at his former acquaintances, so that you might think that a Marcellus was returning after the taking of Syracuse.

Many of them, who deny that there are higher powers in heaven, neither appear in public nor eat a meal nor think they can with due caution take a bath, until they have critically examined the calendar and learned where, for example, the planet Mercury is, or what degree of the constellation of the Crab the moon occupies in its course through the heavens.

· · ·

Let us now turn to the idle and slothful commons. Among them some who have no shoes are conspicuous as though they have cultured names, such as the Messores, Statarii, Semicupae and Serapini, and Cicymbricus, with Gluturinus and Trula, and Lucanicus with Porclaca and Salsula, and countless others. These spend all their life with wine and dice, in low haunts, pleasures, and the games. Their temple, their dwelling, their assembly, and the height of all their hopes is the Circus Maximus. You may see some groups of them gathered in the fora, the cross-roads, the streets, and their other meeting-places, engaged in quarrelsome arguments with one another, some (as usual) defending this, others that. Among them those who have enjoyed a surfeit of life, influential through long experience, often swear by their hoary hair and wrinkles that the state cannot exist if in the coming race the chari-oteer whom each favours is not first to rush forth from the barriers, and fails to round the turning-point closely with his ill-omened horses. And when there is such a dry rot of thoughtlessness, as soon as the longed-for day of the chariot-races begins to dawn, before the sun is yet shining clearly they all hasten in crowds to the spot at top speed, as if they would outstrip the very chariots that are to take part in the con-test; and torn by their conflicting hopes about the result of the race, the great number of them in their anxiety pass sleepless nights.

If from there they come to worthless theatrical pieces, any actor is hissed off the boards who has not won the favour of the low rabble with money. And if this noisy form of demonstration is lacking, they cry in imitation of the Tauric race that all strangers—on whose aid they have always depended and stood upright—ought to be driven from the city. All this in foul and absurd terms, very different from the expression of their interests and desires made by your commons of old, of whose many witty and happy sayings tradition tells us.

2.   Imperial Regimentation: The Theodosian Code

The code of laws promulgated by the emperor Theodosius II in 438 pro-vides much incidental information about social and economic conditions in the late Roman empire.

I, 5, 11. All persons who govern provinces shall exact payment of the delinquent taxes for their term of office when they have laid aside their administration. Those landlords whom no sense of shame can move to fulfill their public obligations shall be notified three times within a year, and if they do not complete all such public obligations, they shall pay double the amount of the debt through the office of Your Magnificence.

V, 17, 1. Any person in whose possession a colonus that belongs to another is found not only shall restore the aforesaid colonus to his birth status but also shall assume the capitation tax for his man for the time that he was with him.

1. Coloni also who meditate flight must be bound with chains and reduced to a servile condition, so that by virtue of their condemnation to slavery, they shall be compelled to fulfill the duties that befit freemen.

V, 19, 1. There is no doubt that coloni do not have the right to alienate the fields that they cultivate, to the extent that even if they have any belongings of their own, they may not transfer them to others without the advice and knowledge of their patrons.

VI, 2, 14. We order that exemption from the payment of the glebal tax shall be granted to all those persons from Macedonia . . .who have been added to the Most August Order of the City of Constantinople [the Senate], according to the precedent of the Senators who were chosen from Thrace.

VII, 2, 2. If any man should desire to take the oaths of imperial service, first of all, in that city in which he was born or in which he has established residence he shall execute formal records and shall thus prove that neither his father nor his grandfather was a decurion and that he is completely free from obligations to the compulsory services of the municipal senate. If he should not do this, he shall know that he will be recalled to perpetual service as a decurion.

XI, 2, 4. Whenever, in accordance with custom, payment is demanded in the case of regular taxes or of taxes due, not the prices of natural products demanded shall be paid, but the natural products themselves. . . .

XI, 24, 3. If any person from your office or from any order of men should be discovered to have received villages into his protection, he shall suffer the established penalties. Moreover, landholders shall be duly coerced to obey the imperial statutes, even against their will, and they shall be forced to satisfy the compulsory public services. But if it should appear that any villages, depending on the power of their protectors or on their own numbers, have resisted the performance of their compulsory public services, they must be subjected to the retribution that is dictated by reason itself.

XII, 1, 13. Since we have learned that the municipal councils are being left desolate by those persons who are obligated to them through birth status and who are requesting imperial services for themselves through supplications to the Emperor and are running away to the legions and various governmental offices, We order all municipal councils to be admonished that if they should apprehend any persons with less than twenty terms of service in governmental offices . . . they shall drag such persons back to the municipal councils. . . .

XII, 1, 62. If a decurion should steal into a guild of artisans for the purpose of evading other duties, he shall be restored to his pristine status, and in the future no person who derives his birth status from decurions shall dare to aspire to the duties of such a guild.

XIV, 3, 8. The office of Your Sincerity shall be on guard that if any man should once and for all be assigned to the guild of breadmakers, he shall not be granted the opportunity and power in any way to withdraw, even if the assent of all the breadmakers should strive to obtain his release and their assembly should appear to have agreed. Not even this privilege shall be granted to any breadmaker, namely, that he may pass from one breadmaking establishment to another.

XIV, 3, 14. If a daughter of a breadmaker should marry any man and afterward, when her fortune had been squandered, he should suppose that she may be released from the guild, We command that he shall be bound to the compulsory duties and guild of breadmaking by the same law and reason as if he were held by the bond of birth service to such compulsory status.

3.   Salvianus: The Burden of Taxation

The Christian priest Salvianus (ca 400–ca. 480) wrote the following description of conditions in Gaul during the middle years of the fifth century. He sought to explain the barbarian invasions as a judgment of God that the Romans had brought upon themselves by their own wickedness.

But what else can these wretched people wish for, they who suffer the incessant and even continuous destruction of public tax levies. To them there is always imminent a heavy and relentless proscription. They desert their homes, lest they be tortured in their very homes.

From *The Writing of Salvian the Presbyter*, J. F. O'Sullivan, trans. (Washington, D.C.: Catholic University of America Press, 1947), pp. 138–141. Reprinted by permission of the publisher.

They seek exile, lest they suffer torture. The enemy is more lenient to them than the tax collectors. This is proved by this very fact, that they flee to the enemy in order to avoid the full force of the heavy tax levy. This very tax levying, athough hard and inhuman, would nevertheless be less heavy and harsh if all would bear it equally and in common. Taxation is made more shameful and burdensome because all do not bear the burden of all. They extort tribute from the poor man for the taxes of the rich, and the weaker carry the load for the stronger. There is no other reason that they cannot bear all the taxation except that the burden imposed on the wretched is greater than their resources.

They suffer from envy and want, which are misfortunes most diverse and unlike. Envy is bound up with payment of the tax; need, with the ability to pay. If you look at what they pay, you will think them abundant in riches, but if you look at what they actually possess, you will find them poverty stricken. Who can judge an affair of this wretchedness? They bear the payment of the rich and endure the poverty of beggars. Much more serious is the following: the rich themselves occasionally make tributary levies which the poor pay.

But, you say, when the assessment due from the rich is very heavy and the taxes due from them are very heavy, how does it happen that they wish to increase their own debt? I do not say that they increase the taxes for themselves. They increase them because they do not increase them for themselves. I will tell you how this is done. Commonly, new envoys, new bearers of letters, come from the imperial offices and those men are recommended to a few well-known men for the mischief of many. For them new gifts are decreed, new taxes are decreed. The powerful levy what the poor are to pay, the courtesy of the rich decrees what the multitude of the wretched are to lose. They themselves in no way feel what they levy.

You say they who were sent by our superiors cannot be honored and generously entertained otherwise. Therefore, you rich men, you who are the first to levy, be the first to give. Be the first in generosity of goods, you who are the first in profusion of words. You who give of mine, give of thine. Most justly, whoever you are, you who alone wish to receive favor, you alone should bear the expense. But to your will, O rich men, we the poor accede. What you, the few, order, we all pay. What is so just, so humane? Your decrees burden us with new debts; at least make your debt common to us all. What is more wicked and more unworthy than that you alone are free from debt, you who make us all debtors?

Indeed, the most wretched poor thus pay all that I have mentioned, but for what cause or for what reason they pay, they are completely ignorant. For, to whom is it lawful to discuss why they pay; to whom is permitted to find out what is owed? Then it is given out most publicly when the rich get angry with each other, when some of them get indignant because some levies a e made without their advice and handling.

Then you may hear it said by some of them, "What an unworthy crime! Two or three decree what kills many; what is paid by many wretched men is decreed by a few powerful men." Each rich man maintains his honor by being unwilling that anything is decreed in his absence, yet he does not maintain justice by being unwilling that evil things be done when he is present. Lastly, what these very men consider base in others they themselves later legalize, either in punishment of a past contempt or in proof of their power. Therefore, the most unfortunate poor are, as it were, in the midst of the sea, between conflicting, violent winds. They are swamped by the waves rolling now from one side, now from the other.

• • •

Do we think we are unworthy of the punishment of divine severity when we thus constantly punish the poor? Do we think, when we are constantly wicked, that God should not exercise His justice against all of us? Where or in whom are evils so great, except among the Romans? Whose injustice so great except our own? The Franks are ignorant of this crime of injustice. The Huns are immune to these crimes. There are no wrongs among the Vandals and none among the Goths. So far are the barbarians from tolerating these injustices among the Goths, that not even the Romans who live among them suffer them.

Therefore, in the districts taken over by the barbarians, there is one desire among all the Romans, that they should never again find it necessary to pass under Roman jurisdiction. In those regions, it is the one and general prayer of the Roman people that they be allowed to carry on the life they lead with the barbarians. And we wonder why the Goths are not conquered by our portion of the population, when the Romans prefer to live among them rather than with us. Our brothers, therefore, are not only altogether unwilling to flee to us from them, but they even cast us aside in order to flee to them.

4.   *Sidonius Apollinaris: Country House Life in Gaul*

Another view of life in fifth-century Gaul was presented in a letter of the aristocratic Sidonius Apollinaris (ca. 431–ca. 488) in about 465. The pleasant routine he described did not last much longer. Sidonius himself was captured and imprisoned by the Visigothic king Euric in 484.

Reprinted by permission of the publisher of The Loeb Classical Library from Sidonius, Poems and Letters, W. B. Anderson, trans. (Cambridge, Mass.: Harvard University Press, 1936), Vol. I, pp. 451-461.

Sidonius to His Friend Donidius, Greeting

You ask me why, having started long ago for Nemausus, I am causing you so long a disappointment by my tardiness in arriving. I will give you my reasons for my belated return, and I will not be slow to explain my slowness, for what is pleasurable to me is to you also. I have spent the most delicious time in visiting two charming properties and two most sympathetic hosts, Ferreolus and Apollinaris. Their estates have a common boundary, and their residences are near, being connected by a road which is long enough to tire the pedestrian but hardly long enough for a ride. The hills which rise above the buildings are cultivated by the vine-dresser and the olivegrower: you would think them Aracynthus and Nysa, those heights so greatly lauded in poetic song. One house has a view over flat and open ground, the other looks out on woods; yet though they differ in their situation they are alike in their charm. But why should I say more of the lie of the farms when there remains to be disclosed the whole scheme of my entertainment? First of all, the cleverest scouts were sent out to keep watch on the route of my return journey, and the two household staffs took up positions not only on the various courses of the public highways but also on the rough tracks with their intricate short cuts and on the bypaths used by shepherds, in order to leave men no chance of eluding the traps which their kindness had arranged. I admit that I was caught, but by no means against my will, and I was at once forced to take an oath that I would not give a thought to the resumption of my journey till seven days were passed. Each morning saw the start of a really charming contest between the two parties about their guest, to decide which of the two kitchens should be the earlier to steam with my meal; and it was really impossible to keep the balance even by alternation, although one house had the tie of kinship with myself, the other with my family; because Ferreolus is of prefectorian rank, and his age and standing, added to the just claims of his relationship, gave him a prior right to invite me. Well, I was hurried from bliss to bliss. Hardly had I entered one vestibule or the other when behold! I found on one side opposing ball-players bending low amid the whirling evolutions of the *catastrophae;* in another quarter I would hear the clatter of rattling dice-boxes and of dice mingled with the rival shouts of the gamesters; in another part were books in any number ready to hand; you might have imagined yourself looking at the shelves of a professional scholar or at the tiers in the Athenaeum or at the towering presses of the booksellers. The arrangement was such that the manuscripts near the ladies' seats were of a devotional type, while those among the gentlemens' benches were works distinguished by the grandeur of Latin eloquence; the latter, however, included certain writings of particular authors which preserve a similarity of style though their doctrines are different; for it was a frequent practice to read writers whose artistry was of a similar kind — here Augustine, there Varro here Horace, there Prudentius. Amongst these books, the translation of the *Adamantius* of Origen by Turranius Rufinus was diligently studied by readers of our faith. We would all join in a discussion, expressing our various views just as we felt inclined. We debated why Origen was condemned by some of our chief hierophants as an inept and dangerous expositor, and yet his works had been translated into Latin with such faithfulness to the letter and the spirit that Apuleius could not be said to have turned Plato's *Phaedo* or Tully Demosthenes' *Ctesiphon* into such a perfect expression of the theory and the usage of Latin speech. While all and sundry occupied themselves in these pursuits according to their individual tastes, a messenger would approach from the head cook to tell us that the time for refreshment was at hand. He had his eye on the passage of the hours as marked by the water-clock, and as the fifth hour was just departing he was proved to have arrived just at the right moment. The luncheon was at once short and lavish, in the style of senators, who have an inherited and established practice of having abundant viands served up on few dishes, although the meal is varied by having some of the meats roasted and others stewed. As we sat over our wine there were short stories, for amusement or instruction; they were started in two sets, bringing mirth and edification respectively. To sum up, our entertainment was moral, elegant, and profuse. We then rose from table, and if we were at Vorocingus (this was the name of one of the estates) we returned to our baggage and our lodging; if we were at Prusianum (so the other property was called) we turned out of their beds Tonantius and his brothers, the flower of all the young nobles of their age, because it was not easy to carry our own sleeping-kit so often from place to place. After shaking off the midday drowsiness we took short rides to whet our appetites, jaded with eating, to the keenness needful for dinner. Both my entertainers had baths in course of erection; in neither case were they in working order. However, when the convivial crowd consisting of my attendants and the household servants, whose heads the hospitable bowl was wont to souse and overpower, had left off drinking, at least for the moment, a trench would be hastily dug close to the spring or the river, and a pile of heated stones poured into it. Then while the ditch was heating it was roofed over with a dome constructed of pliant hazel twigs twined into a hemispherical shape; in addition, rugs of hair-cloth were thrown over this roof, shutting out the light and darkening the open spaces between the twigs, so as to keep in the rising steam which is created by pouring boiling water on hot stones. Here we while away the hours with no lack of witty and humorous conversation, in the course of which we became wrapped and choked in the breath of the hissing mist, which drew forth a wholesome perspiration. When this had poured out sufficiently to please us we plunged into the hot water. Its kindly warmth relaxed us and cleared our clogged digestions, and then we braced ourselves in turn with the cold water of the spring and the well or in the full flow of the river; for I should explain that the river Vardo flows midway between the houses. Except when it is swollen by the melting of the snows and turns yellowish, it has a red tinge caused by the brownish shingle, and it passes down its channels transparent, smooth, and pebbly, but is none the less on that account prolific in choice fishes. I should have gone on to tell you of our dinners — sumptuous ones, I assure you — had not my paper imposed upon my chatter a limit which my sense of decency is failing to set. The record of these feasts would indeed form a pleasant tale, did I not blush to disfigure the back of my letter with a "soaked" pen. But as I am now approaching you in person and intend with Christ's help to visit you immediately, the dinners of my friends will be more expeditiously related when you and I are dining together. I only hope that the completion of a week's interval will see the prompt restoration of that feeling of hunger for which I yearn; when the stomach is upset by a debauch, nothing repairs it so well as abstemiousness. Farewell.

chapter
II

Christianity and the Pagan Tradition

5. The Nicene Creed

During the fourth century the religious life of the Roman empire was transformed by the rise of Christianity. The essential beliefs of the new faith are set out in the following text, a doctrinal statement based on the decisions of the Council of Nicea (325).

We believe in one God, the Father Almighty, maker of all things visible and invisible; and in one Lord Jesus Christ, the Son of God, the only-begotten of his Father, of the substance of the Father, God of God, Light of Light, very God of very God, begotten not made, being of one substance with the Father. By whom all things were made, both which be in heaven and in earth. Who for us men and for our salvation came down [from heaven] and was incarnate and was made man. He suffered and the third day he rose again, and ascended into heaven. And he shall come again to judge both the quick and the dead. And [we believe] in the Holy Ghost. And whosoever shall say that there was time when the Son of God was not, or that before he was begotten he was not, or that he was made of things that were not, or that he is of a different substance or essence [from the Father] or that he is a creature, or subject to change or conversion—all that so say, the Catholic and Apostolic Church anathematizes them.

From *The Seven Ecumenical Councils*, A. C. McGiffert and E. C. Richardson, trans., in Library of the Nicene and Post-Nicene Fathers (2nd Series; New York: Charles Scribner's, 1900), Vol. XIV, p. 3.

6. Two Famous Conversions: Constantine and Augustine

Men abandoned the old pagan religions for a variety of different reasons. Eusebius (ca. 260–ca. 339), bishop of Caesarea, declared that the following description of the conversion of the emperor Constantine was recounted by the emperor himself. However, this account was written more than twenty years after the event it describes, and modern historians have understandably been sceptical about the colorful details. Another Christian author, Lactantius, recorded simply that Constantine had a dream in which he was commanded to paint Christian symbols on his soldiers' shields. This possibly represents the core of historical truth in the story. Certainly men of the fourth century attached great importance to dreams. (See, for example, Ambrose, p. 26, and Jerome, p. 31.)

Being convinced, however, that he [Constantine] needed some more powerful aid than his military forces could afford him, on account of the wicked and magical enchantments which were so diligently practiced by the tyrant [Maxentius], he sought Divine assistance, deeming the possession of arms and a numerous soldiery of secondary importance, but believing the cooperating power of Deity invincible and not to be shaken. He considered, therefore, on what God he might rely for protection and assistance. While engaged in this enquiry, the thought occurred to him, that, of the many emperors who had preceded him, those who had rested their hopes in a multitude of gods, and served them with sacrifices and offerings, had in the first place been deceived by flattering predictions, and oracles which promised them all prosperity, and at last had met with an unhappy end, while not one of their gods had stood by to warn them of the impending wrath of heaven; while one alone who had pursued an entirely opposite course, who had condemned their error, and honored the Supreme God during his whole life, had found him to be the Saviour and Protector of his empire, and the Giver of every good thing. Reflecting on this . . . he judged it to be folly indeed to join in the idle worship of those who were no gods, and after such convincing evidence, to err from the truth; and therefore felt it incumbent on him to honor his father's God alone.

Accordingly he called on Him with earnest prayer and supplications that he would reveal to him who He was, and stretch forth His right

From Eusebius, *Life of Constantine*, E. C. Richardson, trans., in Library of Nicene and Post-Nicene Fathers (2nd Series; New York: Christian Literature Company, 1890), Vol. I, pp. 489–491. *The Confessions of St. Augustine*, J. G. Pilkington, trans., in Library of the Nicene and Post-Nicene Fathers (1st Series; Buffalo: Christian Literature Company, 1896), Vol. I, pp. 60, 61–62, 88, 127–128.

hand to help him in his present difficulties. And while he was thus praying with fervent entreaty, a most marvelous sign appeared to him from heaven, the account of which it might have been hard to believe had it been related by any other person. But since the victorious emperor himself long afterwards declared it to the writer of this history, when he was honored with his acquaintance and society, and confirmed his statement by an oath, who could hesitate to accredit the relation, especially since the testimony of after-time has established its truth? He said that about noon, when the day was already beginning to decline, he saw with his own eyes the trophy of a cross of light in the heavens, above the sun, and bearing the inscription, CONQUER BY THIS. At this sight he himself was struck with amazement, and his whole army also, which followed him on this expedition, and witnessed the miracle.

He said, moreover, that he doubted within himself what the import of this apparition could be. And while he continued to ponder and reason on its meaning, night suddenly came on; then in his sleep the Christ of God appeared to him with the same sign which he had seen in the heavens, and commanded him to make a likeness of that sign which he had seen in the heavens, and to use it as a safeguard in all engagements with his enemies.

At the dawn of day he arose, and communicated the marvel to his friends: and then, calling together the workers in gold and precious stones, he sat in the midst of them, and described to them the figure of the sign he had seen, bidding them represent it in gold and precious stones. And this representation I myself have had an opportunity of seeing.

Now it was made in the following manner. A long spear, overlaid with gold, formed the figure of the cross by means of a transverse bar laid over it. On the top of the whole was fixed a wreath of gold and precious stones; and within this, the symbol of the Saviour's name, two letters indicating the name of Christ by means of its initial characters, the letter P being intersected by X in its centre [i.e., the Greek Chi Rho]: and these letters the emperor was in the habit of wearing on his helmet at a later period. From the cross-bar of the spear was suspended a cloth, a royal piece, covered with a profuse embroidery of most brilliant precious stones; and which, being also richly interlaced with gold, presented an indescribable degree of beauty to the beholder. This banner was of a square form, and the upright staff, whose lower section was of great length, bore a golden half-length portrait of the pious emperor and his children on its upper part, beneath the trophy of the cross, and immediately above the embroidered banner.

The emperor constantly made use of this sign of salvation as a safeguard against every adverse and hostile power, and commanded that others similar to it should be carried at the head of all his armies.

These things were done shortly afterwards. But at the time above specified, being struck with amazement at the extraordinary vision, and resolving to worship no other God save Him who had appeared to him, he sent for those who were acquainted with the mysteries of His doctrines, and enquired who that God was, and what was intended by the sign of the vision he had seen.

They affirmed that He was God, the only begotten Son of the one and only God: that the sign which had appeared was the symbol of immortality, and the trophy of that victory over death which He had gained in time past when sojourning on earth. They taught him also the causes of His advent, and explained to him the true account of His incarnation. Thus he was instructed in these matters, and was impressed with wonder at the divine manifestation which had been presented to his sight. Comparing, therefore, the heavenly vision with the interpretation given, he found his judgment confirmed; and, in the persuasion that the knowledge of these things had been imparted to him by Divine teaching, he determined thenceforth to devote himself to the reading of the Inspired writings.

Moreover, he made the priests of God his counselors, and deemed it incumbent on him to honor the God who had appeared to him with all devotion. And after this, being fortified by well-grounded hopes in Him, he hastened to quench the threatening fire of tyranny.

St. Augustine of Hippo recounted the course of his own conversion—one of the most famous in the history of Christianity—in his autobiographical Confessions.

To Carthage I came, where a cauldron of unholy loves bubbled up all around me. I loved not as yet, yet I loved to love; and, with a hidden want, I abhorred myself that I wanted not. I searched about for something to love, in love with loving, and hating security, and a way not beset with snares. For within me I had a dearth of that inward food, Thyself, my God, though that dearth caused me no hunger; but I remained without all desire for incorruptible food, not because I was already filled thereby, but the more empty I was the more I loathed it. For this reason my soul was far from well, and, full of ulcers, it miserably cast itself forth, craving to be excited by contact with objects of sense. Yet, had these no soul, they would not surely inspire love. To love and to be loved was sweet to me, and all the more when I succeeded in enjoying the person I loved. I befouled, therefore, the spring of friendship with the filth of concupiscence, and I dimmed its lustre with the hell of lustfulness; and yet, foul and dishonourable as I was, I craved, through an excess of vanity, to be thought elegant and urbane. I fell precipitately, then, into the love in which I longed to be ensnared. My God, my mercy, with how much bitterness didst Thou, out of Thy infinite goodness, besprinkle for me that sweetness! For I was both beloved, and secretly arrived at the bond of enjoying; and was joyfully bound with troublesome ties, and I might be scourged with the burning iron rods of jealousy, suspicion, fear, anger, and strife.

. . .

Among such as these, at that unstable period of my life, I studied books of eloquence, wherein I was eager to be eminent from a damnable and inflated purpose, even a delight in human vanity. In the ordinary course of study, I lighted upon a certain book of Cicero, whose language, though not his heart, almost all admire. This book of his contains an exhortation to philosophy, and is called *Hortensius*. This book, in truth, changed my affections, and turned my prayers to Thyself, O Lord, and made me have other hopes and desires. Worthless suddenly became every vain hope to me; and, with an incredible warmth of heart, I yearned for an immortality of wisdom, and began now to arise that I might return to Thee. Not, then, to improve my language—which I appeared to be purchasing with my mother's means, in that my nineteenth year, my father having died two years before—not to improve my language did I have recourse to that book; nor did it persuade me by its style, but its matter.

How ardent was I then, my God, how ardent to fly from earthly things to Thee! Nor did I know how Thou wouldst deal with me. For with Thee is wisdom. In Greek the love of wisdom is called "philosophy," with which that book inflamed me. There be some who seduce through philosophy, under a great, and alluring, and honourable name colouring and adorning their own errors. And almost all who in that and former times were such, are in that book censured and pointed out.

. . .

When, therefore, they of Milan had sent to Rome to the prefect of the city, to provide them with a teacher of rhetoric for their city, and to despatch him at the public expense, I made interest through those identical persons, drunk with Manichaean vanities, to be freed from whom I was going away,—neither of us, however, being aware of it,—that Symmachus, the then prefect, having proved me by proposing a subject, would send me. And to Milan I came, unto Ambrose the bishop, known to the whole world as among the best of men, Thy devout servant; whose eloquent discourse did at that time strenuously dispense unto Thy people the flour of Thy wheat, the "gladness" of Thy "oil," and the sober intoxication of Thy "wine." To him was I unknowingly led by Thee, that by him I might knowingly be led to Thee. That man of God received me like a father, and looked with a benevolent and episcopal kindliness on my change of abode. And I began to love him, not at first, indeed, as a teacher of truth,—which I entirely despaired of in Thy Church,—but as a man friendly to myself. And I studiously hearkened to him preaching to the people, not with the motive I should, but, as it were, trying to discover whether his eloquence came up to the fame thereof, or flowed fuller or lower than was asserted; and I hung on his words intently, but of the matter I was but as a careless and contemptuous spectator; and I was delighted with the pleasantness of his speech, more erudite, yet less cheerful and soothing in manner, than that of Faustus. Of the matter, however, there could be no comparison; for the latter was straying amid Manichaean deceptions, whilst the former was teaching salvation most soundly. But "salvation is far from the wicked," such as I then stood before him; and yet I was drawing nearer gradually and unconsciously.

• • •

But when a profound reflection had, from the secrets depths of my soul, drawn together and heaped up all my misery before the sight of my heart, there arose a mighty storm, accompanied by as mighty a shower of tears. Which, that I might pour forth fully, with its natural expressions, I stole away from Alypius; for it suggested itself to me that solitude was fitter for the business of weeping. So I retired to such a distance that even his presence could not be oppressive to me. Thus was it with me at that time, and he perceived it; for something, I believe, I had spoken, wherein the sound of my voice appeared choked with weeping, and in that state had I risen up. He then remained where we had been sitting, most completely astonished. I flung myself down, how, I know not, under a certain fig-tree, giving free course to my tears, and the streams of mine eyes gushed out, an acceptable sacrifice unto Thee. And, not indeed in these words, yet to this effect, spake I much unto Thee, — "But Thou, O Lord, how long?" "How long, Lord? Wilt Thou be angry for ever? Oh, remember not against us former iniquities"; for I felt that I was enthralled by them. I sent up these sorrowful cries, — "How long, how long? Tomorrow, and tomorrow? Why not now? Why is there not this hour an end to my uncleanness?"

I was saying these things and weeping in the most bitter contritions of my heart, when, lo, I heard the voice as of a boy or girl, I know not which, coming from a neighbouring house, chanting, and oft repeating, "Take up and read; take up and read." Immediately my countenance was changed, and I began most earnestly to consider whether it was usual for children in any kind of game to sing such words; nor could I remember ever to have heard the like. So, restraining the torrent of my tears, I rose up, interpreting it no other way than as a command to me from Heaven to open the book, and to read the first chapter I should light upon. For I had heard of Antony, that, accidentally coming in whilst the gospel was being read, he received the admonition as if what was read were addressed to him. "Go and sell that thou hast, and give to the poor, and thou shalt have treasure in heaven; and come and follow me." And by such oracle was he forthwith converted unto Thee. So quickly I returned to the place where Alypius was sitting; for there had I put down the volume of the apostles, when I rose thence. I grasped, opened, and in silence read that paragraph on which my eyes first fell —"Not in rioting and drunkenness, not in chambering and wantonness, not in strife and envying; but put ye on the Lord Jesus Christ, and make not provision for the flesh, to fulfil the lusts thereof." No further would I read, nor did I need; for instantly, as the sentence ended, — by a light, as it were, of security infused into my heart, — all the gloom of doubt vanished away.

7.   Church and State: The "Edict of Milan"; The Dispute Between Symmachus and Ambrose; Augustine and Gelasius

The "Edict of Milan"

The last persecution of Christians in the Roman empire was halted by edicts of Galerius (311) and Constantine (312). In 313 the emperors Constantine and Licinius met at Milan and agreed on a policy of general toleration for the future. They also promised restitution of property confiscated from the Christians. Although no actual "Edict" was issued at Milan, the following document preserves the terms of the agreement.

We, Constantinus and Licinius the Emperors, having met in concord at Milan and having set in order everything which pertains to the common good and public security, are of the opinion that among the various things which we perceived would profit men, or which should be set in order first, was to be found the cultivation of religion; we should therefore give both to Christians and to all others free facility to follow the religion which each may desire, so that by this means whatever divinity is enthroned in heaven may be gracious and favourable to us and to all who have been placed under our authority. Therefore we are of the opinion that the following decision is in accordance with sound and true reasoning: that no one who has given his mental assent to the Christian persuasion or to any other which he feels to be suitable to him should be compelled to deny his conviction, so that the Supreme Godhead ("Summa Divinitas"), whose worship we freely observe, can assist us in all things with his wonted favour and benevolence. Wherefore it is necessary for your Excellency to know that it is

From S. Z. Ehler and J. B. Morrall, eds. and trans. *Church and State Through the Centuries* (Westminster, Md.: Newman Press, 1954), pp. 5–6; reprinted by permission of the publisher.

our pleasure that all restrictions which were previously put forward in official pronouncements concerning the sect of the Christians should be removed, and that each one of them who freely and sincerely carries out the purpose of observing the Christian religion may endeavour to practise its precepts without any fear or danger. We believed that these points should be fully brought to your attention, so that you might know that we have given free and absolute permission to practise their religion to the Christians. Now that you perceive what we have granted to them, your Excellency must also learn that for the sake of peace in our time a similar public and free right to practise their religion or cult is granted to others, so that every man may have free opportunity to worship according to his own wish. This has been done by us to avoid any appearance of disfavour to any one religion.

We have decided furthermore to decree the following in respect of the Christians: if those places at which they were accustomed in former times to hold their meetings (concerning which a definite procedure was laid down for your guidance in previous communications) have been at any previous time acquired from our treasury or from any other person, let the persons concerned be willing and swift to restore them to the Christians without financial recompense and without trying to ask a price. Let those who have received such property as a gift restore whatever they have acquired to the Christians in similar manner. If those who have brought such property or received it as a gift seek some recompense from our benevolence, let them apply to the Vicar, by whom their cases will be referred to our clemency. You are to consider it your duty that all these things shall be handed over to the Christian body immediately and without delay by your intervention. And since the aforesaid Christians are known to have possessed not only those places at which they are wont to assemble, but others also pertaining to the law of their body, that is of the churches, not of private individuals, you are to order in accordance with the law which we have described above the return of all those possessions to the aforesaid Christians, that is to their bodies and assemblies without any further hesitation or argument. Our previous statement is to be borne in mind that those who restore this property without price may, as we have said, expect some compensation from our benevolence.

The Dispute Between Symmachus and Ambrose

Many problems arose as Christianity became the favored religion of the Roman emperors. Two great thinkers, St. Ambrose (ca. 340–397) and St. Augustine (354–430), sought to define the right relationship between the Christian church and the institutions of the Roman state. Their works were studied throughout the Middle Ages and profoundly influenced medieval thought. In 384 the imperial authorities commanded that the Statue of Victory, a symbol of the pagan religion, be removed from the Roman senate house. The prefect of the city, Symmachus, protested against this decree, and Ambrose replied for the Christians.

The Memorial of Symmachus, Prefect of the City

It is our task to watch on behalf of your Graces. The glory of these times makes it suitable that we defend the institutions of our ancestors and the rights and destiny of our country. That glory is all the greater when you understand that you may not do anything contrary to the custom of your ancestors. We demand then the restoration of that condition of religious affairs which was so long advantageous to the state. Let the rulers of each sect and of each opinion be counted up; a late one[1] practised the ceremonies of his ancestors, a later[2] did not put them away. If the religion of old times does not make a precedent, let the connivance of the last[3] [emperors] do so.

Who is so friendly with the barbarians as not to require an Altar of Victory? . . .

But even if the avoidance of such an omen were not sufficient, it would at least have been seemly to abstain from injuring us, we beseech you, as old men to leave to posterity what we received as boys. The love of customs is great. Justly did the act of the divine Constantius [who earlier removed the Statue of Victory] last but for a short time. All precedents ought to be avoided by you, which you know were soon abolished. We are anxious for the permanence of your glory and your name, that the time to come may find nothing which needs correction.

. . .

The divine Mind has distributed different guardians and different cults to different cities. As souls are separately given to infants as they are born, so to peoples the genius of their destiny. Here comes in the proof from advantage, which most of all vouches to man for the gods. For, since our reason is wholly clouded, whence does the knowledge of the gods more rightly come to us, than from the memory and evidence of prosperity? Now if a long period gives authority to religious customs, we ought to keep faith with so many centuries, and to follow our ancestors, as they happily followed theirs.

Let us now suppose that Rome is present and address you in these words: "Excellent princes, fathers of your country, respect my years to which pious rites have brought me. Let me use the ancestral ceremonies, for I do not repent of them. Let me live after my own fashion,

Letters of St. Ambrose, based on H. De Romestin, trans., in Library of Nicene and Post-Nicene Fathers (2nd Series; New York: Christian Literature Company, 1896), Vol. X, pp. 4141-416, 417-418, 451-452.

[1]Emperor Julian [Ed.].
[2]Emperor Valentinian I [Ed.].
[3]Emperors Valentian I and Valens [Ed.].

for I am free. This worship subdued the world to my laws, these sacred rites repelled Hannibal from the walls, and the Senones from the Capitol. Have I been reserved for this, that in my old age I should be blamed? I will consider what it is thought should be set in order, but tardy and discreditable is the reformation of old age."

We ask, then, for peace for the gods of our fathers and of our country. It is just that all worship should be considered as one. We look on the same stars, the sky is common, the same world surrounds us. What difference does it make by what pains each seeks the truth? We cannot attain to so great a secret by one road; but this discussion is rather for persons at ease, we offer now prayers not conflict.

. . .

And let no one think that I am defending the cause of religion only, for from deeds of this kind have arisen all the misfortunes of the Roman race. The law of our ancestors honoured the Vestal Virgins and the ministers of the gods with a moderate maintenance and just privileges. This grant remained unassailed till the time of the degenerate money-changers, who turned the fund for the support of sacred chastity into hire for common porters. A general famine followed upon this, and a poor harvest disappointed the hopes of all the provinces. This was not the fault of the earth, we impute no evil influence to the stars. Mildew did not injure the crops, nor wild oats destroy the corn; the year failed through the sacrilege, for it was necessary that what was refused to religion should be denied to all.

Ambrose, bishop of Milan, replied to Symmachus in a letter addressed to Emperor Valentinian II.

Ambrose, Bishop, to the most blessed prince and most gracious Emperor Valentinus, the august.

. . .

The illustrious Prefect of the city has in his Memorial set forth three propositions which he considers of force: that Rome, as he says, asks for her rites again, that pay be given to her priests and Vestal Virgins, and that a general famine followed upon the refusal of the priests' stipends.

In his first proposition Rome complains with sad and tearful words, asking, as he says, for the restoration of the rites of her ancient ceremonies. These sacred rites, he says, repulsed Hannibal from the walls, and the Senones from the Capitol. And so at the same time that the power of the sacred rites is proclaimed, their weakness is betrayed. So that Hannibal long insulted the Roman rites, and while the gods were fighting against him, arrived a conqueror at the very walls of the city. Why did they suffer themselves to be besieged, for whom their gods were fighting in arms?

And why should I say anything of the Senones, whose entrance into the inmost Capitol the remnant of the Romans could not have prevented, had not a goose by its frightened cackling betrayed them? See what sort of protectors the Roman temples have. Where was Jupiter at that time? Was he speaking in the goose?

But why should I deny that their sacred rites fought for the Romans? For Hannibal also worshipped the same gods. Let them choose then which they will. If these sacred rites conquered in the Romans, then they were overcome in the Carthaginians; if they triumphed in the Carthaginians, they certainly did not benefit the Romans.

Let, then, that invidious complaint of the Roman people come to an end. Rome has given no such charge. She speaks with other words. Why do you daily stain me with the useless blood of the harmless herd? Trophies of victory depend not on the entrails of the flocks, but on the strength of those who fight. I subdued the world by a different discipline. Camillus was my soldier, who slew those who had taken the Tarpeian rock, and brought back the standards taken from the Capitol; valour laid those low whom religion had not driven off. What shall I say of Attilius [Regulus], who gave the service of his death? Africanus found his triumphs not amongst the altars of the Capitols, but amongst the lines of Hannibal. Why do you bring forward the rites of our ancestors? I hate the rites of Neros. Why should I speak of the Emperors of two months, and the ends of rulers closely joined to their commencements? Or is it perchance a new thing for the barbarians to cross their boundaries? Were they, too, Christians in whose wretched and unprecedented cases, the one, a captive Emperor, and, under the other, the captive world made manifest that their rites which promised victory were false.* Was there then no Altar of Victory? I mourn over my downfall, my old age is tinged with that shameful bloodshed. I do not blush to be converted with the whole world in my old age. It is undoubtedly true that no age is too late to learn. Let that old age blush which cannot amend itself. Not the old age of years is worthy of praise but that of character. There is no shame in passing to better things. This alone was common to me with the barbarians, that of old I knew not God. Your sacrifice is a rite of being sprinkled with the blood of beasts. Why do you seek the voice of God in dead animals? Come and learn on earth the heavenly warfare; we live here, but our warfare is there. Let God Himself, Who made me, teach me the mystery of heaven, not man, who knew not himself. Whom rather than God should I believe concerning God? How can I believe you, who confess that you know not what you worship?

By one road, says he, one cannot attain to so great a secret. What you know not, that we know by the voice of God. And what you seek by fancies, we have found out from the very Wisdom and Truth of God. Your ways, therefore, do not agree with ours. You implore peace

---

*Ambrose refers to the humiliations suffered by Rome in the time of the emperor Valerian and his son, Gallienus. Valerian was captured by the Persians in 260. Under Gallienus a group of generals known as the "Thirty Tyrants" dominated the empire [Ed.].

for your gods from the Emperors, we ask for peace for the Emperors themselves from Christ. You worship the works of your own hands, we think it an offence that anything which can be made should be esteemed God. God wills not that He should be worshipped in stones. And, in fine, your philosophers themselves have ridiculed these things.

Ambrose wanted the Roman state to protect the church but he also defended the autonomy of the church against the state. The following letter was written to Emperor Valentinian II in 386.

Ambrose, Bishop, to the most gracious Emperor and Blessed Augustus, Valentianian.

. . . No one ought to consider me contumacious when I affirm what you father of august memory not only replied by word of mouth, but also sanctioned by his laws, that, in a matter of faith, or any ecclesiastical ordinance, he should judge who was not unsuited by office, nor disqualified by equity, for these are the words of the rescript. That is, it was his desire that priests should judge concerning priests. Moreover, if a bishop were accused of other matters also, and a question of character was to be enquired into, it was also his will that this should be reserved for the judgment of bishops.

Who, then, has answered your Clemency contumaciously? He who desires that you should be like your father, or he that wishes you to be unlike him? Unless, perhaps, the judgment of so great an Emperor seems to any persons of small account, whose faith has been proved by the constancy of his profession, and his wisdom declared by the continual improvement of the State.

When have you heard, most gracious Emperor, that laymen gave judgment concerning a bishop in a matter of faith? Are we so prostrate through the flattery of some as to be unmindful of the rights of the priesthood, and do I think that I can entrust to others what God has given me? If a bishop is to be taught by a layman, what will follow? Let the layman argue, and the bishop listen, let the bishop learn of the layman. But undoubtedly, whether we go through the series of the holy Scriptures, or the times of old, who is there who can deny that, in a matter of faith, — in a matter I say of faith, — bishops are wont to judge of Christian emperors, not emperors of bishops.

The same spirit of independence appears in a letter of Ambrose to Theodosius I, written in 390, rebuking the emperor for commanding a massacre in the city of Thessalonica.

Listen, august Emperor. I cannot deny that you have a zeal for the faith; I do confess that you have the fear of God. But you have a natural vehemence, which, if any one endeavours to soothe, you quickly turn to mercy; if any one stirs it up, you rouse it so much more that you can scarcely restrain it. Would that if no one soothe it, at least no one may inflame it! To yourself I willingly entrust it, you restrain yourself, and overcome your natural vehemence by the love of piety.

This vehemence of yours I preferred to commend privately to your own consideration, rather than possibly raise it by any action of mine in public. And so I have preferred to be somewhat wanting in duty rather than in humility, and that others should rather think me wanting in priestly authority than that you should find me lacking in most loving reverence, that having restrained your vehemence your power of deciding on your counsel should not be weakened. I excuse myself by bodily sickness, which was in truth severe, and scarcely to be lightened but by great care. Yet I would rather have died than not wait two or three days for your arrival. But it was not possible for me to do so.

There was that done in the city of the Thessalonians of which no similar record exists, which I was not able to prevent happening; which, indeed, I had before said would be most atrocious when I so often petitioned against it, and that which you yourself show by revoking it too late you consider to be grave, this I could not extenuate when done.

• • •

You are a man, and [temptation] has come upon you, conquer it. Sin is not done away but by tears and penitence. Neither angel can do it, nor archangel. The Lord Himself, Who alone can say, "I am with you," if we have sinned, does not forgive any but those who repent.

I urge, I beg, I exhort, I warn, for it is a grief to me, that you who were an example of unusual piety, who were conspicuous for clemency, who would not suffer single offenders to be put in peril, should not mourn that so many have perished. Though you have waged battle most successfully, though in other matters, too, you are worthy of praise, yet piety was ever the crown of your actions. The devil envied that which was your most excellent possession. Conquer him whilst you still possess that wherewith you may conquer. Do not add another sin to your sin by a course of action which has injured many.

I, indeed, though a debtor to your kindness, for which I cannot be ungrateful, that kindness which has surpassed that of many emperors, and has been equalled by one only; I, I say, have no cause for a charge of contumacy against you, but have cause of fear; I dare not offer the sacrifice if you intend to be present. Is that which is not allowed after shedding blood of one innocent person, allowed after shedding the blood of many? I do not think so.

Lastly, I am writing with my own hand that which you alone may read. As I hope that the Lord will deliver me from all troubles, I have been warned, not by man, nor through man, but plainly by Himself that this is forbidden me. For when I was anxious, in the very night in which I was preparing to set out, you appeared to me in a dream to have come into the Church, and I was not permitted to offer sacrifice.

I pass over other things, which I could have avoided, but I bore them for love of you, as I believe. May the Lord cause all things to pass peaceably. Our God gives warnings in many ways, by heavenly signs, by the precepts of the prophets; by the visions even of sinners He wills that we should understand, that we should entreat Him to take away all disturbances, to preserve peace for you emperors, that the faith and peace of the Church, whose advantage it is that emperors should be Christians and devout, may continue.

Augustine and Gelasius

The most profound discussion of the relationship between the Christian church and the Roman empire was Augustine's City of God. *It was not so much a theory of church and state as a philosophy of history. Augustine saw the whole human race divided into two "cities"—one made up of those who loved God and the other of those who rejected him.*

. . . This race we have distributed into two parts, the one consisting of those who live according to man, the other of those who live according to God. And these we also mystically call the two cities, or the two communities of men, of which one is predestined to reign eternally with God, and the other to suffer eternal punishment with the devil. This, however, is their end, and of it we are to speak afterwards. At present, as we have said enough about their reign, whether among the angels, whose numbers we know not, or in the two first human beings, it seems suitable to attempt an account of their career, from the time when our two first parents began to propagate the race until all human generation shall cease. For this whole time or world-age, in which the dying give place and those who are born succeed, is the career of these two cities concerning which we treat.

Of these two first parents of the human race, then, Cain was the first-born, and he belonged to the city of man; after him was born Abel, who belonged to the city of God. For as in the individual the truth of the apostle's statement is discerned, "that is not first which is spiritual, but that which is natural, and afterward that which is spiritual," whence it comes to pass that each man, being derived from a condemned stock, is first of all born of Adam evil and carnal, and becomes good and spiritual only afterwards, when he is grafted into Christ by regeneration: so was it in the human race as a whole. When these two cities began to run their course by a series of deaths and births, the citizen of this world was the first-born, and after him the stranger

From Augustine, *The City of God,* Marcus Dodds, trans. (Edinburgh: T. and T. Clark, 1871), Vol. II, pp. 49–51, 326–328. Pope Gelasius in *The Crisis of Church and State, 1050–1300,* with selected documents. © 1964 (Englewood Cliffs, N.J.: Prentice-Hall, 1964), pp. 13–14; reprinted by permission of Prentice-Hall, Inc., Englewood Cliffs, New Jersey.

in this world, the citizen of the city of God, predestinated by grace, elected by grace, by grace a stranger below, and by grace a citizen above. By grace, — for so far as regards himself he is sprung from the same mass, all of which is condemned in its origin; but God, like a potter (for this comparison is introduced by the apostle judiciously, and not without thought), of the same lump made one vessel to honour, another to dishonour. But first the vessel to dishonour was made, and after it another to honour. For in each individual, as I have already said, there is first of all that which is reprobate, that from which we must begin, but in which we need not necessarily remain; afterwards is that which is well-approved, to which we may by advancing attain, and in which, when we have reached it, we may abide. Not, indeed, that every wicked man shall be good, but that no one will be good who was not first of all wicked; but the sooner any one becomes a good man, the more speedily does he receive this title, and abolish the old name in the new. Accordingly, it is recorded of Cain that he built a city, but Abel, being a sojourner, built none. For the city of the saints is above, although here below it begets citizens, in whom it sojourns till the time of its reign arrives, when it shall gather together all in the day of the resurrection; and then shall the promised kingdom be given to them, in which they shall reign with their Prince, the King of the ages, time without end.

• • •

But the families which do not live by faith seek their peace in the earthly advantages of this life; while the families which live by faith look for those eternal blessings which are promised, and use as pilgrims such advantages of time and of earth as do not fascinate and divert them from God, but rather aid them to endure with greater ease, and to keep down the number of those burdens of the corruptible body which weigh upon the soul. Thus the things necessary for this mortal life are used by both kinds of men and families alike, but each has its own peculiar and widely different aim in using them. The earthly city, which does not live by faith, seeks an earthly peace, and the end it proposes, in the well-ordered concord of civic obedience and rule, is the combination of men's wills to attain the things which are helpful to this life. The heavenly city, or rather the part of it which sojourns on earth and lives by faith, makes use of this peace only because it must, until this mortal condition which necessitates it shall pass away. Consequently, so long as it lives like a captive and a stranger in the earthly city, though it has already received the promise of redemption, and the gift of the Spirit as the earnest of it, it makes no scruple to obey the laws of the earthly city, whereby the things necessary for the maintenance of this mortal life are administered; and thus, as this life is common to both cities, so there is a harmony between them in regard to what belongs to it. But, as the earthly city has had some philosophers whose doctrine is condemned by the divine teaching . . . it has come to pass that the two cities could not have common laws of religion, and that the heavenly city has been compelled in this matter to dissent, and to become obnoxious to those who think differently, and to stand the brunt of their anger and hatred and persecutions, except in so far as the minds of their enemies have been alarmed by the multitude of the Christians and quelled by the manifest protection of God accorded to them. This heavenly city, then, while it sojourns on earth, calls citizens out of all nations, and gathers together a society of pilgrims of all languages, not scrupling about diversities in the manners, laws, and institutions whereby earthly peace is secured and maintained, but recognizing that, however various these are, they all tend to one and the same end of earthly peace. It therefore is so far from rescinding and abolishing these diversities, that it even preserves and adopts them, so long only as no hindrance to the worship of the one supreme and true God is thus introduced. Even the heavenly city, therefore, while in its state of pilgrimage, avails itself of the peace of earth, and, so far as it can without injuring faith and godliness, desires and maintains a common agreement among men regarding the acquisition of the necessaries of life, and makes this earthly peace bear upon the peace of heaven; for this alone can be truly called and esteemed the peace of the reasonable creatures, consisting as it does in the perfectly ordered and harmonious enjoyment of God and of one another in God. When we shall have reached that peace, this mortal life shall give place to one that is eternal, and our body shall be no more this animal body which by its corruption weighs down the soul, but a spiritual body feeling no want, and in all its members subjected to the will. In its pilgrim state the heavenly city possesses this peace by faith; and by this faith it lives righteously when it refers to the attainment of that peace every good action towards God and man; for the life of the city is a social life.

Pope Gelasius I (492–496) provided a classical definition of the right relationship between priesthood and kingship in this letter written to Emperor Anastasius in 494. The text was included in later collections of canon law and elaborately discussed by medieval jurists.

. . . Two there are, august emperor, by which this world is chiefly ruled, the sacred authority [*auctoritas*] of the priesthood and the royal power [*potestas*]. Of these the responsibility of the priests is more weighty in so far as they will answer for the kings of men themselves at the divine judgment. You know, most clement son, that, although you take precedence over all mankind in dignity, nevertheless you piously bow the neck to those who have charge of divine affairs and seek from them the means of your salvation, and hence you realize that, in the order of religion, in matters concerning the reception and right administration of the heavenly sacraments, you ought to submit yourself rather than rule, and that in these matters you should depend on their judgment rather than seek to bend them to your will. For if the bishops themselves, recognizing that the imperial office was conferred on you by divine disposition, obey your laws so far as the sphere of public order is concerned lest they seem to obstruct your decrees in mundane matters, with what zeal, I ask you, ought you to obey those who have been charged with administering the sacred mysteries? Moreover, just as no light risk attends pontiffs who keep silent in matters concerning the service of God, so too no little danger threatens those who show scorn—which God forbid—when they ought to obey. And if the hearts of the faithful should be submitted to all priests in general who rightly administer divine things, how much more should assent be given to the bishop of that see which the Most High wished to be preeminent over all priests, and which the devotion of the whole church has honored ever since. As Your Piety is certainly well aware, no one can ever raise himself by purely human means to the privilege and place of him whom the voice of Christ has set before all, whom the church has always venerated and held in devotion as its primate. The things which are established by divine judgement can be assailed by human presumption; they cannot be overthrown by anyone's power.

8.   Jerome on Classical Literature

The third of the three great Western fathers (along with Ambrose and Augustine) was St. Jerome (354–420). One of his major works was a translation of the Bible into Latin, and naturally he was much concerned about the right attitude of Christians to the literary tradition of Rome. His acceptance of the need for literary studies—although somewhat grudging—was important for the future development of Christian scholarship.

To Eustochium

Many years ago, when for the kingdom of heaven's sake I had cut myself off from home, parents, sisters, relations, and—harder still—from the dainty food to which I had been accustomed; and when I was on my way to Jerusalem to wage my warfare, I still could not bring myself to forego the library which I had formed for myself at Rome with great care and toil. And so, miserable man that I was, I would fast only that I might afterwards read Cicero. After many nights spent in vigil, after floods of tears called from my inmost heart, after the recollection of my past sins, I would once more take up Plautus. And when at times I

From Jerome, *Letters*, W. H. Fremantle, trans., Library of Nicene and Post-Nicene Fathers (2nd Series; New York: Christian Literature Company, 1893), Vol. VI, pp. 35, 149.

returned to my right mind, and began to read the prophets, their style seemed rude and repellent. I failed to see the light with my blinded eyes; but I attributed the fault not to them, but to the sun. While the old serpent was thus making me his plaything, about the the middle of Lent a deep-seated fever fell upon my weakened body, and while it destroyed my rest completely—the story seems hardly credible—it so wasted my unhappy frame that scarcely anything was left of me but skin and bone. Meantime preparations for my funeral went on; my body grew gradually colder, and the warmth of life lingered only in my throbbing breast. Suddenly I was caught up in the spirit and dragged before the judgement seat of the Judge; and here the light was so bright, and those who stood around were so radiant, that I cast myself upon the ground and did not dare to look up. Asked who and what I was I replied: "I am a Christian." But He who presided said: "Thou liest, thou art a follower of Cicero and not of Christ. For 'where thy treasure is, there will thy heart be also.' " Instantly I became dumb, and amid the strokes of the lash—for He had ordered me to be scourged—I was tortured more severely still by the fire of conscience, considering with myself that verse, "In the grave who shall give thee thanks?" Yet for all that I began to cry and to bewail myself, saying: "Have mercy upon me, O Lord: have mercy upon me."

To Magnus, an Orator of Rome:

You ask me at the close of your letter why it is that sometimes in my writings I quote examples from secular literature and thus defile the whiteness of the church with the foulness of heathenism. I will now briefly answer your question. You would never have asked it, had not your mind been wholly taken up with Tully; you would never have asked it had you made it a practice instead of studying Volcatius to read the holy scriptures and the commentators upon them. For who is there who does not know that both in Moses and in the prophets there are passages cited from Gentile books and that Solomon proposed questions to the philosophers of Tyre and answered others put to him by them. In the commencement of the book of Proverbs he charges us to understand prudent maxims and shrewd adages, parables and obscure discourse, the words of the wise and their dark sayings; all of which belong by right to the sphere of the dialectician and the philosopher. The Apostle Paul also, in writing to Titus, has used a line of the poet Epimenides: "The Cretians are always liars, evil beasts, slow bellies." Half of which line was afterwareds adopted by Callimachus.

• • •

And as if this were not enough, that leader of the Christian army, that unvanquished pleader for the cause of Christ [Paul], skilfully turns a chance inscription into a proof of the faith. For he had learned from the true David to wrench the sword of the enemy out of his hand and with his own blade to cut off the head of the arrogant Goliath. He had read in Deuteronomy the command given by the voice of the Lord that when a captive woman had had her head shaved, her eyebrows and all her hair cut off, and her nails pared, she might then be taken to wife. Is it surprising that I too, admiring the fairness of her form and the grace of her eloquence, desire to make that secular wisdom which is my captive and my handmaid, a matron of the true Israel? Or that shaving off and cutting away all in her that is dead whether this be idolatry, pleasure, error, or lust, I take her to myself clean and pure and beget by her servants for the Lord of Sabaoth? My efforts promote the advantage of Christ's family, my so-called defilement with an alien increases the number of my fellow-servants. Hosea took a wife of whoredoms, Gomer the daughter of Diblaim, and this harlot bore him a son called Jezreel or the seed of God. Isaiah speaks of a sharp razor which shaves "the head of sinners and the hair of their feet": and Ezekiel shaves his head as a type of that Jerusalem which has been an harlot, in sign that whatever in her is devoid of sense and life must be removed.

III

The Barbarians

9. The Germania of Tacitus

*The earliest detailed description of the Germanic peoples was written by the
Roman historian Tacitus at the end of the first century after Christ.*

Boundaries of Germany. Germany is separared from the Galli, the
Rhaeti, and Pannonii, by the rivers Rhine and Danube; mountain
ranges, or the fear which each feels for the other, divide it from the
Sarmatae and Daci. Elsewhere ocean girds it, embracing broad penin-
sulas and islands of unexplored extent, where certain tribes and kingdoms are newly known to us, revealed by war. The Rhine springs from
a precipitous and inaccessible height of the Rhaetian Alps, bends
slightly westward, and mingles with the Northern Ocean. The Danube
pours down from the gradual and gently rising slope of Mount Ab-
noba, and visits many nations, to force its way at last through six
channels into the Pontus; a seventh mouth is lost in marshes.

The Inhabitants. Origins of the Name "Germany." The Germans
themselves I should regard as aborignal, and not mixed at all with
other races through immigration or intercourse. For, in former times,
it was not by land but on shipboard that those who sought to emigrate
would arrive; and the boundless and, so to speak, hostile ocean beyond
us, is seldom entered by a sail from our world. And, beside the perils
of rough and unknown seas, who would leave Asia, or Africa, or Italy
for Germany, with its wild country, its inclement skies, its sullen manners and aspect, unless indeed it were his home? In their ancient

From Tacitus, *The Agricola and Germany,* A. J. Church and W. J. Brodribb, trans.
(London: Macmillan, 1877), pp. 87-107.

songs, their only way of remembering or recording the past, they celebrate an earth-born god Tuisco, and his son Mannus, as the origin of
their race, as their founders. To Mannus they assign three sons, from
whose names, they say, the coast tribes are called Ingaevones; those of
the interior, Herminones; all the rest, Istaevones. Some, with the freedom of conjecture permitted by antiquity, assert that the god had several descendants, and the nation several appellations, as Marsi, Gam-
brivii, Suevi, Vandilii, and that these are genuine old names. The
name Germany, on the other hand, they say, is modern and newly introduced, from the fact that the tribes which first crossed the Rhine
and drove out the Gauls, and are now called Tungrians, were then
called Germans. Thus what was the name of a tribe, and not of a race,
gradually prevailed, till all called themselves by this self-invented
name of Germans, which the conquerors had first employed to inspire
terror.

The National War-Songs. Legend of Ulysses.   They say that Hercules, too, once visited them; and when going into battle, they sing of
him first of all heroes. They have also those songs of theirs, by the re-
cital of which ("baritus," they call it), they rouse their courage, while
from the note they augur the result of the approaching conflict. For,
as their line shouts, they inspire or feel alarm. It is not so much an ar-
ticulate sound, as a general cry of valor. They aim chiefly at a harsh
note and a confused roar, putting their shields to their mouth, so that,
by reverberation, it may swell into a fuller and deeper sound. Ulysses,
too, is believed by some, in his long legendary wanderings, to have
found his way into this ocean, and, having visited German soil, to have
founded and named the town of Asciburgium, which stands on the
bank of the Rhine, and is to this day inhabited. They even say that an
altar dedicated to Ulysses, with the addition of the name of his father,
Laertes, was formerly discovered on this same spot, and that certain
monuments and tombs, with Greek inscriptions, still exist on the borders of Germany and Rhaetia. These statements I have no intention of
sustaining by proofs, or of refuting; every one may believe or disbelieve
them as he feels inclined.

Physical Characteristics.   For my own past, I agree with those who
think that the tribes of Germany are free from all taint of intermar-
riages with foreign nations, and that they appear as a distinct, unmixed
race, like none but themselves. Hence, too, the same physical pecu-
liarities throughout so vast a population. All have fierce blue eyes, red
hair, huge frames, fit only for a sudden exertion. They are less able to
bear laborious work. Heat and thirst they cannot in the least endure;
to cold and hunger their climate and their soil inure them.

Climate and Soil. Precious Metals.   Their country, though somewhat various in appearance, yet generally either bristles with forests or
reeks with swamps; it is more rainy on the side of Gaul, bleaker on that
of Noricum and Pannonia. It is productive of grain, but unfavourable

to fruit-bearing trees; it is rich in flocks and herds, but these are for the most part undersized, and even the cattle have not their usual beauty or noble head. It is number that is chiefly valued; they are in fact the most highly prized, indeed the only riches of the people. Silver and gold the gods have refused to them, whether in kindness or in anger I cannot say. I would not, however, affirm that no vein of German soil produces gold or silver, for who has ever made a search? They care but little to possess or use them. You may see among them vessels of silver, which have been presented to their envoys and chieftains, held as cheap as those of the clay. The border population, however, value gold and silver for their commerical utility, and are familiar with, and show preference for, some of our coins. The tribes of the interior use the simpler and more ancient practice of the barter of commodities. They like the old and well-known money, coins milled, or showing a two-horse chariot. They likewise prefer silver to gold, not from any special liking, but because a large number of silver pieces is more convenient for use among dealers in cheap and common articles.

Arms, Military Manoeuvres, and Discipline. Even iron is not plentiful with them, as we infer from the character of their weapons. But few use swords or long lances. They carry a spear (*framea* is their name for it), with a narrow and short head, but so sharp and easy to wield that the same weapon serves, according to circumstances, for close or distant conflict. As for the horse-soldier, he is satisfied with a shield and spear; the foot-soldiers also scatter showers of missiles, each man having several and hurling them to an immense distance, and being naked or lightly clad with a little cloak. There is no display about their equipment; their shields alone are marked with very choice colours. A few only have corslets, and just one or two here and there a metal or leathern helmet. Their horses are remarkable neither for beauty nor for fleetness. Nor are they taught various evolutions after our fashion, but are driven straight forward, or so as to make one wheel to the right in such a compact body that none is left behind another. On the whole, one would say that their chief strength is in their infantry, which fights along with the cavalry; admirably adapted to the action of the latter is the swiftness of certain foot-soldiers, who are picked from the entire youth of their country, and stationed in front of the line. Their number is fixed—a hundred from each canton; and from this they take their name among their countrymen, so that what was originally a mere number has now become a title of distinction. Their line of battle is drawn up in a wedge-like formation. To give ground, provided you return to the attack, is considered prudence rather than cowardice. The bodies of their slain they carry off even in indecisive engagements. To abandon your shield is the basest of crimes; nor may a man thus disgraced be present at the sacred rites, or enter their council; many, indeed, after escaping from battle, have ended their infamy with the halter.

Government. Influence of Women.   They choose their kings by birth, their generals for merit. These kings have not unlimited or arbitrary power, and the generals do more by example than by authority. If they are energetic, if they are conspicuous, if they fight in the front, they lead because they are admired. But to reprimand, to imprison, even to flog, is permitted to the priests alone, and that not as a punishment, or at the general's bidding, but, as it were, by the mandate of the god whom they believe to inspire the warrior. They also carry with them into battle certain figures and images taken from their sacred groves. And what most stimulates their courage is, that their squadrons or battalions, instead of being formed by chance or by a fortuitous gathering, are composed of families and clans. Close by them, too, are those dearest to them, so that they hear the shrieks of women, the cries of infants. *They* are to every man the most sacred witnesses of his bravery—*they* are his most generous applauders. The soldier brings his wounds to mother and wife, who shrink not from counting or even demanding them and who administer food and encouragement to the combatants.

Tradition says that armies already wavering and giving way have been rallied by women who, with earnest entreaties and bosoms laid bare, have vividly represented the horrors of captivity, which the Germans fear with such extreme dread on behalf of their women, that the strongest tie by which a state can be bound is the being required to give, among the number of hostages, maidens of noble birth. They even believe that the sex has a certain sanctity and prescience, and they do not despise their counsels, or make light of their answers. In Vespasian's days we saw Veleda, long regarded by many as a divinity. In former times, too, they venerated Aurinia, and many other women, but not with servile flatteries, or with sham deification.

Deities.   Mercury is the deity whom they chiefly worship, and on certain days they deem it right to sacrifice to him even with human victims. Hercules and Mars they appease with more lawful offerings. Some of the Suevi also sacrifice to Isis. Of the occassion and origin of this foreign rite I have discovered nothing, but that the image, which is fashioned like a light galley, indicates an imported worship. The Germans, however, do not consider it consistent with the grandeur of celestial beings to confine the gods within walls, or to liken them to the form of any human countenance. They consecrate woods and groves, and they apply the names of deities to the abstraction which they see only in spiritual worship.

Auguries and Method of Divination.   Augury and divination by lot no people practise more diligently. The use of the lots is simple. A little bough is lopped off a fruit-bearing tree, and cut into small pieces; these are distinguished by certain marks, and thrown carelessly and at random over a white garment. In public questions the priest of the particular state, in private the father of the family, invokes the gods, and, with his eyes toward heaven, takes up each piece three times, and finds in them a meaning according to the mark previously impressed on them. If they prove unfavourable, there is no further consultation that day about the matter; if they sanction it, the confirmation of augury is still required. For they are also familiar with the practice of consulting the notes and the flight of birds. It is peculiar to this people to seek omens and monitions from horses. Kept at the public expense, in these same woods and groves, are white horses, pure from the taint of earthly labour; these are yoked to a sacred car, and accompanied by the priest and the king, or chief of the tribe, who note their neighings and snortings. No species of augury is more trusted, not only by the people and by the nobility, but also by the priests, who regard themselves as the ministers of the gods, and the horses as acquainted with their will. They have also another method of observing auspices, by which they seek to learn the result of an important war. Having taken, by whatever means, a prisoner from the tribe with whom they are at war, they pit him against a picked man of their own tribe, each combatant using the weapons of their country. The victory of the one or the other is accepted as an indication of the issue.

Councils. About minor matters the chiefs deliberate, about the more important the whole tribe. Yet even when the final decision rests with the people, the affair is always thoroughly discussed by the chiefs. They assemble, except in the case of a sudden emergency, on certain fixed days, either at new or at full moon; for this they consider the most auspicious season for the transaction of business. Instead of reckoning by days as we do, they reckon by nights, and in this manner fix both their ordinary and their legal appointments. Night they regard as bringing on day. Their freedom has this disadvantage, that they do not meet simultaneously or as they are bidden, but two or three days are wasted in the delays of assembling. When the multitude think proper, they sit down armed. Silence is proclaimed by the priests, who have on these occassions the right of keeping order. Then the king or the chief, according to age, birth, distinction in war, or eloquence, is heard, more because he has influence to persuade than because he has power to command. If his sentiments displease them, they reject them with murmurs; if they are satisfied, they brandish their spears. The most complimentary form of assent is to express approbation with their spears.

Punishments. Administration of Justice. In their councils an accusation may be preferred or a capital crime prosecuted. Penalties are distinguished according to the offence. Traitors and deserters are hanged on trees; the coward, the unwarlike, the man stained with abominable vices, is plunged into the mire of the morass with a hurdle put over him. This distinction in punishment means that crime, they think, ought, in being punished, to be exposed, while infamy ought to be buried out of sight. Lighter offences, too, have penalties proportioned to them; he who is convicted, is fined in a certain number of horses or of cattle. Half of the fine is paid to the king or to the state, half to the person whose wrongs are avenged and to his relatives. In these same councils they also elect the chief migistrates, who administer law in the cantons and the towns. Each of these has a hundred associates chosen from the people, who support him with their advice and influence.

Training of the Youth.   They transact no public or private business without being armed. It is not, however, usual for anyone to wear arms till the state has recognized his power to use them. Then in the presence of the council one of the chiefs, or the young man's father, or some kinsman, equips him with a shield and a spear. These arms are what the "toga" is with us, the first honour with which youth is invested. Up to this time he is regarded as a member of a household, afterwards as a member of the commonwealth. Very noble birth or great services rendered by the father secure for lads the rank of a chief; such lads attach themselves to men of mature strength and of long approved valour. It is no shame to be seen among a chief's followers. Even in his escort there are gradations of rank, dependent on the choice of the man to whom they are attached. These followers vie keenly with each other as to who shall rank first with his chiefs, the chiefs as to who shall have the most numerous and the bravest followers. It is an honour as well as a source of strength to be thus always surrounded by a large body of picked youths; it is an ornament in peace and a defence in war. And not only in his own tribe but also in the neighboring states it is the renown and glory of a chief to be distinguished for the number and valour of his followers, for such a man is courted by embassies, is honoured with presents, and the very prestige of his name often settles a war.

Warlike Ardour of the People.   When they go into battle, it is a disgrace for the chief to be surpassed in valour, a disgrace for his followers not to equal the valour of the chief. And it is an infamy and a reproach for life to have survived the chief, and returned from the field. To defend, to protect him, to ascribe one's own brave deeds to his renown, is the height of loyalty. The chief fights for victory; his vassals fight for their chief. If their native state sinks into the sloth of prolonged peace and repose, many of its noble youths voluntarily seek those tribes which are waging some war, both because inaction is odious to their race, and because they win renown more readily in the midst of peril, and cannot maintain a numerous following except by violence and war. Indeed, men look to the liberality of their chief for their war-horse and their bloodstained and victorious lance. Feasts and entertainments, which, though inelegant, are plentifully furnished, are their only pay. The means of this bounty come from war and rapine. Nor are they as easily persuaded to plough the earth and to wait for the year's produce as to challenge an enemy and earn the honour of wounds. Nay, they actually think it tame and stupid to acquire by the sweat of toil what they might win by their blood.

Habits in Time of Peace.   Whenever they are not fighting, they pass much of their time in the chase, and still more in idleness, giving themselves up to sleep and to feasting, the bravest and the most warlike doing nothing, and surrendering the management of the household, of the home, and of the land, to the women, the old men, and all the weakest members of the family. They themselves lie buried in sloth, a strange combination in their nature that the same men should be so fond of idleness, so averse to peace. It is the custom of the states to bestow by voluntary and individual contribution on the chiefs a present of cattle or of grain, which, while accepted as a compliment, supplies their wants. They are particularly delighted by gifts from neighbouring tribes, which are sent not only by individuals but also by the state, such as choice steeds, heavy armour, trappings, and neck-chains. We have now taught them to accept money also.

Arrangement of Their Towns. Subterranean Dwellings.   It is well known that the nations of Germany have not cities, and that they do not even tolerate closely contiguous dwellings. They live scattered and apart, just as a spring, a meadow, or a wood has attracted them. Their village they do not arrange in our fashion, with the buildings connected and joined together, but every person surrounds his dwelling with an open space, either as a precaution against the disasters of fire, or because they do not know how to build. No use is made by them of stone or tile; they employ timber for all purposes, rude masses without ornament or attractiveness. Some parts of their buildings they stain more carefully with a clay so clear and bright that it resembles painting, or a coloured design. They are wont also to dig out subterranean caves, and pile on them great heaps of dung, as a shelter from winter and as a receptacle for the year's produce, for by such places they mitigate the rigour of the cold. And should an enemy approach, he lays waste the open country, while what is hidden and buried is either not known to exist, or escapes him from the very fact that it has to be searched for.

Dress.   They all wrap themselves in a cloak which is fastened with a clasp, or, if this is not forthcoming, with a thorn, leaving the rest of their persons bare. They pass whole days on the hearth by the fire. The wealthiest are distinguished by a dress which is not flowing, like that of the Sarmatæ and Parthi, but is tight, and exhibits each limb. They also wear the skins of wild beasts; the tribes on the Rhine and Danube in a careless fashion, those of the interior with more elegance, as not obtaining other clothing by commerce. These select certain animals, the hides of which they strip off and vary them with the spotted skins of beasts, the produce of the outer ocean, and of seas unknown to us. The women have the same dress as the men, except that they generally wrap themselves in linen garments, which they embroider with purple, and do not lengthen out the upper part of their clothing into sleeves. The upper and lower arm is thus bare, and the nearest part of the bosom is also exposed.

Marriage Laws.   Their marriage code, however, is strict, and indeed no part of their manners is more praiseworthy. Almost alone among barbarians they are content with one wife, except a very few among them, and these not from sensuality, but because their noble birth procures for them many offers of alliance. The wife does not bring a dower to the husband, but the husband to the wife. The parents and relatives are present, and pass judgment on the marriage-gifts, gifts not meant to suit a woman's taste, nor such as a bride would deck herself with, but oxen, a caparisoned steed, a shield, a lance, and a sword. With these presents the wife is espoused, and she herself in her turn brings her husband a gift of arms. This they count their strongest bond of union, these their sacred mysteries, these their gods of marriage. Lest the woman should think herself to stand apart from aspirations after noble deeds and from the perils of war, she is reminded by the ceremony which inaugurates marriage that she is her husband's partner in toil and danger, destined to suffer and to dare with him alike both in peace and in war. The yoked oxen, the harnessed steed, the gift of arms, proclaim this fact. She must live and die with the feeling that she is receiving what she must hand down to her children neither tarnished nor depreciated, what future daughters-in-law may receive, and may be so passed on to her grandchildren.

Thus with their virtue protected they live uncorrupted by the allurements of public shows or the stimulant of feastings. Clandestine correspondence is equally unknown to men and women. Very rare for so numerous a population is adultery, the punishment for which is prompt, and in the husband's power. Having cut off the hair of the adulteress and stripped her naked, he expels her from the house in the presence of her kinsfolk, and then flogs her through the whole village. The loss of chastity meets with no indulgence; neither beauty, youth, nor wealth will procure the culprit a husband. No one in Germany laughs at vice, nor do they call it the fashion to corrupt and to be corrupted. Still better is the condition of those states in which only maidens are given in marriage, and where the hopes and expectations of a bride are then finally terminated. They receive one husband, as having one body and one life, that they may have no thoughts beyond, no further-reaching desires, that they may love not so much the husband as the married state. To limit the number of children or to destroy any of their subsequent offspring is accounted infamous, and good habits are here more effectual than good laws elsewhere.

Their Children. Laws of Succession.   In every household the children, naked and filthy, grow up with those stout frames and limbs which we so much admire. Every mother suckles her own offspring and never entrusts it to servants and nurses. The master is not distinguished from the slave by being brought up with greater delicacy.

Both live amid the same flocks and lie on the same ground till the free-born are distinguished by age and recognised by merit. The young men marry late, and their vigour is thus unimpaired. Nor are the maidens hurried into marriage; the same age and a similar stature is required; well-matched and vigorous they wed, and the offspring reproduce the strength of the parents. Sister's sons are held in as much esteem by their uncles as by their fathers; indeed, some regard the relation as even more sacred and binding, and prefer it in receiving hostages, thinking thus to secure a stronger hold on the affections and a wider bond for the family. But every man's own children are his heirs and successors, and there are no wills. Should there be no issue, the next in succession to the property are his brothers and his uncles on either side. The more relatives he has, the more numerous his connections, the more honoured is his old age; nor are there any advantages in childlessness.

Hereditary Feuds. Fines for Homicide. Hospitality.   It is a duty among them to adopt the feuds as well as the friendships of a father or a kinsman. These feuds are not implacable; even homicide is expiated by the payment of a certain number of cattle and of sheep, and the satisfaction is accepted by the entire family, greatly to the advantage of the state, since feuds are dangerous in proportion to the people's freedom.

No nation indulges more profusely in entertainments and hospitality. To exclude any human being from their roof is thought impious; every German, according to his means, receives his guest with a well-furnished table. When his supplies are exhausted, he who was but now the host becomes the guide and companion to further hospitality, and without invitation they go to the next house. It matters not; they are entertained with like cordiality. No one distinguishes between an acquaintance and a stranger, as regards the rights of hospitality. It is usual to give the departing guest whatever he may ask for, and a present in return is asked with as little hesitation. They are greatly charmed with gifts, but they expect no return for what they give, nor feel any obligation for what they receive.

Habits of Life.   On waking from sleep, which they generally prolong for a late hour of the day, they take a bath, oftenest of warm water, which suits a country where winter is the longest of the seasons. After their bath they take their meal, each having a separate seat and table of his own. Then they go armed to business, or no less often to their festal meetings. To pass an entire day and night in drinking disgraces no one. Their quarrels, as might be expected with intoxicated people, are seldom fought out with mere abuse, but commonly with wounds and bloodshed. Yet it is at their feasts that they generally consult on the reconciliation of enemies, on the forming of matrimonial alliances, on the choice of chiefs, finally even on peace and war, for they think that at no time is the mind more open to simplicity of purpose or more warmed to noble aspirations. A race without either natural or acquired cunning, they disclose their hidden thoughts in the freedom of the festivity. Thus the sentiments of all having been discovered and laid bare, the discussion is renewed on the following day, and from each occasion its own peculiar advantage is derived. They deliberate when they have no power to dissemble; they resolve when error is impossible.

Food.   A liquor for drinking is made of barley or other grain, and fermented into a certain resemblance to wine. The dwellers on the river-bank also buy wine. Their food is of a simple kind, consisting of wild fruit, fresh game, and curdled milk. They satisfy their hunger without elaborate preparation and without delicacies. In quenching their thirst they are equally moderate. If you indulge their love of drinking by supplying them with as much as they desire, they will be overcome by their own vices as easily as by the arms of an enemy.

Sports. Passion for Gambling.   One and the same kind of spectacle is always exhibited at every gathering. Naked youths who practise the sport bound in the dance amid swords and lances that threaten their lives. Experience gives them skill and skill again gives grace; profit or pay are out of the question; however reckless their pastime, its reward is the pleasure of the spectators. Strangely enough they make games of hazard a serious occupation even when sober, and so venturesome are they about gaining or losing, that, when every other resource has failed, on the last and final throw they stake the freedom of their own persons. The loser goes into voluntary slavery; though the younger and stronger, he suffers himself to be bound and sold. Such is their stubborn persistency in a bad practice; they themselves call it honour. Slaves of this kind the owners part with in the way of commerce, and also to relieve themselves from the scandal of such a victory.

Slavery.   The other slaves are not employed after our manner with distinct domestic duties assigned to them, but each one has the management of a house and home of his own. The master requires from the slave a certain quantity of grain, of cattle, and of clothing, as he would from a tenant, and this is the limit of subjection. All other household functions are discharged by the wife and children. To strike a slave or to punish him with bonds or with hard labour is a rare occurrence. They often kill them, not in enforcing strict discipline, but on the impulse of passion, as they would an enemy, only it is done with impunity. The freedmen do not rank much above slaves, and are seldom of any weight in the family, never in the state, with the exception of those tribes which are ruled by kings. There indeed they rise above the freeborn and the noble; elsewhere the inferiority of the freedman marks the freedom of the state.

Occupation of Land. Tillage.   Of lending money on interest and increasing it by compounding interest they know nothing—a more effectual safeguard than if it was prohibited.

Land proportioned to the number of inhabitants is occupied by the whole community in turn, and afterwards divided among them according to rank. A wide expanse of plains makes the partition easy. They till fresh fields every year, and they have still more land than enough; with the richness and extent of their soil, they do not laboriously exert themselves in planting orchards, inclosing meadows, and watering gardens. Corn is the only produce required from the earth; hence even the year itself is not divided by them into as many seasons as with us. Winter, spring, and summer have both a meaning and a name; the name and blessings of autumn are alike unknown.

Funeral Rites.   In their funerals there is no pomp; they simply observe the custom of burning the bodies of illustrious men with certain kinds of wood. They do not heap garments or spices on the funeral pile. The arms of the dead man and in some cases his horse are consigned to the fire. A turf mound forms the tomb. Monuments with their lofty elaborate splendour they reject as oppressive to the dead. Tears and lamentations they soon dismiss; grief and sorrow but slowly. It is thought becoming for women to bewail, for men to remember, the dead.

Such on the whole is the account which I have received of the origin and manners of the entire German people.

10. A Romanized Ostrogoth: Theodoric

The Ostrogoth Theodoric, king of Italy from 493 to 526, was the most civilized ruler among the barbarian invaders of the empire. He was brought up at the court of Constantinople where he was held as a hostage during his youth. The following letters were written on the king's behalf by his secretary, Cassiodorus. The composition of the letters reflects the style of Cassiodorus, but they describe the policies that Theodoric actually pursued.

King Theodoric to Maximian, Vir Illustris; and Andreas, Vir Spectabilis

If the people of Rome will beautify their City we will help them.

Institute a strict audit (of which no one need be ashamed) of the money given by us to the different workmen for the beautification of the City. See that we are receiving money's worth for the money spent. If there is embezzlement anywhere, cause the funds so embezzled to be disgorged. We expect the Romans to help from their own resources in this patriotic work, and certainly not to intercept our contributions for the purpose.

From *Letters of Cassiodorus,* Thomas Hodgkin, trans. (London: H. Frowde, 1886), pp. 156–219.

The wandering birds love their own nests; the beasts haste to their own lodgings in the brake; the voluptuous fish, roaming the fields of ocean, returns to its own well-known cavern. How much more should Rome be loved by her children!

King Theodoric to Faustus, Praepositus

It should be only the surplus of the crops of any Province, beyond what is needed for the supply of its own wants, that should be exported. Station persons in the harbours to see that foreign ships do not take away produce to foreign shores until the Public Providers have got all that they require.

King Theodoric to Suna, Vir Illustris and Comes

Let nothing lie useless which may rebound to the beauty of the City. Let your Illustrious Magnificence therefore cause the blocks of marble which are everywhere lying about in ruins to be wrought up into the walls by the hands of the workmen whom I send herewith. Only take care to use only those stones which have really fallen from public buildings, as we do not wish to appropriate private property, even for the glorification of the City.

King Theodoric to the Senate of the City of Rome

We hear with sorrow, by the report of the Provincial Judges, that you the Fathers of the State, who ought to set an example to your sons (the ordinary citizens), have been so remiss in the payment of taxes that on this first collection nothing, or next to nothing, has been brought in from any Senatorial house. Thus a crushing weight has fallen on the lower orders, who have had to make good your deficiencies and have been distraught by the violence of the tax gatherers.

Now then, oh Conscript Fathers, who owe as much duty to the Republic as we do, pay the taxes for which each of you is liable, to the Procurators appointed in each Province, by three instalments. Or, if you prefer to do so—and it used to be accounted a privilege—pay all at once into the chest of the Vicarius. And let this following edict be published, that all the Provincials may know that they are not to be imposed upon and that they are invited to state their grievances.

King Theodoric to Colossaeus, Vir Illustris and Comes

We delight to entrust our mandates to persons of approved character.

We are sending you with the dignity of the illustrious belt to Pannonia Sirmiensis, an old habitation of the Goths. Let that Province be induced to welcome her old defenders, even as she used gladly to obey our ancestors. Show forth the justice of the Goths, a nation happily situated for praise, since it is theirs to unite the forethought of the Romans and the virtue of the Barbarians. Remove all ill-planted customs, and impress upon all your subordinates that we would rather that our Treasury lost a suit than that it gained one wrongfully, rather that we lost money than the taxpayer was driven to suicide.

King Theodoric to Unigis, the Sword-Bearer

We delight to live after the law of the Romans, whom we seek to defend with our arms; and we are as much interested in the maintenance of morality as we can possibly be in war. For what profit is there in having removed the turmoil of the Barbarians, unless we live according to law? . . . Let other kings desire the glory of battles won, of cities taken, of ruins made; our purpose is, God helping us, so to rule that our subjects shall grieve that they did not earlier acquire the blessings of our dominion.

King Theodoric to All the Jews of Genoa

. . . We cannot command the religion of our subjects, since no-one can be forced to believe against his will.

11. A Barbarous Frank: Clovis

The founder of the Frankish monarchy, Clovis, was a more typical barbarian leader than Theodoric. The following account of his career is from the Chronicle of Bishop Gregory of Tours, which was completed about 590. Clovis himself died in 511.

The queen did not cease to urge him to recognize the true God and cease worshipping idols. But he could not be influenced in any way to this belief, until at last a war arose with the Alemanni, in which he was driven by necessity to confess what before he had of his free will denied. It came about as the two armies were fighting fiercely, there was much slaughter, and Clovis's army began to be in danger of destruction. He saw it and raised his eyes to heaven, and with remorse in his heart he burst into tears and cried: "Jesus Christ, whom Clotilda asserts to be the son of the living God, who art said to give aid to those in distress, and to bestow victory on those who hope in thee, I beseech

From Gregory of Tours, *History of the Franks*, E. Brehaut, trans. (New York: Columbia University Press, 1916), pp. 39–40, 45–50; Copyright 1916 by Columbia University Press; reprinted by permission of the publisher.

the glory of thy aid, with the vow that if thou wilt grant me victory over these enemies, and I shall know that power which she says that people dedicated in thy name have had from thee, I will believe in thee and be baptized in thy name. For I have invoked my own gods, but, as I find, they have withdrawn from aiding me; and therefore I believe that they possess no power, since they do not help those who obey them. I now call upon thee, I desire to believe thee, only let me be rescued from my adversaries." And when he said this, the Alemanni turned their backs, and began to disperse in flight. And when they saw that their king was killed, they submitted to the domination of Clovis, saying: "Let not the people perish further, we pray; we are yours now." And he stopped the fighting, and after encouraging his men, retired in peace and told the queen how he had merit to win the victory by calling on the name of Christ. This happened in the fifteenth year of his reign.

• • •

Now Clovis the king said to his people: "I take it very hard that these Arians hold part of the Gauls. Let us go with God's help and conquer them and bring the land under our control." Since these words pleased all, he set his army in motion and made for Poitiers where Alaric was at the time. But since part of the host was passing through Touraine, he issued an edict out of respect to the blessed Martin that no one should take anything from that country except grass for fodder, and water. But one from the army found a poor man's hay and said: "Did not the king order grass only to be taken, nothing else? And this," said he, "is grass. We shall not be transgressing his command if we take it." And when he had done violence to the poor man and taken his hay by force, the deed came to the king. And quicker than speech the offender was slain by the sword, and the king said: "And where shall our hope of victory be if we offend the blessed Martin? It would be better for the army to take nothing else from this country." . . .

Meantime king Clovis met with Alaric, king of Goths, in the plain of Vouillé at the tenth mile-stone from Poitiers, and while the one army was for fighting at a distance the other tried to come to close combat. And when the Goths had fled as was their custom, king Clovis won the victory by God's aid. He had to help him the son of Sigibert the lame, named Chloderic. This Sigibert was lame from a wound in the leg, received in a battle with the Alemanni near the town of Zülpich. Now when the king had put the Goths to flight and slain king Alaric, two of the enemy suddenly appeared and struck him with their lances, one on each side. But he was saved from death by the help of his coat of mail, as well as by his fast horse. At that time there perished a very great number of the people of Auvergne, who had come with Apollinaris and the leading senators. From this battle Amalaric, son of Alaric, fled to Spain and wisely seized his father's kingdom. Clovis sent his son Theodoric to Clermont by way of Albi and Rodez. He went, and brought under his father's dominion the cities from the boundaries of the Goths to the limit of the Burgundians. Alaric reigned twenty-two years. When Clovis had spent the winter in Bordeaux and taken all the treasures of Alaric at Toulouse, he went to Angoulême. And the Lord gave him such grace that the walls fell down of their own accord when he gazed at them. Then he drove the Goths out and brought the city under his own dominion. Thereupon after completing his victory he returned to Tours, bringing many gifts to the holy church of the blessed Martin.

Clovis received an appointment to the consulship from the emperor Anastasius, and in the church of the blessed Martin he clad himself in the purple tunic and chlamys, and placed a diadem on his head. Then he mounted his horse, and in the most generous manner he gave gold and silver as he passed along the way which is between the gate of the entrance [of the church of St. Martin] and the church of the city, scattering it among the people who were there with his own hand, and from that day he was called *consul* or *Augustus*. Leaving Tours he went to Paris and there he established the seat of his kingdom. There also Theodoric came to him.

• • •

When king Clovis was dwelling at Paris he sent secretly to the son of Sigibert saying: "Behold your father has become an old man and limps in his weak foot. If he should die," said he, "of due right his kingdom would be yours together with our friendship." Led on by greed the son plotted to kill his father. And when his father went out from the city of Cologne and crossed the Rhine and was intending to journey through the wood Buchaw, as he slept at midday in his tent his son sent assassins in against him, and killed him there, in the idea that he would get his kingdom. But by God's judgment he walked into the pit that he had cruelly dug for his father. He sent messengers to king Clovis to tell about his father's death, and to say: "My father is dead, and I have his treasures in my possession, and also his kingdom. Send men to me, and I shall gladly transmit to you from his treasures whatever pleases you." And Clovis replied: "I thank you for your good will, and I ask that you possess all yourself." When they came, he showed his father's treasures. And when they were looking at the different things he said: "It was in this little chest that my father used to put his gold coins." "Thrust in your hand," said they, "to the bottom, and uncover the whole." When he did so, and was much bent over, one of them lifted his hand and dashed his battle-ax against his head, and so in a shameful manner he incurred the death which he had brought on his father. Clovis heard that Sigibert and his son had been slain, and came to the place and summoned all the people saying: "Hear what has happened. When I," said he, "was sailing down the river Scheldt, Chloderic, son of my kinsman, was in pursuit of his own father, asserting that I wished him killed. And when his father was fleeing through the forest of

Buchaw, he set highwaymen upon him, and gave him over to death, and slew him. And when he was opening the treasures, he was slain himself by some one or other. Now I know nothing at all of these matters. For I cannot shed the blood of my own kinsmen, which it is a crime to do. But since this has happened. I give you my advice, if it seems acceptable; turn to me, that you may be under my protection." They listened to this, and giving applause with both shields and voices, they raised him on a shield, and made him king over them. He received Sigibert's kingdom with his treasures, and placed the people, too, under his rule. For God was laying his enemies low every day under his hand, and was increasing his kingdom, because he walked with an upright heart before him, and did what was pleasing in his eyes.

After this he turned to Chararic. When he had fought with Siagrius this Chararic had been summoned to help Clovis, but stood at a distance, aiding neither side, but awaiting the outcome, in order to form a league of friendship with him to whom victory came. For this reason Clovis was angry, and went out against him. He entrapped and captured him and his son also, and kept them in prison, and gave them the tonsure; he gave orders to ordain Chararic priest and his son deacon. And when Chararic complained of his degradation and wept, it is said that his son remarked: "It was on green wood,' said he, "that these twigs were cut, and they are not altogether withered. They will shoot out quickly, and be able to grow; may he perish as swiftly who has done this." This utterance was reported to the ears of Clovis, namely, that they were threatening to let their hair grow, and kill him. And he ordered them both to be put to death. When they were dead, he took their kingdom with the treasures and people.

Ragnachar was then king at Cambrai, a man so unrestrained in his wantonness that he scarcely had mercy for his own near relatives. He had a counsellor Farro, who defiled himself with a like vileness. And it was said that when food, or a gift, or anything whatever was brought to the king, he was wont to say that it was enough for him and his Farro. And at this thing the Franks were in a great rage. And so it happened that Clovis gave golden armlets and belts, but all only made to resemble gold—for it was bronze gilded so as to deceive—these he gave to Ragnachar's *leudes* to be invited to attack him. Moreover, when Clovis had set his army in motion against him, and Ragnachar was continually sending spies to get information, on the return of his messengers he used to ask how strong the force was. And they would answer: "It is a great sufficiency for you and your Farro." Clovis came and made war on him, and he saw that his army was beaten and prepared to slip away in flight, but was seized by his army, and with his hands tied behind his back, he was taken with Ricchar his brother before Clovis. And Clovis said to him: "Why have you humiliated our family in permitting yourself to be bound? It would have been better for you to die." And raising his ax he dashed it against his head, and he turned to his brother and said: "If you had aided your brother, he would not have been bound." And in the same way he smote him with his ax and killed him. After their death their betrayers perceived that the gold which they had received from the king was false. When they told the king of this, it is said that he answered: "Rightly," said he, "does he receive this kind of gold, who of his own will brings his own master to death"; it ought to suffice them that they were alive, and were not put to death, to mourn amid torments the wicked betrayal of their masters. When they heard this, they prayed for mercy, saying it was enough for them if they were allowed to live. The kings named above were kinsmen of Clovis, and their brother, Rignomer by name, was slain by Clovis's order at the city of Mans. When they were dead Clovis received all their kingdom and treasures. And having killed many other kings and his nearest relatives, of whom he was jealous lest they take the kingdom from him, he extended his rule over all the Gauls. However he gathered his people together at one time, it is said, and spoke of the kinsmen whom he had himself destroyed. "Woe to me, who have remained as a stranger among foreigners, and have none of my kinsmen to give me aid if adversity comes." But he said this not because of grief at their death but by way of a ruse, if perchance he should be able to find some one still to kill.

chapter IV

Roman, Christian, and Teutonic Conceptions of Law

12. The Corpus Juris Civilis of Justinian

Medieval law grew out of a fusion of Roman, Christian, and Teutonic concepts. Roman law claimed to be based on abstract principles of justice that were translated into concrete rules of law by legislative authority of the emperor or the Roman people. These ideas were transmitted to the Middle Ages in the great codification of Roman law carried through by the emperor Justinian (527–565).

The Digest: Prologue

The Emperor Caesar, Flavius, Justinianus, Pious, Fortunate, Renowned, Conqueror, and Triumpher, Ever Augustus, to Tribonianus His Quaestor: Greeting

With the aid of God governing Our Empire which was delivered to Us by His Celestial Majesty, We carry on war successfully. We adorn peace and maintain the Constitution of the State, and have such confidence in the protection of Almighty God that We do not depend upon Our arms, or upon Our soldiers, or upon those who conduct Our Wars, or upon Our own genius, but We solely, place Our reliance upon the providence of the Holy Trinity, from which are derived the elements of the entire world and their disposition throughout the globe.

Therefore, since there is nothing to be found in all things so worthy

From *The Digest of Justinian*, C. H. Monro, ed. (Cambridge, Mass.: Cambridge University Press, 1904).

of attention as the authority of the law, which properly regulates all affairs both divine and human, and expels all injustice; We have found the entire arrangement of the law which has come down to us from the foundation of the City of Rome and the times of Romulus, to be so confused that it is extended to an infinite length and is not within the grasp of human capacity; and hence We were first induced to begin by examining what had been enacted by former most venerated princes, to correct their constitutions, and make them more easily understood; to the end that being included in a single Code, and having had removed all that is superfluous in resemblance and all iniquitous discord, they may afford to all men the ready assistance of their true meaning.

After having concluded this work and collected it all in a single volume under Our illustrious name, raising Ourself above small and comparatively insignificant matters, We have hastened to attempt the most complete and thorough amendment of the entire law, to collect and revise the whole body of Roman jurisprudence, and to assemble in one book the scattered treatises of so many authors; which no one else has herebefore ventured to hope for or to expect, and it has indeed been considered by Ourselves a most difficult undertaking, nay, one that was almost impossible; but with Our hands raised to heaven and having invoked the Divine aid, We have kept this object in Our mind, confiding in God who can grant the accomplishment of things which are almost desperate, and can Himself carry them into effect by virtue of the greatness of His power.

• • •

We desire you to be careful with regard to the following: if you find in the old books anything that is not suitably arranged, superfluous, or incomplete, you must remove all superfluities, supply what is lacking, and present the entire work in regular form, and with as excellent an appearance as possible. You must also observe the following, namely: if you find anything which the ancients have inserted in their old laws or constitutions that is incorrectly worded, you must correct this, and place it in its proper order, so that it may appear to be true, expressed in the best language, and written in this way in the first place; so that by comparing it with the original text, no one can venture to call in question as defective what you have selected and arranged. Since by an ancient law, which is styled the *Lex Regia,* all the rights and power of the Roman people were transferred to the Emperor, We do not derive Our authority from that of other different compilations, but wish that it shall all be entirely Ours, for how can antiquity abrogate our laws?

The Institutes: Sources of Law

Justice is the set and constant purpose which gives to every man his

From *The Institutes of Justinian,* J. B. Moyle, trans. (3rd ed.; Oxford: Oxford University Press, 1896), pp. 3–5.

due. Jurisprudence is the knowledge of things divine and human, the science of the just and the unjust. . . .

The precepts of the law are these: to live honestly, to injure no one, and to give every man his due. The study of law consists of two branches, law public and law private. The former relates to the welfare of the Roman State; the latter to the advantage of the individual citizen. Of private law then we may say that it is of threefold origin, being collected from the precepts of nature, from those of the law of nations, or from those of the civil law of Rome.

The law of nature is that which she has taught all animals; a law not peculiar to the human race, but shared by all living creatures, whether denizens of the air, the dry land, or the sea. Hence comes the union of male and female, which we call marriage; hence the procreation and rearing of children, for this is a law by the knowlege of which we see even the lower animals are distinguished. The civil law of Rome, and the law of all nations, differ from each other thus. The laws of every people governed by statutes and customs are partly peculiar to itself, partly common to all mankind. Those rules which a state enacts for its own members are peculiar to itself, and are called civil law: those rules prescribed by natural reason for all men are observed by all people alike, and are called the law of nations. Thus the laws of the Roman people are partly peculiar to itself, partly common to all nations; a distinction of which we shall take notice as occasion offers. . . .

Our law is partly written, partly unwritten, as among the Greeks. The written law consists of statutes, plebiscites, senatusconsults, enactments of the Emperors, edicts of the magistrates, and answers of those learned in the law. A statute is an enactment of the Roman people, which it used to make on the motion of a senatorial magistrate, as for instance a consul. A plebiscite is an enactment of the commonalty, such as was made on the motion of one of their own magistrates, as a tribune. . . . A senatusconsult is a command and ordinance of the senate, for when the Roman people had been so increased that it was difficult to assemble it together for the purpose of enacting statutes, it seemed right that the senate should be consulted instead of the people. Again, what the Emperor determines has the force of a statute, the people having conferred on him all their authority and power by the *lex regia,* which was passed concerning his office and authority. Consequently, whatever the Emperor settles by rescript, or decides in his judicial capacity, or ordains by edicts, is clearly a statute: and these are what are called constitutions.

13.   Canons of the Council of Nicea

The Christian bishops who assembled at Nicea for the first general council of the church in 325 also assumed the right to confirm old customs or abolish them as they saw fit. In addition, they enacted new laws to deal with new problems that were arising.

Since many things have taken place that are contrary to the ecclesiastical canons, either through necessity or through the pressure of men, so that persons just converted from heathenism to the faith and instructed only for a short time are led directly to the spiritual bath and at the same time with baptism are promoted to the sacerdotal or episcopal dignity, it appeared just that in the future such things should not be done, since for catechetical instruction and for further probation after baptism time is necessary. For it is a wise saying of the apostle: a bishop should be "not a neophyte; lest being puffed up with pride, he fall into the judgment and snare of the devil." If in the future, however, a grave sin be discovered in a cleric and he be convicted by two or three witnesses, he must lay aside his clerical office. Any one who acts contrary to the ordinance and dares to be disobedient to this great council runs the risk of being disposed from the clerical state.

• • •

Let the ancient custom that obtains in Egypt, Libya, and Pentapolis, namely, that the bishop of Alexandria has the supervision of all these provinces, be strictly adhered to, since this is also the custom of the bishop of Rome. In like manner, in respect to Antioch and the other provinces, let each Church retain its prerogatives. It is unmistakably clear that if anyone has been made bishop without the approval of the metropolitan, this great council does not permit him to exercise the office of bishop. If, however, the election, which was participated in by all with discernment and in accordance with the rules of the Church, is by reason of a contentious spirit opposed by two or three, the votes of the majority shall prevail.

• • •

In regard to those who call themselves *Cathari*, should they desire to enter the Catholic and Apostolic Church, this holy and great council decrees that they receive the imposition of hands and then remain in the clerical state; above all, however, they must certify in writing that they will accept and follow the teachings of the Catholic and Apostolic Church, that is, hold communion with those who have married a second time, as well as with those who lapse in time of persecution and for whom a definite period of penance has been fixed and an occasion

From *The Disciplinary Decrees of the General Councils,* H. J. Schroeder, trans. (St. Louis: B. Herder, 1937), pp. 29-30, 34, 39, 44; reprinted by permission of the publisher.

of reconciliation determined. In all things, therefore, must they follow the teachings of the Catholic Church. In places, then, where there are only ecclesiastics of their party, be it in villages or in cities, these are to remain in the clerical state and retain their positions; but if a Catholic bishop or priest be already there, and there come to him clerics from that party, it is clear that the bishop of the Catholic Church retains his episcopal dignity, but the bishop of the so-called *Cathari* is to have the sacerdotal dignity of the episcopal title. If he is dissatisfied with this, then he, the Catholic bishop, is to assign him as a rural bishop or priest, so that he may appear as a regular member of the clergy and thus avoid the presence of two bishops in a city.

• • •

With regard to those who during the tyranny of Licinius apostatized without compulsion or confiscation of property or peril or any other pressure, the council has decided to treat them with kindness, though they have shown themselves unworthy of it. Those, therefore, who are truly repentant and were believers before their fall, shall do three years of penance among the *audientes* and seven years among the *substrati;* for two years more they shall take part with the people in the prayers, but without offering sacrifice themselves.

• • •

On account of the many disorders and divisions, it was thought well to abolish everywhere the custom which has been established in some localities contrary to the canon; namely, that no bishop, priest, or deacon is to pass from one city to another. Should, however, anyone dare to act contrary to this decision of the holy and great council and follow the old custom, his action shall be regarded as absolutely null, and he is to return to the Church for which he was ordained bishop or priest.

14.   The Law of the Salian Franks

Primitive Teutonic codes of law were bodies of tribal practices handed down at first by word of mouth. They were not thought of as enactments of a legislator, but as customs of the folk that had existed from time immemorial. Such codes began to be set down in writing from the early seventh century onward.

Title I. Concerning Summonses.

1. If any one be summoned before the "Thing" by the king's law, and do not come, he shall be sentenced to 600 denars, which make 15 shillings (solidi).

From "The Salic Law," in E. F. Henderson, ed., *Select Historical Documents of the Middle Ages* (London: George Bell, 1892), pp. 176-189.

2. But he who summons another, and does not come himself, shall, if a lawful impediment have not delayed him, be sentenced to 15 shillings, to be paid to him whom he summoned.

Title III. Concerning Thefts of Cattle.

4. If any one steal that bull which rules the herd and never has been yoked, he shall be sentenced to 1800 denars, which make 45 shillings.

5. But if that bull is used for the cows of three villages in common, he who stole him shall be sentenced to three times 45 shillings.

6. If any one steal a bull belonging to the king he shall be sentenced to 3600 denars, which make 90 shillings.

Title XI. Concerning Thefts or Housebreakings of Freemen.

1. If any freeman steal, outside of the house, something worth 2 denars, he shall be sentenced to 600 denars, which make 15 shillings.

2. But if he steal, outside of the house, something worth 40 denars, and it be proved on him, he shall be sentenced, besides the amount and the fines for delay, to 1400 denars, which make 35 shillings.

3. If a freeman break into a house and steal something worth 2 denars, and it be proved on him, he shall be sentenced to 15 shillings.

4. But if he shall have stolen something worth more than 5 denars, and it have been proved on him, he shall be sentenced, besides the worth of the object and the fines for delay, to 1400 denars, which make 35 shillings.

5. But if he have broken, or tampered with, the lock, and thus have entered the house and stolen anything from it, he shall be sentenced, besides the worth of the object and the fines for delay, to 1800 denars, which make 45 shillings.

6. And if he have taken nothing, or have escaped by flight, he shall, for the housebreaking alone, be sentenced to 1200 denars, which make 30 shillings.

Title XIII. Concerning Rape Committed by Freemen.

1. If three men carry off a free born girl, they shall be compelled to pay 30 shillings.

2. If there are more than three, each one shall pay 5 shillings.

3. Those who shall have been present with boats shall be sentenced to three shillings.

4. But those who commit rape shall be compelled to pay 2500 denars, which make 63 shillings.

5. But if they have carried off that girl from behind lock and key, or from the spinning room, they shall be sentenced to the above price and penalty.

6. But if the girl who is carried off be under the king's protection, then the "firth" (peace-money) shall be 2500 denars, which make 63 shillings.

Title XIV. *Concerning Assault and Robbery.*

1. If any one have assaulted and plundered a freeman, and it be proved on him, he shall be sentenced to 2500 denars, which make 63 shillings.

2. If a Roman have plundered a Salian Frank, the above law shall be ordered.

3. But if a Frank have plundered a Roman, he shall be sentenced to 35 shillings.

4. If any man should wish to migrate, and has permission from the king, and shall have shown this in the public "Thing": whoever, contrary to the decree of the king, shall presume to oppose him, shall be sentenced to 8000 denars, which make 200 shillings.

Title XVII. *Concerning Wounds.*

1. If any one have wished to kill another person, and the blow have missed, he on whom it was proved shall be sentenced to 2500 denars, which make 63 shillings.

2. If any person have wished to strike another with a poisoned arrow, and the arrow have glanced aside, and it shall be proved on him: he shall be sentenced to 2500 denars, which make 63 shillings.

3. If any person strike another on the head so that the brain appears, and the three bones which lie above the brain shall project, he shall be sentenced to 1200 denars, which make 30 shillings.

4. But if it shall have been between the ribs or in the stomach, so that the wound appears and reaches to the entrails, he shall be sentenced to 1200 denars—which make 30 shillings—besides five shillings for the physician's pay.

5. If any one shall have struck a man so that blood falls to the floor, and it be proved on him, he shall be sentenced to 600 denars, which make 15 shillings.

6. But if a freeman strike a freeman with his fist so that blood does not flow, he shall be sentenced for each blow—up to 3 blows—to 120 denars, which make 3 shillings.

Title XXIV. *Concerning the Killing of Little Children and Women.*

1. If any one have slain a boy under 10 years—up to the end of the tenth—and it shall have been proved on him, he shall be sentenced to 24000 denars, which make 600 shillings.

3. If any one have hit a free woman who is pregnant, and she dies, he shall be sentenced to 28000 denars, which makes 700 shillings.

6. If any one have killed a free woman after she has begun bearing children, he shall be sentenced to 24000 denars, which make 600 shillings.

7. After she can have no more children, he who kills her shall be sentenced to 8000 denars, which make 200 shillings.

Title XXX. *Concerning Insults.*

3. If any one, man or woman, shall have called a woman harlot, and shall not have been able to prove it, he shall be sentenced to 1800 denars, which make 45 shillings.

4. If any person shall have called another "fox," he shall be sentenced to 3 shillings.

5. If any man shall have called another "hare," he shall be sentenced to 3 shillings.

Title XLI. *Concerning the Murder of Freemen.*

1. If any one shall have killed a free Frank, or a barbarian living under the Salic law, and it have been proved on him, he shall be sentenced to 8000 denars.

2. But if he shall have thrown him into a well or into the water, or shall have covered him with branches or anything else, to conceal him, he shall be sentenced to 24000 denars, which make 600 shillings.

3. But if any one has slain a man who is in the service of the king, he shall be sentenced to 24000 denars, which make 600 shillings.

4. But if he have put him in the water or in a well, and covered him with anything to conceal him, he shall be sentenced to 72000 denars, which make 1800 shillings.

5. If any one have slain a Roman who eats in the king's palace, and it have been proved on him, he shall be sentenced to 12000 denars, which make 300 shillings.

6. But if the Roman shall not have been a landed proprietor and table companion of the king, he who killed him shall be sentenced to 4000 denars, which make 100 shillings.

Title LVII. *Concerning the "Chrenecruda."*

1. If any one have killed a man, and, having given up all his property, has not enough to comply with the full terms of the law, he shall present 12 sworn witnesses to the effect that, neither above the earth nor under it, has he any more property than he has already given, And he shall afterwards go into his house, and shall collect in his hand dust from the four corners of it, and shall afterwards stand upon the

threshold, looking inwards into the house. And then, with his left hand, he shall throw over his shoulder some of that dust on the nearest relative that he has. But if his father and (his father's) brothers have already paid, he shall then throw that dust on their (the brothers') children—that is, over three (relatives) who are nearest on the father's and three on the mother's side. And after that, in his shirt, without girdle and without shoes, a staff in his hand, he shall spring over the hedge. And then those three shall pay half of what is lacking of the compounding money or the legal fine; that is, those others who are descended in the paternal line shall do this.

2. But if there be one of those relatives who has not enough to pay his whole indebtedness, he, the poorer one, shall in turn throw the "chrenecruda" on him of them who has the most, so that he shall pay the whole fine.

3. But if he also have not enough to pay the whole, then he who has charge of the murderer shall bring him before the "Thing," and afterwards to 4 Things, in order that they (his friends) may take him under their protection. And if no one have taken him under his protection— that is, so as to redeem him for what he can not pay—then he shall have to atone with his life.

Title LIX. *Concerning Private Property.*

1. If any man die and leave no sons, if the father and mother survive, they shall inherit.

2. If the father and mother do not survive, and he leave brothers or sisters, they shall inherit.

3. But if there are none, the sisters of the father shall inherit.

4. But if there are no sisters of the father, the sisters of the mother shall claim the inheritance.

5. If there are none of these, the nearest relative on the father's side shall succeed to that inheritance.

6. But of Salic land no portion of the inheritance shall come to a woman: but the whole inheritance of the land shall come to the male sex.

Title LXII. *Concerning Wergeld.*

1. If any one's father have been killed, the sons shall have half the compounding money (wergeld); and the other half the nearest relatives, as well on the mother's as on the father's side, shall divide among themselves.

2. But if there are no relatives, paternal or maternal, that portion shall go to the fisc.

15. Formulae Concerning Ordeals

The only methods of proof used in early Germanic law were compurgation and ordeal. In compurgation the accused swore to his own innocence together with a group of "oath-helpers." Two typical types of ordeal—in their Christianized form—are described in the following liturgical formulae.

The Judgment of the Glowing Iron

After the accusation has been lawfully made, and three days have been passed in fasting and prayer, the priest, clad in his sacred vestments with the exception of his outside garment, shall take with a tongs the iron placed before the altar; and, singing the hymn of the three youths, namely, "Bless him all his works," he shall bear it to the fire, and shall say this prayer over the place where the fire is to carry out the judgment: "Bless, O Lord God, this place, that there may be for us in it sanctity, chastity, virtue and victory, and sanctimony, humility, goodness, gentleness and plentitude of law, and obedience to God the Father and the Son and the Holy Ghost."—After this, the iron shall be placed in the fire and shall be sprinkled with holy water; and while it is heating, he shall celebrate mass. But when the priest shall have taken the Eucharist, he shall adjure the man who is to be tried . . . and shall cause him to take the communion.—Then the priest shall sprinkle holy water above the iron and shall say: "The blessing of God the Father, the Son, and the Holy Ghost descend upon this iron for the discerning of the right judgment of God." And straightway the accused shall carry the iron to a distance of nine feet. Finally his hand shall be covered under seal for three days, and if festering blood be found in the track of the iron, he shall be judged guilty. But if, however, he shall go forth uninjured, praise shall be rendered to God.

Test of the Cold Water

Consecration to be said over the man.   May omnipotent God, who did order baptism to made by water, and did grant remission of sins to men through baptism: may He, through His mercy, decree a right judgment through that water. If, namely, thou art guilty in that matter, may the water which received thee in baptism not receive thee now; if however, thou art innocent, may the water which received thee in baptism receive thee now. Through Christ our Lord.

Afterwards he shall exorcise the water thus: I adjure thee, water, in name of the Father Almighty, who did create thee in the beginning,

From "'Formulae Liturgicae' in Use at Ordeals," in E. F. Henderson, ed., *Select Historical Documents of the Middle Ages* (London: George Bell, 1892), pp. 314-317.

who also did order thee to be separated from the waters above, . . . that in no manner thou receive this man, if he be in any way guilty of the charge that is brought against him; by deed, namely, or by consent, or by knowledge, or in any way: but make him to swim above thee. And may no process be employed against thee, and no magic which may be able to conceal that (fact of his guilt).

The Rise of the Papacy

16. The Primacy of the Roman See

From very early times the Roman church claimed a position of preeminence both because Rome was the capital city of the empire and because Peter, the first pope, was considered the chief of the apostles. The first church synod that attributed a primacy of jurisdiction to the bishop of Rome was the Council of Sardica (343).

Canon V. Bishop Hosius said: Resolved, that if a bishop has been accused and the assembled bishops of that region have deposed him, and he has appealed and had recourse to the most blessed bishop of the Roman church, and is desirous that he should hear his case; then if he should think it just that his case should be reopened, let him think fit to write to the appellant's fellow-bishops of the adjacent provinces, that they may make careful and exact enquiry into the details, and give sentence according to what they believe to be the truth. But if anyone who claims a fresh trial should by his entreaty move the Roman bishop to send one of the presbyters of his personal suite, then it shall be in the power of the bishop [of Rome] if he so decide, to send representatives to sit in judgment with the bishops; such representatives to have the authority of him from whom they were sent. If he think the bishops competent to judge the matter and to decide on the bishop's case, then he shall act as it seems best to his most wise counsel.

From *Documents of the Christian Church*, edited by H. Bettenson, published by the Oxford University Press (2nd ed.; London: Oxford University Press, 1963), pp. 113, 32–33; reprinted by permission of the publisher.

The emperor Valentinian III acknowledged the primacy of Rome in an edict promulgated in 445.

We are convinced that the only defence for us and for our Empire is in the favour of the God of heaven: and in order to deserve this favour it is our first care to support the Christian faith and its venerable religion. Therefore, inasmuch as the pre-eminence of the Apostolic See is assured by the merit of S. Peter, the first of the bishops, by the leading position of the city of Rome and also by the authority of the holy Synod, let not presumption strive to attempt anything contrary to the authority of that See. For the peace of the churches will only then be everywhere preserved when the whole body acknowledge its ruler. Hitherto this has been observed without violation: but Hilary, Bishop of Arles, as we have learnt from the report of that venerable man Leo, the pope of Rome, has with contumacious presumption ventured upon certain unlawful proceedings; and thus an abominable confusion has invaded the church beyond the Alps. . . . By such presumptuous acts confidence in the the Empire, and respect for our rule is destroyed. Therefore in the first place we put down so great a crime: and, beyond that, in order that no disturbance, however slight, may arise among the churches, and the discipline of religion may not appear to be impaired in any case whatever, we decree, by a perpetual edict, that nothing shall be attempted by the Gallican bishops, or by those of any other province, contrary to the ancient custom, without the authority of the venerable pope of the Eternal City. But whatsoever the authority of the Apostolic See has enacted, or shall enact, let that be held as law for all. So that if any bishop summoned before the pope of Rome shall neglect to attend, let him be compelled to appear by the governor of the province. . . .

17.   *The Petrine Doctrine According to Leo I*

From the fifth century onward papal claims came to be based more exclusively on the primacy of Peter. Pope Leo I (440–461) gave a considered exposition of the Petrine doctrine of papal authority in one of his sermons.

II. From Christ and through S. Peter the priesthood is handed on in perpetuity.

Although, therefore, dearly beloved, we be found both weak and slothful in fulfilling the duties of our office, because, whatever devoted and

From *Sermons of Leo the Great*, C. L. Feltoe, trans., in Library of Nicene and Post-Nicene Fathers (2nd Series; New York: Christian Literature Company, 1895), Vol. XII, p. 117.

vigorous action we desire to do, we are hindered by the frailty of our very condition; yet having the increasing propitiation of the Almighty and perpetual Priest, who being like us and yet equal with the Father, brought down His Godhead even to things human, and raised His Manhood even to things Divine, we worthily and piously rejoice over His dispensation, whereby, though He has delegated the care of His sheep to many shepherds, yet He has not Himself abandoned the guardianship of His beloved flock. And from His overruling and eternal protection we have received the support of the Apostles' aid also, which assuredly does not cease from its operation: and the strength of the foundation, on which the whole superstructure of the Church is reared, is not weakened by the weight of the temple that rests upon it. For the solidity of that faith which was praised in the chief of the Apostles is perpetual: and as that remains which Peter believed in Christ, so that remains which Christ instituted in Peter. For when, as has been read in the Gospel lesson, the LORD had asked the disciples whom they believed Him to be amid the various opinions that were held, and the blessed Peter had replied, saying, "Thou art the Christ, the Son of the living GOD," the LORD says, "Blessed art thou, Simon Bar-Jona, because flesh and blood hath not revealed it to thee, but My Father, which is in heaven. And I say to thee, that thou art Peter, and upon this rock I will build My church, and the gates of Hades shall not prevail against it. And I will give unto thee the keys of the kingdom of heaven. And whatsoever thou shalt bind on earth, shall be bound in heaven; and whatsoever thou shalt loose on earth, shall be loosed also in heaven."

III. S. Peter's work is still carried out by his successors.

The dispensation of Truth therefore abides, and the blessed Peter persevering in the strength of the Rock, which he has received, has not abandoned the helm of the Church, which he undertook. For he was ordained before the rest in such a way that from his being called the Rock, from his being pronounced the Foundation, from his being constituted the Doorkeeper on the kingdom of heaven, from his being set as the Umpire to bind and to loose, whose judgments shall retain their validity in heaven, from all these mystical titles we might know the nature of his association with Christ. And still to-day he more fully and effectually performs what is entrusted to him, and carries out every part of his duty and charge in Him and with Him, through Whom he has been glorified. And so if anything is rightly done and rightly decreed by us, if anything is won from the mercy of GOD by our daily supplications, it is of his work and merits whose power lives and whose authority prevails in his See. For this, dearly-beloved, was gained by that confession, which, inspired in the Apostle's heart by GOD the Father, transcended all the uncertainty of human opinions, and was endued with the firmness of a rock, which no assaults could shake. For throughout the Church Peter daily says, "Thou art the Christ, the Son of the living GOD." and every tongue which confesses the LORD, accepts the instruction his voice conveys. This Faith conquers the devil, and breaks the bonds of his prisoners. It uproots us from this earth and plants us in heaven, and the gates of Hades cannot prevail against it. For with such solidity is it endued by GOD that the depravity of heretics cannot mar it nor the belief of the heathen overcome it.

18. Papal Headship in Action: Gregory the Great

Pope Gregory I (590–604) has been called " the founder of the medieval papacy." He influenced the Western church both as a teacher and as a vigorous leader. His attitude to the imperial authority is illustrated in the following letter addressed to the emperor Maurice, which protested against a recent law forbidding soldiers to become monks.

To Mauricius Augustus

Gregory to Mauricius, &c.

He is guilty before Almighty God who is not pure of offence towards our most serene lords in all he does and says. . . . Yet still, feeling that this ordinance makes against God, who is the Author of all, I cannot keep silence to my lords. For power over all men has been given from heaven to the piety of my lords to this end, that they who aspire to what is good may be helped, and that the way to heaven may be more widely open, so that an earthly kingdom may wait upon the heavenly kingdom. And lo, it is said in plain words that one who has once been marked to serve as an earthly soldier may not, unless he has either completed his service or been rejected for weakness of body, serve as the soldier of our Lord Jesus Christ.

To this, behold, Christ through me the last of His servants and of yours will answer, saying; From a notary I made thee a Count of the body-guard; from Count of the body-guard I made thee a Caesar; from a Caesar I made thee Emperor; and not only so, but also a father of emperors. I have committed my priests into thy hand; and dost thou withdraw thy soldiers from my service? Answer thy servant, most pious lord, I beseech thee; what wilt thou answer to thy Lord when He comes and thus speaks?

From *Selected Epistles of Gregory the Great,* J. Barmby, trans., in Library of Nicene and Post-Nicene Fathers (2nd Series; New York: Christian Literature Company, 1895), Vo. XII, pp. 140–141; Vol. XIII, pp.84–85, 81. Gregory I, *The Book of Pastoral Rule,* J. Barmby, trans., in Library of Nicene and Post-Nicene Fathers (2nd Series; New York: Christian Literature Company, 1895). Vo. XII, pp. 9–15, 20.

But peradventure it is believed that no one among them turns monk with a pure motive. I, your unworthy servant, know how many soldiers who have become monks in my own days have done miracles, have wrought signs and mighty deeds. But by this law it is forbidden that even one of such as these should become a monk.

Let my lord enquire, I beg, what former emperor ever enacted such a law, and consider more thoroughly whether it ought to have been enacted. And indeed it is a very serious consideration, that now at this time any are forbidden to leave the world; a time when the end of the world is drawing nigh. For lo! there will be no delay: the heavens on fire, the earth on fire, the elements blazing, with angels and arch-angels, thrones and dominions, principalities and powers, the tremendous Judge will appear. Should He remit all sins, and say only that this law has been promulged against Himself, what excuse, pray, will there be? Wherefore by the same tremendous Judge I beseech you, that all those tears, all those prayers, all those fasts, all those alms of my lord, may not on any ground lose their lustre before the eyes of Almighty God: but let your Piety, either by interpretation or alteration, modify the force of this law, since the army of my lords against their enemies increases the more when the army of God has been increased in prayer.

I indeed, being subject to your command, have caused this law to be transmitted through various parts of the world; and, inasmuch as the law itself is by no means agreeable to Almighty God, lo, I have by this my representation declared this to my most serene lords. On both sides, then, I have discharged my duty, having both yielded obedience to the Emperor, and not kept silence as to what I feel in behalf of God.

Gregory's concern for the churches north of the Alps was evident in many of his letters. He adopted an upbraiding tone in addressing the Frankish queen, Brunhild.

To Brunichild, Queen of the Franks

Gregory to Brunichild, &c.

Since it is written, *Righteousness exalteth a nation; but sin maketh people miserable* (Prov. xiv. 34), a kingdom is then believed to be stable when a fault that is known of is quickly amended. Now it has come to our ears by the report of many, what we cannot mention without exceeding affliction of heart, that certain priests in those parts live so immodestly and wickedly that it is a shame for us to hear of it and lamentable to tell it. Lest, then, now that the rumour of this iniquity has extended as far as here, the wrong doing of others should smite either our soul or your kingdom with the dart of its sin, we ought to arise with ardour to avenge these things, lest the wickedness of a few should be the perdition of many. For bad priests are the cause of the ruin of a people. For who may offer himself as an intercessor for a people's sins, if the priest who ought to have prayed for it commits more grievous offences? But, since those whose place it is to prosecute these things are stirred neither by care to enquire into them nor by zeal to punish them, let letters from you be addressed to us, and let us send over, if you order it, a person with the assent of your authority, who together with other priests may search into these things thoroughly, and amend them according to the will of God. For indeed what we speak of is not a thing to be winked at, since one who can amend a fault and neglects to do so without doubt makes himself partaker in it. See therefore to your own soul, see to your grandsons, whom you wish to reign happily, see to the provinces; and, before our Creator stretches out His hand to smite, take most earnest thought for the correction of this wickedness, lest He afterwards smite by so much the more sharply as He now waits longer and more mercifully. Know moreover that you will offer a great sacrifice of expiation to our God, if you cut off speedily from your territories the infections of so great a sin.

The next two letters concern the mission to the English sent by Gregory from Rome in 596.

To Mellitus, Abbot

Gregory to Mellitus, Abbot in France.

Since the departure of our congregation, which is with thee, we have been in a state of great suspense from having heard nothing of the success of your journey. But when Almighty God shall have brought you to our most reverend brother the bishop Augustine, tell him that I have long been considering with myself about the case of the Angli; to wit, that the temples of idols in that nation should not be destroyed, but that the idols themselves that are in them should be. Let blessed water be prepared, and sprinkled in these temples, and altars constructed, and relics deposited, since, if these same temples are well built, it is needful that they should be transferred from the worship of idols to the service of the true God; that, when the people themselves see that these temples are not destroyed, they may put away error from their heart and, knowing and adoring the true God, may have recourse with the more familiarity to the places they have been accustomed to. And, since they are wont to kill many oxen in sacrifice to demons, they should have also some solemnity of this kind in a changed form, so that on the day of dedication, or on the anniversaries of the holy martyrs whose relics are deposited there, they may make for themselves tents of the branches of trees around these temples that have been changed into churches, and celebrate the solemnity with religious feasts. Nor let them any longer sacrifice animals to the devil, but slay animals to the praise of God for their own eating, and return thanks to the Giver of all for their fulness, so that, while some joys are reserved to them outwardly, they may be able the more easily to incline their minds to inward joys. For it is undoubtedly impossible to cut away everything at once from hard hearts, since one who strives to ascend to the highest place must needs rise by steps or paces, and not by leaps. Thus to the people of Israel in Egypt the Lord did indeed make Himself known; but still He reserved to them in His own worship the use of the sacrifices which they were accustomed to offer to the devil, enjoining them to immolate animals in sacrifice to Himself; to the end that, their hearts being changed, they should omit some things in the sacrifice and retain others, so that, though the animals were the same as what they had been accustomed to offer, nevertheless, as they immolated them to God and not to idols, they should be no longer the same sacrifices. This then it is necessary for thy Love to say to our aforesaid brother, that he, being now in that country, may consider well how he should arrange all things. God keep thee safe, most beloved son. Given this 15th day of the Kalends of July, the 19th year of the empire of our most pious lord Mauricius Tiberius Augustus, the 18th year after the consulship of the same our lord, Indiction 4.

To Augustine, Bishop of the Angli

Gregory to Augustine, &c.

Though it is certain that for those who labour for Almighty God ineffable rewards of an eternal kingdom are reserved, yet we must needs bestow honours upon them, that by reason of remuneration they may apply themselves the more manifoldly in devotion to spiritual work. And, since the new Church of the Angli has been brought to the grace of Almighty God through the bountifulness of the same Lord and thy labours, we grant to thee the use of the pallium therein for the solemnization of mass only, so that thou mayest ordain bishops in twelve several places, to be subject to thy jurisdiction, with the view of a bishop of the city of London being always consecrated in future by his own synod, and receiving the dignity of the pallium from this holy and Apostolical See which by the grace of God I serve. Further, to the city of York we desire thee to send a bishop whom thou mayest judge fit to be ordained; so that, if this same city with the neighbouring places should receive the word of God, he also may ordain twelve bishops, so as to enjoy the dignity of a metropolitan: for to him also, if our life is continued, we propose, with the favour of God, to send a pallium; but yet we desire to subject him to the control of thy Fraternity. But after thy death let him be over the bishops whom he shall have ordained, so as to be in no wise subject to the jurisdiction of the bishop of London. Further, between the bishops of London and York in the future let there be this distinction of dignity, that he be accounted first who has been first ordained. But let them arrange by council in common, and with concordant action, whatever things may have to be done in zeal for Christ; let them be of one mind in what is right, and accomplish what they are minded to do without disagreement with each other.

But let they Fraternity have subject to thyself under our God not only those bishops whom thous shalt ordain, and those whom the bishop of York may ordain, but also all the priests of Britain, to the end that they may learn the form of right belief and good living from the tongue and life of thy Holiness, and, executing their office well in their faith and manners, may attain to heavenly kingdoms when it may please the Lord. God keep thee safe, most reverend brother. Given on the tenth day of the Kalends of July, in the 19th year of the empire of our lord Mauricius Tiberius, the 18th year after the consulship of the same lord, Indiction 4.

The following excerpts from Gregory's Book of Pastoral Rule *describe the characteristics of a good bishop. Gregory's book provided a model for the Western episcopate throughout the Middle Ages.*

The conduct of a prelate ought so far to transcend the conduct of the people as the life of a shepherd is wont to exalt him above the flock. For one whose estimation is such that the people are called his flock is bound anxiously to consider what great necessity is laid upon him to maintain rectitude. It is necessary, then, that in thought he should be pure, in action chief; discreet in keeping silence, profitable in speech; a near neighbour to every one in sympathy, exalted above all in contemplation; a familiar friend of good livers through humility, unbending against the vices of evil-doers through zeal for righteousness; not relaxing in his care for what is inward from being occupied in outward things, nor neglecting to provide for outward things in his solicitude for what is inward. But the things which we have thus briefly touched on let us now unfold and discuss more at length.

The ruler should always be pure in thought, inasmuch as no impurity ought to pollute him who has undertaken the office of wiping away the stains of pollution in the hearts of others also; for the hand that would cleanse from dirt must needs be clean, lest, being itself sordid with clinging mire, it soil whatever it touches all the more. . . .

The ruler should always be chief in action, that by his living he may point out the way of life to those that are put under him, and that the flock, which follows the voice and manners of the shepherd, may learn how to walk better through example than through words. For he who is required by the necessity of his position to speak the highest things is compelled by the same necessity to exhibit the highest things. . . .

The ruler should be a near neighbour to every one in sympathy, and exalted above all in contemplation, so that through the bowels of loving-kindness he may transfer the infirmities of others to himself, and by loftiness of speculation transcend even himself in his aspiration after the invisible; lest either in seeking high things he despise the weak things of his neighbours, or in suiting himself to the weak things of his neighbours he relinquish his aspiration after high things. . . .

Supreme rule, then, is ordered well, when he who presides lords it over vices, rather than over his brethren. But, when superiors correct their delinquent subordinates, it remains for them anxiously to take heed how far, while in right of their authority they smite faults with due discipline, they still, through custody of humility, acknowledge themselves to be on a par with the very brethen who are corrected; although for the most part it is becoming that in our silent thought we even prefer the brethen whom we correct to ourselves. For their vices are through us smitten with the vigour of discipline; but in those which we ourselves commit we are lacerated by not even a word of upbraiding. Wherefore we are by so much the more bounden before the Lord as among men we sin unpunished; but our discipline renders our subordinates by so much the freer from divine judgment, as it leaves not their faults without retribution here. Therefore, in the heart humility should be maintained, and in action discipline.

. . .

It is to be borne in mind also, that it is right for good rulers to desire to please men; but this in order to draw their neighbours by the sweetness of their own character to affection for the truth; not that they should long to be themselves loved, but should make affection for themselves as a sort of road by which to lead the hearts of their hearers to the love of the Creator. For it is indeed difficult for a preacher who is not loved, however well he may preach, to be willingly listened to. He, then, who is over others ought to study to be loved to the end that he may be listened to, and still not seek love for its own sake, lest he be found in the hidden usurpation of his thought to rebel against Him whom in his office he appears to serve. Which things Paul insinuates well, when, manifesting the secret of his affection for us, he says, *Even as I please all men in all things* (1 Cor. x. *33*). And yet he says again, *If I yet pleased men, I should not be the servant of Christ* (Gal. i. 10). Thus Paul pleases, and pleases not; because in that he desires to please he seeks that not he himself should please men, but truth through him.

VI

Monasticism and the Conversion of the North

19.   Ireland: Monks and Missionaries

During the turmoil of the early Middle Ages, monasteries became the principal centers of Christian piety and culture. The monastic movement of Ireland influenced much of Western Europe because the Irish monks often adopted a life of voluntary exile as wandering preachers. St. Columba (521–597) and his followers converted Scotland and much of northern England. Columba did not leave a written Rule. The following Rule, traditionally attributed to him, was set down much later, but it reflects faithfully the spirit of early Irish monasticism.

Rule of S. Columba

Be alone in a separate place near a chief city,* if thy conscience is not prepared to be in common with the crowd.

Be always naked in imitation of Christ and the Evangelists.

Whatsoever little or much thou possessest of anything, whether clothing, or food, or drink, let it be at the command of the senior and at his disposal, for it is not befitting a religious to have any distinction of property with his own free brother.

Let a fast place, with one door, enclose thee.

A few religious men to converse with thee of God and his Testament; to visit thee on days of solemnity; to strengthen thee in the Testaments of God, and the narratives of the Scriptures.

From A. W. Haddan and W. Stubbs, *Councils and Ecclesiastical Documents Relating to Great Britain and Ireland* II, i (Oxford: Oxford University Press, 1873), pp. 119–121.

*That is, an Episcopal church or city.

A person too who would talk with thee in idle words, or of the world; or who murmurs at what he cannot remedy or prevent, but who would distress thee more should he be a tattler between friends and foes, thou shalt not admit him to thee, but at once give him thy benediction should he deserve it.

Let thy servant be a discreet, religious, not tale-telling man, who is to attend continually on thee, with moderate labour of course, but always ready.

Yield submission to every rule that is of devotion.

A mind prepared for red martyrdom.

A mind fortified and steadfast for white martyrdom.*

Forgiveness from the heart of every one.

Constant prayers for those who trouble thee.

Fervour in singing the office for the dead, as if every faithful dead was a particular friend of thine.

Hymns for souls *to be sung* standing.

Let thy vigils be constant from eve to eve, under the direction of another person.

Three labours in the day, viz., prayers, work, and reading.

The work to be divided into three parts, viz., thine own work, and the work of thy place, as regards its real wants; secondly, thy share of the brethen's [work]; lastly, to help the neighbours, viz. by instruction or writing, or sewing garments, or whatever labour they may be in want of, ut Dominus ait, "Non apparebis ante Me vacuus [as the Lord says, "You shall not appear before me empty."].

Everything in its proper order; Nemo enim coronabitur nisi qui legitime certaverit. [For no one is crowned except he who has striven lawfully.]

Follow alms-giving before all things.

Take not of food till thou art hungry.

Sleep not till thou feelest desire.

Speak not except on business.

Every increase which comes to thee in lawful meals, or in wearing apparel, give it for pity to the brethren that want it, or to the poor in like manner.

The love of God with all thy heart and all thy strength;

The love of thy neighbour as thyself.

Abide in the Testament of God throughout all times.

Thy measure of prayer shall be until thy tears come;

Or thy measure of work of labour till thy tears come;

Or thy measure of thy work of labour, or of thy genuflexions, until thy perspiration often comes, if thy tears are not free.

Other Irish missionaries traveled through Gaul and Germany and as far as Italy. St. Columban (ca. 543–615), founder of the monastery of Bobbio in

---

*That is self-mortification and ascetic practices, or bodily chastisement, as opposed to "red martyrdom," where blood is shed or the life laid down for the truth's sake.

northern Italy, was one of the greatest of them. His Boat Song *captures the mood of adventure and robust faith that animated the Irish monks.*

St. Columban: Boat-Song (c. 600)

Cut in the forests, swept down the two-horned Rhine,
Our keel, tight-caulked, now floats upon the sea.
Heia, men! Let the echoes resound with our heia!
The wild gusts swell, the slashing torrents fall,
But manly strength has force to tame the storm.
Heia, men! Let the echoes resound with our heia!
To earnest effort, clouds and tempest yield;
Zeal and unceasing labor conquer all.
Heia, men! Let the echoes resound with our heia!
Endure and save yourselves for better things;
O you who have suffered worse, this too shall end.
Heia, men! Let the echoes resound with our heia!
So when the loathsome foe assaults our hearts,
Tempting and shaking the depths of our hearts with passion,
Let your souls, men, remembering Christ, cry heia!
In resolution fixed, scorn Satan's wiles.
By virtues armed, defend yourselves with valor.
Let your souls, men, remembering Christ, cry heia!
Firm faith and holy ardor conquer all.
The ancient fiend, defeated, breaks his arrows.
Let your souls, men, remembering Christ, cry heia!
The Source of Good and Being, the Highest Power,
Offers the warrior and gives the victor prizes.
Let your souls, men, remembering Christ, cry heia!

20.   *The Rule of St. Benedict*

The "Holy Rule" of St. Benedict, composed in Italy about 530, defined the form of monastic life that came to be accepted throughout the Western church. In the seventh and eighth centuries, many monasteries in northern Europe that had originally been founded by Irish monks adopted the Benedictine rule.

Prologue.   . . . we are about to found, therefore, a school for the Lord's service; in the organization of which we trust that we shall ordain nothing severe and nothing burdensome. But even if, the demands of justice dictating it, something a little irksome shall be the result, for

From "The Rule of St. Benedict," E. F. Henderson, ed., *Select Historical Documents of the Middle Ages* (London: George Bell, 1892), pp. 274–309.

the purpose of amending vices or preserving charity;—thou shalt not therefore, struck by fear, flee the way of salvation, which can not be entered upon except through a narrow entrance. But as one's way of life and one's faith progresses, the heart becomes broadened, and, with the unutterable sweetness of love, the way of the mandates of the Lord is traversed. Thus, never departing from His guidance, continuing in the monastery in his teaching until death, through patience we are made partakers in Christ's passion, in order that we may merit to be companions in His kingdom.

Concerning the kinds of monks and their manner of living. It is manifest that there are four kinds of monks. The cenobites are the first kind; that is, those living in a monastery, serving under a rule or an abbot. Then the second kind is that of the anchorites; that is, the hermits—those who, not by the new fervour of a conversion but by the long probation of life in a monastery, have learned to fight against the devil, having already been taught by the solace of many. They, having been well prepared in the army of brothers for the solitary fight of the hermit, being secure now without the consolation of another, are able, God helping them, to fight with their own hand or arm against the vices of the flesh or of their thoughts.

But a third very bad kind of monks are the sarabaites, approved by no rule, experience being their teacher, as with the gold which is tried in the furnace. But, softened after the manner of lead, keeping faith with the world by their works, they are known through their tonsure to lie to God. These being shut up by twos or threes, or, indeed, alone, without a shepherd, not in the Lord's but in their own sheep-folds—their law is the satisfaction of their desires. For whatever they think good or choice, this they call holy; and what they do not wish, this they consider unlawful. But the fourth kind of monks is the kind which is called gyratory. During their whole life they are guests, for three or four days at a time, in the cells of the different monasteries, throughout the various provinces; always wandering and never stationary, given over to the service of their own pleasures and the joys of the palate, and in every way worse than the sarabaites. Concerning the most wretched way of living of all such monks it is better to be silent than to speak. These things therefore being omitted, let us proceed, with the aid of God, to treat of the best kind, the cenobites.

What the abbot should be like. An abbot who is worthy to preside over a monastery ought always to remember what he is called, and carry out with his deeds the name of a Superior. For he is believed to be Christ's representative, since he is called by His name, the apostle saying: "Ye have received the spirit of adoption of sons, whereby we call Abba, Father." And so the abbot should not—grant that he may not—teach, or decree, or order, any thing apart from the precept of the Lord; but his order or teaching should be sprinkled with the ferment of divine justice in the minds of his disciples. Let the abbot always be mindful that, at the tremendous judgment of God, both things will be weighed in the balance: his teaching and the obedience of his disciples. And let the abbot know that whatever the father of the family finds of less utility among the sheep is laid to the fault of the shepherd. Only in a case where the whole diligence of their pastor shall have been bestowed on an unruly and disobedient flock, and his whole care given to their morbid actions, shall that pastor, absolved in the judgment of the Lord, be free to say to the Lord with the prophet: "I have not hid Thy righteousness within my heart, I have declared Thy faithfulness and Thy salvation, but they despising have scorned me." And then at length let the punishment for the disobedient sheep under his care be death itself prevailing against them. Therefore, when any one receives the name of abbot, he ought to rule over his disciples with a double teaching; that is, let him show forth all good and holy things by deeds more than by words. So that to ready disciples he may propound the mandates of God in words; but, to the hard-hearted and the more simple-minded, he may show forth the divine precepts by his deeds. But as to all the things that he has taught to his disciples to be wrong, he shall show by his deeds that they are not to be done; lest, preaching to others, he himself shall be found worthy of blame, and lest God may say at some time to him a sinner: "What hast thou to do to declare my statutes or that thou should'st take my covenant in thy mouth. Seeing that thou hatest instruction and casteth my words behind thee; and why beholdest thou the mote that is in thy brother's eye, but considerest not the beam that is in thine own eye?" He shall make no distinction of persons in the monastery. One shall not be more cherished than another, unless it be the one whom he finds excelling in good works or in obedience. A free-born man shall not be preferred to one coming from servitude, unless there be some other reasonable cause. But if, justice demanding that it should be thus, it seems good to the abbot, he shall do this no matter what the rank shall be. But otherwise they shall keep their own places; for whether we be bond or free we are all one in Christ; and, under one God, we perform an equal service of subjection; for God is no respecter of persons. Only in this way is a distinction made by Him concerning us: if we are found humble and surpassing others in good works. Therefore let him (the abbot) have equal charity for all: let the same discipline be administered in all cases according to merit. In his teaching indeed the abbot ought always to observe that form laid down by the apostle when he says: "reprove, rebuke, exhort." That is, mixing seasons with seasons, blandishments with terrors, let him display the feeling of a severe yet devoted master. He should, namely, rebuke more severely the unruly and the turbulent. The obedient, moreover, and the gentle and the patient, he should exhort, that they may progress to higher things. But the negligent and scorners, we warn him to admonish and reprove. . . .

About calling in the brethren to take council. As often as anything especial is to be done in the monastery, the abbot shall call together the whole congregation, and shall himself explain the question at issue. And, having heard the advice of the brethren, he shall think it over by himself, and shall do what he considers most advantageous.

• • •

Concerning obedience. The first grade of humility is obedience without delay. This becomes those who, on account of the holy service which they have professed, or on account of the fear of hell or the glory of eternal life, consider nothing dearer to them than Christ: so that, so soon as anything is commanded by their superior, they may not know how to suffer delay in doing it, even as if it were a divine command. Concerning whom the Lord said: "As soon as he heard of me he obeyed me."

• • •

Concerning humility. . . . The sixth grade of humility is, that a monk be contented with all lowliness or extremity, and consider himself, with regard to everything which is enjoined on him, as a poor and unworthy workman; saying to himself with the prophet: "I was reduced to nothing and was ignorant; I was made as the cattle before thee, and I am always with thee." The seventh grade of humility is, not only that he, with his tongue, pronounce himself viler and more worthless than all; but that he also believe it in the innermost workings of his heart; humbling himself and saying with the prophet, etc. . . . The eighth degree of humility is that a monk do nothing except what the common rule of the monastery, or the example of his elders, urges him to do. The ninth degree of humility is that a monk restrain his tongue from speaking; and, keeping silence, do not speak until he is spoken to. The tenth grade of humility is that he be not ready, and easily inclined, to laugh. . . . The eleventh grade of humility is that a monk, when he speaks, speak slowly and without laughter, humbly with gravity, using few and reasonable words; and that he be not loud of voice. . . . The twelfth grade of humility is that a monk shall, not only with his heart but also with his body, always show humility to all who see him: that is, when at work, in the oratory, in the monastery, in the garden, on the road, in the fields. And everywhere, sitting or walking or standing, let him always be with head inclined, his looks fixed upon the ground; remembering every hour that he is guilty of his sins. Let him think that he is already being presented before the tremendous judgment of God, saying always to himself in his heart what the publican of the gospel, fixing his eyes on the earth, said: "Lord I am not worthy, I a sinner, so much as to lift mine eyes unto Heaven."

Concerning the divine offices at night. In the winter time, that is from the Calends of November until Easter, according to what is reasonable, they must rise at the eighth hour of the night, so that they rest a little more than half the night, and rise when they have already digested. But let the time that remains after vigils be kept for meditation by those brothers who are in any way behind hand with the psalter or lessons. From Easter, moreover, until the aforesaid Calends of November, let the hour of keeeping vigils be so arranged that, a short interval being observed in which the brethren may go out for the necessities of nature, the matins, which are always to take place with the dawning light, may straightway follow.

How many psalms are to be said at night.   In the winter first of all the verse shall be said: "Make haste oh God to deliver me; make haste to help me oh God." Then, secondly, there shall be said three times: "Oh Lord open Thou my lips and my mouth shall show forth Thy praise." To which is to be subjoined the third psalm and the Gloria. After this the ninety-fourth psalm is to be sung antiphonally or in unison. The Ambrosian chant shall then follow: then six psalms antiphonally. These having been said, the abbot shall, with the verse mentioned, give the blessing. And all being seated upon the benches, there shall be read in turn from the Scriptures—following out the analogy—three lessons; between which also three responses shall be sung. Two responses shall be said without the *Gloria;* but, after the third lesson, he who chants shall say the *Gloria.* And, when the cantor begins to say this, all shall straightway rise from their seats out of honour and reverence for the holy Trinity. Books, moreover, of the old as well as the New Testament of Divine authority shall be read at the Vigils; but also expositions of them which have been made by the most celebrated orthodox teachers and catholic Fathers. Moreover, after these three lessons with their responses, shall follow other six psalms to be sung with the Alleluia. After this a lesson of the Apostle shall follow, to be recited by heart; and verses and the supplication of the Litany, that is the Kyrie eleison: and thus shall end the nocturnal vigils.

• • •

How Divine Service shall be held through the day.   As the prophet says: "Seven times in the day so I praise Thee." Which sacred number of seven will thus be fulfilled by us if, at matins, at the first, third, sixth, ninth hours, at vesper time and at "completorium" we perform the duties of our service; for it is of these hours of the day that he said: "Seven times in the day do I praise Thee." For, concerning nocturnal vigils, the same prophet says: "At midnight I arose to confess unto thee." Therefore, at these times, let us give thanks to our Creator concerning the judgments of his righteousness; that is, at matins, etc. . . . , and at night we will rise and confess to him. . . .

• • •

How the monks shall sleep.   They shall sleep separately in separate beds. They shall receive positions for their beds, after the manner of their characters, according to the dispensation of their abbot. If it can be done, they shall all sleep in one place. If, however, their number do not permit it, they shall rest by tens or twenties, with elders who will concern themselves about them. A candle shall always be burning in that same cell until early in the morning. They shall sleep clothed, and girt with belts or with ropes; and they shall not have their knives at their sides while they sleep, lest perchance in a dream they should wound the sleepers. And let the monks be always on the alert; and, when the signal is given, rising without delay, let them hasten to mutually prepare themselves for the service of God—with all gravity and modesty, however. The younger brothers shall not have beds by themselves, but interspersed among those of the elder ones. And when they rise for the service of God, they shall exhort each other mutually with moderation on account of the excuses that those who are sleepy are inclined to make.

• • •

Concerning the cellarer of the monastery, what sort of a person he shall be.   As a cellarer of the monastery there shall be elected from the congregation one who is wise, mature in character, sober, not given to much eating, not proud, not turbulent, not an upbraider, not tardy, not prodigal, but fearing God: a father, as it were, to the whole congregation. He shall take care of everything, he shall do nothing without the order of the abbot. He shall have charge of what things are ordered: he shall not rebuff the brethren. If any brother by chance demand anything unreasonably from him, he shall not, by spurning, rebuff him; but reasonably, with humility, shall deny to him who wrongly seeks.

• • •

Whether the monks should have anything of their own.   More than anything else is this special vice to be cut off root and branch from the monastery, that one should presume to give or receive anything without the order of the abbot, or should have anything of his own. He should have absolutely not anything: neither a book, nor tablets, nor a pen—nothing at all.—For indeed it is not allowed to the monks to have their own bodies or wills in their own power. But all things necessary they must expect from the Father of the monastery; nor is it allowable to have anything which the abbot did not give or permit. All things shall be common to all, as it is written: "Let not any man presume or call anything his own." But if any one shall have been discovered delighting in this most evil vice: being warned once and again, if he do not amend, let him be subjected to punishment.

• • •

Concerning old age and infancy.   . . . Although human nature itself is prone to have pity for these ages—that is, old age and infancy—nevertheless the authority of the Rule also has regard for them. Their weakness shall always be considered, and in the matter of food, the strict tenor of the Rule shall by no means be observed, as far as they are concerned; but they shall be treated with pious consideration, and may anticipate the canonical hours.

• • •

Concerning the amount of food.   . . . We believe, moreover, that, for the daily refection of the sixth as well as of the ninth hour, two cooked dishes, on account of the infirmities of the different ones, are enough for all tables: so that whoever, perchance, can not eat of one may partake of the other. Therefore let two cooked dishes suffice for all the brothers: and, if it is possible to obtain apples or growing vegetables, a third may be added. One full pound of bread shall suffice for a day, whether there be one refection, or a breakfast and a supper. But if they are going to have supper, the third part of that same pound shall be reserved by the cellarer, to be given back to those who are about to sup. But if, perchance, some greater labour shall have been performed, it shall be in the will and power of the abbot, if it is expedient, to increase anything; surfeiting above all things being guarded against, so that indigestion may never seize a monk: for nothing is so contrary to every Christian as surfeiting, as our Lord says: "Take heed to yourselves, lest your hearts be overcharged with surfeiting." But to younger boys the same quantity shall not be served, but less than that to the older ones; moderation being observed in all things. But the eating of the flesh of quadrupeds shall be abstained from altogether by every one, excepting alone the weak and the sick.

• • •

Concerning the amount of drink.   Each one has his own gift from God, the one in this way, the other in that. Therefore it is with some hesitation that the amount of daily sustenance for others is fixed by us. Nevertheless, in view of the weakness of the infirm we believe that a hemina of wine a day is enough for each one. Those moreover to whom God gives the ability of bearing abstinence shall know that they will have their own reward. But the prior shall judge if either the needs of the place, or labour or the heat of summer, requires more; considering in all things lest satiety or drunkenness creep in. Indeed we read that wine is not suitable for monks at all. But because, in our day, it is not possible to persuade the monks of this, let us agree at least as to the fact that we should not drink till we are sated, but sparingly. For wine can make even the wise to go astray. Where, moreover, the necessities of the place are such that the amount written above can not be found — but much less or nothing at all — those who live there shall bless God and shall not murmur. And we admonish them to this above all: that they be without murmuring.

• • •

Concerning the daily manual labour.   Idleness is the enemy of the soul. And therefore, at fixed times, the brothers ought to be occupied in manual labour; and again, at fixed times, in sacred reading. Therefore we believe that, according to this disposition, both seasons ought to be arranged; so that, from Easter until the Calends of October, going out early, from the first until the fourth hour they shall do what labour may be necessary. Moreover, from the fourth hour until about the sixth, they shall be free for reading. After the meal of the sixth hour, moreover, rising from table, they shall rest in their beds with all silence; or, perchance, he that wishes to read may so read to himself that he do not disturb another. And the nona (the second meal) shall be gone through with more moderately about the middle of the eighth hour; and again they shall work at what is to be done until Vespers. But, if the exigency or poverty of the place demands that they be occupied by themselves in picking fruits, they shall not be dismayed: for then they are truly monks if they live by the labours of their hands; as did also our fathers and the apostles. Let all things be done with moderation, however, on account of the faint-hearted. From the Calends of October, moreover, until the beginning of Lent they shall be free for reading until the second full hour. At the second hour the tertia (morning service) shall be held, and all shall labour at the task which is enjoined upon them until the ninth. The first signal, moreover, of the ninth hour having been given, they shall each one leave off his work; and be ready when the second signal strikes. Moreover after the refection they shall be free for their reading or for psalms. But in the days of Lent, from dawn until the third full hour, they shall be free for their readings; and, until the tenth full hour, they shall do the labour that is enjoined on them. In which days of Lent they shall all receive separate books from the library; which they shall read entirely through in order. These books are to be given out on the first day of Lent. Above all there shall certainly be appointed one or two elders, who shall go round the monastery at the hours in which the brothers are engaged in reading, and see to it that no troublesome brother chance to be found who is open to idleness and trifling, and is not intent on his reading; being not only of no use to himself, but also stirring up others.

• • •

Concerning clothes and shoes. . . . Vestments shall be given to the brothers according to the quality of the places where they dwell, or the temperature of the air. For in cold regions more is required; but in warm, less. This, therefore, is a matter for the abbot to decide. We nevertheless consider that for ordinary places there suffices for the monks a cowl and a gown apiece—the cowl, in winter hairy, in summer plain or old—and a working garment, on account of their labours. As clothing for the feet, shoes and boots.

• • •

Concerning the manner of receiving brothers. When any new comer applies for conversion, an easy entrance shall not be granted him: but, as the apostle says, "Try the spirits if they be of God." Therefore, if he who comes perserveres in knocking, and is seen after four or five days to patiently endure the insults inflicted upon him, and the difficulty of ingress, and to persist in his demand: entrance shall be allowed him, and he shall remain for a few days in the cell of the guests. After this, moreover, he shall be in the cell of the novices, where he shall meditate and eat and sleep. And an elder shall be detailed off for him who shall be capable of saving souls, who shall altogether intently watch over him, and make it a care to see if he reverently seek God, if he be zealous in the service of God, in obedience, in suffering shame. And all the harshness and roughness of the means through which God is approached shall be told him in advance. If he promise perseverance in his steadfastness, after the lapse of two months this Rule shall be read to him in order, and it shall be said to him: Behold the law under which thou dost wish to serve; if thou canst observe it, enter; but if thou canst not, depart freely. If he have stood firm thus far, then he shall be led into the aforesaid cell of the novices; and again he shall be proven with all patience. And, after the lapse of six months, the Rule shall be read to him; that he may know upon what he is entering. And, if he stand firm thus far, after four months the same Rule shall again be re-read to him. And if, having deliberated with himself, he shall promise to keep everything, and to obey all the commands that are laid upon him: then he shall be received in the congregation; knowing that it is decreed, by the law of the Rule, that from that day he shall not be allowed to depart from the monastery, nor to shake free his neck from the yoke of the Rule, which, after such tardy deliberation, he was at liberty either to refuse or receive.

• • •

Concerning the ordination of an abbot.   In ordaining an abbot this consideration shall always be observed: that such a one shall be put into office as the whole congregation, according to the fear of God, with one heart—or even a part, however small, of the congregation with more prudent counsel—shall have chosen. He who is to be ordained, moreover, shall be elected for merit of life and learnedness in wisdom; even though he be the lowest in rank in the congregation. But even if the whole congregation with one consent shall have elected a person consenting to their vices—which God forbid;—and those vices shall in any way come clearly to the knowledge of the bishop to whose diocese that place pertains, or to the neighbouring abbots or Christians: the latter shall not allow the consent of the wicked to prevail, but shall set up a dispenser worthy of the house of God; knowing that they will receive a good reward for this, if they do it chastely and with zeal for God. Just so they shall know, on the contrary, that they have sinned if they neglect it.

21.   *England, Rome, and Germany*

England was converted to Christianity in the seventh century, partly by Irish monks, partly by Benedictine missionaries sent out from Rome (see

From *Bede's Ecclesiastical History*, A. M. Sellar, trans. (London: George Bell and Sons, 1907), pp. 116-117, 195-201.

above, p. 66). Bede (ca. 673–735), the greatest of Anglo-Saxon scholars, described how King Edwin of Northumbria received the Roman missionary Paulinus in 627.

Holding a council with the wise men, [King Edwin] asked of every one in particular what he thought of this doctrine hitherto unknown to them, and the new worship of God that was preached? The chief of his own priests, Coifi, immediately answered him, "O king, consider what this is which is now preached to us; for I verily declare to you what I have learnt beyond doubt, that the religion which we have hitherto professed has no virtue in it and no profit. For none of your people has applied himself more diligently to the worship of our gods than I; and yet there are many who receive greater favours from you, and are more preferred than I, and are more prosperous in all that they undertake to do or to get. Now if the gods were good for any thing, they would rather forward me, who have been careful to serve them with greater zeal. It remains, therefore, that if upon examination you find those new doctrines, which are now preached to us, better and more efficacious, we hasten to receive them without any delay."

Another of the king's chief men, approving of his wise words and exhortations, added thereafter: "The present life of man upon earth, O king, seems to me in comparison with that time which is unknown to us, like to the swift flight of a sparrow through the house wherein you sit at supper in winter, with your ealdormen and thegns, while the fire blazes in the midst, and the hall is warmed, but the wintry storms of rain or snow are raging abroad. The sparrow, flying in at one door and immediately out at another, whilst he is within, is safe from the wintry tempest; but after a short space of fair weather, he immediately vanishes out of your sight, passing from winter into winter again. So this life of man appears for a little while, but of what is to follow or what went before we know nothing at all. If, therefore, this new doctrine tells us something more certain, it seems justly to deserve to be followed." The other elders and king's counsellors, by Divine prompting, spoke to the same effect.

But Coifi added, that he wished more attentively to hear Paulinus discourse concerning the God Whom he preached. When he did so, at the king's command, Coifi, hearing his words, cried out, "This long time I have perceived that what we worshipped was naught; because the more diligently I sought after truth in that worship, the less I found it. But now I freely confess, that such truth evidently appears in this preaching as can confer on us the gifts of life, of salvation, and of eternal happiness. For which reason my counsel is, O king, that we instantly give up to ban and fire those temples and altars which we have consecrated without reaping any benefit from them." In brief, the king openly assented to the preaching of the Gospel by Paulinus, and renouncing idolatry, declared that he received the faith of Christ.

A later king of Northumbria, Oswy, made a choice between the Irish and Roman traditions of Christianity in 664. A major point at issue was the date of Easter.

Then Colman said, "The Easter which I keep, I received from my elders, who sent me hither as bishop; all our forefathers, men beloved of God, are known to have celebrated it after the same manner; and that it may not seem to any contemptible and worthy to be rejected, it is the same which the blessed John the Evangelist, the disciple specially beloved of our Lord, with all the churches over which he presided, is recorded to have celebrated."

Then Wilfrid, being ordered by the king to speak, began thus:— "The Easter which we keep, we saw celebrated by all at Rome, where the blessed Apostles, Peter and Paul, lived, taught, suffered, and were buried; we saw the same done by all in Italy and in Gaul, when we travelled through those countries for the purpose of study and prayer. We found it observed in Africa, Asia, Egypt, Greece, and all the world, wherever the Church of Christ is spread abroad, among divers nations and tongues, at one and the same time; save only among these and their accomplices in obstinacy, I mean the Picts and the Britons, who foolishly, in these two remote islands of the ocean, and only in part even of them, strive to oppose all the rest of the world."

"But as for you and your companions, you certainly sin, if, having heard the decrees of the Apostolic see, nay, of the universal Church, confirmed, as they are, by Holy Scripture, you scorn to follow them; for, though your fathers were holy, do you think that those few men, in a corner of the remotest island, are to be preferred before the universal Church of Christ throughout the world? And if that Columba of yours, (and, I may say, ours also, if he was Christ's servant,) was a holy man and powerful in miracles, yet could he be preferred before the most blessed chief of the Apostles, to whom our Lord said, 'Thou art Peter, and upon this rock I will build my Church, and the gates of hell shall not prevail against it, and I will give unto thee the keys of the kingdom of Heaven.'"

When Wilfrid had ended thus, the king said, "Is it true, Colman, that these words were spoken to Peter by our Lord?" He answered, "It is true, O king!" Then said he, "Can you show any such power given to your Columba?" Colman answered, "None." Then again the king asked, "Do you both agree in this, without any controversy, that these words were said above all to Peter, and that the keys of the kingdom of Heaven were given to him by our Lord?" They both answered, "Yes." Then the king concluded, "And I also say unto you, that he is the door-keeper, and I will not gainsay him, but I desire, as far as I know and am able, in all things to obey his laws, lest haply when I come to the gates of the kingdom of Heaven, there should be none to open them, he being my adversary who is proved to have the keys." The king having said this, all who were seated there or standing by, both great and small, gave their assent, and renouncing the less perfect custom, hastened to conform to that which they had found to be better.

In the eighth century, Anglo-Saxon monks, working in close association with the Roman church, spread Christianity to still-pagan parts of Europe. St. Boniface (ca. 680–755) played a major part in the conversion of Germany.

Letter of Pope Gregory II to Boniface (719)

Gregory, servant of the servants of God, to the devout priest Boniface:

Knowing that thou hast from childhood been devoted to sacred letters, and that thou hast labored to reveal to unbelieving people the mystery of faith, . . . we decree in the name of the indivisible Trinity, through the unshaken authority of Peter, chief of the apostles, whose doctrine it is our charge to teach, and whose holy see is in our keeping, that, since thou seemest to glow with the salvation-bringing fire which our Lord came to send upon the earth, thou shalt hasten to whatsoever tribes are lingering in the error of unbelief, and shalt institute the rites of the kingdom of God. . . . And we desire thee to establish the discipline of the sacraments, according to the observance of our holy apostolic see.

Oath of Boniface to the Papacy (722)

I, Boniface, bishop by the grace of God, promise to you, the blessed, Peter, chief of the apostles, and to thy vicar, the blessed Pope Gregory, and to his successors, by the Father and the Son and the Holy Ghost, the indivisible Trinity, and by this thy most holy body, that, God helping me, I will maintain all the belief and the purity of the holy Catholic faith, and I will remain steadfast in the unity of this faith in which the whole salvation of Christians lies, as is established without doubt.

I will in no wise oppose the unity of the one universal Church, no matter who may seek to persuade me. But as I have said, I will maintain my faith and purity and union with thee and the benefits of thy Church, to whom God has given the power to loose and to bind, and with thy vicar and his successors, in all things. And if it comes to my knowledge that priests have turned from the ancient practices of the holy fathers, I will have no intercourse nor connection with them; but

"Letter of Gregory II," "Oath of Boniface," in J. H. Robinson, ed. and trans., *Readings in European History*, I (Boston: Ginn and Company, 1904), pp. 105–106.

rather, if I can restrain them, I will. If I cannot, I will at once faithfully make known the whole matter to my apostolic lord.

In Germany, Boniface had to contend with persistent loyalty to the old pagan gods. An occasional miracle proved helpful. *

Many of the people of Hesse were converted [by Boniface] to the Catholic faith and confirmed by the grace of the spirit: and they received the laying on of hands. But some there were, not yet strong of soul, who refused to accept wholly the teachings of the true faith. Some men sacrificed secretly, some even openly, to trees and springs. Some secretly practiced divining, soothsaying, and incantations, and some openly. But others, who were of sounder mind, cast aside all heathen profanation and did none of these things, and it was with the advice and consent of these men that Boniface sought to fell a certain tree of great size, at Geismar, and called, in the ancient speech of the region, the oak of Thor.

The man of God was surrounded by the servants of God. When he would cut down the tree, behold a great throng of pagans who were there cursed him bitterly among themselves because he was the enemy of their gods. And when he had cut into the trunk a little way, a breeze sent by God stirred overhead, and suddenly the branching top of the tree was broken off, and the oak in all its huge bulk fell to the ground. And it was broken into four huge sections without any effort of the brethren who stood by. When the pagans who had cursed did see this, they left off cursing and, believing, blessed God. Then the most holy priest took counsel with the brethren: and he built from the wood of the tree an oratory, and dedicated it to the holy apostle Peter.

The Life of Sturmi (a convert of Boniface) describes the establishment of Benedictine monasteries in the wilds of Germany. †

For almost three years Sturmi fulfilled the duties of the priesthood, preaching and baptizing among the people. Then by the inspiration of God the purpose came into his soul to chasten himself by the straiter life and the hardships of the wilderness. He sought counsel thereupon from Boniface,—his master in the spirit,—who, when he understood Sturmi, knew that this purpose was inspired of God and rejoiced that God had designed to lead him by his grace. He gave Sturmi two companions, and when he had prayed and blessed them all he said: "Go forth into that solitude which is called Bochonia and seek a place meet for the servants of God to dwell in. For God is able to prepare for his servants a place in the wilderness."

*From "Willibald's Life of Boniface," in J. H. Robinson, *Readings,* pp. 106-107.
†From "Eigil's Life of Sturmi," in J. H. Robinson, *Readings,* pp. 107-111.

And so those three went forth into the wilderness and entered into places solitary and rough, and saw almost nothing but heaven and earth and great trees; and they prayed Christ fervently that he would direct their feet in the path of peace. On the third day they came to the place which even to this day is called Hersfeld; and when they had seen and explored the region round about, they asked Christ that the place might be blest to the dwellers therein. On the very spot where the monastery now stands they built poor huts of the bark of trees. There they tarried many days, serving God with holy fasts and watching and prayer. . . .

Then after some time spent in holy meditation Sturmi returned to the bishop, and described the lay of the land and the course of the streams, and the hills and valleys. . . . Boniface heard him attentively, and answered: "I fear to have you dwell in this place which ye have found because a barbarous race lives close by, for, as thou knowest, the fell Saxons are near at hand. Wherefore seek a dwelling in the wilderness farther away and higher up the stream, where ye may remain without danger."

Then the holy man Sturmi returned to his companions. With two brethren he entered a boat and traveled along the river Fulda, spying out the land, but they found no place which pleased them. So Sturmi went again to Boniface and said, "For many days did we sail along the river Fulda, but we found nothing that we would dare to praise to you." And the holy bishop saw that God had not yet revealed the place which he had chosen.

Sturmi returned to the cell which had now been built in a place above Herfeld. Here he saluted the brethren and reported to them what the holy bishop had counseled. Then after resting a little he mounted his ass and set forth alone, commending his journey to Christ, who is the way, the truth, and the life. All alone, sitting upon his ass, he began his journey through the vast places of the wilderness. He eagerly explored the region and observed with quick eye the mountains and the hills and the plains, the springs and torrents and rivers. With psalms always upon his lips, he prayed to God with groaning, his soul lifted up to heaven. And wherever night found him, there he rested; and he hewed wood with the sword which he bore in his hand, and laid it in a circle, and set it on fire to protect his ass, lest the wild beasts which were there in great numbers might devour him. For himself, he made on his forehead the sign of the cross of Christ, in the name of God, and rested in safety. . . .

And then he went back a little way and came to the place already made ready and blessed by God, even the place where the holy monastery [of Fulda] now stands. When he had come thither straightway the holy man Sturmi was filled with exceeding great joy, for he knew that through the merits and prayers of the holy bishop Boniface the place had been revealed to him by God.

Then on the second day the man of God came again to Hersfeld and found his brethren there calling upon God with fervent prayers. He told them of the place he had found and bade them make ready to go thither with him. But Sturmi went straightway to the holy bishop Boniface to tell him how he had found a place for the brethren to dwell in. Together they rejoiced and gave God thanks and held sweet converse about the life and conversation of monks. Then did the bishop let Sturmi go back to his wilderness, while he went to the palace of Carloman, the king, to gain from him a grant of the place Sturmi had chosen. . . .

And the brethren decided to follow the rule of the holy father Benedict. They spent many years in holy pursuits; and the number of brethren in the monastery grew greater, for many men gave themselves and all that they had to serve God there. And the holy bishop was zealous to visit them from time to time; and he had compassion upon their poverty, and gave them some lands to furnish them necessary food.

Women played an important role in English religious life, sometimes as rulers of "double monasteries"—a community of men and a community of women living under a single abbess. Boniface summoned the nun, Leoba, from one such house to help in his work in Germany.

In the island of Britain, which is inhabited by the nation of the English, is a place called among that people by the ancient name Wimborne. . . . Here two monasteries were of old founded by kings of that race, surrounded with high and stout walls, and supplied with a sufficiency of income by a reasonable provision; one a monastery of clerics, and the other of women. From the beginning of their foundation, each of them was regulated by that rule of conduct, that neither of them was entered by the opposite sex. For a woman was never permitted to enter the congregation of men, or any man the house of the nuns, except priests only, who used to enter the churches solely to perform the office of Mass, and when the service was solemnly concluded, immediately to return to their own dwelling. . . . Morever, the mother of the congregation herself, when she had need to make arrangements or give orders about any outside affairs for the profit of the monastery, spoke through the window, and from there decided whatever expediency required to be arranged or commanded.

To this place, after some abbesses and spiritual mothers, there was preferred a religious virgin, Tette by name, noble certainly by the dignity of secular family—she was, in fact, the king's sister—but much more noble by the goodness of her behavior and tokens of holy virtues. She ruled both monasteries with great skill and discretion. For she

From "Life of Leoba," edited by Dorothy Whitelock in *English Historical Documents*, I *c.500–1042*, Second Edition (New York: Oxford University Press, 1955), pp. 719-722. Copyright © 1955, 1979 by Eyre Methuen Ltd. Reprinted by permission of Oxford University Press, Inc.

showed all good and holy things more by example than by words, and whatever things she taught to be contrary to the welfare of the soul, she demonstrated by her deeds how to avoid them. . . . Very many tokens of virtue are related of her, which the venerable maiden Leoba, her pupil, used delightfully to recount from memory. . . .

At the time when the blessed maiden Leoba flourished in the monastery in the pursuits of the celestial life, the holy martyr Boniface was ordained bishop by Gregory, bishop of the Roman see (who succeeded Constantine in the pontificate), and was sent to preach the word of God to the people of Germany. And there, since he found the harvest indeed great and the people inclined to the faith, but had few labourers to work with him in the Lord's field, he sent messengers and letters into the land of the English, from which he was himself sprung, and summoned some from the divers orders of the clergy, versed in the divine law and suitable by due probity of life and habits for preaching the word, with whose support he vigorously discharged the mission enjoined on him. . . .

Likewise also he sent messengers into his own country with letters to Abbess Tette, who has been mentioned above, begging her to send to him for the solace of his exile and the support of the mission which had been enjoined on him the maiden Leoba, the fame of whose sanctity and virtuous teaching had been spread abroad through distant lands, and filled the mouths of many with repeated praises. The mother of the community indeed felt her departure very grievously, but yet, since she could not resist the divine dispensation, she sent her with honour to the blessed man just as he had asked. . . . The man of God received her with great respect when she came, loving her not so much for their kinship, in that she was related to him on the maternal side, as for her holiness of life and wise teaching, with which he knew that she would profit many by word and example.

Therefore he regulated the charge of the monasteries and the pattern of life according to the rule, just as he had desired; and he put Abbot Sturmi over the monks and decided that the religious maiden Leoba should be the mother of virgins, and established a monastery for her in place called Bischofsheim, where was collected no small number of handmaids of God, who were set to the study of celestial learning after the example of their blessed mistress, and profited so much by her teaching that many of them were afterwards made mistresses over others; so that there were either very few, or no monasteries of women in those districts which did not desire teachers from her pupils. For she was a woman of great virtues, and so confirmed in the strength of the purpose she had undertaken that she remembered neither her country nor her relations, but employed all her zeal on what she had begun, that she might show herself blameless before God and be to all subject to her a model of salvation in word and way of life. She always took care not to teach other than as she herself acted.

No arrogance, no pride influenced her behavior, but she showed herself affable and kind to all, without regard to persons. For she was of angelic aspect, of pleasant speech, of clear intelligence, great in counsel, orthodox in faith, most patient in hope, most generous in charity; and though she always showed a glad countenance, she never gave way to laughter with too great hilarity. No one ever heard a curse from her mouth, "the sun never went down on her anger." She herself practised very sparingly the use of food and drink, though she showed the greatest kindness to others. Therefore the little cup from which she used to drink was called by the sisters, because of its size, "the little one of the loved one." She applied herself to the pursuit of reading with such diligence that, unless she were occupied in prayer or refreshing the body with food or sleep, the divine Scripture was never out of her hands. For, since she had been educated from early infancy in grammar and in the study of the other liberal arts, she tried to attain to the perfection of spiritual knowledge with such great earnestness in meditation that, as natural gifts combined with diligence, she became most erudite by the double gift of nature and industry. For with a keen mind she went through the volumes of the Old and New Testaments, and committed divine precepts to memory. And she added also the sayings of the holy fathers and the decrees of the canons, as well as the laws of the whole ecclesiastical system in full perfection. Especially she observed discretion in every act and instruction. . . . She truly practised the virtue of humility with so great zeal, that, though she was set above the others by merit of holiness and her position of mistress, she believed in her heart that she was the last of all, and revealed it in her speech and showed it in her bearing. She set particular store by hospitality; for to all, without any exception of person, she opened her house, and produced a feast, the mother herself fasting, and with her own hands washed the feet of all, being guardian and servant of the teaching of our Lord. . . .

chapter
VII

Byzantium and Islam

22. *Justinian: Achievements and Personality*

During the sixth and seventh centuries, Christian culture in the West survived mainly in scattered monastic communities. But in the Eastern Empire a great civilization still flourished. The contemporary Greek historian Procopius depicted the magnificence of Byzantium in his account of the achievements and the architectural program of the emperor Justinian (527–565).

In our own age there has been born the Emperor Justinian, who, taking over the State when it was harrassed by disorder, has not only made it greater in extent, but also much more illustrious, by expelling from it those barbarians who had from of old pressed hard upon it, as I have made clear in detail in the Books on the Wars. Indeed they say that Themistocles, the son of Neocles, once boastfully said that he did not lack the ability to make a small state large. But this Sovereign does not lack the skill to produce completely transformed states—witness the way he has already added to the Roman domain many states which in his own time had belonged to others, and has created countless cities which did not exist before. And finding that the belief in God was, before his time, straying into errors and being forced to go in many di-

From Procopius, *Buildings,* H. B. Dewing, trans. (Cambridge, Mass.: Harvard University Press, 1940), pp. 5-13, 25-27, 33-37. Reprinted by permission of the publishers and The Loeb Classical Library. From Procopius, *Secret History,* R. Atwater, trans. (Ann Arbor: University of Michigan Press, 1961), pp. 42-44. Copyright © 1961 by The University of Michigan.

rections, he completely destroyed all the paths leading to such errors, and brought it about that it stood on the firm foundation of a single faith. Morever, finding the laws obscure because they had become far more numerous than they should be, and in obvious confusion because they disagreed with each other, he preserved them by cleansing them of the mass of their verbal trickery, and by controlling their discrepancies with the greatest firmness;[1] as for those who plotted against him, he of his own volition dismissed the charges against them, and causing those who were in want to have a surfeit of wealth, and crushing the spiteful fortune that oppressed them, he wedded the whole State to a life of prosperity. Furthermore, he strengthened the Roman domain, which everywhere lay exposed to the barbarians, by a multitude of soldiers, and by constructing strongholds he built a wall along its remote frontiers.

However, most the Emperor's other achievements have been described by me in my other writings, so that the subject of the present work will be the benefits which he wrought as a builder. . . . And with good reason the buildings in Byzantium, beyond all the rest, will serve as foundation for my narrative. For "o'er a work's beginnings," as the old saying has it, "we needs must set a front that shines afar."

Some men of the common herd, all the rubbish of the city, once rose up against the Emperor Justinian in Byzantium, when they brought about the rising called the Nika Insurrection, which has been described by me in detail and without any concealment in the Book on the Wars. And by way of shewing that it was not against the Emperor alone that they had taken up arms, but no less against God himself, unholy wretches that they were, they had the hardihood to fire the Church of the Christians, which the people of Byzantium call "Sophia," [Wisdom] an epithet which they have most appropriately invented for God, by which they call His temple; and God permitted them to accomplish this impiety, foreseeing into what an object of beauty this shrine was destined to be transformed. So the whole church at that time lay a charred mass of ruins. But the Emperor Justinian built not long afterwards a church so finely shaped, that if anyone had enquired of the Christians before the burning if it would be their wish that the church should be destroyed and one like this should take its place, shewing them some sort of model of the building we now see, it seems to me that they would have prayed that they might see their church destroyed forthwith, in order that the building might be converted into its present form. At any rate the Emperor, disregarding all questions of expense, eagerly pressed on to begin the work of construction, and began to gather all the artisans from the whole world. And Anthemius of Tralles, the most learned man in the skilled craft which is known as the art of building, not only of all his contemporaries, but also when

[1]On Justinian's legal codification see above, p.50 [Ed.].

compared with those who had lived long before him, ministered to the Emperor's enthusiasm, duly regulating the tasks of the various artisans, and preparing in advance designs of the future construction; and associated with him was another master-builder, Isidorus by name, a Milesian by birth, a man who was intelligent and worthy to assist the Emperor Justinian. Indeed this also was an indication of the honour in which God held the Emperor, that He had already provided the men who would be most serviceable to him in the tasks which were waiting to be carried out. And one might with good reason marvel at the discernment of the Emperor himself, in that out of the whole world he was able to select the men who were most suitable for the most important of his enterprises.

So the church has become a spectacle of marvellous beauty, overwhelming to those who see it, but to those who know it by hearsay altogether incredible. For it soars to a height to match the sky, and as if surging up from amongst the other buildings it stands on high and looks down upon the remainder of the city, adoring it, because it is a part of it, but glorying in its own beauty, because, though a part of the city and dominating it, it at the same time towers above it to such a height that the whole city is viewed from there as from a watch-tower. Both its breadth and its length have been so carefully proportioned, that it may not improperly be said to be exceedingly long and at the same time unusually broad. And it exults in an indescribable beauty.

• • •

The whole ceiling is overlaid with pure gold, which adds glory to the beauty, yet the light reflected from the stones prevails, shining out in rivalry with the gold. And there are two stoa-like colonnades, one on each side, not separated in any way from the structure of the church itself, but actually making the effect of its width greater, and reaching along its whole length, to the very end, while in height they are less than the interior of the building. And they too have vaulted ceilings and decorations of gold. One of these two colonnaded stoas has been assigned to men worshippers, while the other is reserved for women engaged in the same exercise. But they have nothing to distinguish them, nor do they differ from one another in any way, but their very equality serves to beautify the church, and their similarity to adorn it. But who could fittingly describe the galleries of the women's side, or enumerate the many colonnades and the colonnaded aisles by means of which the church is surrounded? Or who could recount the beauty of the columns and the stones with which the church is adorned? One might imagine that he had come upon a meadow with its flowers in full bloom. For he would surely marvel at the purple of some, the green tint of others, and at those on which the crimson glows and those from which the white flashes, and again at those which Nature, like some painter, varies with the most contrasting colours. And whenever anyone enters this church to pray, he understands at once that it is not by any human power or skill, but by the influence of God, that this work has been so finely turned. And so his mind is lifted up toward God and exalted, feeling that He cannot be far away, but must especially love to dwell in this place which He has chosen. And this does not happen only to one who sees the church for the first time, but the same experience comes to him on each successive occasion, as though the sight were new each time. Of this spectacle no one has ever had a surfeit, but when present in the church men rejoice in what they see, and when they leave it they take proud delight in conversing about it.

. . .

Before the Senate House there happened to be a sort of marketplace, which the people of Byzantium call the Augustaeum. In that place there is a structure of stones, which is made up of not less than seven courses, laid in a rectangle, all fitted to each other at their ends, but each course being narrower than that beneath, and set back with the result that each of the stones becomes, from the way it is set, a projecting step, so that people assembled there sit upon them as upon seats. And at the top of the stones there rises a column of extraordinary size, not a monolith, however, but composed of large stones in circular courses, cut so as to form angles on their inner faces, and fitted to one another by the skill of the masons. And finest brass, cast in panels and garlands, covers the stones on every side, both serving to bind them securely, and covering them with adornment, and giving the shaft throughout, but particularly at the base and the capital, the appearance of a column. This brass, in its colour, is softer than pure gold, and its value is not much less than that of an equal weight of silver. And on the summit of the column stands a gigantic bronze horse, facing toward the east, a very noteworthy sight. He seems about to advance, and to be splendidly pressing forward. Indeed he holds his left foot in the air, as though it were about to take a forward step on the ground before him, while the other is pressed down upon the stone on which he stands, as if ready to take the next step; his hind feet he holds close together, so that they may be ready whenever he decides to move. Upon this horse is mounted a colossal bronze figure of the Emperor. And the figure is habited like Achilles, that is, the costume he wears is known by that name. He wears half-boots and his legs are not covered by greaves. Also he wears a breastplate in the heroic fashion, and a helmet covers his head and gives the impression that it moves up and down, and a dazzling light flashes forth from it. One might say, in poetic speech, that here is that star of Autumn. And he looks toward the rising sun, directing his course, I suppose, against the Persians. And in his left hand he holds a globe, by which the sculptor signifies that the whole earth and sea are subject to him, yet he has neither sword nor spear nor any other weapon, but a cross stands upon the globe which he carries, the emblem by which alone he has obtained both his Empire and his victory in war. And stretching forth his right hand toward the rising sun and spreading out his fingers, he commands the barbarians in that quarter to remain at home and to advance no further.

As regards Justinian's personality, Procopius makes an ambiguous witness. He publicly extolled the emperor, but he also wrote a Secret History, *from which the next quotation is taken, and in this he accused Justinian of every kind of vice and folly.*

Now such was Justinian in appearance; but his character was something I could not fully describe. For he was at once villainous and amenable; as people say colloquially, a moron. He was never truthful with anyone, but always guileful in what he said and did, yet easily hoodwinked by any who wanted to deceive him. His nature was an unnatural mixture of folly and wickedness. What in olden times a peripatetic philosopher said was also true of him, that opposite qualities combine in a man as in the mixing of colors. I will try to portray him, however, insofar as I can fathom his complexity.

This Emperor, then, was deceitful, devious, false, hypocritical, two-faced, cruel, skilled in dissembling his thought, never moved to tears by either joy or pain, though he could summon them artfully at will when the occasion demanded, a liar always, not only offhand, but in writing, and when he swore sacred oaths to his subjects in their very hearing. Then he would immediately break his agreements and pledges, like the vilest of slaves, whom indeed only the fear of torture drives to confess their perjury. A faithless friend, he was a treacherous enemy, insane for murder and plunder, quarrelsome and revolutionary, easily led to anything evil, but never willing to listen to good counsel, quick to plan mischief and carry it out, but finding even the hearing of anything good distasteful to his ears.

How could anyone put Justinian's ways into words? These and many even worse vices were disclosed in him as in no other mortal: nature seemed to have taken the wickedness of all other men combined and planted it in this man's soul. And besides this, he was too prone to listen to accusations; and too quick to punish. For he decided such cases without full examinations, naming the punishment when he had heard only the accuser's side of the matter. Without hesitation he wrote decrees for the plundering of countries, sacking of cities, and slavery of whole nations, for no cause whatever. So that if one wished to take all the calamities which had befallen the Romans before this time and weigh them against his crimes, I think it would be found that more men had been murdered by this single man than in all previous history.

He had no scruples about appropriating other people's property, and did not even think any excuse necessary, legal or illegal, for confiscating what did not belong to him. And when it was his, he was more than ready to squander it in insane display, or give it as an unnecessary bribe to the barbarians. In short, he neither held on to any money himself nor let anyone else keep any: as if his reason were not avarice, but jealousy of those who had riches. Driving all wealth from the country of the Romans in this manner, he became the cause of universal poverty.

Now this was the character of Justinian, so far as I can portray it.

23. *Islam: A Fighting Faith*

In the mid-seventh century Byzantium faced a new threat. The forces of Islam, inspired by the prophet Mohammed, conquered most of the eastern provinces of the empire. The following surâh, or chapter, from the Koran conveys some of the essentials of the new faith.

Mohammed

IN THE NAME OF ALLAH, THE COMPASSIONATE, THE MERCIFUL
Allah will bring to nothing the deeds of those who disbelieve and debar others from His path. As for the faithful who do good works and believe in what is revealed to Mohammed—which is the truth from their Lord—He will forgive them their sins and ennoble their state.

This, because the unbelievers follow falsehood, while the faithful follow the truth from their Lord. Thus Allah coins their sayings for mankind.

When you meet the unbelievers in the battlefield strike off their heads and, when you have laid them low, bind your captives firmly. Then grant them their freedom or take ransom from them, until War shall lay down her armour.

Thus shall you do. Had Allah willed, He could Himself have punished them; but He had ordained it thus that He might test you, the one by the other.

As for those who are slain in the cause of Allah, He will not allow their works to perish. He will vouchsafe them guidance and ennoble their state; He will admit them to the Paradise He has made known to them.

Believers, if you help Allah, Allah will help you and make you strong. But the unbelievers shall be consigned to perdition. He will bring their deeds to nothing. Because they have opposed His revelations, He will frustrate their works.

Have they never journeyed through the land and seen what was the end of those who have gone before them? Allah destroyed them utterly.

From *The Koran*, N.J. Dawood, trans. (Baltimore: Penguin Books, 1968), pp. 121- 124. Reprinted by permission of Penguin Books Ltd.

A similar fate awaits the unbelievers, because Allah is the protector of the faithful: because the unbelievers have no protection.

Allah will admit those who embrace the true faith and do good works to gardens watered by running streams. The unbelievers take their fill of pleasure and eat as the beasts eat: but Hell shall be their home.

How many cities were mightier than your own city, which has cast you* out! We destroyed them all, and there was none to help them.

Can he who follows the guidance of his Lord be compared to him who is led by his appetites and whose foul deeds seem fair to him?

This is the Paradise which the righteous have been promised. There shall flow in it rivers of unpolluted water, and rivers of milk for ever fresh; rivers of delectable wine and rivers of clearest honey. They shall eat therein of every fruit and receive forgiveness from their Lord. Is this like the lot of those who shall abide in Hell for ever and drink scalding water which will tear their bowels?

Some of them indeed listen to you, but no sooner do they leave your presence than they ask those to whom knowledge has been given: 'What did he say just now?' Such are the men whose hearts are sealed by Allah and who follow their base desires.

As for those who follow the right path, Allah will increase their guidance and teach them to guard themselves against evil.

Are they waiting for the Hour of Doom to overtake them unawares? Its portents have already come. But how will they be warned when it overtakes them?

Know that there is no god but Allah. Implore Him to forgive your sins and to forgive the true believers, men and women. Allah knows your busy haunts and resting-places.

The faithful say: 'If only a Chapter were revealed!' But when a forthright Chapter is revealed and war is mentioned in it, you see the infirm of heart looking towards you as though they were fainting away for fear of death. Yet obedience and courteous speech would become them more. Indeed, should war be decided upon, it would be better for them to be true to Allah.

If you† renounced the Faith you would surely do evil in the land and violate the ties of blood. Such are those on whom Allah has laid His curse, leaving them bereft of sight and hearing.

Will they not ponder on the Koran? Are there locks upon their hearts?

Those who return to unbelief after Allah's guidance has been revealed to them are seduced by Satan and inspired by him. That is because they say to those who abhor the word of Allah: 'We shall obey you in *some* matters.' Allah knows their secret talk.

What will they do when the angels carry away their souls and strike them on their heads and backs?

*Mohammed.
†The hypocrites.

That is because they follow what has incurred the wrath of Allah and abhor what pleases Him. He will surely bring their works to nothing.

Do the feeble-hearted think that Allah will not reveal their malice? If We please, We could point them out to you and you would recognize them promptly by their looks. But you will surely know them from the tenor of their words. Allah has knowledge of all your actions.

We shall put you to the proof until We know the valiant and the resolute among you and test all that is said about you.

The unbelievers who debar others from the path of Allah and disobey the Apostle after they have seen the light shall in no way harm Allah. He will bring their works to nothing.

Believers, obey Allah and His apostle and never let your labours go in vain.

Those that disbelieve and debar others from Allah's path and in the end die unbelievers shall not be shown forgiveness by Allah. Therefore do not falter or sue for peace when you have gained the upper hand. Allah is on your side and will not grudge you the reward of your labours.

The life of this world is but a sport and a pastime. Allah will reward you if you believe in Him and guard yourselves against evil. He does not ask for all your wealth. If he demanded all and strongly pressed you, you would grow niggardly and this would show your ill-feelings.

You are called upon to give to the cause of Allah. Some of you are ungenerous; yet whoever is ungenerous to this cause is ungenerous to himself. Indeed, Allah does not need you, but you need Him. If you give no heed, He will replace you by others different from you.

chapter VIII

The Frankish-Papal Alliance

24. Rome, Byzantium, and Frankish Gaul

Various circumstances contributed to the formation of a new alliance between the papacy and the Frankish monarchy in the eighth century. Byzantium, the traditional defender of the church, was preoccupied with the threat of Islam. Missionaries like St. Boniface (above, p. 83) were spreading papal influence north of the Alps. Then, in 726, a quarrel broke out between the churches of Rome and Constantinople. It began when the emperor Leo III (717–741) condemned the traditional use of images in Christian worship. The following letter is believed to have been written by Pope Gregory II to Leo III in 727.

. . . You know that the dogmas of holy church are not the concern of emperors but of pontiffs, who ought to teach securely. The pontiffs who preside over the church do not meddle in affairs of state, and likewise the emperors ought not to meddle in ecclesiastical affairs, but to administer the things committed to them. . . .

The Lombards and Sarmatians and others who live in the north have attacked the wretched Decapolis and have occupied the city of Ravenna itself. They have deposed your governors and appointed governors of their own, and they have determined to do the same at other

From "Gregory II," in Brian Tierney, *The Crisis of Church and State, 1050–1300,* with selected documents, © 1964 (Englewood Cliffs, N.J.: Prentice-Hall, 1964), pp. 19–20; reprinted by permission of Prentice-Hall, Inc., Englewood Cliffs, New Jersey. Pope Gregory III and the "Annals of Lorsch," in O. J. Thatcher and E. H. McNeal, trans., *A Source Book for Medieval History* (New York: Charles Scribner's 1905), pp. 102, 37–38.

imperial cities in this neighborhood and even at Rome itself, since you are unable to defend us. All this is the result of your imprudence and stupidity. But you wish to strike terror into them and say, "I will send to Rome and destroy the image of St. Peter and, having overcome Pope Gregory, will carry him off, as Constantine [II] commanded [Pope] Martin to be carried off." You ought rather to know and to hold for certain that the pontiffs who have ruled at Rome preside there in order to maintain peace, like a wall joining East and West, occupying the middle ground between them, and that they are arbitrators and promoters of peace. . . . If you insolently threaten and insult us there is no need for us to descend to fighting with you. The Roman pontiff will withdraw for a few miles into the Campania; then you may go chase the wind.

. . . Would that I might, by God's gift, tread the same path as Pope Martin [who died in exile]. And yet I wish to survive and to live for the sake of the people, since the whole western world has turned its eyes upon our humility and, although we are unworthy, the people greatly trust in us and in him whose statue you threaten to cast down and destroy, namely St. Peter, whom all the kingdoms of the West regard as an earthly God. If you want to put the matter to the test, the people of the West are ready and they will avenge the injuries you have inflicted on the people of the East. But we beseech you in the Lord to turn aside from these puerile follies. . . . One thing we take badly is this, that while the savage and barbarous people become peaceful your peacefulness turns to savagery and cruelty. The whole of the West faithfully offers its fruits to the holy prince of the apostles. If you do send anyone to cast down the image of St. Peter, we protest to you that we shall be innocent of the blood that will be shed. The responsibility will fall on your head. . . .

In 739 Pope Gregory III (731—741) appealed to the Frankish ruler Charles Martel for help against the Lombards in Italy.

Pope Gregory to his most excellent son, Karl, sub-king.

In our great affliction we have thought it necessary to write to you a second time, believing that you are a loving son of St. Peter, the prince of apostles, and of ourselves, and that out of reverence for him you would obey our commands to defend the church of God and his chosen people. We can now no longer endure the persecution of the Lombards, for they have taken from St. Peter all his possessions, even those which were given him by you and your fathers. These Lombards hate and oppress us because we sought protection from you; for the same reason also the church of St. Peter is despoiled and desolated by them. But we have intrusted a more complete account of all our woes to your faithful subject, our present messenger, and he will relate them to you. You, oh son, will receive favor from the same prince of apostles here and in the future life in the presence of God, according as you render speedy aid to his church and to us, that all peoples may recognize the faith and love and singleness of purpose which you display in defending St. Peter and us and his chosen people. For by doing this you will attain lasting fame on earth and eternal life in heaven.

Charles Martel did not respond to the pope's plea, but his son, Pepin, formed an alliance with the papacy. The events leading up to it are described in the contemporary Annals of Lorsch.

Anno 749. Burchard, bishop of Würzburg, and Fulrad, priest and chaplain, were sent [by Pipin] to pope Zacharias to ask his advice in regard to the kings who were then ruling in France, who had the title of king but no real royal authority. The pope replied by these ambassadors that it would be better that he who actually had the power should be called king.

750 [751]. In this year Pipin was named king of the Franks with the sanction of the pope, and in the city of Soissons he was anointed with the holy oil by the hands of Boniface, archbishop and martyr of blessed memory, and was raised to the throne after the custom of the Franks. But Childerich, who had the name of king, was shorn of his locks and sent into a monastery.

753. . . . In this year pope Stephen came to Pipin at Kiersy, to urge him to defend the Roman church from the attacks of the Lombards.

754. And after pope Stephen had received a promise from king Pipin that he would defend the Roman church, he anointed the king and his two sons, Karl and Karlmann, with the holy oil. And the pope remained that winter in France.

25. The Founding of the Papal States

In 756 Pepin reconquered from the Lombards certain imperial territories in Italy that the Lombards had occupied and then conferred them on the Roman church. The transaction was described in a contemporary Life of Pope Stephen II (752–757).

. . . [An imperial messenger] hastened after the aforementioned most

From "Life of Pope Stephen II," in Brian Tierney, *The Crisis of Church and State, 1050–1300,* with selected documents, © 1964 (Englewood Cliffs, N.J.: Prentice-Hall, 1964), pp. 20–21; reprinted by permission of Prentice-Hall, Inc., Englewood Cliffs, New Jersey. "Donation of Constantine," in *Documents of the Christian Church,* edited by H. Bettenson, published by the Oxford University Press (2nd ed.; London: Oxford University Press, 1963), pp. 139-140; reprinted by permission of the publisher.

Christian king of the Franks. He found him within the Lombard borders, not far from the city of Pavia, and urgently besought him, with the promise of many imperial gifts, to surrender to the imperial authorities the city of Ravenna and the other cities and fortified places of the Exarchate. But he was not able to persuade the steadfast heart of that most Christian and benevolent king, who was faithful to God and loved St. Peter, namely Pepin the king of the Franks, to surrender those cities and places to the imperial authority. That same friend of God and most benevolent king absolutely refused to alienate those cities from the power of St. Peter and the jurisdiction of the Roman church or from the pontiff of the apostolic see. He affirmed under oath that he had not engaged in war so often to win the favor of any man but for the love of St. Peter and for the remission of his sins, and he declared that no enrichment of his treasury would persuade him to snatch away what he had once offered to St. Peter. . . .

Having acquired all these cities, he issued a document of donation for the perpetual possession of them by St. Peter and the Roman church and all the pontiffs of the apostolic see. This document is still preserved in the archives of our holy church. . . .

Probably about this same time the forged "Donation of Constantine" was written at Rome. It purported to be a grant of the first Christian emperor, Constantine, to Pope Sylvester I. The principal clauses of the "Donation" are given below.

. . . To the holy apostles, my lords the most blessed Peter and Paul, and through them also to blessed Silvester, our father, supreme pontiff and universal pope of the city of Rome, and to the pontiffs, his successors, who to the end of the world shall sit in the seat of the blessed Peter, we grant and by this present we convey our imperial Lateran palace, which is superior to and excels all palaces in the whole world; and further the diadem, which is the crown of our head; and the miter; as also the superhumeral, that is, the stole which usually surrounds our imperial neck; and the purple cloak and the scarlet tunic and all the imperial robes; also the rank of commanders of the imperial cavalry. . . .

And we decree that those most reverend men, the clergy of various orders serving the same most holy Roman Church, shall have that eminence, distinction, power and precedence, with which our illustrious senate is gloriously adorned; that is, they shall be made patricians and consuls. And we ordain that they shall also be adorned with other imperial dignities. Also we decree that the clergy of the sacred Roman Church shall be adorned as are the imperial officers. . . .

Wherefore that the pontifical crown should not be made of less repute, but rather that the dignity of a more than earthly office and the might of its glory should be yet further adorned—lo, we convey to the oft-mentioned and most blessed Silvester, universal pope, both our palace, as preferment, and likewise all provinces, palaces and districts of the city of Rome and Italy and of the regions of the West; and, bequeathing them to the power and sway of him and the pontiffs, his successors, we do (by means of fixed imperial decision through this our divine, sacred and authoritative sanction) determine and decree that the same be placed at his disposal, and do lawfully grant it as a permanent possession to the holy Roman Church.

Wherefore we have perceived that our empire and the power of our government should be transferred and removed to the regions of the East and that a city should be built in our name in the best place in the province of Byzantium and our empire there established; for it is not right that an earthly emperor should have authority there, where the rule of priests and the head of the Christian religion have been established by the Emperor of heaven. . . .

Given at Rome, March 30th, when our lord Flavius Constantinus Augustus, for the fourth time, and Galliganus, most illustrious men. were consuls.

26. *Charlemagne: King and Emperor*

Pepin's son Charlemagne made himself master of almost all Western Europe. A friend and courtier, Einhard, wrote this account of him.

Charles was large and strong, and of lofty stature, though not disproportionately tall (his height is well known to have been seven times the length of his foot); the upper part of his head was round, his eyes very large and animated, nose a little long, hair fair, and face laughing and merry. Thus his appearance was always stately and dignified, whether he was standing or sitting; although his neck was thick and somewhat short, and his belly rather prominent; but the symmetry of the rest of his body concealed these defects. His gait was firm, his whole carriage manly, and his voice clear, but not so strong as his size led one to expect. His health was excellent, except during the four years preceding his death, when he was subject to frequent fevers; at the last he even limped a little with one foot. Even in those years he consulted rather his own inclinations than the advice of physicians, who were almost hateful to him, because they wanted him to give up roasts, to which he was accustomed, and to eat boiled meat instead. In accordance with the national custom, he took frequent exercise on

From Einhard, *Life of Charlemagne*, S. E. Turner, trans. (New York: Harper and Brothers, 1880), pp. 56-62, 51-54, 64-66.

horseback and in the chase, accomplishments in which scarcely any people in the world can equal the Franks. He enjoyed the exhalations from natural warm springs, and often practised swimming, in which he was such an adept that none could surpass him; and hence it was that he built his palace at Aix-la-Chapelle, and lived there constantly during his latter years until his death. He used not only to invite his sons to his bath, but his nobles and friends, and now and then a troop of his retinue or body-guard, so that a hundred or more persons sometimes bathed with him.

He used to wear the national, that is to say, the Frank, dress—next his skin a linen shirt and linen breeches, and above these a tunic fringed with silk; while hose fastened by bands covered his lower limbs, and shoes his feet, and he protected his shoulders and chest in winter by a close-fitting coat of otter or marten skins. Over all he flung a blue cloak, and he always had a sword girt about him, usually one with a gold or silver hilt and belt; he sometimes carried a jewelled sword, but only on great feast-days or at the reception of ambassadors from foreign nations. He despised foreign costumes, however handsome, and never allowed himself to be robed in them, except twice in Rome, when he donned the Roman tunic, chlamys, and shoes; the first time at the request of Pope Hadrian, the second to gratify Leo, Hadrian's successor. On great feast-days he made use of embroidered clothes, and shoes bedecked with precious stones; his cloak was fastened by a golden buckle, and he appeared crowned with a diadem of gold and gems: but on other days his dress varied little from the common dress of the people.

Charles was temperate in eating, and particularly so in drinking, for he abominated drunkenness in anybody, much more in himself and those of his household; but he could not easily abstain from food, and often complained that fasts injured his health. He very rarely gave entertainments, only on great feast-days, and then to large numbers of people. His meals ordinarily consisted of four courses, not counting the roast, which his huntsmen used to bring in on the spit; he was more fond of this than of any other dish. While at table, he listened to reading or music. The subjects of the readings were the stories and deeds of olden time: he was fond, too, of St. Augustine's books, and especially of the one entitled "The City of God." He was so moderate in the use of wine and all sorts of drink that he rarely allowed himself more than three cups in the course of a meal. In summer, after the midday meal, he would eat some fruit, drain a single cup, put off his clothes and shoes, just as he did for the night, and rest for two or three hours. He was in the habit of awaking and rising from bed four or five times during the night. While he was dressing and putting on his shoes, he not only gave audience to his friends, but if the Count of the Palace told him of any suit in which his judgment was necessary, he had the parties brought before him forthwith, took cognizance of the case, and gave his decision, just as if he were sitting on the judgment-seat. This was not the only business that he transacted at this time, but he performed any duty of the day whatever, whether he had to attend to the matter himself, or to give commands concerning it to his officers.

Charles had the gift of ready and fluent speech, and could express whatever he had to say with the utmost clearness. He was not satisfied with command of his native language merely, but gave attention to the study of foreign ones, and in particular was such a master of Latin that he could speak it as well as his native tongue; but he could understand Greek better than he could speak it. He was so eloquent, indeed, that he might have passed for a teacher of eloquence. He most zealously cultivated the liberal arts, held those who taught them in great esteem, and conferred great honours upon them. He took lessons in grammar of the deacon Peter of Pisa, at that time an aged man. Another deacon, Albin of Britain, surnamed Alcuin, a man of Saxon extraction, who was the greatest scholar of the day, was his teacher in other branches of learning. The King spent much time and labour with him studying rhetoric, dialectics, and especially astronomy; he learned to reckon, and used to investigate the motions of the heavenly bodies most curiously, with an intelligent scrutiny. He also tried to write, and used to keep tablets and blanks in bed under his pillow, that at leisure hours he might accustom his hand to form the letters; however, as he did not begin his efforts in due season, but late in life, they met with ill success.

· · ·

The plan that he adopted for his children's education was, first of all, to have both boys and girls instructed in the liberal arts, to which he also turned his own attention. As soon as their years admitted, in accordance with the custom of the Franks, the boys had to learn horsemanship, and to practise war and the chase, and the girls to familiarize themselves with cloth-making, and to handle distaff and spindle, that they might not grow indolent through idleness, and he fostered in them every virtuous sentiment. He only lost three of all his children before his death, two sons and one daughter, Charles, who was the eldest, Pepin, whom he had made King of Italy, and Hruodrud, his oldest daughter. . . .

He was so careful of the training of his sons and daughters that he never took his meals without them when he was at home, and never made a journey without them; his sons would ride at his side, and his daughters follow him, while a number of his body-guard, detailed for their protection, brought up the rear. Strange to say, although they were very handsome women, and he loved them very dearly, he was never willing to marry any of them to a man of their own nation or to a foreigner, but kept them all at home until his death, saying that he could not dispense with their society. Hence, though otherwise happy, he experienced the malignity of fortune as far as they were concerned;

yet he concealed his knowledge of the rumours current in regard to them, and of the suspicions entertained of their honour.

• • •

He cherished the Church of St. Peter the Apostle at Rome above all other holy and sacred places, and heaped its treasury with a vast wealth of gold, silver, and precious stones. He sent great and countless gifts to the popes; and throughout his whole reign the wish that he had nearest at heart was to re-establish the ancient authority of the city of Rome under his care and by his influence, and to defend and protect the Church of St. Peter, and to beautify and enrich it out of his own store above all other churches. Although he held it in such veneration, he only repaired to Rome to pay his vows and make his supplications four times during the whole forty-seven years that he reigned.

When he made his last journey thither, he had also other ends in view. The Romans had inflicted many injuries upon the Pontiff Leo, tearing out his eyes and cutting out his tongue, so that he had been compelled to call upon the King for help. Charles accordingly went to Rome, to set in order the affairs of the Church, which were in great confusion, and passed the whole winter there. It was then that he received the titles of Emperor and Augustus, to which he at first had such an aversion that he declared that he would not have set foot in the Church the day that they were conferred, although it was a great feast-day, if he could have foreseen the design of the Pope. He bore very patiently with the jealousy which the Roman emperors showed upon his assuming these titles, for they took this step very ill; and by dint of frequent embassies and letters, in which he addressed them as brothers, he made their haughtiness yield to his magnanimity, a quality in which he was unquestionably much their superior.

The following accounts of Charlemagne's coronation are all from sources of the early ninth century. Each tells a slightly different story.

(*According to the* Annals of Lorsch)

Now since the title of emperor had become extinct among the Greeks and a woman claimed the imperial authority it seemed to the apostle Leo and to all the holy fathers who were present at the council and to the rest of the Christian people that Charles, king of the Franks, ought to be named emperor, for he held Rome itself where the Caesars were always wont to reside and also other cities in Italy, Gaul, and Germany. Since almighty God had put all these places in his power it seemed to them that, with the help of God, and in accordance with the request

From "Annals of Lorsch," "Frankish Royal Annals," and "Life of Pope Leo III," translated by Brian Tierney, in Brian Tierney, Donald Kagan, and L. Pearce Williams, eds., *Great Issues in Western Civilization* (2nd ed.; New York: Random House, 1972), Vol. I, pp. 319–320, 322; reprinted by permission of the publisher.

of all the Christian people, he should hold this title. King Charles did not wish to refuse their petition, and, humbly submitting himself to God and to the petition of all the Christian priests and people, he accepted the title of emperor on the day of the nativity of our Lord Jesus Christ and was consecrated by the lord Pope Leo.

(*According to the* Frankish Royal Annals)

On the most holy day of the nativity of the Lord, as the king rose from praying at Mass before the tomb of the blessed apostle Peter, pope Leo placed a crown on his head and all the Roman people cried out, "To Charles Augustus, crowned by God, great and peace-giving emperor of the Romans, life and victory." And after the laudation he was adored by the pope in the manner of the ancient princes and, the title of patrician being set aside, he was called emperor and Augustus. A few days later he commanded the men who had deposed the pope the year before to be brought before him. They were examined according to Roman law on a charge of treason and condemned to death. However, the pope interceded for them with the emperor and they were spared in life and limb. Subsequently they were sent into exile for so great a crime.

(*According to the* Life of Pope Leo III)

On a later day, in the same church of the blessed apostle Peter, when all were present, namely the archbishops, bishops, abbots, all the Franks who were in the service of the great king and all the Romans, the venerable pontiff mounted to the altar holding the four Gospels of Christ and in a clear voice declared under oath, "I have no knowledge of these false crimes which the Romans who have persecuted me have basely charged me with, nor any knowledge of having done such things." When this was done all the archbishops, bishops, abbots and all the clergy chanted litanies and gave praise to God and to our lady the ever-virgin Mary, Mother of God, and to the blessed apostle Peter, prince of the apostles and to all the saints of God.

After this, on the day of the nativity of our Lord Jesus Christ, all were again gathered together in the basilica of the blessed apostle Peter. And then the venerable holy pontiff with his own hands crowned Charles with a most precious crown. Then all the faithful Romans, seeing how he loved the holy Roman church and its vicar and how he defended them, cried out with one voice by the will of God and of St. Peter, the key-bearer of the kingdom of Heaven, "To Charles, most pious Augustus, crowned by God, great and peace-giving emperor, life and victory." This was proclaimed three times before the tomb of blessed Peter the apostle, with the invocation of many saints, and he was instituted by all as the emperor of the Romans. . . .

chapter IX

The Early Medieval Empire

27. Carolingian Government

The two following excerpts illustrate aspects of Charlemagne's administration in military and civil affairs. The second one (Capitulary for the Missi) sets out a general program for the reform of the realm. It may be noted that he took for granted his right to regulate the affairs of the church as well as matters of secular administration.

A Summons to Charlemagne's Army

In the name of the Father, Son and Holy Ghost. Charles, most serene, august, crowned by God, great pacific Emperor, and also, by God's mercy, King of the Franks and Lombards, to Abbot Fulrad.

Be it known to you that we have decided to hold our general assembly this year in the eastern part of Saxony, on the river Bode, at the place which is called Stassfurt. Therefore, we have commanded you to come to the aforesaid place, with all your men well armed and prepared, on the fifteenth day before the Kalends of July, that is, seven days before the festival of St. John the Baptist. Come, accordingly, so equipped with your men to the aforesaid place that thence you may be able to go well prepared in any direction whither our summons shall direct; that is, with arms and gear also, and other equipment for war in food and clothing. So that each horseman shall have a shield, lance, sword, dagger, bow and quivers with arrows; and in your carts utensils of various kinds, that is, axes, planes, augers,

From D. C. Munro, trans., *University of Pennsylvania Translations and Reprints* (Philadelphia: University of Pennsylvania, 1900), Vol. VI, No. 5, pp. 11-12, 16-18, 2-4.

boards, spades, iron shovels, and other utensils which are necessary in an army. In the carts also supplies of food for three months, dating from the time of the assembly, arms and clothing for a half-year. And we command this in general, that you cause it to be observed that you proceed peacefully to the aforesaid place, through whatever part of our realm your journey shall take you, that is, that you presume to take nothing except fodder, wood and water; and let the men of each one of your vassals march along with the carts and horsemen, and let the leader always be with them until they reach the aforesaid place, so that the absence of a lord may not give an opportunity to his men of doing evil.

Send your gifts, which you ought to present to us at our assembly in the middle of the month of May, to the place where we then shall be; if perchance your journey shall so shape itself that on your march you are able in person to present these gifts of yours to us, we greatly desire it. See that you show no negligence in the future if you desire to have our favor.

General Capitulary of the Missi (802)

First chapter. Concerning the embassy sent out by the lord emperor. Therefore, the most serene and most Christian lord emperor Charles has chosen from his nobles the wisest and most prudent men, both archbishops and some of the other bishops also, and venerable abbots and pious laymen, and has sent them throughout his whole kingdom, and through them by all the following chapters has allowed men to live in accordance with the correct law. Moreover, where anything which is not right and just has been enacted in the law, he has ordered them to inquire into this most diligently and to inform him of it; he desires, God granting, to reform it. And let no one, through his cleverness or astuteness, dare to oppose or thwart the written law, as many are wont to do, or the judicial sentence passed upon him, or to do injury to the churches of God or the poor or the widows or the wards or any Christian. But all shall live entirely in accordance with God's precept, justly and under a just rule, and each one shall be admonished to live in harmony with his fellows in his business or profession; the canonical clergy ought to observe in every respect a canonical life without heeding base gain, nuns ought to keep diligent watch over their lives, laymen and the secular clergy ought rightly to observe their laws without malicious fraud, and all ought to live in mutual charity and perfect peace. And let the *missi* themselves make a diligent investigation whenever any man claims that an injustice has been done to him by any one, just as they desire to deserve the grace of omnipotent God and to keep their fidelity promised to Him, so that entirely in all cases everywhere, in accordance with the will and fear of God, they shall administer the law fully and justly in the case of the holy churches of God and of the poor, of wards and widows and of the whole people. And if there shall be anything of such a nature that they, together with the provincial counts, are not able of themselves to correct it and to do justice concerning it, they shall, without any ambiguity, refer this, together with their reports, to the judgment of the emperor; and the straight path of justice shall not be impeded by any one on account of flattery or gifts from any one, or on account of any relationship, or from fear of the powerful.

2. Concerning the fidelity to be promised to the lord emperor. And he commanded that every man in his whole kingdom, whether ecclesiastic or layman, and each one according to his vow and occupation, should now promise to him as emperor the fidelity which he had previously promised to him as king; and all of those who had not yet made that promise should do likewise, down to those who were twelve years old. And that it shall be announced to all in public, so that each one might know, how great and how many things are comprehended in that oath; not merely, as many have thought hitherto, fidelity to the lord emperor as regards his life, and not introducing any enemy into his kingdom out of enmity, and not consenting to or concealing another's faithlessness to him; but that all may know that this oath contains in itself this meaning:

3. First, that each one voluntarily shall strive, in accordance with his knowledge and ability, to live wholly in the holy service of God in accordance with the precept of God and in accordance with his own promise, because the lord emperor is unable to give to all individually the necessary care and discipline.

4. Secondly, that no man, either through perjury or any other wile or fraud, on account of the flattery or gift of any one, shall refuse to give back or dare to abstract or conceal a serf of the lord emperor or a district or land or anything that belongs to him; and that no one shall presume, through perjury or other wile, to conceal or abstract his fugitive fiscaline serfs who unjustly and fradulently say that they are free.

5. That no one shall presume to rob or do any injury fraudulently to the churches of God or widows or orphans or pilgrims; for the lord emperor himself, after God and His saints, has constituted himself their protector and defender.

6. That no one shall dare to lay waste a benefice of the lord emperor, or to make it his own property.

7. That no one shall presume to neglect a summons to war from the lord emperor; and that no one of the counts shall be so presumptuous as to dare to dismiss thence any one of those who owe military service, either on account of relationship or flattery or gifts from any one.

8. That no one shall presume to impede at all in any way a ban or command of the lord emperor, or to dally with his work or to impede or to lessen or in any way to act contrary to his will or commands. And that no one shall dare to neglect to pay his dues or tax

9. That no one, for any reason, shall make a practice in court of defending another unjustly, either from any desire of gain when the cause is weak, or by impeding a just judgment by his skill in reasoning, or by a desire of oppressing when the cause is weak. But each one shall answer for his own cause or tax or debt unless any one is infirm or ignorant of pleading; for these the *missi* or the chiefs who are in the court or the judge who knows the case in question shall plead before the court; or if it is necessary, such a person may be allowed as is acceptable to all and knows the case well; but this shall be done wholly according to the convenience of the chiefs or *missi* who are present. But in every case it shall be done in accordance with justice and the law; and that no one shall have the power to impede justice by a gift, reward, or any kind of evil flattery or from any hindrance of relationship. And that no one shall unjustly consent to another in anything, but that with all zeal and goodwill all shall be prepared to carry out justice.

For all the above mentioned ought to be observed by the imperial oath.

Thirty detailed regulations followed to implement these general principles. Charlemagne's most savage military campaigns were waged against the pagans of Saxony. After subjugating the Saxons, he compelled them to accept Christianity and imposed a kind of martial law on them.

Capitulary for Saxony

1. It was pleasing to all that the churches of Christ, which are now being built in Saxony and consecrated to God, should not have less, but greater and more illustrious honor, than the fanes of the idols had had.

2. If any one shall have fled to a church for refuge, let no one presume to expel him from the church by violence, but he shall be left in peace until he shall be brought to the judicial assemblage; and on account of the honor due to God and the saints, and the reverence due to the church itself, let his life and all his members be granted to him. Moreover, let him plead his cause as best he can and he shall be judged; and so let him be led to the presence of the lord king, and the latter shall send him where it shall have seemed fitting to his clemency.

3. If any one shall have entered a church by violence and shall have carried off anything in it by force or theft, or shall have burned the church itself, let him be punished by death.

4. If any one, out of contempt for Christianity, shall have despised the holy Lenten fast and shall have eaten flesh, let him be punished by death. But, nevertheless, let it be taken into consideration by a priest, lest perchance any one from necessity has been led to eat flesh.

5. If any one shall have killed a bishop or priest or deacon, let him likewise be punished capitally.

6. If any one deceived by the devil shall have believed, after the manner of the pagans, that any man or woman is a witch and eats men,

and on this account shall have burned the person, or shall have given the person's flesh to others to eat, or shall have eaten it himself, let him be punished by a capital sentence.

7. If any one, in accordance with pagan rites, shall have caused the body of a dead man to be burned and shall have reduced his bones to ashes, let him be punished capitally.

8. If any one of the race of the Saxons hereafter concealed among them shall have wished to hide himself unbaptized, and shall have scorned to come to baptism and shall have wished to remain a pagan, let him be punished by death.

9. If any one shall have sacrificed a man to the devil, and after the manner of the pagans shall have presented him as a victim to the demons, let him be punished by death.

10. If any one shall have formed a conspiracy with the pagans against the Christians, or shall have wished to join with them in opposition to the Christians, let him be punished by death; and whoever shall have consented to this same fraudulently against the king and the Christian people, let him be punished by death.

11. If any one shall have shown himself unfaithful to the lord king, let him be punished with a capital sentence.

12. If any one shall have ravished the daughter of his lord, let him be punished by death.

13. If any one shall have killed his lord or lady, let him be punished in a like manner.

14. If, indeed, for these mortal crimes secretly committed any one shall have fled of his own accord to a priest, and after confession shall have wished to do penance, let him be freed by the testimony of the priest from death.

15. Concerning the lesser chapter all have consented. To each church let the parishioners present a house and two mansi of land, and for each one hundred and twenty men, noble and free, and likewise liti [freedmen], let them give to the same church a man-servant and a maid-servant.

16. And this has been pleasing, Christ being propitious, that whencesoever any receipts shall have come into the treasury, either for a breach of the peace or for any penalty of any kind, and in all income pertaining to the king, a tithe shall be rendered to the churches and priests.

17. Likewise, in accordance with the mandate of God, we command that all shall give a tithe of their property and labor to the churches and priests; let the nobles as well as the freemen, and likewise the liti, according to that which God shall have given to each Christian, return a part to God.

18. That on the Lord's day no meetings and public judicial assemblages shall be held, unless perchance in a case of great necessity or when war compels it, but all shall go to the church to hear the word of

God, and shall be free for prayers or good works. Likewise, also, on the especial festivals they shall devote themselves to God and to the services of the church, and shall refrain from secular assemblies.

19. Likewise, it has been pleasing to insert in these decrees that all infants shall be baptized within a year; and we have decreed this, that if any one shall have despised to bring his infant to baptism within the course of a year, without the advice or permission of the priest, if he is a noble he shall pay 120 solidi to the treasury, if a freeman 60, if a litus 30.

20. If any shall have made a prohibited or illegal marriage, if a noble 60 solidi, if a freeman 30, if a litus 15.

21. If any one shall have made a vow at springs or trees or groves, or shall have made any offerings after the manner of the heathen and shall have partaken of a repast in honor of the demons, if he shall be a noble 60 solidi, if a freeman 30, if a litus 15. If, indeed they have not the means of paying at once, they shall be given into the service of the church until the solidi are paid.

22. We command that the bodies of Saxon Christians shall be carried to the church cemeteries and not to the mounds of the pagans.

23. We have ordered that diviners and soothsayers shall be given to the church and priests.

33. Concerning perjuries, let it be according to the law of the Saxons.

34. We have forbidden that all the Saxons shall hold public assemblies in general, unless perchance our *missus* shall have caused them to come together in accordance with our command; but each count shall hold judicial assemblies and administer justice in his jurisdiction. And this shall be cared for by the priests, lest it be done otherwise.

28.   *Monastic Life and Culture*

Charlemagne's interest in promoting learning and culture throughout his realm is evident in this letter to Baugulf, abbot of Fulda.

Charles, by the grace of God, King of the Franks and Lombards and Patrician of the Romans, to Abbot Baugulf and to all the congregation, also to the faithful committed to you, we have directed a loving greeting by our ambassadors in the name of omnipotent God.

Be it known, therefore, to your devotion pleasing to God, that we, together with our faithful, have considered it to be useful that the bishoprics and monasteries entrusted by the favor of Christ to our con-

From "Charlemagne," in D. C. Munro, trans., *University of Pennsylvania Translations and Reprints* (Philadelphia: University of Pennsylvania, 1900), Vol. VI, No. 5, pp. 12-14, 20-21.

trol, in addition, in the culture of letters also ought to be zealous in teaching those who by the gift of God are able to learn, according to the capacity of each individual, so that just as the observance of the rule imparts order and grace to honesty of morals, so also zeal in teaching and learning may do the same for sentences, so that those who desire to please God by living rightly should not neglect to please him also by speaking correctly. For it is written: "Either from thy words thou shalt be justified or from thy words thou shalt be condemned." For although correct conduct may be better than knowledge, nevertheless knowledge precedes conduct. Therefore, each one ought to study what he desires to accomplish, so that so much the more fully the mind may know what ought to be done, as the tongue hastens in the praises of omnipotent God without the hindrances of errors. For since errors should be shunned by all men, so much the more ought they to be avoided as far as possible by those who are chosen for this very purpose alone, so that they ought to be the especial servants of truth. For when in the years just passed letters were often written to us from several monasteries in which it was stated that the brethren who dwelt there offered up in our behalf sacred and pious prayers, we have recognized in most of these letters both correct thoughts and uncouth expressions; because what pious devotion dictated faithfully to the mind, the tongue, uneducated on account of the neglect of study, was not able to express in the letter without error. Whence it happened that we began to fear lest perchance, as the skill in writing was less, so also the wisdom for understanding the Holy Scriptures might be much less than it rightly ought to be. And we all know well that, although errors of speech are dangerous, far more dangerous are errors of the understanding. Therefore, we exhort you not only not to neglect the study of letters, but also with most humble mind, pleasing to God, to study earnestly in order that you may be able more easily and more correctly to penetrate the mysteries of the divine Scriptures. Since, moreover, images, tropes and similar figures are found in the sacred pages, no one doubts that each one in reading these will understand the spiritual sense more quickly if previously he shall have been fully instructed in the mastery of letters. Such men truly are to be chosen for this work as have both the will and the ability to learn and a desire to instruct others. And may this be done with a zeal as great as the earnestness with which we command it. For we desire you to be, as it is fitting that soldiers of the church should be, devout in mind, learned in discourse, chaste in conduct and eloquent in speech, so that whosoever shall seek to see you out of reverence of God, or on account of your reputation for holy conduct, just as he is edified by your appearance, may also be instructed by your wisdom, which he has learned from your reading or singing, and may go away joyfully giving thanks to omnipotent God. Do not neglect, therefore, if you wish to have our favor, to send copies of this letter to all your suffragans and fellow-bishops and to all the monasteries.

Charlemagne also insisted on strict discipline in monastic houses in his General Capitulary of 802.

Moreover, that the monks shall live firmly and strictly in accordance with the rule, because we know that any one whose goodwill is lukewarm is displeasing to God, as John bears witness in the Apocalypse: "I would that thou wert cold or hot. So then, because thou art lukewarm, and neither cold nor hot, I will spue thee out of my mouth." Let them in no way usurp to themselves secular business. They shall not have leave to go outside of their monastery at all, unless compelled by a very great necessity; but nevertheless the bishops, in whose diocese they shall be, shall take care in every way that they do not get accustomed to wandering outside of the monastery. . . .

Let them entirely shun drunkenness and feasting, because it is known to all that from these men are especially polluted by lust. For a most pernicious rumor has come to our ears that many in the monasteries have already been detected in fornication and in abomination and uncleanness. It especially saddens and disturbs us that it can be said, without a great mistake, that some of the monks are understood to be sodomites, so that whereas the greatest hope of salvation to all Christians is believed to arise from the life and chastity of the monks, damage has been incurred instead. . . . Certainly, if any such report shall have come to our ears in the future, we shall inflict such a penalty, not only on the guilty but also on those who have consented to such deeds, that no Christian who shall have heard of it will ever dare in the future to perpetrate such acts.

Even after Charlemagne's death the arts of peace that he had encouraged continued to flourish in the great abbeys. This tranquil little poem was written by Walafrid Strabo (809–849), a great scholar and abbot of Reichenau.

To Grimold, Abbot of St. Gall, with his book "Of Gardening"
WALAFRID STRABO

Haec tibi servitii munuscula vilia parvi
Strabo tuus, Grimalde pater doctissime, servus. . . .

A very paltry gift, of no account,
My father, for a scholar like to thee,
But Strabo sends it to thee with his heart.
So might you sit in the small garden close

From H. Waddell, trans., *Mediaeval Latin Lyrics* (London: Constable, 1933), p. 115; reprinted by permission of Constable and Company Limited and Barnes & Noble Books, Division of Harper & Row, Publishers, Inc.

In the green darkness of the apple trees
Just where the peach tree casts its broken shade,
And they would gather you the shining fruit
With the soft down upon it; all your boys,
Your little laughing boys, your happy school,
And bring huge apples clasped in their two hands.
Something the book may have of use to thee.
Read it, my father, prune it of its faults,
And strengthen with they praise what pleases thee.
And my God give thee in thy hands the green
Unwithering palm of everlasting life.

The three monks described below lived in the abbey of St. Gall at the end of the ninth century. The story of their lives survives in a chronicle compiled by Ekkehard of St. Gall a century later. It can serve to remind us that medieval monks were real flesh and blood people with human affections and human failings.

I will tell now of Notker, Ratpert, and Tutilo, since they were one heart and soul, and formed together a sort of trinity in unity. . . . Yet, though so close in heart, in their natures (as it often happens) they were most diverse. Notker was frail in body, though not in mind, a stammerer in voice but not in spirit; lofty in divine thoughts, patient in adversity, gentle in everything, strict in enforcing the discipline of our convent, yet somewhat timid in sudden and unexpected alarms, except in the assaults of demons, whom he always withstood manfully. He was most assiduous in illuminating, reading, and composing; and (that I may embrace all his gifts of holiness within a brief compass) he was a vessel of the Holy Ghost, as full as any other of his own time. But Tutilo was widely different. He was strong and supple in arm and limb, such a man as Fabius tells us to choose for an athlete; ready of speech, clear of voice, a delicate carver and painter; musical, with especial skill on the harp and the flute; for the Abbot gave him a cell wherein he taught the harp to the sons of noble families around. He was a crafty messenger, to run far or near; skilled in building and all the kindred arts; he had a natural gift of ready and forcible expression whether in German or in Latin, in earnest or in jest; so that the emperor Charles [the Fat] once said, "Devil take the fellow who made so gifted a man into a monk!" But with all this he had higher gifts: in choir he was mighty, and in secret prayer he had the gift of tears; a most excellent composer of poetry and melodies, yet chaste, as became the disciple of our Master Marcellus, who shut his eyes against women. Ratpert, again, was midway between the other two. Master of the Schools from his youth, a straightforward and kindly teacher, he was

Ekkehard, "History of the Vicissitudes of St. Gallen," in G. G. Coulton, ed., *A Medieval Garner* (London: Constable, 1910), pp. 18-22.

somewhat harsh in discipline, more loth than all the other Brethren to set foot without the cloister, and wearing but two pairs of shoes in the twelvemonth. He called it death to go forth, and oftentimes warned Tutilo to take heed to himself upon his journeys; in the schools he was most assiduous. He oftentimes omitted the services and the mass, and would say, "We hear good masses when we teach others to sing them." Though he would say that impunity was the worst plague of cloister-life, yet he never came to the Chapter-house* without special summons, since he bore that most heavy burden (as he called it) of reproving and punishing.

These three senators of our Republic being such as they were, yet they suffered constantly (as learned and strenuous men must ever suffer) the detractions and backbiting of such as stagnated in sloth or walked in frivolity; more especially, since he was the less ready to defend himself, that saint (as indeed he was) Dom Notker; for Tutilo and Ratpert, who were of sharper temper and less patient under contumely, were more rarely attacked by such folk. But Notker, the gentlest of men, learned in his own person what insults meant: I will here cite but one example, wherefrom thou mayest judge the rest and know how great is Satan's presumption in such things. There was here a certain Refectorer named Sindolf, who afterwards by feigned obsequiousness (for there was no other use in the man), and by bringing false accusations against the Brethren, wormed himself into the grace of Abbot Solomon, who promoted him to the Clerkship of the Works. Yet even as Refectorer he showed evil for good so far as he had dared, and more especially against Notker. Now Solomon was busied with many things and unable to look closely into every matter; wherefore many of the Brethren, seeing their food sometimes withdrawn and sometimes tainted, would accuse him of injustice; among whom these Three seemed sometimes to have said something [of the kind]. But Sindolf, who ever fomented discord, knowing that ancient spark which had kindled ill-will between these schoolfellows,† wormed himself into Solomon's confidence as one who would tell him a matter concerning his own honour; and he, though he knew that nothing is more harmful for prelates than to give ear to whisperings from their subjects, yet asked of Sindolf's tidings. Then the liar told how those Three, ever wont to speak against the Abbot, had on the day before uttered things intolerable to God. The Abbot believed his words, and conceived against his unsuspecting fellows a grudge which he soon showed openly. They, unable to learn aught from him concerning the ground of their offence, guessed that they had been ensnared by Sindolf's wiles. At length, when the concurrent testimony of the rest, had convinced the Bishop‡

---

*In which faults were daily confessed or pointed out, and "discipline" inflicted in public, after morning mass.

†The four had been schoolfellows in the monastery under Marcellus; and Solomon, the aptest of them all for worldly business, was now promoted far above the others' heads.

‡Solomon's final promotion was to the See of Constance.

that they had said nothing whatever against him, then all demanded vengeance upon the false witness; but the Bishop dissembled, and they tacitly acquiesced. Now these Three inseparable Brethren were wont to meet in the Scriptorium, by the Prior's permission, in the nightly interval before Lauds, and there to hold debates of Holy Scripture, most suited to such a time. But Sindolf, knowing of their colloquies at this time, crept stealthily one night to the glazed window by which Tutilo sat, whereunto he closely applied his ear and listened whether he might catch something which he might twist to evil and bear to the Bishop. Tutilo became aware of this; and, being a resolute man who trusted in the strength of his arms, he spoke to his companions in the Latin tongue (for Sindolf knew no Latin), saying, "The rascal is here, with his ear glued to the window! Thou, Notker, who are a timid fellow, go into the church; but thou, my Ratpert, seize the Brethren's scourge which hangeth in the calefactory, and hasten forth. I, when I hear thine approach, will suddenly open the window, catch him by the hair, and drag him to me here by main force; and thou, dear friend, be strong and of a good courage, and lay upon him with all thy might, that we may avenge God on his body!" So Ratpert, who was ever most ready to discipline, crept softly forth, caught the scourge, and hastened swiftly to the spot, where he found the fellow caught up by the head, and hailed blows upon that defenceless back with all his might; when lo! Sindolf, struggling with arms and legs together, caught the scourge as it fell upon him and held it fast. But Ratpert was aware of a rod that lay hard by, wherewith he now laid on most lustily again; until the victim, after fruitless prayers for mercy, thought within himself, "Now is the time to cry!" and roared aloud for the Brethren. Part of the convent, amazed to hear these unwonted sounds at such an hour, hastened up with lanterns, and asked what was amiss. Whereupon Tutilo cried again and again, "I hold the Devil, I hold the Devil, bring hither a light, that I may see more clearly in whose form I hold him." Then, turning that unwilling head hither and thither to the beholders, he asked as though in astonishment: "What! Is this Sindolf?" "Yea, indeed!" cried they, and prayed for his liberty: at which Tutilo released him, and said: "Woe is me! for I have laid hands upon the bishop's intimate and privy whisperer!" But Ratpert, when the Brethren hastened up, had gone aside and withdrawn himself privily, nor could the victim know who it was that had smitten him. When, therefore, some enquired whither Dom Notker and Dom Ratpert had gone, Tutilo answered, "Both departed to worship God when they heard the Devil, and left me alone with that fiend prowling in the darkness. Know ye all, therefore, that it was an angel of the Lord whose hand dealt him those stripes." The Brethren therefore departed, and the matter was much debated (as was natural enough) by the partisans of their side; some said that it had befallen by God's justice, that privy eavesdroppers might be brought to light; others, again, argued that such a man should not thus have been handled unless it were true that an angel of God had smitten him.

29. *Rural Life*

Charlemagne's capitulary De Villis *provides a description (somewhat idealized perhaps) of the great self-supporting estates that were typical of ninth-century agriculture.*

The Capitulary De Villis

We desire that each steward shall make an annual statement of all our income, giving an account of our lands cultivated by the oxen which our own plowmen drive and of our lands which the tenants of farms ought to plow; of the pigs, of the rents, of the obligations and fines; of the game taken in our forests without our permission; of the various compositions; of the mills, of the forest, of the fields, of the bridges and ships; of the free men and the districts under obligations to our treasury; of markets, vineyards, and those who owe wine to us; of the hay, firewood, torches, planks, and other kinds of lumber; of the waste lands; of the vegetables, millet, panic; of the wool, flax, and hemp; of the fruits of the trees; of the nut trees, larger and smaller; of the grafted trees of all kinds; of the gardens; of the turnips; of the fish ponds; of the hides, skins, and horns; of the honey and wax; of the fat, tallow, and soap; of the mulberry wine, cooked wine, mead, vinegar, beer, and wine, new and old; of the new grain and the old; of the hens and eggs; of the geese; of the number of fishermen, workers in metal, sword makers, and shoemakers; of the bins and boxes; of the turners and saddlers; of the forges and mines—that is, of iron, lead, or other substances; of the colts and fillies. They shall make all these known to us, set forth separately and in order, at Christmas, so that we may know what and how much of each thing we have.

The greatest care must be taken that whatever is prepared or made with the hands—that is, bacon, smoked meat, sausage, partially salted meat, wine, vinegar, mulberry wine, cooked wine, garum, mustard, cheese, butter, malt, beer, mead, honey, wax, flour—all should be prepared and made with the greatest cleanliness.

Each steward on each of our domains shall always have, for the sake of ornament, peacocks, pheasants, ducks, pigeons, partridges, and turtle-doves.

From J. H. Robinson, ed. and trans., *Readings in European History* (Boston: Ginn, 1904), Vol. I, pp. 137-139.

In each of our estates the chambers shall be provided with counter-panes, cushions, pillows, bedclothes, coverings for the tables and benches; vessels of brass, lead, iron, and wood; and irons, chains, pothooks, adzes, axes, augers, cutlasses, and all other kinds of tools, so that it shall never be necessary to go elsewhere for them, or to borrow them. And the weapons which are carried against the enemy shall be well cared for, so as to keep them in good condition; and when they are brought back they shall be placed in the chamber.

For our women's work they are to give at the proper time, as has been ordered, the materials—that is, the linen, wool, woad, vermilion, madder, wool combs, teasels, soap, grease, vessels, and the other objects which are necessary.

Of the kinds of food not forbidden on fast days, two thirds shall be sent each year for our own use—that is, of the vegetables, fish, cheese, butter, honey, mustard, vinegar, millet, panic, dried and green herbs, radishes, and, in addition, of the wax, soap, and other small products; and let it be reported to us, by a statement, how much is left, as we have said above; and this statement must not be omitted as in the past, because after those two thirds we wish to know how much remains.

Each steward shall have in his district good workmen, namely, black-smiths, a goldsmith, a silversmith, shoemakers, turners, carpenters, sword makers, fisherman, foilers, soap makers, men who know how to make beer, cider, perry, or other kind of liquor good to drink, bakers to make pastry for our table, net makers who know how to make nets for hunting, fishing, and fowling, and other sorts of workmen too numerous to be designated.

The following survey of the manor of Neuillay illustrates the social structure of a medieval village community. It was made early in the tenth century for the great abbey of Saint-Germain near Paris, which included the manor of Neuillay among its numerous estates. The terms coloni *and* lidi *refer to peasants who were bound to the soil, but above the level of* servi *(translated as "slaves" below). However, even the* servi *usually had a family holding of land in the village fields. The "bunuarium" was a land measure of 3.16 acres. An "arpent" was one-tenth of a bunuarium.*

The Manor of Neuillay

There is in Neuillay a seigneurial manor amply equipped with other buildings. There are on the estate 10 fields, which are 40 bunuaria in size and which can be sown with 200 modia of oats. There are 9 arpents of meadow, from which 10 loads of hay can be harvested. There is a forest there; it is estimated to be 3 leagues long and 1 league wide. In it 800 pigs can find forage.

1. Electeus a slave and his wife a colona, by the name of Landina.

From D. Herlihy, ed. and trans., *Medieval Culture and Society* (Harper & Row: New York, 1968), pp. 53-55.

They are dependents of Saint-Germain. They live in Neuillay. He holds half a farm, which has in arable land 6 bunuaria, in meadow one-half an arpent. He plows in the winter field 4 perches and in the spring field 13. He carts manure to the lord's field, and performs no other services nor pays anything in addition, for the service that he provides.

2. Abrahil a slave and his wife, a lida, by the name of Berthildis. They are dependents of Saint-Germain. These are their children: Abram, Avremarus, and Bertrada. And Ceslinus a lidus and his wife a lida, named Leutberga. These are their children: Leutgardis, and Ingohildis. And Godalbertus a lidus. These are their children: Gedalcaus, Celsovildis and Bladovildis. These three [families] live in Neuillay. They hold a farm, which has in arable land 15 bunuaria and in meadow 4 arpents. They do carting to Anjou, and in the month of May to Paris. They pay for the army tax 2 muttons, 8 chickens, 30 eggs, 100 planks and as many shingles, 12 staves, 6 hoops and 12 torches. They bring 2 loads of wood to Sutré. They inclose, in the lord's court, 4 perches with a palisade, in the meadow 4 perches with a fence, and at the harvest as much as is necessary. They plow in the winter field 8 perches and in the spring field 26 perches. Along with their corvées and labor services, they cart manure into the lord's field. Each pays a head tax of 4 pennies.

3. Gislevertus a slave and his wife a lida, by name Gotberga. These are their children: Ragno, Gausbertus, Gaujoinus, and Gautlindis. And Sinopus a slave and his wife a slave, by name Frolaica. These are their children: Siclandus, Frothardus, Marellus, Adaluildis and Frotlildis. And Ansegudis a slave. These are their children: Ingalbertus, Frobertus, Frotlaicus, and Frotberga. These three [families] live in Neuillay. They hold one farm, which has in arable land 26 bunuaria, and in meadow 8 arpents. They pay as the above.

4. Maurifius a lidus and his wife a colona, by name Ermengardis. Ermengildis is their child. And Guadulfus a lidus and his wife a lida, by name Celsa. Gaudildis is their child. These two [families] live in Neuillay. They hold one farm, having in arable land 28 bunuaria and in meadow 4 arpents. They pay as the above.

5. Ragenardus a slave and his wife a colona, by name Dagena. Ragenaus is their son. And Gausboldus a slave and his wife a lida, by name Faregildis. These two [families] live in Neuillay. They hold one farm, which has in arable land 11 bunuaria and in meadow 4 arpents. They perform services as the above.

6. Feremundus a slave and his wife a colona, by name Creada. And Feroardus a slave and his wife a lida, by name Adalgardis. Illegardis is their daughter. And Foroenus a slave. And Adalgrimus a slave. These four [families] live in Neuillay. They hold one farm, which has in arable land 8 bunuaria and in meadow 4 arpents. They perform services as the above.

7. Gautmarus a slave and his wife a lida, by name Sigalsis. These are their children: Siclevoldus and Sicleardus. He lives in Neuillay. He

holds a fourth part of a farm, which has in arable land 1 and one-half bunuaria and in meadow 1 arpent. He pays the fourth part of a full farm.

8. Hildeboldus a slave and his wife a lida, by name Bertenildis. These are their children: Aldedramnus, Adalbertus, Hildegaudus, Trutgaudus, Bernardus, Bertramnus, Hildoinus, Halderudis and Martinga. And Haldemarus a slave and his wife a colona, by name Morberga. These are their children: Martinus, Siclehildis and Bernegildis. These two live in Neuillay. They hold one-half a farm, having in land 6 bunuaria and in meadow one-half arpent. They pay half the obligation of an entire farm.

9. Bertlinus a lidus and his wife a colona, by name Lantsida. These are their children: Creatus, Martinus and Lantbertus. He lives in Neuillay. He holds a quarter part of a whole farm, which has in arable land 3 bunuaria, and in meadow 2 arpents. He does service. He must pay a quarter part of an entire farm, but for this obligation he looks after the pigs.

10. There are in Neuillay 6 and one-half inhabited farms, and one-half is not occupied. They are distributed among 16 families. They pay to the army tax 12 muttons; in head tax, 5 shillings and 4 pennies; 48 chickens, 160 eggs, 600 planks and as many shingles, 54 staves and as many hoops, and 72 torches. They make 2 cartings for wine, and during May 2 and one-half cartings, and give half an ox.

11. These are the slaves: Electus, Gislevertus, Sinopus, Ragenardus, Gausboldus, Feremundus, Gedalbertus, Faroardus, Abrahil, Faroinus, Adalgrimus, Gautmarus, and Hildevoldus. They pay torches and do portage.

12. These are the lidi: Maurifius, Gaudulfus, Bertlinus, Ceslinus, and Gedalbertus.

13. These are the women slaves: Frotlina, Ansegundis, Alda and Framberta. They feed chickens and make cloth, if wool is given to them.

14. These are the women lidae: Berthildis, Leutberga, Gotberga, Celsa, Faregildis, Sigalsis and Bertenildis. They pay 4 pennies in tax.

15. Ragenardus holds of the seigneurial property 1 bunuaria. Gislevertus keeps on his farm 2 geese.

30. *The Western Empire and Byzantium*

The Eastern emperors of Constantinople eventually recognized Charlemagne's imperial title. But they were always very reluctant to recognize

From *The Works of Liudprand of Cremona*, translated by F. A. Wright (London: George Routledge and Sons, 1930), pp. 235–243; reprinted by permission of Routledge & Kegan Paul Ltd.

Charlemagne's successors as emperors. In 968 Bishop Liudprand of Cremona led an embassy from the Western emperor Otto I (936–973) to the Byzantine emperor Nicephorus Phocas (963–969). Liudprand's account of his experiences in Constantinople illustrates the growing estrangement between Byzantium and the West.

Liudprand's Embassy to Constantinople

On the fourth of June we arrived at Constantinople, and after a miserable reception, meant as an insult to yourselves, we were given the most miserable and disgusting quarters. The palace where we were confined was certainly large and open, but it neither kept out the cold nor afforded shelter from the heat. Armed soldiers were set to guard us and prevent my people from going out, and any others from coming in. This dwelling, only accessible to us who were shut inside it, was so far distant from the emperor's residence that we were quite out of breath when we walked there — we did not ride. To add to our troubles, the Greek wine we found undrinkable because of the mixture in it of pitch, resin and plaster. The house itself had no water and we could not even buy any to quench our thirst. All this was a serious "Oh dear me!" but there was another "Oh dear me" even worse, and that was our warden, the man who provided us with our daily wants. If you were to seek another like him, you certainly would not find him on earth; you might perhaps in hell. Like a raging torrent he poured upon us every calamity, every extortion, every expense, every grief and every misery that he could invent. In our hundred and twenty days not one passed without bringing to us groaning and lamentation.

On the fourth of June, as I said above, we arrived at Constantinople and waited with our horses in heavy rain outside the Carian gate until five o'clock in the afternoon. At five o'clock Nicephorus ordered us to be admitted on foot, for he did not think us worthy to use the horses with which your clemency had provided us, and we were escorted to the aforesaid hateful, waterless, draughty stone house. On the sixth of June, which was the Saturday before Pentecost, I was brought before the emperor's brother Leo, marshal of the court and chancellor; and there we tired ourselves with a fierce argument over your imperial title. He called you no emperor, which is Basileus in his tongue, but insultingly Rex, which is king in ours. I told him that the thing meant was the same though the word was different, and he then said that I had come not make peace but to stir up strife. Finally he got up in a rage, and really wishing to insult us received your letter not in his own hand but through an interpreter. He is a man commanding enough in person but feigning humility: whereon if a man lean it will pierce his hand.

On the seventh of June, the sacred day of Pentecost, I was brought before Nicephorus himself in the palace called Stephana, that is, the Crown Palace. He is a monstrosity of a man, a dwarf, fat-headed and with tiny mole's eyes; disfigured by a short, broad, thick beard half going gray; disgraced by a neck scarcely an inch long: piglike by reason of the big close bristles on his head; in colour an Ethiopian and, as the poet says, "you would not like to meet him in the dark"; a big belly, a lean posterior, very long in the hip considering his short stature, small legs, fair sized heels and feet; dressed in a robe made of fine linen, but old, foul smelling, and discoloured by age; shod with Sicyonian slippers; bold of tongue, a fox by nature, in perjury and falsehood a Ulysses. My lords and august emperors, you always seemed comely to me; but how much more comely now! Always magnificent; how much more magnificent now! Always mighty; how much more mighty now! Always clement; how much more clement now! Always full of virtues; how much fuller now! At his left, not on a line with him, but much lower down, sat the two child emperors, once his masters, now his subjects. He began his speech as follows: —

It was our duty and our desire to give you a courteous and magnificent reception. That, however, has been rendered impossible by the impiety of your master, who in the guise of an hostile invader has laid claim to Rome; has robbed Berengar and Adalbert of their kingdom contrary to law and right; has slain some of the Romans by the sword, some by hanging, while others he has either blinded or sent into exile; and furthermore has tried to subdue to himself by massacre and conflagration cities belonging to our empire. His wicked attempts have proved unsuccessful, and so he has sent you, the instigator and furtherer of this villainy, under pretence of peace to act *comme un espion,* that is, as a spy upon us.

To him I made this reply: "My master did not invade the city of Rome by force nor as a tyrant; he freed her from a tyrant's yoke, or rather from the yoke of many tyrants. Was she not ruled by effeminate debauchers, and what is even worse and more shameful, by harlots? Your power, methinks, was fast asleep then; and the power of your predecessors, who in name alone are called emperors of the Romans, while the reality is far different. If they were powerful, if they were emperors of the Romans, why did they allow Rome to be in the hands of harlots? . . ."

". . . Come, let us clear away all trickeries and speak the plain truth. My master has sent me to you to see if you will give the daughter of the emperor Romanos and the empress Theophano to his son, my master the august emperor Otto. If you give me your oath that the marriage shall take place, I am to affirm to you under oath that my master in grateful return will observe to do this and this for you. Moreover he has already given you, his brother ruler, the best pledge of friendship by handing over Apulia, which was subject to his rule. I, to whose suggestion you declare this mischief was due, intervened in this matter, and there are as many witnesses to this as there are people in Apulia."

"It is past seven o'clock," said Nicephorus "and there is a church procession which I must attend. Let us keep to the business before us. We will give you a reply at some convenient season."

. . . As Nicephorus, like some crawling monster, walked along, the singers began to cry out in adulation: "Behold the morning star approaches; the day star rises: in his eyes the sun's rays are reflected: Nicephorus our prince, the pale death of the Saracens." And then they cried again: "Long life, long life to our prince Nicephorus. Adore him, ye nations, worship him, bow the neck to his greatness." How much more truly might they have sung: — "Come, you miserable burnt-out coal; old woman in your walk, wood-devil in your look; clodhopper, haunter of byres, goat-footed, horned, double-limbed; bristly, wild, rough, barbarian, harsh, hairy, a rebel, a Cappadocian!" So, puffed up by these lying ditties, he entered St. Sophia, his masters the emperors following at a distance and doing him homage on the ground with the kiss of peace. His armour bearer, with an arrow for pen, recorded in the church the era in progress since the beginning of his reign. So those who did not see the ceremony know what era it is.

On this same day he ordered me to be his guest. But as he did not think me worthy to be placed above any of his nobles, I sat fifteenth from him and without a table cloth. Not only did no one of my suite sit at table with me; they did not even set eyes upon the house where I was entertained. At the dinner, which was fairly foul and disgusting, washed down with oil after the fashion of drunkards and moistened also with an exceedingly bad fish liquor, the emperor asked me many questions concerning your power, your dominions and your army. My answers were sober and truthful; but he shouted out: — "You lie. Your master's soldiers cannot ride and they do not know how to fight on foot. The size of their shields, the weight of their cuirasses, the length of their swords, and the heaviness of their helmets, does not allow them to fight either way." Then with a smile he added: "Their gluttony also prevents them. Their God is their belly, their courage but wind, their bravery drunkenness. Fasting for them means dissolution, sobriety, panic. Nor has your master any force of ships on the sea. I alone have really stout sailors, and I will attack him with my fleets, destroy his maritime cities and reduce to ashes those which have a river near them. Tell me, how with his small forces will he be able to resist me even on land? His son was there: his wife was there: his Saxons, Swabians, Bavarians and Italians were all there with him: and yet they had not the skill nor the strength to take one little city that resisted them. How then will they resist me when I come followed by as many forces as there are

> Corn fields on Gargarus, grapes on Lesbian vine,
> Waves in the ocean, stars in heaven that shine?"

I wanted to answer and make such a speech in our defense as his boasting deserved; but he would not let me and added this final insult: "You are not Romans but Lombards." He even then was anxious to say more and waved his hand to secure my silence, but I was worked up and cried: "History tells us that Romulus, from whom the Romans get their name, was a fratricide born in adultery. He made a place of refuge for himself and received into it solvent debtors, runaway slaves, murderers and men who deserved death for their crimes. This was the sort of crowd whom he enrolled as citizens and gave them the name of Romans. From this nobility are descended those men whom you style 'rulers of the world.' But we Lombards, Saxons, Franks, Lotharingians, Bavarians, Swabians and Burgundians, so despise these fellows that when we are angry with an enemy we can find nothing more insulting to say than—'You Roman!' For us in the word Roman is comprehended every form of lowness, timidity, avarice, luxury, falsehood and vice. You say that we are unwarlike and know nothing of horsemanship. Well, if the sins of the Christians merit that you keep this stiff neck, the next war will prove what manner of men you are, and how warlike we."

chapter

X

The Development of Feudal Institutions

31. Lordship and Vassalage

During the ninth century Charlemagne's empire disintegrated. In the disorders of the times a new pattern of social and political life that historians designate as "feudalism" began to emerge. Some of the elements of feudalism were very ancient—for instance, relationship of special loyalty between lord and vassal. The following early formulas of commendation are from England and France respectively.

Thus shall one take the oath of fidelity:

By the Lord before whom this sanctuary is holy, I will to N. be true and faithful, and love all which he loves and shun all which he shuns, according to the laws of God and the order of the world. Nor will I ever with will or action, through word or deed, do anything which is unpleasing to him, on condition that he will hold to me as I shall deserve it, and that he will perform everything as it was in our agreement when I submitted myself to him and chose his will.

It is right that those who offer to us unbroken fidelity should be protected by our aid. And since *such and such* a faithful one of ours, by the favor of God, coming here in our palace with his arms, has seen fit to swear trust and fidelity to us in our hand, therefore we decree and command by the present precept that for the future *such and such*

From documents in E. P. Cheyney, trans., *University of Pennsylvania Translations and Reprints* (Philadelphia: University of Pennsylvania Press, 1898), Vol. IV, No. 3, pp. 3-5, 18, 15. "De Moribus et Actis Primorum Normanniae Ducum," translated by Brian Tierney in Brian Tierney, Donald Kagan, and L. Pearce Williams, eds., *Great Issues in Western Civilization* (2nd ed.; New York: Random House, 1972), Vol. I, pp. 372-373; reprinted by permission of the publisher.

above mentioned be counted with the number of antrustions. And if anyone perchance should presume to kill him, let him know that he will be judged guilty of his wergild of 600 shillings.

The Frankish kings of the early ninth century tried to regulate relationships between lords and vassals by royal capitularies.

Capitulary Concerning Freemen and Vassals (816)

If anyone shall wish to leave his lord (*seniorem*), and is able to prove against him one of these crimes, that is, in the first place, if the lord has wished to reduce him unjustly into servitude; in the second place, if he has taken counsel against his life; in the third place, if the lord has committed adultery with the wife of his vassal; in the fourth place, if he has wilfully attacked him with a drawn sword; in the fifth place, if the lord has been able to bring defence to his vassal after he has commended his hands to him, and has not done so; it is allowed to the vassal to leave him. If the lord has perpetrated anything against the vassal in these five points it is allowed the vassal to leave him.

Capitulary of Mersen (Kings Lothar, Lewis, and Charles, 847)

We will moreover that each free man in our kingdom shall choose a lord, from us or our faithful, such a one as he wishes.

We command moreover that no man shall leave his lord without just cause, nor should any one receive him, except in such a way as was customary in the time of our predecessors.

And we wish you to know that we want to grant right to our faithful subjects and we do not wish to do anything to them against reason. Similarly we admonish you and the rest of our faithful subjects that you grant right to your men and do not act against reason toward them.

And we will that the man of each one of us in whosoever kingdom he is, shall go with his lord against the enemy, or in his other needs unless there shall have been (as may there not be) such an invasion of the kingdom as is called a *landwer,* so that the whole people of that kingdom shall go together to repel it.

In the tenth century elaborate formulas of commendation often concealed simple usurpations of crown lands. The founding of the Duchy of Normandy provides a famous example.

The Franks, not having the strength to resist the pagans and seeing all France brought to nothing, came to the king and said unanimously, "Why do you not aid the kingdom which you are bound by your scepter to care for and rule? Why is peace not made by negotiation since we cannot achieve it either by giving battle or by defensive fortifications? Royal honor and power is cast down; the insolence of the pagans is raised up. The land of France is almost a desert for its people are dying by famine or by the sword or are taken captive. Care for the kingdom, if not by arms then by taking counsel." . . .

Immediately Charles, having consulted with them, sent Franco, Archbishop of Rouen, to Rollo, Duke of the Pagans. Coming to him he began to speak with mild words. "Most exalted and distinguished of dukes, will you quarrel with the Franks as long as you live? Will you always wage war on them? What will become of you when you are seized by death? Whose creature are you? Do you think you are God? Are you not a man formed from filth? Are you not dust and ashes and food for worms? Remember what you are and will be and by whose judgment you will be condemned. You will experience Hell I think, and no longer injure anyone by your wars. If you are willing to become a Christian you will be able to enjoy peace in the present and the future and to dwell in this world with great riches. Charles, a long-suffering king, persuaded by the counsel of his men, is willing to give you this coastal province that you and Halstigno have grievously ravaged. He will also give you his daughter, Gisela, for a wife in order that peace and concord and a firm, stable and continuous friendship may endure for all time between you and him. . . ."

At the agreed time Charles and Rollo came together at the place that had been decided on. . . . Looking on Rollo, the invader of France, the Franks said to one another, "This duke who has fought such battles against the warriors of this realm is a man of great power and great courage and prowess and good counsel and of great energy too." Then, persuaded by the words of the Franks, Rollo put his hands between the hands of the king, a thing which his father and grandfather and great-grandfather had never done; and so the king gave his daughter Gisela in marriage to the duke and conferred on him the agreed lands from the River Epte to the sea as his property in hereditary right, together with all Brittany from which he could live.

Rollo was not willing to kiss the foot of the king. The bishops said, "Anyone who receives such a gift ought to be eager to kiss the king's foot." He replied, "I have never bent my knees at anyone's knees, nor will I kiss anyone's foot." But, urged by the entreaties of the Franks, he commanded one of his warriors to kiss the foot of the king. The warrior promptly seized the king's foot, carried it to his mouth and kissed it standing up while the king was thrown flat on his back. At that there was a great outburst of laughter and great excitement among the people. Nevertheless King Charles, Duke Robert, the counts and nobles, the bishops and abbots swore by the Catholic faith and by their lives, limbs and the honor of the whole kingdom to the noble Rollo that he should hold and possess the land described above and pass it on to his heirs.

A more conventional ceremony of homage took place in Flanders in 1127. It was described by the chronicler Galbert of Bruges.

Through the whole remaining part of the day those who had been previously enfeoffed by the most pious count Charles, did homage to the count, taking up now again their fiefs and offices and whatever they had before rightfully and legitimately obtained. On Thursday the seventh of April, homages were again made to the count being completed in the following order of faith and security.

First they did their homage thus, the count asked if he was willing to become completely his man, and the other replied, "I am willing"; and with clasped hands, surrounded by the hands of the count, they were bound together by a kiss. Secondly, he who had done homage gave his fealty to the representative of the count in these words, "I promise on my faith that I will in future be faithful to count William, and will observe my homage to him completely against all persons in good faith and without deceit." and thirdly, he took his oath to this upon the relics of the saints. Afterward, with a little rod which the count held in his hand, he gave investitures to all who by this agreement had given their security and homage and accompanying oath.

Sometimes a vassal commended himself to several lords. It was then necessary to specify the order in which he owed loyalty to them, as in this grant of a fief in France (1200).

I, Thiebault, count palatine of Troyes, make known to those present and to come that I have given in fee to Jocelyn d'Avalon and his heirs the manor which is called Gillencourt, which is of the castellanerie of La Ferte sur Aube; and whatever the same Jocelyn shall be able to acquire in the same manor I have granted to him and his heirs in augmentation of that fief. I have granted, moreover, to him that in no free manor of mine will I retain men who are of this gift. The same Jocelyn, moreover, on account of this has become my liege man, saving however, his allegiance to Gerard d'Arcy, and to the lord duke of Burgundy, and to Peter, count of Auxerre. Done at Chouaude, by my own witness, in the year of the Incarnation of our Lord 1200 in the month of January. Given by the hand of Walter, my chancellor; note of Milo.

32.   The Fief and Private Jurisdiction

Another major characteristic of feudalism was a system of landholding in return for specified services. Such a holding of land became known as a fief. Earlier it was called a beneficium *or* precarium, *as in the following formula of the seventh century.*

In the name of God, I abbot *so and so,* with our commissioned brethren. Since it is not unknown how you, *such and such a one,* by the suggestion of divine exhortation did grant to *such and such* a monastery, to the church which is known to be constructed in honor of *such and such a saint,* where we by God's authority exercise our pastoral care, all your possessions which you seemed to have in the district named, in the vill named, which your father on his death bequeathed to you there, or which by your own labor you were able to gain there, or which as against your brother or against *such and such* a co-heir, a just division gave you, with courtyard and buildings, gardens and orchards, with various slaves, *so and so* by name, houses, lands, meadows, woods, cultivated and uncultivated, or with all the dependencies and appurtenances belonging to it, which it would be extremely long to enumerate, in all their completeness; but afterwards, at your request, it has seemed proper to us to cede to you the same possessions to be held for usufruct; and you will not neglect to pay at annual periods the due *censum* hence, that is *so and so much.* And if God should give you a son by your legal wife, he shall have the same possessions for the days of his life only, and shall not presume to neglect the above named payment, and similarly your sons which you are seen to have at present, shall do for the days of their life; after the death of whom all the possessions above named shall revert to us and our successors perpetually. Moreover, if no sons shall have been begotten by you, immediately after your death, without any prejudicial contention, they shall revert to the rulers or guardians of the above named church, forever. Nor may any one, either ourselves or our successors, be successful in a rash attempt inordinately to destroy these agreements, but just as the time has demanded in the present *precaria,* may that be sure to endure unchanged which we, with the consent of our brothers, have decided to corroborate.

From E. P. Cheyney, trans., *University of Pennsylvania Translations and Reprints* (Philadelphia: University of Pennsylvania, 1898), Vol. IV, No. 3, pp. 8, 21, 14. O. J. Thatcher and E. H. McNeal, trans., *A Source Book for Mediaeval History* (New York: Charles Scribner's, 1905), pp. 357, 352-353. *Sources of English Constitutional History,* translated by C. Stephenson and F. G. Marcham: "Laws of Henry I" (New York: Harper and Brothers, 1937), pp. 56-57; Copyright 1937, 1965 by Harper & Row, Publishers, Incorporated; reprinted by permission of the publishers.

Done *in such and such a place*, in the presence of *so and so* and of others whom it is not worth while to enumerate. Seal of the same abbot, who has ordered this *precaria* to be made.

The use of church lands to support warriors in the service of the king contributed greatly to the growth of precaria *in the eighth century. The practice is illustrated in the Frankish "Capitulary of Lestinnes" of 743.*

Because of the threats of war and the attacks of certain tribes on our borders, we have determined, with the consent of God and by the advice of our clergy and people, to appropriate for a time part of the ecclesiastical property for the support of our army. The lands are to be held as *precaria* for a fixed rent; one solidus, or twelve denarii, shall be paid annually to the church or monastery for each *casata* [farm]. When the holder dies the whole possession shall return to the church. If, however, the exigency of the time makes it necessary, the prince may require the *precarium* to be renewed and given out again. Care shall be taken, however, that the churches and monasteries do not incur suffering or poverty through the granting of *precaria*. If the poverty of the church makes it necessry, the whole possession shall be restored to the church.

Often the grant of a benefice included immunity from royal juristiction in the lands conferred, as in this seventh-century formula.

Those who from their early youth have served us or our parents faithfully are justly rewarded by the gifts of our munificence. Know therefore that we have granted to that illustrious man (name), with greatest good will, the villa called (name), situated in the county of (name), with all its possessions and extent, in full as it was formerly held by him *or* by our treasury. Therefore by the present charter which we command to be observed forever, we decree that the said (name) shall possess the villa of (name), as has been said, in its entirety, with lands, houses, buildings, inhabitants, slaves, woods, pastures, meadows, streams, mills, and all its appurtenances and belonging, and with all the subjects of the royal treasury who dwell on the lands, and he shall hold it forever with full immunity from the entrance of any public official for the purpose of exacting the royal portion of the fines from cases arising there; to the extent finally that he shall have, hold, and possess it in full ownership, no one having the right to expect its transfer, and with the right of leaving it to his successors or to anyone whom he desires, and to do with it whatever else he wishes.

In ninth-century France counts who exercised rights of jurisdiction over a given region were commonly vassals of the king and held fiefs from him. Both the countships and the fiefs often passed from father to son. In 877 Charles the Bald gave official recognition to the principle of heritability.

Capitulary of Kiersey

If a count of this kingdom, whose son is with us, shall die, our son with the rest of our faithful shall appoint some one of the nearest relatives of the same count, who, along with the officials of his province and with the bishop in whose diocese the same province is, shall administer that province until announcement is made to us, so that we may honor his son who is with us with his honors.

If, however, he had a minor son, this same son, along with the officials of that province and with the bishop in whose diocese it is, shall make provision for the same province until the notice of the death of the same count shall come to us, that his son may be honored, by our concession, with his honors.

If, however, he had no son, our son along with the rest of the faithful, shall take charge, who, along with the officials of the same province and with the proper bishop shall make provision for the same province until our order may be made in regard to it. Therefore, let him not be angry who shall provide for the province if we give the same province to another whom it pleases us, rather than to him who has so far provided for it.

Similarly also shall this be done concerning our vassals. And we will and command that as well the bishops as the abbots and the counts, and any others of our faithful also, shall study to preserve this toward their men.

Immunity from royal jurisdiction (even without a formal grant of count's rights) implied the right of a lord to exercise control over his own men. The following regulation is from an English law collection of the early twelfth century, the Leges Henrici Primi.

Concerning the privilege of a lord with regard to his man. It is lawful for every lord to summon his man for judgment in his court. Even if the man is residing at a more remote manor in the honour of which he holds, he shall go to court when his lord summons him. If the lord holds various fiefs, a man of one honour is not compelled by law to go to court in another, unless it is a case affecting some one else to which his lord summons him. If a man holds of various lords and honours, no matter how much he holds of the others, his primary obligation . . . is to the lord whose liegeman he is. Every man owes fealty to his lord for life and limbs and earthly honour and the keeping of counsel in all that is honest and worthy, saving fealty to God and to the prince of the land. Theft, treason, murder, and whatever is opposed to God and the catholic faith are, indeed, to be undertaken and carried out for no one. But fealty is to be kept toward all lords, and especially toward the lord of whom he is the liegeman, saving fealty to those mentioned above. . . .

The preceding document indicates again some of the complexities that arose when a man held lands from several lords. Other complications arose from the practice of sub-infeudation as indicated in this extract from the English Exchequer Rolls *(1254).*

Commandment is given to the sheriff of Worcester, that if Baldwin de Frivill does not hold from the king *in capite*, but from Alexander de Abetot, and Alexander from William de Beauchamp, and William from the bishop of Worcester, and the bishop from the king *in capite*, as the same Baldwin says; then the said Baldwin is to have peace from the distraint which has been made upon him for the aid to make the king's son a knight.

33.   Feudal Obligations

The mutual obligations of lords and vassals were described in a letter of Fulbert, bishop of Chartres, written in 1020.

To William most glorious duke of the Aquitanians, bishop Fulbert the favor of his prayers.

Asked to write something concerning the form of fealty, I have noted briefly for you on the authority of the books the things which follow. He who swears fealty to his lord ought always to have these six things in memory; what is harmless, safe, honorable, useful, easy, practicable. Harmless, that is to say that he should not be injurious to his lord in his body; safe, that he should not be injurious to him in his secrets or in the defenses through which he is able to be secure; honorable, that he should not be injurious to him in his justice or in other matters to him in his possessions; easy or practicable, that that good which his lord is able to do easily, he make not difficult, nor that which is practicable he make impossible to him.

However, that the faithful vassal should avoid these injuries is proper, but not for this does he deserve his holding; for it is not sufficient to abstain from evil, unless what is good is done also. It remains, therefore, that in the same six things mentioned above he should faithfully counsel and aid his lord, if he wishes to be looked upon as worthy of his benefice and to be safe concerning the fealty which he has sworn.

From E. P. Cheyney, trans., *University of Pennsylvania Translations and Reprints* (Philadelphia: University of Pennsylvania, 1898), Vol. IV, No. 3, pp. 23–24, 26. "William I," "William II," "Henry I," in Carl Stephenson and Frederick George Marcham, *Sources of English Constitutional History* (rev. ed.; New York: Harper & Row, 1972), pp. 58–60; Copyright © 1972 by Frederick George Marcham; reprinted by permission of Harper & Row, Publishers, Inc.

The lord also ought to act toward his faithful vassal reciprocally in all these things. And if he does not do this he will be justly considered guilty of bad faith, just as the former, if he should be detected in the avoidance of or the doing of or the consenting to them, would be perfidious and perjured.

I would have written to you at greater length, if I had not been occupied with many other things, including the rebuilding of our city and church which was lately entirely consumed in a great fire; from which loss though we could not for a while be diverted, yet by the hope of the comfort of God and of you we breathe again.

The rather idyllic relationship of mutual trust and loyalty portrayed by Fulbert hardened into a complex of military and financial obligations. The most important ones are indicated in these royal writs from Norman England.

William I: Summons for Military Service (1072)

William, king of the English, to Aethelwig, abbot of Evesham, greeting. I command you to summon all those who are under your charge and administration that they shall have ready before me at Clarendon on the octave of Pentecost all the knights that they owe me. Come to me likewise yourself on that day, and bring ready with you those five knights that you owe me from your abbey.

Witness, Eudo the Steward. At Winchester.

William II: Writ for the Collection of Relief (1095–1096)

William, king of the English, to all French and English who hold free lands of the bishopric of Worcester, greeting. Know that, since the bishop has died, the honour has reverted into my own hand. It is now my will that from your lands you give me such relief as I have assessed through my barons: [namely,] Hugh de Lacy £20; Walter Punther £20; Gilbert Fitz-Turold £5; Robert, bishop [of Hereford], £10; the abbot of Evesham £30; Walter of Gloucester £20; Roger Fitz-Duran £10. . . . And if any one refuses to do this, Urse and Bernard are to take both his lands and his chattels into my hand.

Witnesses: Ranulf the Chaplain, Odo the Steward, Urse d'Abeto.

Henry I: Grant Concerning Scutage (1127)

Henry, king of the English, his archbishops, bishops, abbots, earls, etc., greeting. Know that to the church of St. Aetheldreda of Ely, for the love of God, for the souls of my father and mother, for the redemption of my sins, and on the petition of Hervey, bishop of the same church, I have forgiven £40 of those £100 which the aforesaid church was accustomed to give for scutage whenever scutage was assessed throughout my land of England; so that henceforth forever the church shall on that account give no more than £60 when scutage is levied throughout the land. And so let the aforesaid church be quit in perpetuity of the aforesaid [40] pounds.

Witnesses: Roger, bishop of Salisbury; Geoffrey, my chancellor; Robert, [keeper] of the seal; William de Tancarville; William d'Aubigny, steward; Ralph Basset, Geoffrey de Clinton, William de Pont-de-l'Arche. At Eling during my crossing.

The English Exchequer Rolls provide ample evidence of how feudal practices such as the rights of wardship and marriage—originally adopted for social reasons—could be turned to the lord's financial advantage.

Alice, countess of Warwick, renders account of £1000 and 10 palfreys to be allowed to remain a widow as long as she pleases, and not to be forced to marry by the king. And if perchance she should wish to marry, she shall not marry except with the assent and on the grant of the king, where the king shall be satisfied; and to have the custody of her sons whom she has from the earl of Warwick her late husband.

Hawisa, who was wife of William Fitz Robert renders account of 130 marks and 4 palfreys that she may have peace from Peter of Borough to whom the king has given permission to marry her; and that she may not be compelled to marry.

Geoffrey de Mandeville owes 20,000 marks to have as his wife Isabella, countess of Gloucester, with all the lands and tenements and fiefs which fall to her.

Thomas de Colville renders an account of 100 marks for having the custody of the sons of Roger Torpel and their land until they come of age.

William, bishop of Ely, owes 220 marks for having the custody of Stephen de Beauchamp with his inheritance and for marrying him where he wishes.

William of St. Mary's church, renders an account of 500 marks for having the custody of the heir of Robert Young, son of Robert Fitzharding, with all his inheritance and all its appurtenances and franchises; that is to say with the services of knights and gifts of churches and marriages of women, and to be allowed to marry him to whatever one of his relatives he wishes; and that all his land is to revert to him freely when he comes of age.

34. The Peace and Truce of God

A major problem of early feudal society was endemic warfare. The church tried to mitigate feudal violence by proclamations of a Peace of God or Truce of God.

Peace of God, Proclaimed in the Synod of Charroux (989)

Following the example of my predecessors, I, Gunbald, archbishop of Bordeaux, called together the bishops of my diocese in a synod at Charroux, . . . and we, assembled there in the name of God, made the following decrees:

1. Anathema against those who break into churches. If anyone breaks into or robs a church, he shall be anathema unless he makes satisfaction.

2. Anathema against those who rob the poor. If anyone robs a peasant or any other poor person of a sheep, ox, ass, cow, goat, or pig, he shall be anathema unless he makes satisfaction.

3. Anathema against those who injure clergymen. If anyone attacks, seizes, or beats a priest, deacon, or any other clergyman, who is not bearing arms (shield, sword, coat of mail, or helmet), but is going along peacefully or staying in the house, the sacrilegious person shall be excommunicated and cut off from the church, unless he makes satisfaction, or unless the bishop discovers that the clergyman brought it upon himself by his own fault.

Truce for the Bishopric of Terouanne (1063)

Drogo, bishop of Terouanne, and count Baldwin [of Hainault] have established this peace with the cooperation of the clergy and people of the land.

Dearest brothers in the Lord, these are the conditions which you must observe during the time of the peace which is commonly called the truce of God, and which begins with sunset on Wednesday and lasts until sunrise on Monday.

1. During those four days and five nights no man or woman shall assault, wound, or slay another, or attack, seize, or destroy a castle, burg, or villa, by craft or by violence.

2. If anyone violates this peace and disobeys these commands of ours, he shall be exiled for thirty years as a penance, and before he leaves the bishopric he shall make compensation for the injury which he committed. Otherwise he shall be excommunicated by the Lord God and excluded from all Christian fellowship.

From O. J. Thatcher and E. H. McNeal, trans., *A Source Book for Mediaeval History* (New York: Charles Scribner's, 1905), pp. 412, 417–418.

3. All who associate with him in any way, who give him advice or aid, or hold converse with him, unless it be to advise him to do penance and to leave the bishopric, shall be under excommunication until they have made satisfaction.

4. If any violator of the peace shall fall sick and die before he completes his penance, no Christian shall visit him or move his body from the place where it lay, or receive any of his possessions.

5. In addition, brethren, you should observe the peace in regard to lands and animals and all things that can be possessed. If anyone takes from another an animal, a coin, or a garment, during the days of the truce, he shall be excommunicated unless he makes satisfaction. If he desires to make satisfaction for his crime he shall first restore the thing which he stole or its value in money, and shall do penance for seven years within the bishopric. If he should die before he makes satisfaction and completes his penance, his body shall not be buried or removed from the place where it lay, unless his family shall make satisfaction for him to the person whom he injured.

6. During the days of the peace, no one shall make a hostile expedition on horseback, except when summoned by the count; and all who go with the count shall take for their support only as much as is necessary for themselves and their horses.

7. All merchants and other men who pass through your territory from other lands shall have peace from you.

8. You shall also keep this peace every day of the week from the beginning of Advent to the octave of Epiphany and from the beginning of Lent to the octave of Easter, and from the feast of Rogations [the Monday before Ascension Day] to the octave of Pentecost.

9. We command all priests on feast days and Sundays to pray for all who keep the peace, and to curse all who violate it or support its violators.

10. If anyone has been accused of violating the peace and denies the charge, he shall take the communion and undergo the ordeal of hot iron. If he is found guilty, he shall do penance within the bishopric for seven years.

chapter XI

The Investiture Contest

35. Church Reform and Royal Theocracy

During the ninth century many churches and monasteries fell under the control of lay lords with unfortunate results for ecclesiastical discipline. A major movement of monastic reform began with the founding of the abbey of Cluny in 910. The principal provisions of its foundation charter are given below.

To all right thinkers it is clear that the providence of God has so provided for certain rich men that, by means of their transitory possessions, if they use them well, they may be able to merit everlasting rewards. As to which thing, indeed, the divine word, showing it to be possible and altogether advising it, says: "The riches of a man are the redemption of his soul." (Prov. xiii.) I, William, count and duke by the grace of God, diligently pondering this, and desiring to provide for my own safety while I am still able, have considered it advisable — nay, most necessary, that from the temporal goods which have been conferred upon me I should give some little portion for the gain of my soul. . . . Therefore be it known to all who live in the unity of the faith and who await the mercy of Christ, and to those who shall succeed them and who shall continue to exist until the end of the world, that, for the love of God and of our Saviour Jesus Christ, I hand over from my own rule to the holy apostles, Peter, namely, and Paul, the possessions over which I hold sway, the town of Cluny, namely, with the court and

From "Charter of Abbey of Cluny," in E. F. Henderson, ed., *Select Historical Documents of the Middle Ages* (London: George Bell, 1892), pp. 329-332.

demesne manor, and the church in honour of St. Mary the mother of God and of St. Peter the prince of the apostles, together with all the things pertaining to it, the vills, indeed, the chapels, the serfs of both sexes, the vines, the fields, the meadows, the woods, the waters and their outlets, the mills, the incomes and revenues, what is cultivated and what is not, all in their entirety. Which things are situated in or about the country of Macon, each one surrounded by its own bounds. . . .

I give these things, moreover, with this understanding, that in Cluny a regular monastery shall be constructed in honour of the holy apostles Peter and Paul, and that there the monks shall congregate and live according to the rule of St. Benedict, and that they shall possess, hold, have and order these same things unto all time. In such wise, however, that the venerable house of prayer which is there shall be faithfully frequented with vows and supplications, and the celestial converse shall be sought and striven after with all desire and with the deepest ardour; and also that there shall be sedulously directed to God prayers, beseechings and exhortations as well for me as for all, according to the order in which mention has been made of them above. And let the monks themselves, together with all the aforesaid possessions, be under the power and dominion of the abbot Berno, who, as long as he shall live, shall preside over them regularly according to his knowledge and ability. But after his death, those same monks shall have power and permission to elect any one of their order whom they please as abbot and rector, following the will of God and the rule promulgated by St. Benedict — in such wise that neither by the intervention of our own or of any other power may they be impeded from making a purely canonical election. Every five years, moreover, the aforesaid monks shall pay to the church of the apostles at Rome ten shillings to supply them with lights; and they shall have the protection of those same apostles and the defence of the Roman pontiff; and those monks may, with their whole heart and soul, according to their ability and knowledge, build up the aforesaid place. We will, further, that in our times and in those of our successors, according as the opportunities and possibilities of that place shall allow, there shall daily, with the greatest zeal be performed there works of mercy towards the poor, the needy, strangers and pilgrims. It has pleased us also to insert in this document that, from this day, those same monks there congregated shall be subject neither to our yoke, nor to that of our relatives, nor to the sway of the royal might, nor to that of any earthly power. And, through God and all his saints, and by the awful day of judgment, I warn and abjure that no one of the secular princes, no count, no bishop whatever, not the pontiff of the aforesaid Roman see, shall invade the property of these servants of God, or alienate it, or diminish it, or exchange it, or give it as a benefice to any one, or constitute any prelate over them against their will.

In the tenth and eleventh centuries the church greatly emphasized the sanctity of kingship. Thus Conrad II of Germany (1024–1039) was hailed at his coronation as "vicar of Christ." Theocratic monarchs like Conrad normally appointed the bishops of their kingdoms by "investing" them with the symbols of episcopal office, a ring and a staff.

On the Consecration of the King

If Charlemagne had been present, alive, with his scepter, the people would not have been more eager, nor could they have rejoiced more at the return of so great a man than at the first coming of this King. The King arrived at Mainz. And there, received with due honor, he waited devoutly for his consecration, [as one] desirable to all. When the Archbishop of Mainz and all the clergy solemnly prepared themselves to bless him on the day of the birth of St. Mary, the Archbishop delivered this sermon to the King during the sacred offices of regal unction:

"All power of this transient age is derived from one most pure font. It is usually the case, however, that when several rivulets spring forth from the same source, at one time they are turbulent, at another, clear, while at their head, the font stays fast in its purity. In the same way, inasmuch as the human state dares to set Creator and creation side by side for comparison, we have the power to conjecture in a similar way about God the Immortal King and about earthly kings. For it has been written: 'All power is of God.' When this Omnipotent King of kings, the author and the beginning of all honor, pours the grace of some dignity upon princes of the earth, insofar as it is in accord with the nature of its origin, it is pure and unstained. When, however, it has come to those who wield this dignity unworthily and pollute it with pride, malice, lust, avarice, wrath, impatient willfullness, and cruelty, they will serve the perilous potion of iniquity to themselves and to all subject to them, unless they purge themselves by doing penance. O let the whole Church of the Saints pray and intercede before God that the dignity which is offered pure today by God to our present lord and king, Conrad, be preserved inviolate by him as far as is humanly possible.

"Our sermon is with you and for you, O Lord King. The Lord, who elected you to be king over His people, has wished first to test you and to have you rule afterwards. . . . Divine Piety has been unwilling for you to be without preparatory discipline, so that after this instruction from Heaven you might take up the Christian Empire. You have come to the highest dignity: you are the vicar of Christ."

From "The Deeds of Conrad II," in T. E. Mommsen and K. F. Morrison, trans., *Imperial Lives and Letters of the Eleventh Century* (New York: Columbia University Press, 1962), pp. 66–67; reprinted by permission of the publisher. "Libri III Adversus Simoniacos," in *Libelli de Lite* (Hanover: Monumenta Germaniae Historica, 1891), I, pp. 205, 225, translated by Brian Tierney.

Conrad II's successor, Henry III, used his powers over ecclesiastical appoint-ments to establish in Rome a great reforming pope, Leo IX (1040–1054). Leo and his successors directed a major movement of church reform throughout Europe. After Leo's death, however, the reform party at Rome began to turn against the imperial authority. In a work written in 1054–1058 Cardinal Humbert sharply condemned the practice of royal investiture of bishops.

How does it pertain to a lay person to distribute ecclesiastical sacra-ments and pontifical or pastoral grace, namely crozier staffs and rings? . . . Anyone who appoints a prelate with these two symbols undoubt-edly claims all pastoral authority for himself in presuming to do so. For after this institution what free judgment concerning such prelates (who are already appointed) can be exercised by clergy, people and nobles or by the metropolitan who is to consecrate them? . . . One so instituted imposes himself by violence on the clergy, people and nobles to dominate them instead of being acknowledged, sought out and re-quested by them. So too he encroaches on the metropolitan, not being judged by him but rather judging him; for he does not require or re-ceive the metropolitan's approval but only demands and extorts the service of prayer and anointing which is all that is left of him. . . . Why should the metropolitan reconfer what he already has [the ring and staff] unless it is to sell anew the goods of the church under this form of appointment or donation or to confirm the former sale by the subscription of the metropolitan and his bishops or to cloak the pre-sumption of lay ordination under a veil of clerical discipline? . . .

If anyone wishes to compare the priestly and royal dignities in a use-ful and blameless fashion he may say that in the present church the priesthood is like the soul, the kingship like the body; for they esteem one another and each in turn needs the other and demands services and renders them to the other. Hence just as the soul excels and com-mands the body, so is the priestly dignity to the royal or, rather, the heavenly dignity to the earthly.

To maintain the independence of the papacy from outside interference, a new method of electing popes was devised in the pontificate of Nicholas II (1059–1061). For the first time a decisive voice was given to the cardinals of the Roman church. The following decree was promulgated at a council held in Rome in 1059.

. . . Supported by the authority of our predecessors and the other holy fathers, we decree and order that:

When the pontiff of this universal Roman church dies the cardinal

1059 Council at Rome, in Brian Tierney, *The Crisis of Church and State, 1050–1300*, with selected documents. © 1964 (Englewood Cliffs, N. J.: Prentice-Hall, 1964), pp. 42–43. Reprinted by permission of Prentice-Hall, Inc., Englewood Cliffs, New Jersey.

bishops shall first confer together most diligently concerning the election; next they shall summon the other cardinal clergy; and then the rest of the clergy and the people shall approach to give their assent to the new election, the greatest care being taken lest the evil of venality creep in by any way whatsoever. The most eminent churchmen shall be the leaders in carrying out the election of a pope, the others followers. Certainly this order of election will be found right and lawful if anyone examines the rules and acts of the various fathers and also calls to mind the judgment of our holy predecessor Leo. "No reason permits," he says, "that men should be regarded as bishops who have not been chosen by the clergy or requested by the people or consecrated by the bishops of the province with the approval of the metropolitan." But since the apostolic see is superior to all the churches in the world it can have no metropolitan set over it, and so the cardinal bishops who raise the chosen pontiff to the summit of the apostolic dignity undoubtedly act in place of a metropolitan. They shall make their choice from the members of this church if a suitable man is to be found there, but if not they shall take one from another church, saving the honor and reverence due to our beloved son Henry who is now king and who, it is hoped, will in future become emperor with God's grace, according as we have now conceded this to him and to his successors who shall personally obtain this right from the apostolic see.

If, however, the perversity of corrupt and evil men so prevails that a pure, sincere and free election cannot be made in the City, the cardinal bishops, together with the God-fearing clergy and the Catholic laity, even though they are few, may have the right and power of electing a pontiff for the apostolic see in any convenient place.

If, after an election has been made, a time of war or the efforts of any malignant men shall make it impossible for the person elected to be enthroned in the apostolic see according to custom, it is clear that, nonetheless, the person elected shall acquire authority to rule the Roman church and to dispose of all its resources as a true pope, for we know that the blessed Gregory acted thus before his consecration. . . .

36.   *The Program of Gregory VII*

The principal abuses which church reformers sought to eradicate were simony and clerical marriage. Both practices were condemned by a Roman council held in 1074 early in the pontificate of Pope Gregory VII (1073–1085).

Decree of 1074 Council at Rome, in O. J. Thatcher and E. H. McNeal, trans., *A Source Book for Mediaeval History* (New York: Charles Scribner's, 1905), pp. 134–135. Pope Gregory VII, in E. F. Henderson, ed., *Select Historical Documents of the Middle Ages* (London: George Bell, 1892), pp. 366–367, 365.

Those who have been advanced to any grade of holy orders, or to any office, through simony, that is, by the payment of money, shall hereafter have no right to officiate in the holy church. Those also who have secured churches by giving money shall certainly be deprived of them. And in the future it shall be illegal for anyone to buy or to sell [any ecclesiastical office, position, etc.].

Nor shall clergymen who are married say mass or serve the altar in any way. We decree also that if they refuse to obey our orders, or rather those of the holy fathers, the people shall refuse to receive their ministrations, in order that those who disregard the love of God and the dignity of their office may be brought to their senses through feeling the shame of the world and the reproof of the people.

Pope Gregory VII was interested not only in moral reform but also in asserting high claims for papal power. The propositions usually known as the Dictatus Papae *were included in the pope's official Register in the year 1075.*

The Dictate of the Pope

1. That the Roman church was founded by God alone.
2. That the Roman pontiff alone can with right be called universal.
3. That he alone can depose or reinstate bishops.
4. That, in a council, his legate, even if a lower grade, is above all bishops, and can pass sentence of deposition against them.
5. That the pope may depose the absent.
6. That, among other things, we ought not to remain in the same house with those excommunicated by him.
7. That for him alone is it lawful, according to the needs of the time, to make new laws, to assemble together new congregations, to make an abbey of a canonry; and, on the other hand, to divide a rich bishopric and unite the poor ones.
8. That he alone may use the imperial insignia.
9. That of the pope alone all princes shall kiss the feet.
10. That his name alone shall be spoken in the churches.
11. That this is the only name in the world.
12. That it may be permitted to him to depose emperors.
13. That he may be permitted to transfer bishops if need be.
14. That he has power to ordain a clerk of any church he may wish.
15. That he who is ordained by him may *preside* over another church, but may not hold a subordinate position; and that such a one may not receive a higher grade from any bishop.
16. That no synod shall be called a general one without his order.
17. That no chapter and no book shall be considered canonical without his authority.
18. That a sentence passed by him may be retracted by no one; and that he himself, alone of all, may retract it.

19. That he himself may be judged by no one.

20. That no one shall dare to condemn one who appeals to the apostolic chair.

21. That to the latter should be referred the more important cases of every church.

22. That the Roman church has never erred; nor will it err to all eternity, the Scripture bearing witness.

23. That the Roman pontiff, if he have been canonically ordained, is undoubtedly made a saint by the merits of St. Peter; St. Ennodius, bishop of Pavia, bearing witness, and many holy fathers agreeing with him. As is contained in the decrees of St. Symmachus the pope.

24. That, by his command and consent, it may be lawful for subordinates to bring accusations.

25. That he may depose and reinstate bishops without assembling a synod.

26. That he who is not at peace with the Roman church shall not be considered catholic.

27. That he may absolve subjects from their fealty to wicked men.

In 1075 Gregory promulgated a decree forbidding prelates to receive their churches from lay rulers. The text of this decree against "lay investiture" has been lost. The following text is a reenactment of the same prohibition in 1078.

Inasmuch as we have learned that, contrary to the establishments of the holy fathers, the investiture with churches is, in many places, performed by lay persons; and that from this case many disturbances arise in the church by which the Christian religion is trodden under foot: we decree that no one of the clergy shall receive the investiture with a bishopric or abbey or church from the hand of an emperor or king or of any lay person, male or female. But if he shall presume to do so he shall clearly know that such investiture is bereft of apostolic authority, and that he himself shall lie under excommunication until fitting satisfaction shall have been rendered.

37. *Gregory VII and Henry IV*

King Henry IV of Germany (1056–1106) refused to obey the pope's decree and, in January 1076, condemned Gregory as a usurper.

From Henry IV and Gregory VII, in E. F. Henderson, ed., *Select Historical Documents of the Middle Ages* (London: George Bell, 1892), pp. 372-373, 376-377, 388-391.

Henry IV's Letter to Gregory VII (Jan. 24, 1076)

Henry, king not through usurpation but through the holy ordination of God, to Hildebrand, at present not pope but false monk. Such greeting as this hast thou merited through thy disturbances, inasmuch as there is no grade in the church which thou hast omitted to make a partaker not of honour but of confusion, not of benediction but of malediction. For, to mention few and especial cases out of many, not only hast thou not feared to lay hands upon the rulers of the holy church, the anointed of the Lord—the archbishops, namely, bishops and priests—but thou hast trodden them under foot like slaves ignorant of what their master is doing. Thou hast won favour from the common herd by crushing them; thou hast looked upon all of them as knowing nothing, upon thy sole self, moreover, as knowing all things. This knowledge, however, thou hast used not for edification but for destruction; so that with reason we believe that St. Gregory, whose name thou hast usurped for thyself, was prophesying concerning thee when he said: "The pride of him who is in power increases the more, the greater the number of those subject to him; and he thinks that he himself can do more than all." And we, indeed, have endured all this, being eager to guard the honour of the apostolic see; thou, however, has understood our humility to be fear, and hast not, accordingly, shunned to rise up against the royal power conferred upon us by God, daring to threaten to divest us of it. As if we had received our kingdom from thee! As if the kingdom and the empire were in thine and not in God's hand! And this although our Lord Jesus Christ did call us to the kingdom, did not, however, call thee to the priesthood. For thou has ascended by the following steps. By wiles, namely, which the profession of monk abhors, thou hast achieved money; by money, favour; by the sword, the throne of peace. And from the throne of peace thou hast disturbed peace, inasmuch as thou hast armed subjects against those in authority over them; inasmuch as thou, who wert not called, hast taught that our bishops called of God are to be despised; inasmuch as thou hast usurped for laymen the ministry over their priests, allowing them to depose or condemn those whom they themselves had received as teachers from the hand of God through the laying on of hands of the bishops. On me also who, although unworthy to be among the anointed, have nevertheless been anointed to the kingdom, thou hast lain thy hand; me who—as the tradition of the holy Fathers teaches, declaring that I am not to be deposed for any crime unless, which God forbid, I should have strayed from the faith—am subject to the judgment of God alone. For the wisdom of the holy fathers committed even Julian the apostate not to themselves, but to God alone, to be judged and to be deposed. For himself the true pope, Peter, also exclaims: "Fear God, honour the king." But thou who does not fear God, dost dishonour in me his appointed one. Wherefore St. Paul, when he has not spared an angel of Heaven if he shall have preached otherwise, has not excepted thee also who dost teach otherwise upon earth. For he says: "If any one, either I or an angel from Heaven, should preach a gospel other than that which has been preached to you, he shall be damned." Thou, therefore, damned by this curse and by the judgment of all our bishops and by our own, descend and relinquish the apostolic chair which thou hast usurped. Let another ascend the throne of St. Peter, who shall not practise violence under the cloak of religion, but shall teach the sound doctrine of St. Peter. I Henry, king by the grace of God, do say unto thee, together with all our bishops: Descend, descend, to be damned throughout the ages.

Gregory replied by declaring Henry IV excommunicated and deposed.

First Deposition and Banning of Henry IV by Gregory VII (February 22, 1076)

O St. Peter, chief of the apostles, incline to us, I beg, thy holy ears, and hear me thy servant whom thou hast nourished from infancy, and whom, until this day, thou hast freed from the hand of the wicked, who have hated and do hate me for my faithfulness to thee. Thou, and my mistress the mother of God, and thy brother St. Paul are witnesses for me among all the saints that thy holy Roman church drew me to its helm against my will; that I had no thought of ascending thy chair through force, and that I would rather have ended my life as a pilgrim than, by secular means, to have seized thy throne for the sake of earthly glory. And therefore I believe it to be through thy grace and not through my own deeds that it has pleased and does please thee that the Christian people, who have been especially committed to thee, should obey me. And especially to me, as thy representative and by thy favour, has the power been granted by God of binding and loosing in Heaven and on earth. On the strength of this belief therefore, for the honour and security of thy church, in the name of Almighty God, Father, Son and Holy Ghost, I withdraw, through thy power and authority, from Henry the king, son of Henry the emperor, who has risen against thy church with unheard of insolence, the rule over the whole kingdom of the Germans and over Italy. And I absolve all Christians from the bonds of the oath which they have made or shall make to him; and I forbid any one to serve him as king. For it is fitting that he who strives to lessen the honour of thy church should himself lose the honour which belongs to him. And since he has scorned to obey as a Christian, and has not returned to God whom he had deserted — holding intercourse with the excommunicated; practising manifold iniquities; spurning my commands which, as thou dost bear witness, I issued to him for his own salvation; separating himself from thy church and striving to rend it — I bind him in thy stead with the chain of the anathema. And, leaning on thee, I so bind him that the people may know and have proof that thou art Peter, and above thy rock the Son of the living God hath built His church, and the gates of Hell shall not prevail against it.

After an attempted reconciliation at Canossa (mentioned in the text below), Gregory excommunicated Henry a second time in 1080.

Second Banning and Dethronement of Henry IV by Gregory VII (March 7, 1080)

St. Peter, chief of the apostles, and thou St. Paul, teacher of the nations, deign, I beg, to incline your ears to me and mercifully to hear me. Do ye who are the disciples and lovers of truth aid me to tell the truth to ye without any of the falsehood which we together detest: to the end that my brothers may better acquiesce with me and may know and learn that, after God and his mother the ever-virgin Mary, it is in ye I trust when I resist the wicked and unholy but lend aid to your faithful followers. For ye know that I did not willingly take holy orders. And unwillingly I went with my master Gregory beyond the mountains; but more unwillingly I returned with my master pope Leo to your especial church, in which I served ye as always. Then, greatly against my will, with much grieving and groaning and wailing I was placed upon your throne, although thoroughly unworthy. I say these things thus because I did not choose ye but ye chose me and did place upon me the very heavy burden of your church. And because ye did order me to go up into a high mountain and call out and proclaim to the people of God their crimes and to the sons of the earth their sins, the members of the devil have commenced to rise up against me and have presumed, even unto blood, to lay their hands upon me. For the kings of the earth stood by, and the secular and ecclesiastical princes; the men of the palace, also, and the common herd came together against the Lord and against ye His anointed, saying: "Let us break their chains and cast off their yoke from us." And they have in many ways attempted to rise up against me in order to utterly confound me with death or with exile.

Among them, especially, Henry whom they call king, son of Henry the emperor, did raise his heel against your church and strive, by casting me down, to subjugate it, having made a conspiracy with many ultramontane bishops. But your authority resisted and your power destroyed their pride. He, confounded and humbled, came to me in Lombardy and sought absolution from the bann. I seeing him humiliated, having received many promises from him concerning the bettering of his way of living, restored to him the communion. But only that; I did not reinstate him in his kingdom from which I had deposed him in a Roman synod, nor did I order that the fealty from which, in that synod, I have absolved all those who had sworn it to him, or were about to swear it, should be observed towards him. And my reason for not doing so was that I might do justice in the matter or arrange peace—as Henry himself, by an oath before two bishops, had promised me should be done—between him and the ultramontane bishops or princes who, being commanded to do so by your church, had resisted him. But the said ultramontane bishops and princes, hearing that he had not kept his promise to me, and, as it were, despairing of him, elected for themselves without my advice—ye are my witnesses—duke Rudolf as king. This king Rudolf hastily sent an envoy to intimate to me that he had been compelled to accept the helm of state but that he was ready to obey me in every way. And to make this the more credible, he has continued from that time to send me words to the same effect, adding also that he was ready to confirm what he had promised by giving his own son and the son of his faithful follower duke Bertald as hostages. Meanwhile Henry commenced to implore my aid against the said Rudolf. I answered that I would willingly grant it if I could hear the arguments on both sides so as to know whom justice most favoured. But he, thinking to conquer by his own strength, scorned my reply. But when he found that he could not do as he had hoped he sent to Rome two of his partizans, the bishops, namely, of Verdun and of Osnabruck, who asked me in a synod to do justice to him. This also the envoys of Rudolf pressed me to do. At length, by God's inspiration as I believe, I decreed in that synod that an assembly should take place beyond the mountains, where either peace should be established or it should be made known which side justice the most favoured. For I—as ye, my fathers and masters, can testify—have taken care up to this time to aid no party save the one on whose side justice should be found to be. And, thinking that the weaker side would wish the assembly not to take place, whereas justice would hold its own, I excommunicated and bound with the anathema the person of one— whether king, duke, bishop or ordinary man—who should by any means contrive to prevent the assembly from taking place. But the said Henry with his partizans, not fearing the danger from disobedience, which is the crime of idolatry, incurred the excommunication by impeding the assembly. And he bound himself with the chain of the anathema, causing a great multitude of Christians to be given over to death and of churches to be ruined, and rendering desolate almost the whole realm of the Germans. Wherefore, trusting in the judgment and mercy of God and of his most holy mother the evervirgin Mary, armed with your authority, I lay under excommunication and bind with the chains of the anathema the oft-mentioned Henry—the so-called king —and all his followers. And again, on the part of God Almighty and of yourselves, I deny to him the kingdom of the Germans and of Italy and I take away from him all royal power and dignity. And I forbid any Christian to obey him as king, and absolve from their oath all who have sworn or shall swear to him as ruler of the land. May this same Henry, moreover, — as well as his partizans, — be powerless in any war-like encounter and obtain no victory during his life. Whereas I grant and concede in your name that Rudolf, whom, as a mark of fidelity to ye, the Germans have chosen to be their king, may rule and defend the land of the Germans. To all of those who faithfully adhere to him I, trusting in your support, grant absolution of all their sins and your benediction in this life and the life to come. For as Henry, on account of his pride, disobedience and falseness, is justly cast down from his royal dignity, so to Rudolf, for his humility, obedience and truthful-ness, the power and dignity of kingship are granted.

Proceed now, I beg, O fathers and most holy princes, in such way that all the world may learn and know that, if ye can bind and loose in Heaven, so ye can on earth take away empires, kingdoms, principali-ties, duchies, margravates, counties and all possessions of men, and grant them to any man ye please according to his merits. For often have ye taken away patriarchates, primateships, archbishoprics and bishoprics from the wicked and unworthy and given them to devout men. And if ye judge spiritual offices what are we to believe of your power in secular ones? And if ye shall judge angels, who rule over all proud princes, how will it be with those subject to them? Let kings and all secular princes now learn how great ye are and what your power is; and let them dread to disregard the command of your church. And, in the case of the said Henry, exercise such swift judgment that all may know him to fall not by chance but by your power. Let him be con-founded; — would it were to repentance, that his soul may be safe at the day of the Lord!

Given at Rome, on the Nones of March, in the third indiction.

38.   *The End of the Conflict*

The conflict over lay investiture dragged on under the successors of Greg-ory VII. The canonist Ivo of Chartres suggested a compromise solution in 1097. He argued that it was quite legitimate for kings to invest bishops pro-vided that they did not intend to grant spiritual power by doing so but only to grant the royal estates held by the bishopric. The following letter was written to the archbishop of Lyons.

So far as we have heard, a person of noble birth, sufficiently learned,

From "Epistola ad Hugonem," in *Libelli de Lite* (Hanover: Monuments Germaniae Historica, 1892), II, pp. 644-645, translated by Brian Tierney, Paschal II, Calixtus II, and Henry V, in E. F. Henderson, ed., *Select Historical Documents of the Middle Ages* (London: George Bell, 1892), pp. 405-407, 408-409.

of good repute when he exercised the office of deacon in the church, was freely and without discord elected bishop. As to your statement that he accepted episcopal investiture from the hand of the king, this has not been related to us by anyone who saw it. But even if such were the case, we do not see how the faith or holy religion is injured whether this investiture was included or omitted, since it has no sacramental force in the making of a bishop. For it does not seem that kings are prohibited by apostolic authority from conferring bishoprics after a canonical election has been held. . . . What does it matter whether this conferral is made by hand or by gesture, by word or by staff since kings do not intend to confer anything spiritual but only to approve the choice of the electors or to concede to those elected the ecclesiastical estates and the external goods which churches acquire through the munificence of kings?

Pope Paschal II (1099–1118) proposed a more radical solution for the dispute in 1111, but it was promptly rejected by the imperial bishops.

Paschal's Privilege (February 12, 1111)

Bishop Paschal, servant of the servants of God. To his beloved son Henry and his successors, forever. It is both decreed against by the institutions of the divine law, and interdicted by the sacred canons, that priests should busy themselves with secular cases, or should go to the public court except to rescue the condemned, or for the sake of others who suffer injury. Wherefore also the apostle Paul says: "If ye have secular judgments constitute as judges those who are of low degree in the church." Moreover in portions of your kingdom bishops and abbots are so occupied by secular cares that they are compelled assiduously to frequent the court, and to perform military service. Which things, indeed, are scarcely if at all carried on without plunder, sacrilege, arson. For ministers of the altar are made ministers of the king's court: inasmuch as they receive cities, duchies, margravates, monies and other things which belong to the service of the king. Whence also the custom has grown up—intolerably for the church—that elected bishops should by no means receive consecration unless they had first been invested through the hand of the king. From which cause both the wickedness of simoniacal heresy and, at times, so great an ambition has prevailed that the episcopal sees were invaded without any previous election. At times, even, they have been invested while the bishops were alive. Aroused by these and very many other evils which had happened for the most part through investitures, our predecessors the pontiffs Gregory VII. and Urban II. of blessed memory, frequently calling together episcopal councils did condemn those investitures of the lay hand, and did decree that those who should have obtained churches through them should be deposed, and the donors also be deprived of communion — according to that chapter of the apostolic canons which runs thus: "If any bishop, employing the powers of the world, do through them obtain a church: he shall be deposed and isolated, as well as all who communicate with him." Following in the traces of which (canons), we also, in an episcopal council, have confirmed their sentence. And so, most beloved son, king Henry, — now through our office, by the grace of God, emperor of the Romans, — we decree that those royal appurtenances are to be given back to thee and to thy kingdom which manifestly belonged to that kingdom in the time of Charles, Louis, and of thy other predecessors. We forbid, and under sentence of anathema prohibit, that any bishop or abbot, present or future, invade these same royal appurtenances. In which are included the cities, duchies, margravates, counties, monies, toll, market, advowsons of the kingdom, rights of the judges of the hundred courts, and the courts which manifestly belonged to the king together with what pertained to them, the military posts and camps of the kingdom. Nor shall they, henceforth, unless by favour of the king, concern themselves with those royal appurtenances. But neither shall it be allowed our successors, who shall follow us in the apostolic chair, to disturb thee or thy kingdom in this matter. Furthermore, we decree that the churches, with the offerings and hereditary possessions which manifestly did not belong to the kingdom, shall remain free; as, on the day of thy coronation, in the sight of the whole church, thou didst promise that they should be. For it is fitting that the bishops, freed from secular cares, should take care of their people, and not any longer be absent from their churches. For, according to the apostle Paul, let them watch, being about to render account, as it were, for the souls of these (their people).

Later in 1111 Pope Paschal, acting under duress, conceded to King Henry V (1106–1125) the right of investing prelates with ring and staff. This arrangement was also repudiated by many bishops and subsequently annulled by the pope.

Paschal's Privilege (April 12, 1111)

That prerogative, therefore, of dignity which our predecessors did grant to thy predecessors the catholic emperors, and did confirm by their charters, we also do concede to thee, beloved, and do confirm by the page of this present privilege: that, namely, thou may'st confer the investiture of staff and ring, freely, except through simony and with violence to the elected, on the bishops and abbots of thy kingdom. But after the investiture they shall receive the canonical consecration from the bishop to whom they belong. If any one, moreover, without thy consent, shall have been elected by the clergy and people, he shall be consecrated by no one unless he be invested by thee.

The dispute was finally settled by a compromise arrived at in the Concordat of Worms (1122)

Privilege of Pope Calixtus II

I, bishop Calixtus, servant of the servants of God, do grant to thee beloved son, Henry—by the grace of God august emperor of the Romans —that the elections of the bishops and abbots of the German kingdom, who belong to the kingdom, shall take place in thy presence, without simony and without any violence; so that if any discord shall arise between the parties concerned, thou, by the counsel or judgment of the metropolitan and the co-provincials, may'st give consent and aid to the party which has the more right. The one elected, moreover, without any exaction may receive the regalia from thee through the lance, and shall do unto thee for these what he rightfully should. But he who is consecrated in the other parts of the empire (*i.e.* Burgundy and Italy) shall, within six months, and without any exaction, receive the regalia from thee through the lance, and shall do unto thee for these what he rightfully should. Excepting all things which are known to belong to the Roman church. Concerning matters, however, in which thou dost make complaint to me, and dost demand aid—I, according to the duty of my office, will furnish aid to thee. I give unto thee true peace, and to all who are or have been on thy side in the time of this discord.

Edict of the Emperor Henry V

In the name of the holy and indivisible Trinity, I, Henry, by the grace of God august emperor of the Romans, for the love of God and of the holy Roman church and of our master pope Calixtus, and for the healing of my soul, do remit to God, and to the holy apostles of God, Peter and Paul, and to the holy catholic church, all investiture through ring and staff; and do grant that in all the churches that are in my kingdom or empire there may be canonical election and free consecration. All the possessions and regalia of St. Peter which, from the beginning of this discord unto this day, whether in the time of my father or also in mine, have been abstracted, and which I hold: I restore to that same holy Roman church. As to those things, moreover, which I do not hold, I will faithfully aid in their restoration. As to the possessions also of all other churches and princes, and of all other lay and clerical persons which have been lost in that war: according to the counsel of the princes, or according to justice, I will restore the things that I hold; and of those things which I do not hold I will faithfully aid in the restoration. And I grant true peace to our master pope Calixtus, and to the holy Roman church, and to all those who are or have been on its side. And in matters where the holy Roman church shall demand aid I will grant it; and in matters concerning which it shall make complaint to me I will duly grant to it justice.

THE TWELFTH CENTURY

The First Crusaders

39. Pope Urban Proclaims a Crusade

The first Crusade was launched by Pope Urban II at the council of Clermont. Fulcher of Chartres, who was present at the council, wrote this account of the pope's speech.

1. These and many other things having been suitably disposed of, all those present, both clergy and people, at the words of Lord Urban, the Pope, voluntarily gave thanks to God and confirmed by a faithful promise that his decrees would be well kept. But straightway he added that another thing not less than the tribulation already spoken of, but even greater and more oppressive, was injuring Christianity in another part of the world, saying:

2. "Now that you, O sons of God, have consecrated yourselves to God to maintain peace among yourselves more vigorously and to uphold the laws of the Church faithfully, there is work to do, for you must turn the strength of your sincerity, now that you are aroused by divine correction, to another affair that concerns you and God. Hastening to the way, you must help your brothers living in the Orient, who need your aid for which they have already cried out many times.

3. "For, as most of you have been told, the Turks, a race of Persians, who have penetrated within the boundaries of Romania even to the Mediterranean to that point which they call the Arm of Saint George, in occupying more and more of the lands of the Christians,

From Fulcher of Chartres, *Chronicle of the First Crusade,* M. E. McGinty, trans. (Philadelphia: University of Pennsylvania Press, 1941), pp. 15-17; reprinted by permission of the publisher.

have overcome them, already victims of seven battles, and have killed and captured them, have overthrown churches, and have laid waste God's kingdom. If you permit this supinely for very long, God's faithful ones will be still further subjected.

4. "Concerning this affiar, I, with suppliant prayer — not I, but the Lord — exhort you, heralds of Christ, to persuade all of whatever class, both knights and footmen, both rich and poor, in numerous edicts, to strive to help expel that wicked race from our Christian lands before it is too late.

5. "I speak to those present, I send word to those not here; moreover, Christ commands it. Remission of sins will be granted for those going thither, if they end a shackled life either on land or in crossing the sea, or in struggling against the heathen. I, being vested with that gift from God, grant this to those who go.

6. "O what a shame, if a people, so despised, degenerate, and enslaved by demons would thus overcome a people endowed with the trust of almighty God, and shining in the name of Christ! O how many evils will be imputed to you by the Lord Himself, if you do not help those who, like you, profess Christianity!

7. "Let those," he said, "who are accustomed to wage private wars wastefully even against Believers, go forth against the Infidels in a battle worthy to be undertaken now and to be finished in victory. Now, let those, who until recently existed as plunderers, be soldiers of Christ; now, let those, who formerly contended against brothers and relations, rightly fight barbarians; now, let those, who recently were hired for a few pieces of silver, win their eternal reward. Let those, who wearied themselves to the detriment of body and soul, labor for a twofold honor. Nay, more, the sorrowful here will be glad there, the poor here will be rich there, and the enemies of the Lord here will be His friends there.

8. "Let no delay postpone the journey of those about to go, but when they have collected the money owed to them and the expenses for the journey, and when winter has ended and spring has come, let them enter the crossroads courageously with the Lord going on before."

40. *The Capture of Jerusalem*

Fulcher subsequently accompanied the Crusaders to the Holy Land and left this description of the climax of the Crusade, the seige of Jerusalem.

From Fulcher of Chartres, *Chronicle of the First Crusade*, M. E. McGinty, trans. (Philadelphia: University of Pennsylvania Press, 1941), pp. 66–69; reprinted by permission of the publisher.

1. When the Franks viewed the city, and saw that it would be difficult to take, our princes ordered wooden ladders to be made. By erecting them against the wall they hoped to scale it, and by a fierce attack enter the city, with God helping.

2. After they had done this, when the leaders gave the signal and the trumpets sounded, in morning's bright light of the seventh day following they rushed upon the city from all sides in an astonishing attack. But when they had rushed upon it until the sixth hour of the day, and were unable to enter by means of the scaling ladders because there were few of them, they sadly abandoned the assault.

3. After consultation, craftsmen were ordered to make machines, so that by moving them to the wall they might, with God's aid, obtain the desired end. So this was done.

4. Meanwhile they suffered lack of neither bread nor meat; but, because that place was dry, unirrigated, and without rivers, both the men and the beasts of burden were very much in need of water to drink. This necessity forced them to seek water at a distance, and daily they laboriously carried it in skins from four or five miles to the siege.

5. After the machines were prepared, namely, the battering-rams and the sows, they again prepared to assail the city. In addition to other kinds of siege craft, they constructed a tower from small pieces of wood, because large pieces could not be secured in those regions. When the order was given, they carried the tower piecemeal to a corner of the city. Early in the same morning, when they had gathered the machines and other auxiliary weapons, they very quickly erected the tower in compact shape not far from the wall. After it was set up and well covered by hides on the outside, by pushing it they slowly moved it nearer to the wall.

6. Then a few but brave soldiers, at a signal from the horn, climbed on the tower. Nevertheless the Saracens defended themselves from these soldiers and, with slings, hurled firebrands dipped in oil and grease at the tower and at the soldiers, who were in it. Thereafter death was present and sudden for many on both sides.

7. From their position on Mount Zion, Count Raymond and his men likewise made a great assault with their machines. From another position, where Duke Godfrey, Robert, Count of the Normans, and Robert of Flanders, were situated, an even greater assault was made on the wall. This was what was done on that day.

8. On the following day, at the blast of the trumpets, they undertook the same work more vigorously, so that by hammering in one place with the battering-rams, they breached the wall. The Saracens had suspended two beams before the battlement and secured them by ropes as a protection against the stones hurled at them by their assailants. But what they did for their advantage later turned to their detriment, with God's providence. For when the tower was moved to the wall, the ropes, by which the aforesaid beams were suspended, were

cut by falchions, and the Franks constructed a bridge for themselves out of the same timber, which they cleverly extended from the tower to the wall.

9. Already one stone tower on the wall, at which those working our machines had thrown flaming firebrands, was afire. The fire, little by little replenished by the wooden material in the tower, produced so much smoke and flame that not one of the citizens on guard could remain near it.

10. Then the Franks entered the city magnificently at the noon-day hour on Friday, the day of the week when Christ redeemed the whole world on the cross. With trumpets sounding and with everything in an uproar, exclaiming: "Help, God!" they vigorously pushed into the city, and straightway raised the banner on the top of the wall. All the heathen, completely terrified, changed their boldness to swift flight through the narrow streets of the quarters. The more quickly they fled, the more quickly were they put to flight.

11. Count Raymond and his men, who were bravely assailing the city in another section, did not perceive this until they saw the Saracens jumping from the top of the wall. Seeing this, they joyfully ran to the city as quickly as they could, and helped the others pursue and kill the wicked enemy.

12. Then some, both Arabs and Ethiopians, fled into the Tower of David; others shut themselves in the Temple of the Lord and of Solomon, where in the halls a very great attack was made on them. Nowhere was there a place where the Saracens could escape the swordsmen.

13. On the top of Solomon's Temple, to which they had climbed in fleeing, many were shot to death with arrows and cast down headlong from the roof. Within this Temple about ten thousand were beheaded. If you had been there, your feet would have been stained up to the ankles with the blood of the slain. What more shall I tell? Not one of them was allowed to live. They did not spare the women and children.

41.   An Arab View of the Crusaders

Ousama Ibn Mounkidh was an Arab gentleman whose long life spanned almost the whole of the twelfth century. His references to the Crusaders' attitudes and behavior provide an interesting complement to the accounts of Western chroniclers.

Glory be to Allâh, the creator and author of all things! Anyone who is acquainted with what concerns the Franks can only glorify and sanctify

From *The Autobiography of Ousama* (1095-1188), G. R. Potter, trans. (London: George Routledge, 1929), pp. 172-183; reprinted by permission of the publisher.

Allâh the All-Powerful; for he has seen in them animals who are superior in courage and in zeal for fighting but in nothing else, just as beasts are superior in strength and aggressiveness.

I will report some Frankish characteristics and my surprise as to their intelligence.

In the army of King Fulk, the son of Fulk, there was a respectable Frankish knight who had come from their country to make a pilgrimage and then return. He made my acquaintance and became so intimate with me that he called me "My brother." We liked one another and were often together. When he got ready to go back over the sea and return to his own country, he said to me, "My brother, I am returning home and I should like, with your permission, to take your son with me to bring him to our countries (I had with me my son aged fourteen). He will see our knights, and he will learn wisdom and knowledge of chivalry there. When he returns, he will have taken on the bearing of an intelligent man." My ear was hurt by his words, which did not come from a wise head. If my son had been taken prisoner, captivity could have brought him no worse fate than to be taken to the Frankish countries. I answered, "By your life, that was my intention, but I have been prevented by the affection that his grandmother, my mother, has towards my son. She let him leave with me only after making me swear to bring him back to her." "Is your mother still living then?" he asked. "Yes," I replied. He said to me; "Don't disappoint her."

Among the curiosities of medicine among the Franks, I will tell how the governor of Al-Mounaiṭira wrote to my uncle to ask him to send him a doctor who would look after some urgent cases. My uncle chose a Christian doctor named Thâbit (?). He remained absent only ten days and then returned to us. There was a general exclamation: "How rapidly you have cured your patients!" Thâbit replied: "They brought before me a knight with an abscess which had formed in his leg and a woman who was wasting away with a consumptive fever. I applied a little plaster to the knight; his abscess opened and took a turn for the better; the women I forbade certain food and improved her condition. It was at this point that a Frankish doctor came up and said: 'This man is incapable of curing them.' Then, turning to the knight, he asked, 'Which do you prefer, to live with one leg or die with two?' 'I would rather live with one leg,' the knight answered. 'Bring a stalwart knight,' said the Frankish doctor, 'and a sharp hatchet.' Knight and hatchet soon appeared. I was present at the scene. The doctor stretched the patient's leg on the block of wood and then said to the knight, 'Strike off his leg with the hatchet; take it off at one blow.' Under my eyes the knight aimed a violent blow at it without cutting through the leg. He aimed another blow at the unfortunate man, as a result of which his marrow came from his leg and the knight died instantly. As for the woman, the doctor examined her and said, 'She is a woman in whose head there is a devil who has taken possession of her. Shave off her hair!' His prescription was carried out, and like her fellows, she began once again to eat garlic and mustard. Her consumption became worse. The doctor then said, 'It is because the devil has entered her head.' Taking a razor, the doctor cut open her head in the shape of a cross and scraped away the skin in the centre so deeply that her very bones were showing. He then rubbed the head with salt. In her turn, the woman died instantly. After having asked them whether my services were still required and obtained an answer in the negative, I came back, having learnt to know what I had formerly been ignorant of about their medicine."

. . .

It is always those who have recently come to live in Frankish territory who show themselves more inhuman than their predecessors who have been established amongst us and become familiarised with the Mohammedans.

A proof of the harshness of the Franks (the scourge of Allâh upon them!) is to be seen in what happened to me when I visited Jerusalem. I went into the mosque Al-Aḳsâ. By the side of this was a little mosque which the Frank had converted into a church. When I went into the mosque Al-Aḳsâ, which was occupied by the Templars, who were my friends, they assigned me this little mosque in which to say my prayers. One day I went into it and glorified Allâh. I was engrossed in my praying when one of the Franks rushed at me, seized me and turned my face to the East, saying, "That is how to pray!" The Templars again made for him and ejected him, then they apologised to me and said to me, "He is a stranger who has only recently arrived from Frankish lands. He has never seen anyone praying without turning to the East." I answered, "I have prayed sufficiently for to-day." I went out and was astounded to see how put out this demon was, how he trembled and how deeply he had been affected by seeing anyone pray in the direction of the *Ḳibla*.

I saw one of the Templars go up to the emir Mou'în ad-Dîn (may Allâh have mercy upon him!) when he was in the cathedral of the Rock (Aṣ-Sakhra). "Would you like," he asked him, "to see God as a child?" "Yes, certainly," answered Mou'în ad-Dîn. The Templar went before us until he showed us an image of Mary with the Messiah as a child (may he be saved!) on her lap. "Here," said the Templar, "is God as a child." May Allâh raise himself high above those who speak such impious things!

The Franks understand neither the feeling of honour nor the nature of jealousy. . . .

One day, going to his bedroom, [a] wine-merchant found a man in bed with his wife. "What has induced you to come in to my wife?" he asked. "I was tired," the other said, "and I came in to rest myself." "But how," said the Frank, "did you dare to go in to my bed?" "I

found a couch smoothed over like a rug and I went to sleep on it."
"But my wife was sleeping by your side." "The bed belonged to her,
could I turn her away from it?" "By the truth of my religion," the husband answered, "I swear to you that if you do it again we shall see an
estrangement between us." That is what discontent is with a Frank
and this is the measure of his jealousy. . . .

Consider this absolute contradiction. Here are men without jealousy
and without a feeling of honour. On the other hand they are endowed
with great courage. Generally speaking, courage originates solely in
feelings of honour and the care people take to avoid any slur on their
reputation. . . .

At Neapolis, I was once present at a curious sight. They brought in
two men for trial by battle, the cause being the following. Some Mohammedan brigands had raided some property in the neighbourhood
of Neapolis. A farmer was suspected of having guided the brigands to
this spot. The farmer took flight but soon returned, the king having
had his children imprisoned. "Treat me with equity," said the accused,
"and allow me to fight with him who has named me as the person who
brought the brigands into the village." The king then said to the lord
who had received the village as a fief: "Send for his opponent." The
lord returned to his village, picked out a blacksmith who was working
there, and said to him, "You must go and fight a duel." For the owner
of the fief was primarily anxious to see that none of his labourers got
himself killed, for fear his crops should suffer.

I saw this blacksmith. He was a strong young man, but one who,
walking or sitting, was always wanting something to drink. As for the
other, the challenger to single combat, he was an old man of great
courage, who snapped his fingers as a token of defiance and prepared
for the fight without perturbation. The sheriff (*al-biskound*), governor
(*schihna*) of the town, appeared, gave each of the two fighters a
cudgel and shield and made the crowd form a ring around them.

The fight started. The old man forced the blacksmith backwards,
throwing him on to the edge of the crowd, and then returned to the
middle of the ring. The exchange of blows was so violent that the
rivals, who remained standing, seemed to make up one pillar of blood.

The fight continued, while the sheriff urged them to force a conclusion. "Quicker," he shouted to them. The blacksmith profited by his
experience at wielding a hammer. When the old man was exhausted,
the blacksmith aimed a blow at him which overthrew him, making the
cudgel, which he was holding in his hand, fall behind him. The blacksmith crouched over the old man so as to put his fingers into his eyes,
but he could not reach them because of the streams of blood which
were flowing from them; he got up and struck his head so violently
with his cudgel that he finished him off.

At once they put a rope around the neck of the corpse, which they
took away and hung on a gibbet.

The lord who had chosen the blacksmith gave him a considerable piece of property, made him get on a horse with his followers, took him off and went away. See from this example what law and judicial proceedings mean among the Franks (the curse of Allâh upon them!).

On another occasion, I happened to go with the emir Mou'in ad-Dîn to Jerusalem. We stopped at Neapolis. There a blind man came to him, still young, wearing a fine dress, a Mohammedan, who brought him gifts and asked leave to enter his service at Damascus. Mou'in ad-Dîn agreed.

I made enquiries about this man and learnt that his mother had married a Frank and had killed her husband. Her son used trickery against Frankish pilgrims and employed her to help him to kill them. The Franks in the end suspected him of such behaviour and treated him according to Frankish custom.

They fitted up a enormous cask, filled it with water and placed a wooden plank across it. Then the suspect was bound, hung by a rope from his shoulders, and thrown into the cask. If he were innocent, he would sink into the water and would be pulled out by means of this rope without being allowed to die. On the other hand, if he had committed any fault, it would be impossible for him to sink in the water. The unfortunate man when thrown into the cask tried hard to reach the bottom but did not succeed, and had to submit to the rigour of their judgment (the curse of Allâh upon them!). They passed a red-hot silver stiletto over his eyes and blinded him.

chapter XIII

Ways of Thought and Feeling

42. St. Anselm: Proof of the Existence of God

During the twelfth century new forms of theological argumentation grew up along with new movements of religious reform. St. Anselm, archbishop of Canterbury from 1093 to 1109, is remembered in the history of philosophy especially for his "ontological proof" of the existence of God.

Truly there is a God, although the fool hath said in his heart, There is no God.

And so, Lord, do thou, who dost give understanding to faith, give me, so far as thou knowest it to be profitable, to understand that thou art as we believe; and that thou art that which we believe. And, indeed, we believe that thou art a being than which nothing greater can be conceived. Or is there no such nature, since the fool hath said in his heart, there is no God? (Psalms xiv. 1). But, at any rate, this very fool, when he hears of this being of which I speak—a being than which nothing greater can be conceived—understands what he hears, and what he understands is in his understanding; although he does not understand it to exist.

For, it is one thing for an object to be in the understanding, and another to understand that the object exists. When a painter first conceives of what he will afterwards perform, he has it in his understanding, but he does not yet understand it to be, because he has not yet performed

From *St. Anselm, Basic Writings: Proslogium, Monologium*, etc., translated by S. N. Dean, with an Introduction by Charles Hartshorne (LaSalle, Ill.: Open Court Publishing Co., 1962); reprinted by permission of the publisher.

it. But after he has made the painting, he both has it in his understanding, and he understands that it exists, because he has made it.

Hence, even the fool is convinced that something exists in the understanding, at least, than which nothing greater can be conceived. For, when he hears of this, he understands it. And whatever is understood, exists in the understanding. And assuredly that, than which nothing greater can be conceived, cannot exist in the understanding alone. For, suppose it exists in the understanding alone: then it can be conceived to exist in reality; which is greater.

Therefore, if that, than which nothing greater can be conceived, exists in the understanding alone, the very being, than which nothing greater can be conceived, is one, than which a greater can be conceived. But obviously this is impossible. Hence, there is no doubt that there exists a being, than which nothing greater can be conceived, and it exists both in the understanding and in reality.

God cannot be conceived not to exist.—God is that, than which nothing greater can be conceived.—That which can be conceived not to exist is not God.

And it assuredly exists so truly, that it cannot be conceived not to exist. For, it is possible to conceive of a being which cannot be conceived not to exist; and this is greater than one which can be conceived not to exist. Hence, if that, than which nothing greater can be conceived, can be conceived not to exist, it is not that, than which nothing greater can be conceived. But this is an irreconcilable contradiction. There is, then, so truly a being than which nothing greater can be conceived to exist, that it cannot even be conceived not to exist; and this being thou art, O Lord, our God.

So truly, therefore, dost thou exist, O Lord, my God, that thou canst not be conceived not to exist; and rightly. For, if a mind could conceive of a being better than thee, the creature would rise above the Creator; and this is most absurd. And, indeed, whatever else there is, except thee alone, can be conceived not to exist. To thee alone, therefore, it belongs to exist more truly than all other beings, and hence in higher degree than all others. For, whatever else exists does not exist so truly, and hence in a less degree it belongs to it to exist. Why then, has the fool said in his heart, there is no God (Psalms xiv.1), since it is so evident, to a rational mind, that thou dost exist in the highest degree of all? Why, except that he is dull and a fool?

How the fool has said in his heart what cannot be conceived.—A thing may be conceived in two ways: (1) when the word signifying it is conceived; (2) when the thing itself is understood. As far as the word goes, God can be conceived not to exist; in reality he cannot.

But how has the fool said in his heart what he could not conceive; or how is it that he could not conceive what he said in his heart? since it is the same to say in the heart, and to conceive.

But, if really, nay, since really, he both conceived, because he said in his heart; and did not say in his heart, because he could not conceive; there is more than one way in which a thing is said in the heart or conceived. For, in one sense, an object is conceived, when the word signifying it is conceived; and in another, when the very entity, which the object is, is understood.

In the former sense, then, God can be conceived not to exist; but in the latter, not at all. For no one who understands what fire and water are can conceive fire to be water, in accordance with the nature of the facts themselves, although this is possible according to the words. So, then, no one who understands what God is can conceive that God does not exist; although he says these words in his heart, either without any, or with some foreign, signification. For, God is that than which greater cannot be conceived. And he who thoroughly understands this, assuredly understands that this being so truly exists, that not even in concept can it be non-existent. Therefore, he who understands that God so exists, cannot conceive that he does not exist.

I thank thee, gracious Lord, I thank thee; because what I formerly believed by thy bounty, I now so understand by thine illumination, that if I were unwilling to believe that thou dost exist, I should not be able not to understand this to be true.

43. *Peter Abelard: Yes and No*

Peter Abelard (1079–1142) was famous in his own day, and in later times, both for his stormy intellectual career and for his love affair with Heloise. He wrote of both in an autobiography that he called "A History of Calamities."

Chapter II. *Of the Persecution of Him by His Master* William.

I came at length to Paris, where this study had long been greatly flourishing, to *William* styled "of Champeau," my preceptor, a man at that time pre-eminent, rightly and by common repute, in this teaching: with whom I stayed for a while, welcomed by him at first but afterwards a grave burden to him, since I endeavoured to refute certain of his opinions and often ventured to reason with him, and at times shewed myself his superior in debate. Which things indeed those who among our fellow-scholars were esteemed the foremost suffered with all the more indignation in that I was junior to them in age and in length of study. Hence arose the beginnings of my calamities which have continued up to the present time, and the more widely my fame extended,

From "The Calamities of Abelard," in *The Letters of Heloise and Abelard*, C. K. Scott Moncrieff, trans. (New York: Alfred A. Knopf, 1942), pp. 4, 9–13, 19–20, 23–24, 27–28. Copyright 1926 and renewed 1954 by Alfred A. Knopf, Inc. Reprinted by permission of Alfred A. Knopf, Inc.

the more the envy of others was kindled against me. At length it came to pass that, presuming upon my talents beyond the capacity of my years, I aspired, boy as I was, to the mastership of a school, and found myself a place in which to practise, namely Melun, at that time a town of note and a royal abode. . . .

Abelard moved on from philosphy to the study of theology, but again he quarreled with his master.

Chapter IV. Of the Persecution of Him by His Master Anselm.

Wherefore the old man aforesaid, being stirred by vehement envy, and having already been stimulated against me by the persuasion of divers persons, as I have before recounted, began no less to persecute me over the Holy Scriptures than our *William* had aforetime done over philosophy. Now there were at the time in this old man's school two who appeared to predominate over the rest, namely *Alberic* of Rheims and *Lotulph,* a Lombard: who, the more they presumed upon themselves, were the more kindled against me. And so, his mind greatly perturbed by their suggestions, as later it came to light, this old man boldly forbade me to continue further the work of interpretation which I had begun in his place of teaching. Advancing this pretext forsooth, that if perchance I were to write anything in error in my work, being still untrained in that study, it might be imputed to him. This coming to the ears of the scholars, they were moved with the utmost indignation against so manifest a calumny of envy, the like of which had never befallen any man yet. Which, the more manifest it was, the more honourable was it to me, so by persecution my fame increased.

Chapter V. How, Having Returned to Paris, He Completed the Interpretations which He Had Begun to Deliver at Laon.

So, after a few days, returning to Paris, the schools that had long before been intended for me and offered to me, from which I had at first been driven out, I held for some years in quiet, and there at the opening of my course I strove to complete those interpretations of *Ezekiel* which I had begun at Laon. Which indeed were so acceptable to their readers that they believed me to be no less adept in the Holy Scriptures than they had seen me to be in philosophy. Whence in both kinds of study our school vehemently multiplying, what pecuniary gain and what reputation it brought me cannot have failed to reach your ears. But inasmuch as prosperity ever puffs up fools, and worldly tranquillity enervates the vigour of the mind, and easily loosens it by carnal allurements, when now I esteemed myself as reigning alone in the world as a philosopher, nor was afraid of any further disturbance, I began to give rein to my lust, who hitherto had lived in the greatest continence.

Chapter VI. How Having Fallen in Love with Heloise *He Was Thereby Wounded as Well in Body as in Mind.*

Now there was in this city of Paris a certain young maiden by the name of *Heloise,* the niece of a certain Canon who was called *Fulbert,* who, so great was his love for her, was all the more diligent in his zeal to instruct her, so far as was in his power, in the knowledge of letters. Who, while in face she was not inferior to other women, in the abundance of her learning was supreme. For inasmuch as this advantage, namely literary knowledge, is rare in women, so much the more did it commend the girl and had won her the greatest renown throughout the realm. Seeing in her, therefore, all those things which are wont to attract lovers, I thought it suitable to join her with myself in love, and believed that I could effect this most easily. For such renown had I then, and so excelled in grace of youth and form, that I feared no refusal from whatever woman I might deem worthy of my love. All the more easily did I believe that this girl would consent to me in that I knew her both to possess and to delight in the knowledge of letters; even in absence it would be possible for us to reach one another's presence by written intermediaries, and to express many things more boldly in writing than in speech, and so ever to indulge in pleasing discussions.

So, being wholly inflamed with love for this girl, I sought an opportunity whereby I might make her familiar with me in intimate and daily conversation, and so the more easily lead her to consent. With which object in view, I came to terms with the aforesaid uncle of the girl, certain of his friends intervening, that he should take me into his house, which was hard by our school, at whatever price he might ask. . . .

What more need I say? First in one house we are united, then in one mind. So, under the pretext of discipline, we abandoned ourselves utterly to love, and those secret retreats which love demands, the study of our texts afforded us. And so, our books lying open before us, more words of love rose to our lips than of literature, kisses were more frequent than speech. Oftener went our hands to each other's bosom than to the pages; love turned our eyes more frequently to itself than it directed them to the study of the texts. That we might be the less suspected, blows were given at times, by love, not by anger, affection, not indignation, which surpassed all ointments in their sweetness. What more shall I say? No stage of love was omitted by us in our cupidity, and, if love could elaborate anything new, that we took in addition. The less experienced we were in these joys, the more ardently we persisted in them and the less satiety did they bring us. And the more this pleasure occupied me the less leisure could I find for my philosophy and to attend to my school. Most tedious was it for me to go to school or to stay there; laborious likewise when I was keeping nightly vigils of love and daily of study. Which also so negligently and tepidly I now performed that I produced nothing from my mind but everything from memory; nor was I anything now save a reciter of things learned in the past, and if I found time to compose a few verses, they were amorous, and not secret hymns of philosophy. Of which songs the greater part are to this day, as thou knowest, repeated and sung in many parts, principally by those to whom a like manner of life appeals. . . .

Heloise had a child and Abelard married her. He tried, however, to keep the marriage secret.

Presently we withdrew privily apart, nor did we see each other afterwards save seldom and by stealth, concealing as far as possible what we had done. Her uncle, however, and his servants, seeking a solace for their ignominy began to divulge the marriage that had been celebrated, and to break the promise they had given me on that head. But she began to anathematise to the contrary, and to swear that their story was altogether false. Whereby he being vehemently moved began to visit her with frequent contumely.

On learning of this I removed her to a certain Abbey of nuns near Paris, which is called Argenteuil, where she herself as a young girl had been bred up and schooled. The garments also of religion, which befitted the monastic profession, except the veil, I had fashioned for her and put them on her. Hearing which, the uncle and his kinsmen and associates were of the opinion that I had played a trick on them, and had taken an easy way to rid myself of *Heloise*, making her a nun. Whereat vehemently indignant, and conspiring together against me, on a certain night while I slumbered and slept in an inner room of my lodging, having corrupted a servant of mine with money, they punished me with a most cruel and shameful vengeance, and one that the world received with the utmost amazement: amputating, to wit, those parts of my body wherewith I had committed that of which they complained. Who presently taking flight, two of them who could be caught were deprived of their eyes and genitals. One of whom was the servant afore-mentioned, who while he remained with me in my service was by cupidity led to my betrayal.

Chapter VIII. Of the Injury to His Body. He Becomes a Monk in the Monastery of Saint Denis: Heloise a Nun at Argenteuil.

. . . Plunged in so wretched a contrition, it was the confusion of shame, I confess, rather than the devotion of conversion that drove me to the retirement of a monastic cloister. She, moreover, had already at my command willingly taken the veil and entered a convent. And so both the two of us at one time put on the sacred habit, I in the Abbey of Saint Denis and she in the Convent of Argenteuil aforesaid. Who indeed, I remember, when divers in compassion of her tried vainly to deter so young a woman from the yoke of the monastic rule, as from an intolerable burden, breaking out, as best she could amid her tears and sobs, into that famous complaint of *Cornelia,* answered:

Great husband, undeserving of my bed!
What right had I to bow so lofty a head?
Why, impious female, did I marry thee,
To cause thy hurt? Accept the penalty
That of my own free will I'll undergo . . .

And with these words she hastened to the altar and straightway, before the Bishop, took the blessed veil from the altar and publicly bound herself to the monastic profession.

Chapter IX. Of the Book of His Theology, and of the Persecution which He Bore from His Fellow-students. A Council Is Held against Him.

Now it so happend that I applied myself first to lecturing on the fundamentals of our faith by the analogy of human reason, and composed a certain tractate of theology, Of Unity and the Holy Trinity, for our scholars, who were asking for human and philosophical reasons, and demanded rather what could be understood than what could be stated, saying indeed that the utterance of words was superfluous which the intelligence did not follow, nor could anything be believed unless first it had been understood, and that it was ridiculous for anyone to preach to others what neither he himself nor they whom he taught could comprehend with their intellect, Our Lord Himself complaining that such were "blind leaders of the blind." Which tractate indeed, when numbers had seen and read it, began generally to please its readers, because it appeared to satisfy all alike upon these questions. And inasmuch as these questions appeared difficult beyond all others, the more their gravity was admitted, the more subtle my solution of them was considered to be, whereupon my rivals, vehemently incensed, assembled a Council against me, princially those two old plotters, namely *Alberic* and *Lotulph,* who now that their and my masters, to wit *William* and *Anselm,* were defunct, sought as it were to reign alone in their room and also to succeed them as if they had been their heirs. Since moreover both of them were conducting schools at Rheims, by repeated suggestions they moved their Archbishop *Rodulph* against me, that associating with himself *Cono* Bishop of Palestrina, who then held the office of Legate in France, he should assemble a conventicle under the name of Council in the city of Soissons, and should invite me to appear there, bringing with me that famous work which I had written about the Holy Trinity. And so it came to pass. But before I came there, those two rivals of mine so diffamed me among the clergy and the people, that almost the people stoned me and the few of my disciples who had come with me on the first day of our arrival· saying that I preached and had written that there were three Gods, as they themselves had been assured.

The papal legate was inclined to defer the case to another council.

Then my rivals, considering that they had achieved nothing if this business should be carried on outside their diocese, where forsooth they would not be able to sit in judgment, little trusting evidently in justice, persuaded the Archbishop that it was assuredly ignominious to himself if this case were to be transferred to another audience, and that it would be most dangerous if in that way I escaped. And straight-way hastening to the Legate, they succeeded in altering his opinion and brought him reluctantly to the position that he should condemn the book without any inquiry, and at once burn it in the sight of all, and condemn me to perpetual enclosure in a strange monastery. For they said that for the condemnation of the book this ought to be suffi-cient, that I had ventured publicly to read it, though commended by the authority neither of the Roman Pontiff nor of the Church, and had given it to be copied by many. And this would be of great benefit to the Christian faith, if by my example a similar presumption were prevented in others. And because the Legate was less a scholar than he should have been he relied principally on the Archbishop's advice, as the Archbishop on theirs. . . . And so being summoned I went straight way before the Council, and without any process of discussion they compelled me to cast my aforesaid book upon the fire.

Heloise sent a letter to Abelard after reading his "History of Calamities," asking him to write to her. Heloise's letter depicts the famous love affair from her point of view.

To her master, nay father, to her husband, nay brother; his hand-maid, nay daughter, his spouse, nay sister: to ABELARD, HELOISE.
   Your letter written to a friend for his comfort, beloved, was lately brought to me by chance. Seeing at once from the title that it was yours, I began the more ardently to read it in that the writer was so dear to me, that I might at least be refreshed by his words as by a pic-ture of him whose presence I have lost. Almost every line of that letter, I remember, was filled with gall and wormwood, to wit those that re-lated the miserable story of our conversion, and thy unceasing crosses, my all. Thou didst indeed fulfil in that letter what at the beginning of it thou hadst promised thy friend, namely that in comparison with thy troubles he should deem his own to be nothing or but a small matter.

From C. K. Scott Moncrieff, *Letters of Heloise and Abelard,* pp. 53-61.

. . . And so in His Name Who still protects thee in a certain measure for Himself, in the Name of Christ, as His handmaids and thine,* we beseech thee to deign to inform us by frequent letters of those ship-wrecks in which thou still art tossed, that thou mayest have us at least, who alone have remained to thee, as partners in thy grief or joy. . . .

For it is thou alone that canst make me sad, canst make me joyful or canst comfort me. And it is thou alone that owest me this great debt, and for this reason above all that I have at once performed all things that you didst order, till that when I could not offend thee in anything I had the strength to lose myself at thy behest. And what is more, and strange it is to relate, to such madness did my love turn that what alone it sought it cast from itself without hope of recovery when, straightway obeying thy command, I changed both my habit and my heart, that I might shew thee to be the one possessor both of my body and of my mind. Nothing have I ever (God wot) required of thee save thyself, desiring thee purely, not what was thine Not for the pledge of matrimony, nor for any dowry did I look, nor my own passions or wishes but thine (as thou thyself knowest) was I zealous to gratify.

And if the name of wife appears more sacred and more valid, sweeter to me is ever the word friend, or, if thou be not ashamed, concubine or whore. To wit that the more I humbled myself before thee the fuller grace I might obtain from thee, and so also damage less the fame of thine excellence. And thou thyself wert not wholly unmindful of that kindness in the letter of which I have spoken, written to thy friend for his comfort. Wherein thou hast not disdained to set forth sundry rea-sons by which I tried to dissuade thee from our marriage, from an ill-starred bed; but wert silent as to many, in which I preferred love to wedlock, freedom to a bond. I call God to witness, if *Augustus,* ruling over the whole world, were to deem me worthy of the honour of mar-riage, and to confirm the whole world to me, to be ruled by me for ever, dearer to me and of greater dignity would it seem to be called thy strumpet than his empress. . . .

For who among kings or philosophers could equal thee in fame? What kingdom or city or village did not burn to see thee? Who, I ask, did not hasten to gaze upon thee when thou appearedst in public, nor on thy departure with straining neck and fixed eye follow thee? What wife, what maiden did not yearn for thee in thine absence, nor burn in thy presence? What queen or powerful lady did not envy me my joys and my bed? There were two things, I confess, in thee especially, wherewith thou couldst at once captivate the heart of any woman; namely the arts of making songs and of singing them. Which we know that other philosophers have seldom followed. . . . And as the greater part of thy songs descanted of our love, they spread my fame in a short time through many lands, and inflamed the jealousy of many women

*Heloise was head of a community of nuns at this time.

against me. For what excellence of mind or body did not adorn thy youth? What woman who envied me then does not my calamity now compel to pity one deprived of such delights? What man or woman, albeit an enemy at first, is not now softened by the compassion due to me?

Give thy attention, I beseech thee, to what I demand; and thou wilt see this to be a small matter and most easy for thee. While I am cheated of thy presence, at least by written words, whereof thou hast an abundance, present to me the sweetness of thine image. . . . While with thee I enjoyed carnal pleasures, many were uncertain whether I did so from love or from desire. But now the end shews in what spirit I began. I have forbidden myself all pleasures that I might obey thy will. I have reserved nothing for myself, save this, to be now entirely thine. Consider therefore how great is thine injustice, if to me who deserve more thou payest less, nay nothing at all, especially when it is a small thing is demanded of thee, and right easy for thee to perform.

And so in His Name to whom thou hast offered thyself, before God I beseech thee that in whatsoever way thou canst thou restore to me thy presence, to wit by writing me some word of comfort. To this end alone that, thus refreshed, I may give myself with more alacrity to the service of God. When in time past thou soughtest me out for temporal pleasures, thou visitedst me with endless letters, and by frequent songs didst set thy *Heloise* on the lips of all men. With me every public place, each house resounded. How more rightly shouldst thou excite me now towards God, whom thou excitedst then to desire. Consider, I beseech thee, what thou owest me, pay heed to what I demand; and my long letter with a brief ending I conclude. Farewell, my all.

Abelard made a major contribution to medieval philosophical methodology by his use of the "dialectical method" of juxtaposing apparently conflicting authorities. He discussed this technique in the prologue to his Sic et Non (Yes and No).

Among the multitudinous words of the holy Fathers some sayings seem not only to differ from one another but even to contradict one another. Hence it is not presumptuous to judge concerning those by whom the world itself will be judged, as it is written, "They shall judge nations" (Wisdom 3:8) and, again, "You shall sit and judge" (Luke 22:30). We do not presume to rebuke as untruthful or to denounce as erroneous those to whom the Lord said, "He who hears you hears me; he who despises you despises me" (Luke 10:16). Bearing in mind our

From Peter Abelard, "Sic et Non," translated by Brian Tierney, in Brian Tierney, Donald Kagan, and L. Pearce Williams, eds., *Great Issues in Western Civilization* (2nd ed.; New York: Random House, 1972), Vol. I, pp. 412–414; reprinted by permission of the publisher. *Life and Works of Saint Bernard,* S. J. Eales, trans. (London: John Hodges, 1889), Vol. II, pp. 574–575. Peter Abelard in H. O. Taylor, ed., *The Mediaeval Mind* (4th ed.; Cambridge, Mass.: Harvard University Press, 1962), Vol. II, pp. 52–53; reprinted by permission of the publisher.

foolishness we believe that our understanding is defective rather than the writing of those to whom the Truth Himself said, "It is not you who speak but the spirit of your Father who speaks in you" (Matthew 10:20). Why should it seem surprising if we, lacking the guidance of the Holy Spirit through whom those things were written and spoken, the Spirit impressing them on the writers, fail to understand them? Our achievement of full understanding is impeded especially by unusual modes of expression and by the different significances that can be attached to one and the same word, as a word is used now in one sense, now in another. Just as there are many meanings so there are many words. Tully says that sameness is the mother of satiety in all things, that is to say it gives rise to fastidious distaste, and so it is appropriate to use a variety of words in discussing the same thing and not to express everything in common and vulgar words. . . .

We must also take special care that we are not deceived by corruptions of the text or by false attributions when sayings of the Fathers are quoted that seem to differ from the truth or to be contrary to it; for many apocryphal writings are set down under names of saints to enhance their authority, and even the texts of divine Scripture are corrupted by the errors of scribes. That most faithful writer and true interpreter, Jerome, accordingly warned us, "Beware of apocryphal writings. . . ." Again, on the title of Psalm 77 which is "An Instruction of Asaph," he commented, "It is written according to Matthew that when the Lord had spoken in parables and they did not understand, he said, 'These things are done that it might be fulfilled which was written by the prophet Isaias, *I will open my mouth in parables.*' The Gospels still have it so. Yet it is not Isaias who says this but Asaph." Again, let us explain simply why in Matthew and John it is written that the Lord was crucified at the third hour but in Mark at the sixth hour. There was a scribal error, and in Mark too the sixth hour was mentioned, but many read the Greek *epismo* as *gamma.* So too there was a scribal error where "Isaias" was set down for "Asaph." We know that many churches were gathered together from among ignorant gentiles. When they read in the Gospel, "That it might fulfilled which was written by the prophet Asaph," the one who first wrote down the Gospel began to say, "Who is this prophet Asaph?" for he was not known among the people. And what did he do? In seeking to amend an error he made an error. We would say the same of another text in Matthew. "He took," it says, "the thirty pieces of silver, the price of him that was prized, as was written by the prophet Jeremias." But we do not find this in Jeremias at all. Rather it is in Zacharias. You see then that here, as before, there was an error. If in the Gospels themselves some things are corrupted by the ignorance of scribes, we should not be surprised that the same thing has sometimes happened in the writings of later Fathers who are of much less authority. . . .

It is no less important in my opinion to ascertain whether texts quoted from the Fathers may be ones that they themselves have retracted and corrected after they came to a better understanding of the truth as the blessed Augustine did on many occasions; or whether they are giving the opinion of another rather than their own opinion . . . or whether, in inquiring into certain matters, they left them open to question rather than settled them with a definitive solution. . . .

In order that the way be not blocked and posterity deprived of the healthy labor of treating and debating difficult questions of language and style, a distinction must be drawn between the work of later authors and the supreme canonical authority of the Old and New Testaments. If, in Scripture, anything seems absurd you are not permitted to say, "The author of this book did not hold the truth"—but rather that the codex is defective or that the interpreter erred or that you do not understand. But if anything seems contrary to truth in the works of later authors, which are contained in innumerable books, the reader or auditor is free to judge, so that he may approve what is pleasing and reject what gives offense, unless the matter is established by certain reason or by canonical authority (of the Scriptures). . . .

In view of these considerations we have undertaken to collect various sayings of the Fathers that give rise to questioning because of their apparent contradictions as they occur to our memory. This questioning excites young readers to the maximum of effort in inquiring into the truth, and such inquiry sharpens their minds. Assiduous and frequent questioning is indeed the first key to wisdom. Aristotle, that most perspicacious of all philosophers, exhorted the studious to practice it eagerly, saying, "Perhaps it is difficult to express oneself with confidence on such matters if they have not been much discussed. To entertain doubts on particular points will not be unprofitable." For by doubting we come to inquiry; through inquiring we perceive the truth, according to the Truth Himself. "Seek and you shall find," He says, "Knock and it shall be opened to you." In order to teach us by His example He chose to be found when He was about twelve years old sitting in the midst of the doctors and questioning them, presenting the appearance of a disciple by questioning rather than of a master by teaching, although there was in Him the complete and perfect wisdom of God. Where we have quoted texts of Scripture, the greater the authority attributed to Scripture, the more they should stimulate the reader and attract him to the search for truth. Hence I have prefixed to this my book, compiled in one volume from the sayings of the saints, the decree of Pope Gelasius concerning authentic books, from which it may be known that I have cited nothing from apocryphal books. I have also added excerpts from the Retractations of St. Augustine, from which it will be clear that nothing is included which he later retracted and corrected.

[Abelard then presented 156 questions dealing with such topics as these: "That God is one—and the contrary." "That the Son is without beginning

—and the contrary." "That God can do all things—and the contrary." "That God knows all things—and the contrary." "That our first parents were created mortal—and the contrary." "That Adam was saved—and the contrary." "That Peter and Paul and all the apostles were equal—and the contrary." "That Christ alone is the foundation of the church—and the contrary." "That Peter did not deny Christ—and the contrary." "That without baptism of water no one can be saved—and the contrary." "That all are permitted to marry—and the contrary." "That saintly works do not justify man—and the contrary." "That it is permitted to kill men—and the contrary."]

Abelard's approach to sacred learning was bitterly condemned by his contemporary, the highly influential Bernard of Clairvaux, in the following letter.

It is no wonder if a man who is careless of what he says should, when rushing into the mysteries of the Faith, so irreverently assail and tear asunder the hidden treasures of godliness, since he has neither piety nor faith in his notions about the piety of faith. For instance, on the very threshold of this theology (I should rather say his stultology) he defines faith as private judgment; as though in these mysteries it is to be allowed to each person to think and speak as he pleases, or as though the mysteries of our faith are to hang in uncertainty amongst shifting and varying opinions, when on the contrary they rest on the solid and unshakable foundations of truth. Is not our hope baseless if our faith is subject to change? Fools then were our martyrs for bearing so cruel tortures for an uncertainty, and for entering, without hesitation, on an everlasting exile, through a bitter death, when there was a doubt as to the recompense of their reward. But far be it from us to think that in our faith or hope anything, as he supposes, depends on the fluctuating judgment of the individual, and that the whole of it does not rest on sure and solid truth, having been commended by miracles and revelations from above, founded and consecrated by the Son of the Virgin, by the Blood of the Redeemer, by the glory of the risen Christ. These infallible proofs have been given us in superabundance. But if not, the Spirit itself, lastly, bears witness with our spirit that we are the sons of God. How, then, can any one dare to call faith opinion, unless it be that he has not yet received that Spirit, or unless he either knows not the Gospel or thinks it to be a fable? *I know in whom I have believed, and I am confident* (2 Tim. i. 12), cries the Apostle, and you mutter in my ears that faith is only an opinion. Do you prate to me that that is ambiguous than which there is nothing more certain? But Augustine says otherwise: "Faith is not held by any one in whose heart it is, by conjectures or opinions, but it is sure knowledge and has the assent of the conscience." Far be it from us, then, to suppose that the Christian faith has as its boundaries those opinions of the Academicians, whose boast it is that they doubt of everything, and know nothing. But I for my part walk securely, according to the saying of the teacher of the Gentiles, and I know that I shall not be confounded. I am satisfied, I confess, with his definition of faith, even though this man stealthily accuses it. *Faith,* he says, *is the substance of things hoped for, the evidence of things not seen* (Heb. xi. 1). The substance, he says, of things hoped for, not a phantasy of empty conjectures. You hear, that it is a substance; and therefore it is not allowed you in our faith, to suppose or oppose at your pleasure, nor to wander hither and thither amongst empty opinions, through devious errors. Under the name of substance something certain and fixed is put before you. You are enclosed in known bounds, shut in within fixed limits. For faith is not an opinion, but a certitude.

In spite of all his troubles some great prelates of the twelfth century contin-ued to admire and support Abelard. Peter the Venerable, abbot of Cluny, wrote this letter to Heloise in 1142, telling her of Abelard's death at a Cluniac priory.

. . . It was granted us to enjoy the presence of him—who was yours—Master Peter Abaelard, a man always to be spoken of with honour as a true servant of Christ and a philosopher. The divine dispensation placed him in Cluny for his last years, and through him enriched our monastery with treasure richer than gold. No brief writing could do justice to his holy, humble, and devoted life among us. I have not seen his equal in humility of garb and manner. When in the crowd of our brethren I forced him to take a first place, in meanness of clothing he appeared as the last of all. Often I marvelled, as the monks walked past me, to see a man so great and famous thus depise and abase him-self. He was abstemious in food and drink, refusing and condemning everything beyond the bare necessities. He was assiduous in study, fre-quent in prayer, always silent unless compelled to answer the question of some brother or expound sacred themes before us. He partook of the sacrament as often as possible. Truly his mind, his tongue, his act, taught and exemplified religion, fearing God, turning from evil, con-secrating to God the latter days of his life. At last, because of his bod-ily infirmities, I sent him to a quiet and salubrious retreat on the banks of the Saone. There he bent over his books, as long as his strength lasted, always praying, reading, writing, or dictating. In these sacred exercises, not sleeping but watching, he was found by the heavenly Visitor; who summoned him to the eternal wedding feast not as a foolish but as a wise virgin, bearing his lamp filled with oil—the consciousness of a holy life. When he came to pay humanity's last debt, his illness was brief. With holy devotion he made confession of the Catholic Faith, then of his sins. The brothers who were with him can testify how devoutly he received the viaticum of that last journey, and with what fervent faith he commended his body and soul to his

Redeemer. Thus this master, Peter, completed his days. He who was known throughout the world by the fame of his teaching, entered the school of Him who said, "Learn of me, for I am meek and lowly of heart"; and continuing meek and lowly he passed to Him, as we may believe.

Venerable and dearest sister in the Lord, the man who was once joined to thee in the flesh, and then by the stronger chain of divine love, him in thy stead, or as another thee, the Lord holds in His bosom; and at the day of His coming, His grace will restore him to thee.

44.   Bernard of Clairvaux: The Love of God

St. Bernard of Clairvaux (1090–1153), the dominant figure in the new Cistercian Order of monks, opposed an intuitive mysticism to Abelard's rationalism. In one of his most characteristic works, called On the Love of God, *he used the love imagery of the* Song of Solomon *to describe the love between Christ and the church.*

You would hear from me, then, why and how God is to be loved? I answer: The cause of loving God is God; the manner is to love without measure. Is this enough? Yes, perhaps, for the wise. But I am debtor to the unwise as well; where enough is said for the wise, we must comply with the others also. Therefore I will not refuse to repeat it, more fully rather than more deeply, for the sake of the slower in apprehension. I may say that God is to be loved for His own sake for a double reason: because nothing can be loved more justly, nothing more fruitfully. The question, why God is to be loved, bears a double meaning. For it can be asked what is especially asked; whether for what desert of His, or for what advantage of ours, God is to be loved. But I will give the same answer to either: assuredly I find no other worthy cause of loving Him, save Himself. And first with respect to desert. Verily He has deserved much of us, who gave Himself to us for no deserts of ours. For what better than Himself could even He have given? Therefore, if the desert of God is sought, when the cause of loving Him is sought, it is this above all: that *He hath first loved us.* Worthy, indeed, is He to be loved in return, especially if we consider who loved, whom He loved, and how much. For who? Is it not He to whom every spirit confesses: *Thou art my God, for thou has no need of my goods?* It is the true charity of this Majesty who seeketh not His own. But to whom is love so unalloyed shown? *When we were yet enemies,* it is said, *we were recon-*

From Saint Bernard, *On the Love of God,* E. G. Gardner, trans. (London: J. M. Dent, 1916), pp. 27, 29, 39, 41, 43, 45, 47, 69, 71; reprinted by permission of the publisher.

ciled to God. God loved then, both freely, and His enemies. But how much? As much as John says: *God so loved the world, that he gave his only begotten Son;* and Paul says: *He spared not his own Son, but delivered him up for us all.* That very Son, too, of Himself saith: *Greater love hath no man than this, that a man lay down his life for his friends. . . .*

. . . Those also who know not Christ are sufficiently taught by natural law, from the goods they perceived of body and soul, how they, too, are bound to love God for the sake of God. For, to repeat in brief what has been said on this point, what infidel does not know that those necessary things, whereby he lives, whereby he sees, whereby he breathes, are ministered to his body in this mortal life by no other than by Him *who giveth food to all flesh,* who *maketh his sun to rise on the evil and on the good, and sendeth rain on the just and on the unjust?* What wicked man can think any other the author of the human dignity which shines in the soul, save He Himself who saith in Genesis: *Let us make man in our image, after our likeness?* Who can deem any other the bestower of knowledge, save likewise *he that teacheth man knowledge?* Who, again, can think that the gift of virtue has been given him, or hope for it to be given, from any source save from the hand likewise of the *Lord of virtues?* Therefore God deserves to be loved for His own sake, even by the infidel, who, albeit he knows not Christ, yet knows himself. Hence even every infidel is without excuse, if he love not the Lord his God with all his heart, and with all his soul, and with all his might. Surely that innate justice, which reason knows, cries to him from within, that he is bound with his whole self to love Him from whom he is not ignorant that he owes all that he is. But it is difficult, nay impossible, for anyone, with his own powers of free will, to render wholly to the will of God what he has once received from God, and not rather to twist them back to his own will and keep for himself as though his own; as it is written: *All seek their own;* and again: *The imagination and thought of man's heart are prone to evil.*

On the other hand, the faithful surely know how utterly they need Jesus and Him crucified; whilst, wondering at and embracing the love in Him *which passeth knowledge,* they are confounded that they repay not even that little which they are in return for so great love and condescension. Readily therefore do they love more, who understand themselves more loved; but he to whom less has been given, loveth less. The Jew, forsooth, or the Pagan, is in no wise stirred by such prickings of love as the Church feels, who says: *I am wounded with charity;* and again: *Stay me with flowers, comfort me with apples; for I am sick of love.* She beholds king Solomon *with the crown wherewith his mother crowned him;* she beholds the Only Begotten of the Father, bearing His cross; she beholds the Lord of Majesty buffeted and spat upon; she beholds the Author of life and of glory fastened by nails, pierced by the lance, overwhelmed with reproaches, and at last laying down that dear life of His for His friends. She beholds these things, and the more the sword of love pierces her own soul, and she says: *Stay me with flowers, comfort me with apples; for I am sick of love.* These indeed are the pomegranates, which the bride, brought into the garden of her Beloved, gathers from the tree of life, which have borrowed their taste from the heavenly bread, their colour from the blood of Christ. Then she sees death dead, and the author of death led in triumph. She sees captivity led captive from hell to earth, from earth to heaven, *that at the name of Jesus every knee should bow, of things in heaven, and things in earth, and things under the earth.* She perceives the earth, which had brought forth thorns and thistles under the ancient curse, renewed and flowering again at the grace of a new blessing. And, in all this, she remembers the verse: *And my flesh hath flourished again, and with my will I give praise to him;* she desires to wax strong on the apples of the Passion, which she has plucked from the tree of the Cross, and on the flowers of the Resurrection, whose fragrance especially invites the Bridegroom to visit her more often.

At last she says: *Behold, thou art fair, my beloved, and comely; our bed is flowering.* In showing the bed, she manifests clearly what she desires: and, when she calls it flowering, she clearly indicates whence she expects to obtain what she desires: for it is not from her own merits, but from the flowers of the field which God hath blessed. Christ, who willed to be conceived and nurtured in Nazareth, delights in these flowers. The heavenly Bridegroom rejoices in such fragrance, and often and freely enters the bridal-bed of the heart, which He has found filled with such fruits and strewn with flowers. For where He beholds a soul absorbed in contemplating the grace of His passion or the glory of His resurrection, there straightway He is present, constantly and gladly. The memorials of the Passion are as the fruits of last year, or rather of all times past under the rule of death, and sin, at length appearing in the fulness of time. But the signs of the Resurrection are the new flowers of the season following, in the new summer of its flowering again under grace, the fruit of which the future general resurrection will bring forth to abide without end. *Now,* He saith, *the winter is past, the rain is over and gone, the flowers have appeared on the earth;* meaning that the time of summer is come with Him who was loosed from the cold of death into a spring mildness of new life. *Behold,* He saith, *I make all things new;* whose flesh was sown in death, and flowered again in the Resurrection, at the fragrance whereof straightway in the field of our valley the dry becomes green, the cold grows warm, the dead return to life.

• • •

Here first see in what measure, nay how without measure, God has deserved to be loved by us; He who (to repeat in a few words what has been said) first loved us, so much and freely, He so great, we so small and unworthy. Lo, I remember what I said in the beginning, that the manner of loving God is to love without measure. And since the object of the love of God is immeasurable and infinite (for God is infinite and immeasurable), what, I ask, should be the limit or measure of our love? Our very love is not rendered as a free gift, but repaid as a debt. Immeasurableness loves, eternity loves, *charity which passeth knowledge* loves; God loves, whose greatness is unsearchable, whose wisdom is infinite, whose peace passeth all understanding; and do we pay back again with measure? *I will love thee, O Lord, my strength, my rock, my refuge, and my deliverer;* and my sum of all that is desirable and worthy of love. My God, my helper, I love thee according to Thy gift, and in my measure, less indeed than just, but surely not less than my power; I, who cannot as much as I ought, and yet cannot beyond what I can. I shall, indeed, be able to love more, when Thou shalt deign to give more; though never in proportion to Thy worth. *Thine eyes did see my imperfect being;* but, nevertheless, *in thy book all shall be written,* they who do what they can, albeit they cannot what they should. It is clear enough, methinks, both in what measure God is to be loved, and by what desert of His own. By what desert of His, I say; for the greatness of it, who may fully see? Who may tell? Who may know?

chapter
XIV

Towns and Trade

---

45. The Communal Revolt at Laon

A major feature of economic life in the twelfth century was a great growth of urban communities. The townsmen often sought to liberate themselves from a local lord by forming a "commune" to exact privileges from him. The violence attending the formation of a commune at Laon in 1116 was described by a contemporary abbot, Guibert of Nogent.

. . . Now Commune is a new and bad name of an arrangement for the poorest classes to pay their usual due of servitude to their lords once only in the year, and to make good any breach of the laws they have committed by the payment fixed by law, and to be entirely free from all other exactions usually imposed on serfs. . . . [The Bishop of Laon at first granted such a commune to the townsfolk in return for a large payment but then revoked his grant.]

The compact of the Commune being broken, such rage, such amazement seized the citizens that all the officials abandoned their duties and the stalls of the craftsmen and cobblers were closed and nothing was exposed for sale by the innkeepers and hucksters, who expected to have nothing left when the lords began plundering. For at once the property of all was calculated by the Bishop and nobles, and whatever any man was known to have given to arrange the Commune, so much was demanded of him to procure its annulment. These events took place on the day of the Passover, which is called the preparation, and

From *The Autobiography of Guibert, Abbot of Nogent-sous-Coucy*, C. C. Swinton Bland, trans. (New York: E. P. Dutton, 1925), pp. 153–154, 159–164; reprinted by permission of Routledge & Kegan Paul Ltd.

on the holy Sabbath when their minds were being prepared to receive the body and blood of the Lord, they were made ready for murders only here, for perjury there. Why say more? All the efforts of the prelate and nobles in these days were reserved for fleecing their inferiors. But those inferiors were no longer moved by mere anger, but goaded into a murderous lust for the death of the Bishop and his accomplices and bound themselves by oath to effect their purpose. Now they say that four hundred took the oath. Such a mob could not be secret and when it came to the ears of Anselm towards evening of the holy Sabbath, he sent word to the Bishop, as he was retiring to rest, not to go out to the early morning service, knowing that if he did he must certainly be killed. But he, infatuated with excessive pride said, "Fie, surely I shall not perish at the hands of such." Yet notwithstanding his scornful words, he did not dare to rise for matins or to enter the church. The next day, as he followed the clergy in procession, he ordered his household people and all the soldiers coming behind him to carry short swords under their garments. . . . On the fourth day I went to him, because I had been plundered of my supply of corn and of some legs of pork, called bacon, through his disorders. When interviewed by me and requested to relieve the city of these great disturbances, he replied, "What do ye think they can do by their riots? If John, my moor, were to take by the nose the most powerful man amongst them, he would not dare so much as to grunt. For just now I have compelled them to renounce what they call their Commune for so long as I live." I spoke, and then seeing the man overcome with pride, I refrained from saying more. Yet before I left the city, by reason of his instability we quarrelled with mutual recriminations. But although he was warned by many of the imminent peril, he took no notice of any one.

The next day, that is, the fifth in Easter week, after midday, as he was engaged in business with Archdeacon Walter about the getting of money, behold there arose a disorderly noise throughout the city, men shouting "Commune!" and again through the middle of the chapel of the Blessed Mary through that door by which the murderers of Gerard had come and gone, there citizens now entered the Bishop's court with swords, battle-axes, bows and hatchets, and carrying clubs and spears, a very great company. As soon as this sudden attack was discovered, the nobles rallied from all sides to the Bishop, having sworn to give him aid against such an onset, if it should occur. In this rally Guinimon, the chatelain, an aged nobleman of handsome presence and guiltless character, armed only with shield and spear, ran out through the church and as he entered the Bishop's hall, was the first to fall, struck on the back of the head with a battle-axe by a certain Rainbert, who was his fellow-citizen. Immediately afterwards Regnier, of whom I spoke before as married to my cousin, hurrying to enter the palace, was struck from behind with a spear when trying to enter by mounting on the pulpitum of the Bishop's chapel, and there falling headlong was at once consumed by the fire of the palace from his waist downwards. Ado, the Vidame, quarrelsome, but brave, separated from the rest and able to do little by himself among so many, as he was striving to reach the Bishop's palace, encountered the full force of the attack, but with spear and sword made such a stand that in a moment he struck down two of those who came on. Then mounting the dining-table in the hall, wounded now in the knees and other parts of the body and at last only supporting himself on his knees, whilst striking at his assailants all round him, he kept them off for a long time, until, becoming exhausted, he was struck through the body with a lance and after a little was reduced to ashes by the fire in that house.

Next the outrageous mob attacking the Bishop and howling before the walls of his palace, he with some who were succouring him fought them off by hurling of stones and shooting of arrows. For he now, as at times, shewed great spirit as a fighter; but because he had wrongly and in vain taken up another sword, by the sword he perished. Therefore being unable to stand against the reckless assaults of the people, he put on the clothes of one of his servants and flying to the vaults of the church hid himself in a cask, shut up in which with the head fastened on by a faithful follower he thought himself safely hidden. And as they ran hither and thither demanding where, not the Bishop, but the hangdog, was, they seized one of his pages, but through his faithfulness could not get what they wanted. Laying hands on another, they learned from the traitor's nod where to look for him. Entering the vaults therefore, and searching everywhere, at last they found him in the following manner.

There was a pestilent fellow, a bondman of the church of the Blessed Vincent, but for a long time an official and overseer of Enguerrand of Coucy, who being set over the collection of tolls paid for crossing the bridge called Soord, sometimes watched until there were only a few travellers passing, and having robbed them of all their property, in order that they might make no complaint against him, threw them into the river with a weight round their necks. How often he had done this, God only knows. The number of the thefts and robberies being more than any one could count, the unchecked wickedness of his heart, and one as might say, was displayed also in the truculence of his looks. This man having incurred the displeasure of Enguerrand, went over wholly to the party of the Commune in Laon. He who had spared neither monk nor clerk nor stranger, in fact no sex, was last of all to be the slayer of a bishop. He the leader and instigator of this attack searched most diligently for the Bishop, whom he hated more bitterly than the rest.

And so, as they sought for him in every vessel, this fellow halted in front of that cask, where the man was hiding, and having broken in the head, asked again and again who was there. And he, hardly able to move his frozen lips under his blows, said "A prisoner." Now the

Bishop was wont in mockery to call him Isengrin, I suppose, because of his wolfish look, for so some people call wolves. The wretch, therefore, says to the Bishop, "Is this my Lord Isengrin stored away?" Renulf therefore, sinner though he was, yet the Lord's anointed, was dragged forth from the cask by the hair, beaten with many blows and brought out into the open air in the narrow lane of the clergy's cloister before the house of the chaplain Godfrey. And as he piteously implored them, ready to take oath that he would henceforth cease to be their Bishop, that he would leave the country, and as they with hardened hearts jeered at him, one named Bernard and surnamed de Brueys, lifting his battle-axe brutally dashed out the brains of that sacred, though sinner's, head, and he slipping between the hands of those who held him, was dead before he reached the ground stricken by another thwart blow under the eye-sockets and across the middle of the nose. There brought to his end, his legs were cut off and many another wound inflicted. But Thibaut seeing the ring on the finger of the erstwhile prelate and not being able to draw it off, cut off the dead man's finger and took it. And so stripped to his skin he was thrown into a corner in front of his chaplain's house. My God, who shall recount the mocking words that were thrown at him by passers-by, as he lay there, and with what clods and stones and dirt his corpse was covered?

46.   *Urban Privileges in France, England, and Italy*

Many twelfth-century towns obtained charters of privileges not by violence, but by peaceful negotiations with their lords. The charter of Lorris, granted by King Louis VII in 1155, was widely imitated in northern France.

1. Every one who has a house in the parish of Lorris shall pay as *cens* sixpence only for his house, and for each acre of land that he possesses in the parish.

2. No inhabitant of the parish of Lorris shall be required to pay a toll or any other tax on his provisions; and let him not be made to pay measurage fee on the grain which he has raised by his own labor.

From "The Charter of Lorris" in F. A. Ogg, ed., *A Source Book for Mediaeval History* (New York: American Book Company, 1907), pp. 328–330; used by permission of American Book Company. *Sources of English Constitutional History,* translated by C. Stephenson and F. G. Marcham: "John: Charter to Ipswich" (New York: Harper and Brothers, 1937), pp. 96–97; Copyright 1937, 1965 by Harper and Row Publishers, Incorporated; reprinted by permission of the publishers. Otto of Freising and his continuator, Rahewin, *The Deeds of Frederick Barbarossa,* C. C. Mierow, trans. (New York: Columbia University Press, 1953), pp. 127–128; Copyright 1953 Columbia University Press.

3. No burgher shall go on an expedition, on foot or on horseback, from which he cannot return the same day to his home if he desires.

4. No burgher shall pay toll on the road to Étampes, to Orleans, to Milly (which is in the Gâtinais), or to Melun.

5. No one who has property in the parish of Lorris shall forfeit it for any offense whatsoever, unless the offense shall have been committed against us or any of our *hôtes*.

6. No person while on his way to the fairs and markets of Lorris, or returning, shall be arrested or disturbed, unless he shall have committed an offense on the same day.

9. No one, neither we nor any other, shall exact from the burghers of Lorris any tallage, tax, or subsidy.

12. If a man shall have had a quarrel with another, but without breaking into a fortified house, and if the parties shall have reached an agreement without bringing a suit before the provost, no fine shall be due to us or our provost on account of the affair.

15. No inhabitant of Lorris is to render us the obligation of *corvée*, except twice a year, when our wine is to be carried to Orleans, and not elsewhere.

16. No one shall be detained in prison if he can furnish surety that he will present himself for judgment.

17. Any burgher who wishes to sell his property shall have the privilege of doing so; and, having received the price of the sale, he shall have the right to go from the town freely and without molestation, if he so desires, unless he has committed some offense in it.

18. Any one who shall dwell a year and a day in the parish of Lorris, without any claim having pursued him there, and without having refused to lay his case before us or our provost, shall abide there freely and without molestation.

35. We ordain that every time there shall be a change of provosts in the town the new provost shall take an oath faithfully to observe these regulations; and the same thing shall be done by new sergeants every time that they are installed.

Greater rights of self-government were included in the charter of Ipswich, granted by King John in 1200.

John, by the grace of God king, etc. Know that we have granted and by our present charter have confirmed to our burgesses of Ipswich our borough of Ipswich, with all its appurtenances and with all its liberties and free customs, to be held of us and our heirs by them and their heirs in hereditary right, paying to our exchequer every year at Michaelmas term, by the hand of the reeve of Ipswich, the just and accustomed farm and, at the same time, the increment of 100s. sterling by tale that they used to pay. We have also granted that all burgesses of Ipswich are to be quit of toll, stallage, lastage, pontage, and all other customs throughout all our land and throughout the ports of the sea. We have granted to them that, with the exception of our officials, none of them shall be impleaded in any plea outside the borough of Ipswich, save only in pleas concerning foreign tenures; and that they shall have their gild merchant and their hanse; that no one shall be lodged or shall take anything by force within the borough of Ipswich; that they shall justly have their lands and their pledges and all their debts, by whomsoever owed; that, with regard to their lands and tenures inside the borough, justice shall be assured them according to the custom of the borough of Ipswich and of our free boroughs; that, with regard to their debts established at Ipswich and their pledges made in tne same place, the pleas shall be held at Ipswich; and that none of them shall be adjudged in mercy with respect to his chattels except according to the law of our free boroughs. We also forbid any one in all our land, on pain of £10 forfeiture to us, to exact toll, stallage, or any other custom from the men of Ipswich. Wherefore we will and straitly command that the aforesaid burgesses shall have and hold the aforesaid liberties and free customs well and in peace, as they have been and are best and most freely enjoyed by the other burgesses of our free boroughs in England, saving in all things to our citizens of London their liberties and free customs.

Furthermore, we will and grant that our said burgesses, by the common counsel of their town, shall elect two of the more lawful and discreet men of their town and present them to our chief justice at our exchequer; which men shall well and faithfully keep the reeveship *(preposituram)* of our aforesaid borough of Ipswich. And so long as they well conduct themselves in that office, they shall not be removed except by the common counsel of the aforesaid burgesses. We also will that in the same borough, by the common council of the aforesaid burgesses, four of the more lawful and discreet men of the borough shall be elected to keep the pleas of the crown and other matters that pertain to us and to our crown in the same borough, and to see that the reeves of that borough justly treat both rich and poor.

These are the witnesses. . . . May 25, in the second year of our reign.

In general it was only in Italy that the towns grew into completely autonomous city-states. The unusual degree of political independence enjoyed by the northern Italian communes in the twelfth century was noted in 1154 by the chronicler Bishop Otto of Freising.

But [the Lombards] having put aside crude, barbarous ferocity, perhaps from the fact that when united in marriage with the natives they begat sons who inherited something of the Roman gentleness and keenness from their mother's blood, and from the very quality of the country and climate, retain the refinement of the Latin speech and their elegance of manners. In the governing of their cities, also, and in the conduct of public affairs, they still imitate the wisdom of the ancient Romans. Finally, they are so desirous of liberty that, avoiding the insolence of power, they are governed by the will of consuls rather than rulers. There are known to be three orders among them: captains, vavasors, and commoners. And in order to suppress arrogance, the aforesaid consuls are chosen not from one but from each of the classes. And lest they should exceed bounds by lust for power, they are changed almost every year. The consequence is that, as practically that entire land is divided among the cities, each of them requires its bishops to live in the cities, and scarcely any noble or great man can be found in all the surrounding territory who does not acknowledge the authority of his city. And from this power to force all elements together they are wont to call the several lands of each [noble, or magnate] their contado *(comitatus)*. Also, that they may not lack the means of subduing their neighbors, they do not disdain to give the girdle of knighthood or the grades of distinction to young men of inferior station and even some workers of the vile mechanical arts, whom other peoples bar like the pest from the more respected and honorable pursuits. From this it has resulted that they far surpass all other states of the world in riches and in power. They are aided in this not only, as has been said, by their characteristic industry, but also by the absence of their princes, who are accustomed to remain on the far side of the Alps. In this, however, forgetful of their ancient nobility, they retain traces of their barbaric imperfection, because while boasting that they live in accordance with law, they are not obedient to the laws. For they scarcely if ever respect the prince to whom they should display the voluntary deference of obedience or willingly perform that which they have sworn by the integrity of their laws, unless they sense his authority in the power of his great army. Therefore it often happens that although a citizen must be humbled by the laws and an adversary subdued by arms in accordance with the laws, yet they very frequently receive in hostile fashion him whom they ought to accept as their own gentle prince, when he demands what is rightfully his own. From this arises a twofold loss to the common weal: the prince is obliged to assemble an army for the subjugation of his people, and the people (not without great loss of their own possessions) are forced to obey their prince. Accordingly, by the same process of reasoning whereby impetuosity accuses the people for this situation, so should necessity excuse the prince in the sight of God and men.

47.　*Guild Organization*

The rules of the guild merchant at Southampton provide a typical example

From E. P. Cheyney, trans., *University of Pennsylvania Translations and Reprints* (Philadelphia: University of Pennsylvania, 1897), Vol. II, No. 1, pp. 12-17.

of early guild organization. They refer to both the charitable and the economic activities of the guild.

In the first place, there shall be elected from the gild merchant, and established, an alderman, a steward, a chaplain, four skevins, and an usher. And it is to be known that whosoever shall be alderman shall receive from each one entering into the gild fourpence; the steward, twopence; the chaplain, twopence; and the usher, one penny. And the gild shall meet twice a year: that is to say, on the Sunday next after St. John the Baptist's day, and on the Sunday next after St. Mary's day.

And when the gild shall be sitting no one of the gild is to bring in any stranger, except when required by the alderman or steward. And the alderman shall have a sergeant to serve before him, the steward another sergeant, and the chaplain shall have his clerk.

And when the gild shall sit, the alderman is to have, each night, so long as the gild sits, two gallons of wine and two candles, and the steward the same; and the four skevins and the chaplain, each of them one gallon of wine and one candle, and the usher one gallon of wine.

And when the gild shall sit, the lepers of La Madeleine shall have of the alms of the gild, two sesters (approximately eight gallons) of ale, and the sick of God's House and of St. Julian shall have two sesters of ale. And the Friars Minors shall have two sesters of ale and one sester of wine. And four sesters of ale shall be given to the poor wherever the gild shall meet.

And when the gild is sitting, no one who is of the gild shall go outside the town for any business, without the permission of the steward. And if any does so, let him be fined two shillings, and pay them.

And when the gild sits, and any gildsman is outside of the city so that he does not know when it will happen, he shall have a gallon of wine, if his servants come to get it. And if a gildsman is ill and is in the city, wine shall be sent to him, two loaves of bread and a gallon of wine and a dish from the kitchen; and two approved men of the gild shall go to visit him and look after his condition.

And when a gildsman dies, all those who are of the gild and are in the city shall attend the service of the dead, and the gildsmen shall bear the body and bring it to the place of burial. And whoever will not do this shall pay according to his oath, two pence, to be given to the poor. And those of the ward where the dead man shall be ought to find a man to watch over the body the night that the dead shall lie in his house. And so long as the service of the dead shall last, that is to say the vigil and the mass, there ought to burn four candles of the gild, each candle of two pounds weight or more, until the body is buried. And these four candles shall remain in the keeping of the steward of the gild.

And when a gildsman dies, his eldest son or his next heir shall have the seat of his father, or of his uncle, if his father was not a gildsman, and of no other one; and he shall give nothing for his seat. No husband can have a seat in the gild by right of his wife, nor demand a seat by right of his wife's ancestors.

And no one of the city of Southampton shall buy anything to sell again in the same city, unless he is of the gild merchant or of the franchise. And if anyone shall do so and is convicted of it, all which he has so bought shall be forfeited to the king; and no one shall be quit of custom unless he proves that he is in the gild or in the franchise, and this from year to year.

And no one shall buy honey, fat, salt herrings, or any kind of oil, or millstones, or fresh hides, or any kind of fresh skins, unless he is a gildsman: nor keep a tavern for wine, nor sell cloth at retail, except in market or fair days; nor keep grain in his granary beyond five quarters, to sell at retail, if he is not a gildsman; and whoever shall do this and be convicted, shall forfeit all to the king.

If any gildsman falls into poverty and has not the wherewithal to live, and is not able to work or to provide for himself, he shall have one mark from the gild to relieve his condition when the gild shall sit. No one of the gild nor of the franchise shall avow another's goods for his by which the custom of the city shall be injured. And if any one does so and is convicted, he shall lose the gild and the franchise; and the merchandise so avowed shall be forfeited to the king.

And no private man nor stranger shall bargain for or buy any kind of merchandise coming into the city before a burgess of the gild merchant, so long as the gildsman is present and wishes to bargain for and buy this merchandise; and if anyone does so and is convicted, that which he buys shall be forfeited to the king.

The common chest shall be in the house of the chief alderman or of the steward, and the three keys of it shall be lodged with three discreet men of the aforesaid twelve sworn men, or with three of the skevins, who shall loyally take care of the common seal, and the charters and of the treasure of the town, and the standards, and other muniments of the town; and no letter shall be sealed with the common seal, nor any charter taken out of the common-chest but in the presence of six or twelve sworn men, and of the alderman or steward; and nobody shall sell by any kind of measure or weight that is not sealed, under forfeiture of two shillings.

No one shall go out to meet a ship bringing wine or other merchandise coming to the town, in order to buy anything, before the ship be arrived and come to anchor for unlading; and if any one does so and is convicted, the merchandise which he shall have bought shall be forfeited to the king.

Some crafts were dominated by women. These rules of a women's guild were set down in mid-thirteenth-century Paris.

From Etienne Boileau, "Livre des Métiers," in J. D. O'Faolain and L. Martines, *Not in God's Image* (New York, Harper and Row, 1973), pp. 155-156.

Any woman who wishes to be a silk spinster on large spindles in the city of Paris—i.e., reeling, spinning, doubling and retwisting—may freely do so, provided she observe the following customs and usages of the craft:

No spinster on large spindles may have more than three apprentices, unless they be her own or her husband's children born in true wedlock; nor may she contract with them for an apprenticeship of less than seven years or for a fee of less than 20 Parisian sols to be paid to her, their mistress. The apprenticeship shall be for eight years if there is no fee, but she may accept more years and money if she can get them. . . .

No woman of the said craft may hire an apprentice or work-girl who has not completed her years of service with the mistress to whom she was apprenticed. If a spinster has assumed an apprentice, she may not take on another before the first has completed her seven years unless the apprentice die or forswear the craft forever. If an apprentice spinster buy her freedom before serving the said seven years, she may not herself take on an apprentice until she has practiced the craft for seven years. If any spinster sell her apprentice, she shall owe six deniers to the guardians appointed in the King's name to guard the [standards of the] craft. The buyer shall also owe six deniers. . . .

If a working woman comes from outside Paris and wishes to practice the said craft in the city, she must swear before two guardians of the craft that she will practice it well and loyally and conform to its customs and usages.

If anyone give a woman of the said craft silk to be spun and the woman pawn it and the owner complain, the fine shall be 5 sols.

No workwoman shall farm out another's silk to be worked upon outside her own house.

The said craft has as guardians two men of integrity sworn in the King's name but appointed and changed at the will of the provost of Paris. Taking an oath in the provost's presence, they shall swear to guard the craft truly, loyally, and to their utmost, and to inform him or his agents of all malpractices discovered therein.

48.   A Medieval Merchant's Life

The career of Godric, the merchant described below, was like those of many twelfth-century traders. The unusual thing about Godric was that he ended his life as a saint and so attracted a biographer who left us an unusually detailed account of his life.

From Reginald of Durham, "Life of St. Godric," in G. G. Coulton, ed., *Social Life in Britain from the Conquest to the Reformation* (Cambridge: Cambridge University Press, 1918), pp. 415–420; reprinted by permission of the publisher.

This holy man's father was named Ailward, and his mother Edwenna; both of slender rank and wealth, but abundant in righteousness and virtue. They were born in Norfolk, and had long lived in the township called Walpole. . . . When the boy had passed his childish years quietly at home; then, as he began to grow to manhood, he began to follow more prudent ways of life, and to learn carefully and persistently the teachings of worldly forethought. Wherefore he chose not to follow the life of a husbandman, but rather to study, learn and exercise the rudiment of more subtle conceptions. For this reason, aspiring to the merchant's trade, he began to follow the chapman's way of life, first learning how to gain in small bargains and things of insignificant price; and thence, while yet a youth, his mind advanced little by little to buy and sell and gain from things of greater expense. For, in his beginnings, he was wont to wander with small wares around the villages and farmsteads of his own neighborhood; but, in process of time, he gradually associated himself by compact with city merchants. Hence, within a brief space of time, the youth who had trudged for many weary hours from village to village, from farm to farm, did so profit by his increase of age and wisdom as to travel with associates of his own age through towns and boroughs, fortresses and cities, to fairs and to all the various booths of the market-place, in pursuit of his public chaffer. He went along the high-way, neither puffed up by the good testimony of his conscience nor downcast in the nobler part of his soul by the reproach of poverty. . . .

Yet in all things he walked with simplicity; and, in so far as he yet knew how, it was ever his pleasure to follow in the footsteps of the truth. For, having learned the Lord's Prayer and the Creed from his very cradle, he oftentimes turned them over in his mind, even as he went alone on his longer journeys; and, in so far as the truth was revealed to his mind, he clung thereunto most devoutly in all his thoughts concerning God. At first, he lived as a chapman for four years in Lincolnshire, going on foot and carrying the smallest wares; then he travelled abroad, first to St Andrews in Scotland and then for the first time to Rome. On his return, having formed a familiar friendship with certain other young men who were eager for merchandise, he began to launch upon bolder courses, and to coast frequently by sea to the foreign lands that lay around him. Thus, sailing often to and fro between Scotland and Britain, he traded in many divers wares and, amid these occupations, learned much worldly wisdom. . . . He fell into many perils of the sea, yet by God's mercy he was never wrecked; for He who had upheld St Peter as he walked upon the waves, by that same strong right arm kept this His chosen vessel from all misfortune amid these perils. Thus, having learned by frequent experience his wretchedness amid such dangers, he began to worship certain of the Saints with more ardent zeal, venerating and calling upon their shrines, and giving himself up by wholehearted service to those holy names. In

such invocations his prayers were oftentimes answered by prompt consolation; some of which prayers he learned from his fellows with whom
he shared these frequent perils; others he collected from faithful hearsay; others again from the custom of the place, for he saw and visited
such holy places with frequent assiduity. Thus aspiring ever higher
and higher, and yearning upward with his whole heart, at length his
great labours and cares bore much fruit of worldly gain. For he laboured not only as a merchant but also as a shipman . . . to Denmark
and Flanders and Scotland; in all which lands he found certain rare,
and therefore more precious, wares, which he carried to other parts
wherein he knew them to be least familiar, and coveted by the inhabitants beyond the price of gold itself; wherefore he exchanged these
wares for others coveted by men of other lands; and thus he chaffered
most freely and assiduously. Hence he made great profit in all his bargains, and gathered much wealth in the sweat of his brow; for he sold
dear in one place the wares which he had bought elsewhere at a small
price.

Then he purchased the half of a merchant-ship with certain of his
partners in the trade; and again by his prudence he bought the fourth
part of another ship. At length, by his skill in navigation, wherein he excelled all his fellows, he earned promotion to the post of steersman. . . .

For he was vigorous and strenuous in mind, whole of limb and
strong in body. He was of middle stature, broad-shouldered and deep-
chested, with a long face, grey eyes most clear and piercing, bushy
brows, a broad forehead, long and open nostrils, a nose of comely
curve, and a pointed chin. His beard was thick, and longer than the
ordinary, his mouth well-shaped, with lips of moderate thickness; in
youth his hair was black, in age as white as snow; his neck was short
and thick, knotted with veins and sinews; his legs were somewhat slender, his instep high, his knees hardeneed and horny with frequent
kneeling; his whole skin rough beyond the ordinary, until all this
roughness was softened by old age. . . . In labour he was strenuous, assiduous above all men; and, when by chance his bodily strength proved
insufficient, he compassed his ends with great ease by the skill which
his daily labours had given, and by a prudence born of long experience. . . . He knew, from the aspect of sea and stars, how to foretell
fair or foul weather. In his various voyages he visited many saints'
shrines, to whose protection he was wont most devoutly to commend
himself; more especially the church of St Andrew in Scotland, where
he most frequently made and paid his vows. On the way thither, he
oftentimes touched at the island of Lindisfarne, wherein St Cuthbert
had been bishop, and at the isle of Farne, where that Saint had lived
as an anchoret, and where St Godric (as he himself would tell afterwards) would meditate on the Saint's life with abundant tears. Thence
he began to yearn for solitude, and to hold his merchandise in less esteem than heretofore. . . .

And now he had lived sixteen years as a merchant, and began to think of spending on charity, to God's honour and service, the goods which he had so laboriously acquired. He therefore took the cross as a pilgrim to Jerusalem, and, having visited the Holy Sepulchre, came back to England by way of St James [of Compostella]. Not long afterwards he became steward to a certain rich man of his own country, with the care of his whole house and household. But certain of the younger household were men of iniquity, who stole their neighbours' cattle and thus held luxurious feasts, whereat Godric, in his ignorance, was sometimes present. Afterwards, discovering the truth, he rebuked and admonished them to cease; but they made no account of his warnings; wherefore he concealed not their iniquity, but disclosed it to the lord of the household, who, however, slighted his advice. Wherefore he begged to be dismissed and went on a pilgrimage, first to St Gilles and thence to Rome the abode of the Apostles, that thus he might knowingly pay the penalty for those misdeeds wherein he had ignorantly partaken. I have often seen him, even in his old age, weeping for this unknowing transgression. . . .

On his return from Rome, he abode awhile in his father's house; until, inflamed again with holy zeal, he purposed to revisit the abode of the Apostles and made his desire known unto his parents. Not only did they approve his purpose, but his mother besought his leave to bear him company on this pilgrimage; which he gladly granted, and willingly paid her every filial service that was her due. They came therefore to London; and they had scarcely departed from thence when his mother took off her shoes, going thus barefooted to Rome and back to London. Godric, humbly serving his parent, was wont to bear her on his shoulders. . . .

Godric, when he had restored his mother safe to his father's arms, abode but a brief while at home; for he was now already firmly purposed to give himself entirely to God's service. Wherefore, that he might follow Christ the more freely, he sold all his possessions and distributed them among the poor. Then, telling his parents of this purpose and receiving their blessing, he went forth to no certain abode, but whithersoever the Lord should deign to lead him; for above all things he coveted the life of a hermit.

chapter XV

Varieties of Medieval Literature

*The various types of twelfth-century literature illustrate many aspects of
medieval men's attitudes to love, war, honor, and religion.*

49. Warrior Chivalry: The Song of Roland

*The "Song of Roland" exemplifies the warrior ideals of early feudalism, un-
complicated by later notions of romantic love.*

The Battle at Roncevals

Then Oliver goes up into a high mountain, and looks away to the
right, all down a grassy valley, and sees the host of the heathen coming
on, and he called to Roland, his comrade, saying: "From the side of
Spain I see a great light coming, thousands of white hauberks and thousands of gleaming helms. They will fall upon our Franks with great
wrath. Ganelon the felon has done this treason, and he it was adjudged
us to the rearguard, before the Emperor." "Peace Oliver," saith Count
Roland, "he is my mother's husband, speak thou no ill of him."

Oliver has fared up the mountain, and from the summit thereof he
sees all the kingdom of Spain and the great host of the Saracens. Wondrous is the shrine of helmets studded with gold, of shields and broidered hauberks, of lances and gonfanons. The battles are without
number, and no man may give count thereof, so great is the multitude. Oliver was all astonied at the sight; he got him down the hill as
best he might, and came to the Franks, and gave them his tidings.

"I have seen the paynims," said Oliver; "never was so great a multitude seen of living men. Those of the vanguard are upon a hundred

From "The Song of Roland," I. Butler, trans., in C. W. Jones, ed., *Medieval Literature
in Translation* (New York: Longmans, Green, 1950), pp. 533–535, 537–539, 553–554.

thousand, all armed with shields and helmets, and clad in white hauberks; right straight are the shafts of their lances, and bright the points thereof. Such a battle we shall have as was never before seen of man. Ye lords of France, may God give you might! and stand ye firm that we be not overcome." "Foul fall him who flees!" then say the Franks. "For no peril of death will we fail thee."

"Great is the host of the heathen," saith Oliver, "and few is our fellowship. Roland, fair comrade, I pray thee sound thy horn of ivory that Charles may hear it and return again with all his host." "That were but folly," quoth Roland, "and thereby would I lose all fame in sweet France. Rather will I strike good blows and great with Durendal, that the blade thereof shall be blooded even unto the hilt. Woe worth the paynims that they came into the passes! I pledge thee my faith short life shall be theirs."

"Roland, comrade, blow now thy horn of ivory, and Charles shall hear it, and bring hither his army again, and the King and his barons shall succour us." But Roland answers him, saying: "Now God forfend that through me my kinsman be brought to shame, or aught of dishonour befall fair France. But first I will lay on with Durendal, the good sword that is girded here at my side, and thou shalt see the blade thereof all reddened. Woe worth the paynims when they gathered their hosts! I pledge me they shall all be given over to death."

"Roland, comrade, blow thy horn of ivory, that Charles may hear it as he passes the mountains, and I pledge me the Franks will return hither again." But Roland saith: "Now God forfend it be said of any living man that I sounded my horn for dread of paynims. Nay, that reproach shall never fall upon my kindred. But when I am in the stour I will smite seven hundred blows, or mayhap a thousand, and thou shalt see the blade of Durendal all crimson. The Franks are goodly men, and they will lay on right valiantly, nor shall those of Spain have any surety from death."

Saith Oliver, "I see no shame herein. I have seen the Saracens of Spain, they cover the hills and the valleys, the heaths and the plains. Great are the hosts of this hostile folk, and ours is but a little fellowship." And Roland makes answer: "My desire is the greater thereby. May God and His most holy angels forfend that France should lose aught of worship through me. Liefer had I die than bring dishonour upon me. The Emperor loves us for dealing stout blows."

Roland is brave, and Oliver is wise, and both are good men of their hands; once armed and a-horseback, rather would they die than flee the battle. Hardy are the Counts and high their speech. The felon paynims ride on in great wrath. Saith Oliver: "Roland, prithee look. They are close upon us, but Charles is afar off. Thou wouldst not deign to sound thy horn of ivory; but were the King here we should suffer no hurt. Look up towards the passes of Aspre and thou shalt see the woeful rearguard; they who are of it will do no more service henceforth." But Roland answers him: "Speak not so cowardly. Cursed be the heart that turns coward in the breast! Hold we the field, and ours be the buffets and the slaughter."

When Roland sees that the battle is close upon them he waxes fiercer than lion or leopard. He calls to the Franks, and he saith to Oliver: "Comrade, friend, say not so. When the Emperor left us his Franks he set apart such a twenty thousand of men that, certes, among them is no coward. For his liege lord a man ought to suffer all hardship, and endure great heat and great cold, and give both his blood and his body. Lay on with thy lance, and I will smite with Durendal, my good sword that the King gave me. If I die here, may he to whom it shall fall, say, 'This was the sword of goodly vassal.'"

Nigh at hand is Archbishop Turpin; he now spurs his horse to the crest of a knoll, and speaks to the Franks, and this is his sermon: "Lords, barons, Charles left us here, and it is a man's devoir to die for his King. Now help ye to uphold Christianity. Certes, ye shall have a battle, for here before you are the Saracens. Confess your sins and pray Gold's mercy, and that your souls may be saved I will absolve you. If ye are slain ye will be held martyrs, and ye shall have seats in the higher Paradise." The Franks light off their horses and kneel down, and the Archbishop blesses them, and for a penance bids them that they lay on with their swords.

• • •

And Gerier, the comrade of Gerin, smites the Emir, and shatters his shield and unmails his hauberk, and thrusts his good lance into his heart; so great is the blow his lance drives through the body and with all the force of his shaft he throws him to the ground dead. "Ours is a goodly battle," quoth Oliver.

Samson the Duke rides upon the Almaçur, and breaks his shield all flowered and set with gold, nor doth his good hauberk give him any surety, but Samson pierces him through heart and liver and lungs, and fells him dead, whether any one grieves for him or no. Saith the Archbishop: "That was knightly stricken."

And Anseïs urges on his horse and encounters with Turgis of Tortosa, cleaves his shield below the gold boss, rends asunder his twofold hauberk, and sets the point of his good lance in his body and thrusts so well that the iron passes sheer through him, that the might of the blow hurls him to the ground dead. "That was the buffet of a man of good prowess," saith Roland.

• • •

Count Roland rides through the press; in his hand he hath Durendal, right good for hacking and hewing, and doth great damage upon the Saracens. Lo, how he hurls one dead upon another, and the bright blood flows out on the field. All reddened are his hauberk and his arms, and the neck and shoulders of his good horse. Nor doth Oliver hold back from the battle; the Twelve Peers do not shame themselves, and all the Franks smite and slay, that the paynims perish or fall swooning. Then saith the Archbishop, "Our barons do passing well," and he cries out Montjoy, the war-cry of Charles.

Oliver drives through the stour; his lance is broken and naught is left him but the truncheon; yet he smites the paynim Malsaron that his shield patterned with gold and flowers is broken, and his two eyes fly out from his head, and his brains fall at his feet; among seven hundred of his fellows Oliver smites him dead. Then he slew Turgin and Esturgus, and thereby broke his lance that it splintered even unto the pommel. Thereat Roland saith: "Comrade what does thou? I have no mind for a staff in so great battle, rather a man hath need of iron and steel. Where is thy sword Halteclere?" "I may not draw it," Oliver answered him. "So keen am I to smite."

But now the lord Oliver hath drawn his good sword, even as his comrade had besought him, and hath shown it to him in knightly wise; and therewith he smites the paynim Justin de Val Ferrée that he severs his head in twain, cuts through his broidered hauberk and his body, through his good saddle set with gold, and severs the backbone of his steed, that man and horse fall dead on the field before him. Then said Roland: "Now I hold you as my brother, and 'tis for such buffets the Emperor loves us." And on all sides they cry out Montjoy.

* * *

[Oliver was killed in the battle and Roland received a death wound.]

Now Roland feels that death had come upon him, and that it creeps down from his head to his heart. In all haste he fares under a pine tree, and hath cast himself down upon his face on the green grass. Under him he laid his sword and his horn of ivory; and he turned his face towards the paynim folk, for he would that Charles and all his men should say that the gentle Count had died a conqueror. Speedily and full often he confesses his sins, and in atonement he offers his glove to God.

Roland lies on a high peak looking towards Spain; he feels that his time is spent, and with one hand he beats upon his breast: "O God, I have sinned; forgive me through thy might the wrongs, both great and small, which I have done from the day I was born even to this day on which I was smitten." With his right hand he holds out his glove to God; and lo, the angels of heaven come down to him.

Count Roland lay under the pine tree; he has turned his face towards Spain, and he begins to call many things to remembrance—all the lands he had won by his valour, and sweet France, and the men of his lineage, and Charles, his liege lord, who had brought him up in his household; and he cannot help but weep. But he would not wholly forget himself, and again he confesses his sins and begs forgiveness of God: "Our Father, Who art Truth, Who raised up Lazarus from the dead, and Who defended Daniel from the lions, save Thou my soul from the perils to which it is brought through the sins I wrought in my life days." With his right hand he offers his glove to God, and Saint Gabriel has taken it from his hand. Then his head sinks on his arm, and with clasped hands he hath gone to his end. And God sent him His cherubim, and Saint Michael of the Seas, and with them went Saint Gabriel, and they carried the soul of the Count into Paradise.

50.   *Troubadour Songs*

In the late eleventh and early twelfth centuries a new kind of love song appeared in the south of France. Soon the fashion spread to other parts of Europe. William, Count of Poitou (1071–1127), knew how to write in the new style—and also how to make fun of it.

A Song of Nothing
WILLIAM, COUNT OF POITOU

Farai un vers de dreyt nien:
Non er de me ni d'autra gen,
Non er d'amor ni de joven,
  Ni de ren au,
Qu' enans fo trobatz en durmen
  Sobre chevau.

I'll make some verses just for fun
Not about me nor any one,
Nor deeds that noble knights have done
  Nor love's ado: —
I made them riding in the sun
  (My horse helped, too.)

When I was born I cannot say;
I am not sad, I am not gay,
I am not stiff nor dégagé;
  What can I do?
Long since enchanted by a fay
  Star-touched I grew.

Dreaming for living I mistake
Unless I'm told when I'm awake.
My heart is sad and nigh to break
  With bitter rue—
And I don't care three crumbs of cake
  Or even two.

William, Count of Poitou, "A Song of Nothing," T. G. Bergin, trans., in C. W. Jones, ed., *Medieval Literature in Translation* (New York: Longmans, Green, 1950), pp. 668–669; reprinted by permission of David McKay Company, Inc.

I have a lady, who or where
I cannot tell you, but I swear
She treats me neither ill nor fair
   But I'm not blue
Just so the Normans stay up there
   Out of Poitou.

I have not seen yet I adore
This distant love; she sets no store
By what I think and furthermore
   ('Tis sad but true)
Others there are, some three or four,
   I'm faithful to.

So ill I am that death I fear;
I nothing know but what I hear;
I hope there is a doctor here,
   No matter who.
If he can cure me I'll pay dear,
   If not, he's through.

I've made the verse; if you'll allow
I think I'll send it off right now
To one who'll pass it on somehow
   Up in Anjou;
He'd tell me what it means, I vow,
   If he but knew.

Alba

ANONYMOUS

En un vergier sotz folha d'albespi
Tenc la dompna son amic costa si,
Tro la gaita crida que l'alba vi.
Oi deus, oi deus, de l'alba! tan tost ve.

In orchard where the leaves of hawthorn hide,
The lady holds a lover to her side,
Until the watcher in the dawning cried.
Ah God, ah God, the dawn! it comes how soon.

"Ah, would to God that never night must end,
Nor this my lover far from me should wend,
Nor watcher day nor dawning ever send!
Ah God, ah God, the dawn! it comes how soon.

"Alba," C. C. Abbott, trans., in C. W. Jones, ed., *Medieval Literature in Translation* (New York: Longmans, Green, 1950), pp. 669–670; reprinted by permission of Oxford University Press.

Come let us kiss, dear lover, you and I,
Within the meads where pretty song-birds fly;
We will do all despite the jealous eye:
Ah God, ah God, the dawn! it comes how soon.

Sweet lover come, renew our lovemaking
Within the garden where the light birds sing,
Until the watcher sound the severing.
Ah God, ah God, the dawn! it comes how soon.

Through the soft breezes that are blown from there,
From my own lover, courteous, noble and fair,
From his breath have I drunk a draught most rare.
Ah God, ah God, the dawn! it comes how soon.

Gracious the lady is, and debonaire,
For her beauty a many look at her,
And in her heart is loyal love astir.
Ah God, ah God, the dawn! it comes how soon.

To His Love Afar
JAUFRÉ RUDEL

Lanquan li jorn son lonc en may
M'es belhs dous chans d'auzelhs de lonh,
E quan mi suy partitz de lay
Remembra. m d'un amor de lonh. . . .

When the days lengthen in the month of May,
Well pleased am I to hear the birds
      Sing far away.
And when from that place I am gone,
I hang my head and make dull moan,
Since she my heart is set upon
      Is far away.

So far, that song of birds, flower o' the thorn,
Please me no more than winter morn,
      With ice and sleet.
Ah, would I were a pilgrim over sea,
With staff and scrip and cloak to cover me,
That some day I might kneel me on one knee
      Before her feet.

Jaufré Rudel, "To His Love Afar," in H. Waddell, trans., *The Wandering Scholars* (7th ed.; London: Constable, 1934), pp. 205–206; reprinted by permission of the publisher.

Most sad, most joyous shall I go away,
Let me have seen her for a single day,
     My love afar.
I shall not see her, for her land and mine
Are sundered, and the ways are hard to find,
So many ways, and I shall lose my way,
     So wills it God.

Yet shall I know no other love but hers,
And if not hers, no other love at all.
     She hath surpassed all.
So fair she is, so noble, I would be
A captive with the hosts of paynimrie
In a far land, if so be upon me
     Her eyes might fall.

God, who hath made all things in earth that are,
That made my love, and set her thus afar,
     Grant me this grace,
That I may some day come within a room,
Or in some garden gloom
     Look on her face.

It will not be, for at my birth they said
That one had set this doom upon my head,
     —God curse him among men!—
That I should love, and not till I be dead,
     Be loved again.

*Women as well as men wrote troubadour songs. This one is by the
Countess de Dia (born ca. 1140).*

Estat ai en greu cossirier
per un cavallier qu'ai agut,

I've lately been in great distress
over a knight who once was mine,
and I want it known for all eternity
how I loved him to excess.
Now I see I've been betrayed
because I wouldn't sleep with him;
night and day my mind won't rest
to think of the mistake I made.

How I wish just once I could caress
that chevalier with my bare arms,

Meg Bogin, trans., in *The Woman Troubadours* (New York: Paddington Press Ltd.,
1976), p. 89. Reprinted by permission.

for he would be in ecstasy
if I'd just let him lean his head against my breast.
I'm sure I'm happier with him
than Blancaflor with Floris.
My heart and love I offer him,
my mind, my eyes, my life.

Handsome friend, charming and kind,
when shall I have you in my power?
If only I could lie beside you for an hour
and embrace you lovingly—
know this, that I'd give almost anything
to have you in my husband's place,
but only under the condition
that you swear to do my bidding.

51.   *Goliardic Literature: Songs and Satire*

The Latin lyrics called "Goliardic" were usually songs in praise of love and wine. The name is derived from the Old Testament "Goliath" (or "Golias") —regarded as a symbol of wickedness in the Middle Ages.

The Archpoet

His Confession

*Estuans intrinsecus
ira vehementi
in amaritudine
loquar mee menti. . . .*

Seething over inwardly
   With fierce indignation,
In my bitterness of soul,
   Hear my declaration.
I am of one element,
   Levity my matter,
Like enough a withered leaf
   For the winds to scatter.

Since it is the property
   Of the sapient

From "The Archpoet," in H. Waddell, trans., *Mediaeval Latin Lyrics* (London: Constable, 1933), pp. 171, 173, 177, 179.

To sit firm upon a rock,
   It is evident
That I am a fool, since I
   Am a flowing river,
Never under the same sky,
   Transient for ever.

Hither, thither, masterless
   Ship upon the sea,
Wandering through the ways of air,
   Go the birds like me.
Bound am I by ne'er a bond,
   Prisoner to no key,
Questing go I for my kind,
   Find depravity.

Never yet could I endure
   Soberness and sadness,
Jests I love and sweeter than
   Honey find I gladness.
Whatsoever Venus bids
   Is a joy exciting,
Never in an evil heart
   Did she make her dwelling.

Down the broad way do I go,
   Young and unregretting,
Wrap me in my vices up,
   Virtue all forgetting,
Greedier for all delight
   Than heaven to enter in:
Since the soul in me is dead,
   Better save the skin.

Pardon, pray you, good my lord,
   Master of discretion,
But this death I die is sweet,
   Most delicious poison.
Wounded to the quick am I
   By a young girl's beauty:
She's beyond my touching? Well,
   Can't the mind do duty?

• • •

Yet a second charge they bring:
   I'm for ever gaming.
Yea, the dice hath many a time
   Stripped me to my shaming.
What an if the body's cold,
   If the mind is burning.

On the anvil hammering,
   Rhymes and verses turning.

Look again upon your list.
   Is the tavern on it?
Yea, and never have I scorned,
   Never shall I scorn it,
Till the holy angels come,
   And my eyes discern them,
Singing for the dying soul,
   Requiem aeternam.

For on this my heart is set:
   When the hour is nigh me,
Let me in the tavern die,
   With a tankard by me,
While the angels looking down
   Joyously sing o'er me,
Deus sit propitius
   Huic potatori.

'Tis the fire that's in the cup
   Kindles the soul's torches,
'Tis the heart that drenched in wine
   Flies to heaven's porches.
Sweeter tastes the wine to me
   In a tavern tankard
Than the watered stuff my Lord
   Bishop hath decanted.

Let them fast and water drink,
   All the poets' chorus,
Fly the market and the crowd
   Racketing uproarious.
Sit in quiet spots and think,
   Shun the tavern's portal,
Write, and never having lived,
   Die to be immortal.

Let's Away with Study

Obmittamus studia
dulce est desipere. . . .

Let's away with study,
   Folly's sweet.
Treasure all the pleasure
   Of our youth:

Time enough for age
    To think on Truth.
So short a day,
And life so quickly hasting
And in study wasting
    Youth that would be gay!

'Tis our spring that slipping,
    Winter draweth near,
    Life itself we're losing,
    And this sorry cheer
Dries the blood and chills the heart,
    Shrivels all delight.
Age and all its crowd of ills
    Terrifies our sight.
So short a day,
And life so quickly hasting,
And in study wasting
    Youth that would be gay!

Let us as the gods do,
    'Tis the wiser part:
Leisure and love's pleasure
    Seek the young in heart
Follow the old fashion,
    Down into the street!
Down among the maidens,
    And the dancing feet!
So short a day,
And life so quickly hasting,
And in study wasting
    Youth that would be gay!

There for the seeing
    Is all loveliness,
White limbs moving
    Light in wantonness.
Gay go the dancers,
    I stand and see,
Gaze, till their glances
    Steal myself from me.
So short a day,
And life so quickly hasting,
And in study wasting
    Youth that would be gay!

Now the Fields Are Laughing

Iamiam rident prata,
iamiam virgines
iocundantur, terre
ridet facies. . . .

Now the fields are laughing,
   Now the maidens playing,
The face of earth is smiling,
   Summer now appearing,
Joyous and lovely with all flowers beguiling.

The trees again are green,
Budding the underwood,
And cruel winter passes.
O lads, be gay of mood,
For Love himself now leads you to the lasses.

For the love of Venus
   Go we now to war,
Banish we all sadness,
   We who tender are,
And may lovely faces and soft speeches,
   Love and Hope now bring us into gladness!

O Truth of Christ

Dic Christi Veritas
Dic cara raritas,
Dic rara Caritas,
Ubi nunc habitas?

O truth of Christ,
O most dear rarity,
O most rare Charity,
Where dwell'st thou now?
In the valley of Vision?
On Pharaoh's throne?
On high with Nero?
With Timon alone?
In the bulrush ark
Where Moses wept?
Or in Rome's high places
With lightning swept?

With the lightning of Bulls,
And a thundering judge,
Summoned, accused,

Truth stands oppressed,
Torn asunder and sold,
While Justice sells her body in the street.
Come and go and come again
To the Curia, and when
Stripped to the last farthing, then
Leave the judgment seat.

Then Love replied,
"Man, wherefore didst thou doubt?"
Not where thou wast wont to find
My dwelling in the southern wind;
Not in court and not in cloister,
Not in casque nor yet in cowl,
Not in battle nor in Bull,
But on the road from Jericho
I come with a wounded man.

The Gospel According to the Silver Mark

In those days the Pope spake unto the Romans, "When the son of man cometh to the seat of our majesty, first say unto him, 'Friend, wherefore art thou come?' But if he shall continue knocking and giving nothing unto you, cast him forth into the outer darkness." And it came to pass that a certain poor clerk came to the *curia* of the Lord Pope and cried, saying, "Have mercy on me, ye doorkeepers of the Pope, for the hand of poverty hath touched me. For I am poor and needy, and I pray you that ye should have compassion upon my calamity and my affliction." But they hearing it had indignation among themselves and said, "Friend, thy poverty go with thee to perdition: get thee behind me, Satan, for thou savourest not the things that be of pelf. Verily, verily, I say unto thee, thou shalt not enter into the joy of thy lord, until thou hast given thy uttermost farthing."

And the poor man went away and sold his cloak and his tunic and all that he had, and gave to the cardinals and the doorkeepers and the chamberlains. But they said, "And what is this among so many?" And they cast him out, and he going out wept bitterly and could not be comforted. And thereafter came to the *curia* a certain rich clerk, fat and well-fed and puffed up, who for sedition had committed murder. He first gave to the doorkeeper, and then to the chamberlain, and then to the cardinals. And they took counsel among themselves, which of them should have received most. But the Lord Pope hearing that his cardinals and his servants had received many gifts from the clerk

From "The Gospel According to the Silver Mark," in H. Waddell, trans., *The Wandering Scholars* (7th ed.; London: Constable, 1934), pp. 150–151; reprinted by permission of the publisher.

fell sick nigh unto death. Then sent unto him the rich clerk an electuary of gold and silver, and straightway he was recovered. Then the Lord Pope called unto him his cardinals and his servants and said unto them, "Brethren, see to it that no man seduce you with vain words. For I have given you an example, that even as much as I take, ye should take also."

52. Popular Piety: Our Lady's Tumbler

Many of the most popular stories of the Middle Ages reflect a spirit of naive piety very different from the attitudes found in troubadour and Goliardic writings. In the following tale a wandering entertainer enters a monastery but finds himself too uneducated to join in the monks' Latin prayers. He decides to serve the Virgin in the only way he knows.

. . . By the Mother of God, this will I do, and never shall I be blamed for it. I will do that which I have learnt, and thus, after mine own manner, will I serve the Mother of God in her Church. The others do service with song, and I will do service with tumbling."

And he took off his habit, and then stripped himself, and laid his garments beside the altar, but so that his body should not be uncovered, he kept on a tunic, the which was very clinging and close fitting. Little better was it than a shift; nevertheless was his body wholly covered. And thus was he fitly clad and equipped, and he girded his tunic, and duly prepared him, and he turned him to the image, and gazed on it very humbly. "Lady," said he, "to your keeping I commend my body and my soul. Gentle Queen and Lady, despise not that which I am acquainted with, for, without ado, I will essay me to serve you in good faith, if so be that God will aid me."

Then he began to turn somersaults, now high, now low, first forwards, then backwards, and then he fell on his knees before the image, and bowed his head. "Ah, very gentle Queen!" said he, "of your pity, and of your generosity, despise not my service." Then he tumbled, and leaped, and turned gaily the somersault of Metz. And he bowed to the image, and worshipped it, for he paid homage to it as much as he was able. And anon he turned the French somersault, and then the somersault of Champagne, and after that, those of Spain and of Brittany, and then that of Lorraine. And he laboured to the utmost of his power.

From "Our Lady's Tumbler," A. Kemp-Welch, trans., in C. W. Jones, ed., *Medieval Literature in Translation* (London: Longmans, Green, 1950), pp. 596–602; reprinted by permission of Chatto and Windus.

And after that, he did the Roman somersault, and then he put his hand before his face, and turned him with great grace and looked very humbly at the image of the Mother of God. "Lady," said he, "I do homage to you with my heart, and my body, and my feet, and my hands, for naught beside this do I understand. Now would I be your gleeman. Yonder they are singing, but I am come here to divert you. Lady, you who can protect me, for God's sake do not despise me." Then he beat his breast, and sighed, and mourned very grievously that he knew not how to do service in other manner. And then he turned a somersault backwards. "Lady," said he, "so help me God, never before have I done this. Lady! How that one would have his utmost desire, who could dwell with you in your right glorious mansion! For God's sake, Lady, receive me there. I do this for your sake, and in nowise for mine own." Then he again turned the somersault of Metz, and tumbled and capered full many a time.

And when he heard the monks celebrating, he began to exert himself, and so long as the Mass dured, he ceased not to dance, and to jump, and to leap, until that he was on the point to faint, and he could not stand up, and thus he fell to the ground, and dropped from sheer fatigue. And like as the grease issues from the spitted meat, so the sweat issued from him all over, from head to foot. "Lady," said he, "no more can I do now, but of a surety I shall come back again."

And he was quite overcome of heat. And he took up his clothing, and when that he was dressed, he took his leave, and he bowed to the image, and went his way. "Farewell, very gentle friend," said he. "For God's sake, grieve not at all, for if that I am able, and it is permitted unto me, I will come back, for each hour would I serve you to the utmost of my power, so gracious are you."

And longwhiles he led this life, and, at each hour precisely he repaired to the image, to render service and homage. Certes, so greatly did it please him, and with such right good will did he do this, that never a day was he so tired that he could not do his very utmost to delight the Mother of God, and never did he desire to do other service.

Well known was it that he went each day into the crypt, but no one, save God, knew what he did there, nor would he, for all the riches of the whole world, that any, save the supreme God alone, should know of his doings. . . .

And then [the abbot and a monk] went thither quite quietly, and without delay they hid themselves in a covert nook nigh unto the altar, so that he saw them not. And the abbot, watching there, observed all the service of the novice, and the divers somersaults the which he turned, and how that he capered, and danced, and bowed before the image, and jumped, and leaped, until that he was nigh fainting. And so greatly was he overcome of fatigue, that he fell heavily to the ground, and so exhausted was he, that he sweated all over from his efforts, so that the sweat ran all down the middle of the crypt. But in a little, the Mother of God, whom he served all without guile, came to his succour, and well knew she how to aid him.

And anon the abbot looked, and he saw descend from the vaulting so glorious a lady, that never had he seen one so fair or so richly crowned, and never had another so beautiful been created. Her vesture was all wrought with gold and precious stones, and with her were the angels and the archangels from the heavens above, who came around the tumbler, and solaced and sustained him. And when that they were ranged around him, he was wholly comforted, and they made ready to tend him, for they desired to make recompense unto him for the services the which he had rendered unto their Lady, who is so precious a gem. And the sweet and noble Queen took a white cloth, and with it she very gently fanned her minstrel before the altar. And the noble and gracious Lady fanned his neck and body and face to cool him, and greatly did she concern herself to aid him, and gave herself up to the care of him; but of this the good man took no heed, for he neither perceived, nor did he know, that he was in such fair company.

And the holy angels who remained with him, paid him much honour, but the Lady no longer sojourned there, and she made the sign of the cross as she turned away, and the holy angels, who greatly rejoiced to keep watch over their companion, took charge over him, and they did but await the hour when God would take him from this life, and they might bear away his soul.

• • •

And, as I have told unto you, at last it came to pass that he died. And the abbot was there, and all his monks, and the novices and good folk, who kept watch over him very humbly, and quite clearly did they see a right wondrous miracle. Of a truth they saw how that, at his death, the angels, and the Mother of God, and the archangels, were ranged around him. And there, also, were the very evil and cruel and violent devils, for to possess them of his soul, and no fancy is this. But to no purpose had they so long lain in wait for him, and striven so earnestly for him and pursued him, for now no power had they over his soul. And forthwith his soul quitted his body, but in nowise was it lost, for the Mother of God received it. And the holy angels who were there, sang for joy, and then they departed, and bare it to heaven, and this was seen of all the monks, and of all the others who were there.

Thus died the minstrel. Cheerfully did he tumble and cheerfully did he serve, for the which he merited great honour, and none was there to compare unto him.

And the holy Fathers have related unto us that it thus befel this minstrel. Now let us pray God, without ceasing, that He may grant unto us so worthily to serve Him, that we may be deserving of His love. The story of the Tumbler is set forth.

53. Andreas Capellanus: The Idea of Courtly Love

Andreas Capellanus lived in the household of Countess Marie de Champagne in the last quarter of the twelfth century. His De Amore *presented a detailed (and often satirical) guide to the practice of courtly love.*

What the Effect of Love Is

Now it is the effect of love that a true lover cannot be degraded with any avarice. Love causes a rough and uncouth man to be distinguished for his handsomeness; it can endow a man even of the humblest birth with nobility of character; it blesses the proud with humility; and the man in love becomes accustomed to performing many services gracefully for everyone. O what a wonderful thing is love, which makes a man shine with so many virtues and teaches everyone, no matter who he is, so many good traits of character! There is another thing about love that we should not praise in few words; it adorns a man, so to speak, with the virtue of chastity, because he who shines with the light of one love can hardly think of embracing another woman, even a beautiful one. For when he thinks of his beloved the sight of any other women seems to his mind rough and rude.

A man of the higher nobility speaks with a woman of the simple nobility

When a man of the higher nobility addresses a woman of the simple nobility, let him use the same speeches that a nobleman and a man of the higher nobility use with a woman of the middle class, except that part dealing with commendation of birth, and he must not boast very much of the fact that he is noble. In addition he might begin with this formula:

"I ought to give God greater thanks than any other living man in the whole world because it is now granted me to see with my eyes what my soul has desired above all else to see, and I believe that God has granted it to me because of my great longing and because He has seen fit to hear the prayers of my importunate supplication. For not an hour of the day or night could pass that I did not earnestly pray God to grant me the boon of seeing you near me in the flesh. It is no wonder that I was driven by so great an impulse to see you and was tormented by so great a desire, since the whole world extols your virtue and your wisdom, and in the farthest parts of the world courts are fed upon the tale of your goodness just as though it were a sort of tangible

Andreas Capellanus, *The Art of Courtly Love,* J. J. Parry, trans., F. Locke, ed. (New York: Frederick Ungar, 1954), pp. 4, 15-19, 24.

food. And now I know in very truth that a human tongue is not able to tell the tale of your beauty and your prudence or a human mind to imagine it. And so the mighty desire, which I already had, of seeing you and serving you has greatly increased and will increase still more."

THE WOMAN SAYS: "We are separated by too wide and too rough an expanse of country to be able to offer each other love's solaces or to find proper opportunities for meeting. . . . Besides there is another fact, by no means trivial, which keeps me from loving you. I have a husband who is greatly distinguished by his nobility, his good breeding, and his good character, and it would be wicked for me to violate his bed or submit to the embraces of any other man, since I know that he loves me with his whole heart and I am bound to him with all the devotion of mine. The laws themselves bid me refrain from loving another man when I am blessed with such a reward for my love."

THE MAN SAYS: "I admit it is true that your husband is a very worthy man and that he is more blest than any man in the world because he has been worthy to have the joy of embracing Your Highness. But I am greatly surprised that you wish to misapply the term 'love' to that marital affection which husband and wife are expected to feel for each other after marriage, since everybody knows that love can have no place between husband and wife. They may be bound to each other by a great and immoderate affection, but their feeling cannot take the place of love, because it cannot fit under the true definition of love. For what is love but an inordinate desire to receive passionately a furtive and hidden embrace? But what embrace between husband and wife can be furtive, I ask you, since they may be said to belong to each other and may satisfy each other's desires without fear that anybody will object.

"But there is another reason why husband and wife cannot love each other and that is the very substance of love, without which true love cannot exist—I mean jealousy—is in such a case very much frowned upon and they should avoid it like the pestilence; but lovers should always welcome it as the mother and the nurse of love. From this you may see clearly that love cannot possibly flourish between you and your husband. Therefore, since every woman of character ought to love, prudently, you can without doing yourself any harm accept the prayers of a suppliant and endow your suitor with your love."

THE WOMAN SAYS: "You are trying to take under your protection what all men from early times down have agreed to consider very reprehensible and to reject as hateful. For who can rightly commend envious jealousy or speak in favor of it, since jealousy is nothing but a shameful and evil suspicion of a woman? God forbid, therefore, that any worthy man should feel jealous about anyone, since this proves hostile to every prudent person and throughout the world is hated by everybody good. You are trying also, under cover of defining love, to condemn love between husband and wife, saying that their embraces cannot be furtive, since without fear that anyone may object they can fulfill each other's desires. But if you understood the definition correctly it could not interfere with love between husband and wife, for the expression 'hidden embraces' is simply an explanation in different words of the preceding one, and there seems to be no impossibility in husband and wife giving each other hidden embraces, even though they can do so without the least fear that anybody may raise an objection. Everyone should choose that love which may be fostered by security for continual embraces and, what is more, can be practiced every day without any sin. I ought therefore to choose a man to enjoy my embraces who can be to me both husband and lover, because, no matter what the definition of love may say, love seems to be nothing but a great desire to enjoy carnal pleasure with someone, and nothing prevents this feeling existing between husband and wife."

THE MAN SAYS: "If the theory of love were perfectly clear to you and Love's dart had ever touched you, your own feelings would have shown you that love cannot exist without jealousy, because, as I have already told you in more detail, jealousy between lovers is commended by every man who is experienced in love, while between husband and wife it is condemned throughout the world; the reason for this will be perfectly clear from a description of jealousy. Now jealousy is a true emotion whereby we greatly fear that the substance of our love may be weakened by some defect in serving the desires of our beloved, and it is an anxiety lest our love may not be returned.

"We find many, however, who are deceived in this matter and say falsely that a shameful suspicion is jealousy. As for what you tried to prove by your answer—that the love which can be practiced without sin is far preferable—that, apparently, cannot stand. For whatever solaces married people extend to each other beyond what are inspired by the desire for offspring or the payment of the marriage debt, cannot be free from sin, and the punishment is always greater when the use of a holy thing is perverted by misuse than if we practice the ordinary abuses. It is a more serious offense in a wife than in another woman, for the too ardent lover, as we are taught by the apostolic law, is considered an adulterer with his own wife."

The Love of Peasants

If you should, by some chance, fall in love with a peasant woman, be careful to puff her up with lots of praise and then, when you find a convenient place, do not hesitate to take what you seek and to embrace her by force. For you can hardly soften their outward inflexibility so far that they will grant you their embraces quietly or permit you to have the solaces you desire unless first you use a little compulsion as a convenient cure for their shyness. We do not say these things, however, because we want to persuade you to love such women, but only so that, if through lack of caution you should be driven to love them, you may know, in brief compass, what to do.

chapter

XVI

Feudal Kingship

---

54. France: The Campaigns of Louis VI

King Louis VI (1108–1137) came to the French throne at a low point in the history of the Capetian monarchy. His work in disciplining the barons of the royal demesne was described by the king's great minister Abbot Suger.

The young hero, Prince Louis, gay, gracious, and so friendly to all that he passed with some for a person of no force, had hardly come to man's estate when he proved himself an illustrious and courageous defender of his father's realm. He provided for the needs of the Church, and strove to secure peace for those who pray, for those who work, and for the poor. And no one had done this for a long time.

Now it came to pass at this time that certain disputes arose between Adam, the venerable abbot of St. Denis, and a nobleman, Burchard, lord of Montmorency [his vassal], concerning certain customs. The controversy waxed so hot and reached such extremes of irritation that all ties of homage were broken between vassal and lord, and the two disputants betook themselves to arms, war, and fire.

When the affair came to the ears of Lord Louis he was sorely vexed. He delayed not, but ordered the aforesaid Burchard, duly summoned, to appear before his father in the castle of Poissy for judgment. Burchard lost his cause, but refused to submit to the judgment. He was not taken prisoner, for that is not the custom of the French, but having withdrawn to his estates, he straightway learned what manner of injury and calamity the king's majesty can inflict on his disobedient subjects.

From Suger, "Life of Louis VI," in J. H. Robinson, ed., *Readings in European History* (Cambridge, Mass.: Ginn, 1904), Vol. I, pp. 199, 202–204.

For this famous youth [Prince Louis] carried arms thither against him and his criminal allies, Matthew, count of Beaumont, and Dreux of Mouchy-le-châtel, vigorous and warlike men. He laid waste the land of Burchard with fire, famine, and the sword; and overthrew all the defenses and buildings, except the castle itself, and razed them to the ground. When his enemies undertook to defend themselves in the castle he besieged them with the French and the Flemish troops of his uncle Robert, as well as with his own. By these and the other means he brought the humiliated Burchard to repentance, bent him to his will and pleasure, and satisfactorily adjusted the dispute which had given rise to the trouble.

A king, when he takes the royal power, vows to put down with his strong right arm insolent tyrants whensoever he sees them vex the state with endless wars, rejoice in rapine, oppress the poor, destroy the churches, give themselves over to lawlessness which, and it be not checked, would flame out into ever greater madness; for the evil spirits who instigate them are wont cruelly to strike down those whom they fear to lose, but give free rein to those whom they hope to hold, while they add fuel to the flames which are to devour their victims to all eternity.

Such an utterly abandoned man was Thomas of Marle. While King Louis was busied with many wars, he laid waste the territories of Laon, Rheims, and Amiens, devouring like a raging wolf. He spared not the clergy—fearing not the vengeance of the Church—nor the people for humanity's sake. And the devil aided him, for the success of the foolish does ever lead them to perdition. Slaying all men, spoiling all things, he seized two manors, exceeding rich, from the abbey of the nuns of St. John of Laon. He fortified the two exceeding strong castles, Crécy and Nogent, with a marvelous wall and very high towers, as if they had been his own; and made them like to a den of dragons and a cave of robbers, whence he did waste almost the whole country with fire and pillage; and he had no pity.

The Church of France could no longer bear this great evil; wherefore the clergy, who had met together in a general synod at Beauvais, proceeded to pass sentence of condemnation upon the enemy of the Church's true spouse, Jesus Christ. The venerable Cono, bishop of Praeneste and legate of the holy Roman Church, troubled past endurance by the plaints of churches, of the orphans, of the poor, did smite this ruthless tyrant with the sword of the blessed Peter, which is general anathema. He did also ungird the knightly sword belt from him, though he was absent, and by the judgment of all declared him infamous, a scoundrel, unworthy the name of Christian.

And the king was moved by the plaints of this great council and led an army against him right quickly. He had the clergy, to whom he was ever humbly devoted, in his company, and marched straight against the castle of Crécy. Well fortified was it; yet he took it unprepared because his soldiers smote with an exceeding strong hand; or rather, because the hand of the Lord fought for him. He stormed the strongest tower as if it were the hut of a peasant, and put to confusion the wicked men and piously destroyed the impious. Because they had no pity upon other men, he cut them down without mercy. None could behold the castle tower flaming like the fires of hell and not exclaim, "The whole universe will fight for him against these madmen."

After he had won this victory, the king, who was ever swift to follow up his advantage, pushed forward toward the other castle, called Nogent. There came to him a man who said: "Oh, my lord king, it should be known to thy Serenity that in that wicked castle dwell exceeding wicked men who are worthy to lie in hell, and there only. Those are they who, when thou didst issue commands to destroy the commune of Laon, did burn with fire not only the city of Laon, but the noble church of the Mother of God, and many others beside. And well-nigh all the noble men of the city suffered martyrdom because they were true to their faith and defended their lord the bishop. And these evil men feared not to raise their hands against thy venerable Bishop Gaudin, the anointed of the Lord, defender of the church, but did him most cruelly to death, and exposed his naked body on the open road for beasts and birds of prey to feed upon; but first they cut off his finger with the pontifical ring. And they have agreed together, persuaded by the wicked Thomas, to attack and hold your tower."

The king was doubly animated by these words, and he attacked the wicked castle, broke open the abominable places of confinement, like prisons of hell, and set free the innocent; the guilty he punished with very heavy punishment. He alone avenged the injuries of many. Athirst for justice, he ordained that whatsoever murderous wretches he came upon should be fastened to a gibbet, and left as common food for the greed of kites, crows, and vultures. And this they deserved who had not feared to raise their hand against the Lord's anointed.

When he had taken these two adulterine castles and given back to the monastery of St. John the domains that had been seized, he returned to the city of Amiens and laid siege to a tower of that city which as held by a certain Adam, a cruel tyrant who was laying waste the churches and all the regions round about. He held the place besieged for hard upon two years, and at last forced those who defended it to give themselves up. When he had taken it he destroyed it utterly, and thus brought peace to the realm. He fulfilled most worthily the duty of a king who beareth not the sword in vain, and he deprived the wicked Thomas and his heirs forever of the lordship over that city.

55.   England: Stephen and Henry II

The reigns of Stephen (1135–1154) and Henry II (1154–1189) provide examples of contrasting styles of medieval kingship. The troubles of Stephen's reign were vividly described in the Anglo-Saxon Chronicle.

A.C. 1137. This year King Stephen went over sea to Normandy, and he was received there because it was expected that he would be altogether like his uncle, and because he had gotten possession of his treasure, — but this he distributed and scattered foolishly. King Henry had gathered together much gold and silver, yet did he no good for his soul's sake with the same. When King Stephen came to England he held an assembly at Oxford; and there he seized Roger, bishop of Salisbury, and Alexander, bishop of Lincoln, and Roger the chancellor, his nephew, and he kept them all in prison till they gave up their castles. When the traitors perceived that he was a mild man, and a soft, and a good, and that he did not enforce justice, they did all wonder. They had done homage to him, and sworn oaths, but they no faith kept; all became forsworn, and broke their allegiance, for every rich man built his castles, and defended them against him, and they filled the land full of castles. They greatly oppressed the wretched people by making them work at these castles, and when the castles were finished they filled them with devils and evil men. Then they took those whom they suspected to have any goods, by night and by day, seizing both men and women, and they put them in prison for their gold and silver, and tortured them with pains unspeakable, for never were any martyrs tormented as these were. They hung some up by their feet and smoked them with foul smoke, some by their thumbs or by the head; and they hung burning things at their feet. They put a knotted string about their heads, and twisted it till it went into the brain. They put them into dungeons wherein were adders and snakes, and toads, and thus wore them out. Some they put into a crucet house — that is, into a chest that was short and narrow and not deep; and they put sharp stones in it, and crushed the man therein so that they broke all his limbs. There were hateful and grim things called "sachenteges" in many of the castles, which two or three men had enough to do to carry. The sachentege was made thus: it was fastened to a beam, having a sharp iron to go around a man's throat and neck, so that he might no ways sit, nor lie, nor sleep, but that he must bear all the iron. Many thousands they exhausted with hunger. I cannot and I may not tell of all the wounds and all the tortures that they inflicted upon the wretched men of this land; and this state of things lasted the

From the *Anglo-Saxon Chronicle*, J. A. Giles, trans., and William of Newburgh, in E. P. Cheyney, ed., *Readings in English History* (Cambridge, Mass.: Ginn, 1935), pp. 128–130, 139–141.

nineteen years that Stephen was king, and ever grew worse and worse. They were continually levying an exaction from the towns, which they called "tenserie," and when the miserable inhabitants had no more to give, then plundered they, and burnt all the towns, so that then well mightest thou walk a whole day's journey nor ever shouldest thou find a man seated in a town, or its land tilled.

Then was corn dear, and flesh, and cheese, and butter, for there was none in the land; wretched men starved with hunger; some lived on alms who had been erewhile rich; some fled the country—never was there more misery, and never acted heathens worse than these. At length they spared neither church nor churchyard, but they took all that was valuable therein, and then burned the church and all together. Neither did they spare the lands of bishops, nor of abbots, nor of priests; but they robbed the monks and the clergy, and every man plundered his neighbor as much as he could. If two or three men came riding to a town, all the township fled before them, and thought that they were robbers. The bishops and clergy were ever cursing them, but this to them was nothing, for they were all accursed and forsworn, and reprobate. The earth bare no corn; you might as well have tilled the sea, for the land was all ruined by such deeds, and it was said openly that Christ and his saints slept. These things, and more than we can say, did we suffer during nineteen years because of our sins.

The chronicler William of Newburgh described the restoration of order under Henry II.

In the year 1154 Henry, a grandson of Henry the elder through his daughter, formerly the empress, came into England from Normandy after the death of King Stephen. He received there his hereditary kingdom, and, after being warmly greeted by all, was consecrated king with the holy oil, while all the people throughout the kingdom exclaimed, "Long live the king!" Having experienced the unhappiness of the former reign, in which so many evils had arisen, all hoped for better things from the new king, especially since great wisdom, together with a great zeal for justice, seemed to possess him, and since he already gave the appearance of a great leader in his very first acts. Soon he published an edict that those who had come to England from foreign nations during the reign of Stephen, to enrich themselves under the guise of performing military service, and especially the Flemings, of whom there was a great abundance dwelling in England then, should return to their own countries, and he set a day for their departure, beyond which day it would be very hazardous for them to remain in England. Frightened by this edict, they slipped away in so short a time that they seemed to have disappeared like phantoms, leaving many to wonder how they had vanished so quickly. Presently the new strongholds, which had not existed in the days of his grandfather, he ordered to be demolished, with the exception of a few situated in most excellent positions, which either he himself wished to retain or to be retained for the protection of the kingdom by the peaceable. Especially did he take care of the public order, and that the strength of the law might be felt again in England, which seemed to have been destroyed and buried under Stephen. Thus he had his hands full of weighty matters.

The king, considering that the royal revenue was small which had been large under his grandfather, because the crown lands through the weakness of King Stephen had been transferred for the most part to many other lords, ordered these to be resigned completely, by whomsoever held, and to be returned to their former condition. The men who were prominent in the royal towns and manors brought forward charters, which they had either extorted from King Stephen or bought from him by service. But since the charters of a usurper ought by no means to harm the right of the legitimate prince, they could not be safe with these documents. And so at first angry, then frightened and saddened, with difficulty indeed, but nevertheless wholly, did they resign these things which had been taken and retained so long as if by legitimate right. . . .

The king therefore carried out all these things in this district according to his wish, and then went to the north of England. Here he found that Hugh de Mortimer, a brave and highborn man, had been rebelliously holding for many years the royal stronghold of Bridgenorth. When he was ordered to be content with his own and to return those things which he possessed by royal gift, he refused most obstinately and prepared to resist in whatever ways he could. But that his pride and indignation were more than his courage appeared in the outcome. For the king quickly collected an army and besieged Bridgenorth, which after a days' siege surrendered; and he pardoned this man humbled and a suppliant, whose heart a few days before had been the heart of a lion.

chapter
XVII

Empire and Papacy

---

56.   The Incident at Besançon

A major dispute between empire and papacy broke out in 1157 when Pope Hadrian IV sent a letter to Emperor Frederick Barbarossa which apparently claimed suzerainty over the empire for the popes. (The word "beneficium" which was used by the pope could mean simply "a benefit" but it could also mean "a fief.") The reception of the letter at the Diet of Besançon was described by the chronicler Rahewin.

One day, upon the prince's retiring from the uproar and tumult of the people, the aforesaid messengers [from the pope] were conducted into his presence in the more secluded retreat of a certain oratory and — as was fitting — were received with honor and kindness, claiming (as they did) to be the bearers of good tidings.

But the beginning of their speech appeared notable at the very outset. It is said to have been as follows: "Our most blessed father, Pope Hadrian, salutes you, and the College of Cardinals of the Holy Roman Church, he as father, they as brethren." . . . Now the content of the letter was as follows:

"Bishop Hadrian, the servant of the servants of God, to his beloved

From Otto of Freising and his continuator, Rahewin, *The Deeds of Frederick Barbarossa*, C. C. Mierow, trans. (New York: Columbia University Press, 1953), pp. 180–184; Copyright 1953 Columbia University Press; reprinted by permission of the publisher.

son Frederick, the illustrious emperor of the Romans, greeting and apostolic benediction.

"We recollect having written, a few days since, to the Imperial Majesty, of that dreadful and accursed deed, an offense calling for atonement, committed in our time, and hitherto, we believe, never attempted in the German lands. In recalling it to Your Excellency, we cannot conceal our great amazement that even now you have permitted so pernicious a deed to go unpunished with the severity it deserves. For how our venerable brother E[skil], archbishop of Lund, while returning from the apostolic see, was taken captive in those parts by certain godless and infamous men — a thing we cannot mention without great and heartfelt sorrow — and is still held in confinement; how in taking him captive, as previously mentioned, those men of impiety, a seed of evildoers, children that are corrupters, drew their swords and violently assaulted him and his companions, and how basely and shamefully they treated them, stripping them of all they had, Your Most Serene Highness knows, and the report of so great a crime has already spread abroad to the most distant and remote regions. To avenge this deed of exceptional violence, you, as a man to whom we believe good deeds are pleasing but evil works displeasing, ought with great determination to arise and bring down heavily upon the necks of the wicked the sword which was entrusted by divine providence to you 'for the punishment of evildoers and for the praise of them that do well,' and should most severely punish the presumptuous. But you are reported so to have ignored and indeed been indifferent to this deed, that there is no reason why those men should be repentant at having incurred guilt, because they have long since perceived that they have secured immunity for the sacrilege which they have committed.

"Of the reason for this indifference and negligence we are absolutely ignorant, because no scruple of conscience accuses our heart of having in aught offended the glory of Your Serenity. Rather have we always loved, with sincere affection, and treated with an attitude of due kindness, your person as that of our most dear and specially beloved son and most Christian prince, who, we doubt not, is by the grace of God grounded on the rock of the apostolic confession.

"For you should recall, O most glorious son, before the eyes of your mind, how willingly and how gladly your mother, the Holy Roman Church, received you in another year, with what affection of heart she treated you, what great dignity and honor she bestowed upon you, and with how much pleasure she conferred the emblem of the imperial crown, zealous to cherish in her most kindly bosom the height of Your Sublimity, and doing nothing at all that she knew was in the least at variance with the royal will.

"Nor do we regret that we fulfilled in all respects the ardent desires of your heart; but if Your Excellency had received still greater benefits at our hand (had that been possible), in consideration of the great increase and advantage that might through you accrue to the Church of God and to us, we would have rejoiced, not without reason.

"But now, because you seem to ignore and hide so heinous a crime, which is indeed known to have been committed as an affront to the Church universal and to your empire, we both suspect and fear that perhaps your thoughts were directed toward this indifference and neglect on this account: that at the suggestion of an evil man, sowing tares, you have conceived against your most gracious mother the Holy Roman Church and against ourselves—God forbid!—some displeasure or grievance.

"On this account, therefore, and because of all the other matters of business which we know to impend, we have thought best to dispatch at this time from our side to Your Serenity two of the best and dearest of those whom we have about us, namely, our beloved sons, Bernard, cardinal priest of St. Clement's, and Roland, cardinal priest of St. Mark's and our chancellor, men very notable for piety and wisdom and honor. We very earnestly beseech Your Excellency that you receive them with as much respect as kindness, treat them with all honor, and that whatever they themselves set forth before Your Imperial Dignity on our behalf concerning this and concerning other matters of the honor of God and of the Holy Roman Church, and pertaining also to the glory and exaltation of the empire, you accept without any hesitation as though proceeding from our mouth. Give credence to their words, as if we were uttering them." [September 20, 1157.]

When this letter had been read and carefully set forth by Chancellor Rainald in a faithful interpretation, the princes who were present were moved to great indignation, because the entire content of the letter appeared to have no little sharpness and to offer even at the very outset an occasion for future trouble. But what had particularly aroused them all was the fact that in the aforesaid letter it had been stated, among other things, that the fullness of dignity and honor had been bestowed upon the emperor by the Roman pontiff, that the emperor had received from his hand the imperial crown, and that he would not have regretted conferring even greater benefits (*beneficia*) upon him, in consideration of the great gain and advantage that might through him accrue to the Roman Church. And the hearers were led to accept the literal meaning of these words and to put credence in the aforesaid explanation because they knew that the assertion was rashly made by some Romans that hitherto our kings had possessed the imperial power over the City, and the kingdom of Italy, by gift of the popes, and that they made such representations and handed them down to posterity not only orally but also in writing and in pictures. Hence it is written concerning Emperor Lothar, over a picture of this sort in the Lateran palace:

> Coming before our gates, the king vows to safeguard the City,
> Then, liegeman to the Pope, by him he is granted the crown.

Since such a picture and such an inscription, reported to him by those faithful to the empire, had greatly displeased the prince when he had been near the City in a previous year [1155], he is said to have received from Pope Hadrian, after a friendly remonstrance, the assurance that both the inscription and the picture would be removed, lest so trifling a matter might afford the greatest men in the world an occasion for dispute and discord.

When all these matters were fully considered, and a great tumult and uproar arose from the princes of the realm at so insolent a message, it is said that one of the ambassadors, as though adding sword to flame, inquired: "From whom then does he have the empire, if not from our lord the pope?" Because of this remark, anger reached such a pitch that one of them, namely, Otto, count palatine of Bavaria (it was said), threatened the ambassador with his sword. But Frederick, using his authority to quell the tumult, commanded that the ambassadors, being granted safe-conduct, be led to their quarters and that early in the morning they should set forth on their way; he ordered also that they were not to pause in the territories of the bishops and abbots, but to return to the City by the direct road, turning neither to the right nor to the left.

Rahewin continued his chronicle with an account of the aftermath of the Besançon affair.

And so [the legates] returned without having accomplished their purpose, and what had been done by the emperor was published throughout the realm in the following letter [October, 1157]:

"Whereas the Divine Sovereignty, from which is derived all power in heaven and on earth, has entrusted unto us, His anointed, the kingdom and the empire to rule over, and has ordained that the peace of the churches is to be maintained by the imperial arms, not without the greatest distress of heart are we compelled to complain to Your Benevolence that from the head of the Holy Church, on which Christ has set the imprint of his peace and love, there seem to be emanating causes of dissensions and evils, like a poison, by which, unless God avert it, we fear the body of the Church will be stained, its unity shattered, and a schism created between the temporal and spiritual realms.

"For when we were recently at the diet in Besançon and were dealing with the honor of the empire and the security of the Church with all due solicitude, apostolic legates arrived asserting that they bore to Our Majesty such tidings that the honor of the empire should receive no small increase. After we had honorably received them on the first day of their arrival, and on the second, as is customary, had seated

Otto of Freising and his continuator, Rahewin, *The Deeds of Frederick Barbarossa*, C. C. Mierow, trans. (New York: Columbia University Press, 1953), pp. 184–186, 190–194, 199–200; Copyright 1953 Columbia University Press; reprinted by permission of the publisher.

ourself with our princes to hear their tidings, they, as though inspired by the Mammon of unrighteousness, by lofty pride, by arrogant disdain, by execrable haughtiness, presented a message in the form of a letter from the pope, the content of which was to the effect that we ought always to remember the fact that the lord pope had bestowed upon us the imperial crown and would not even regret it if Our Excellency had received greater benefits (*beneficia*) from him.

"This was the messsage of fatherly kindness, which was to foster the unity of Church and empire, which was to bind them together in the bonds of peace, which was to bring the hearts of its hearers to harmony with both and obedience to both! Certain it is that at that impious message, devoid of all truth, not only did Our Imperial Majesty conceive a righteous indignation, but all the princes who were present were filled with so great fury and wrath that they would undoubtedly have condemned those two wicked priests to death, had not our presence averted this.

"Moreover, because many copies of this letter were found in their possession, and blank parchments with seals affixed that were still to be written on at their discretion, whereby—as has been their practice hitherto—they were endeavoring to scatter the venom of their iniquity throughout the churches of the Teutonic realm, to denude the altars, to carry off the vessels of the house of God, to strip crosses of their coverings, we obliged them to return to the City by the way they had come, lest an opportunity be afforded them of proceeding further.

"And since, through election by the princes, the kingdom and the empire are ours from God alone, Who at the time of the passion of His Son Christ subjected the world to dominion by the two swords, and since the apostle Peter taught the world this doctrine: 'Fear God, honor the king,' whosoever says that we received the imperial crown as a benefice (*pro beneficio*) from the lord pope contradicts the divine ordinance and the doctrine of Peter and is guilty of a lie. But because we have hitherto striven to snatch from the hand of the Egyptians the honor and freedom of the churches, so long oppressed by the yoke of undeserved slavery, and are intent on preserving to them all their rights and dignities, we ask Your University to grieve at so great an insult to us and to the empire, hoping that your unwavering loyalty will not permit the honor of the empire, which has stood, glorious and undiminished, from the founding of the City and the establishment of the Christian religion even down to your days, to be disparaged by so unheard-of a novelty, such presumptuous arrogance, knowing that— all ambiguity aside—we would prefer to encounter the risk of death rather than to endure in our time the reproach of so great a disorder." . . . The following is a copy of a letter sent by the supreme pontiff to the archbishops and bishops concerning these matters:

"As often as any attempt is made in the Church directed against the honor of God and the welfare of the faithful, the solicitude of our brothers and fellow bishops, and of those in particular who are led by the spirit of God, must be aroused, that matters which have been wrongly done may receive the correction that is pleasing to God.

"Now at this time, a matter of which we cannot speak without the deepest sorrow, our very dear son Frederick, emperor of the Romans, has done such a thing as we do not know to have been done in the times of our predecessors. For when we had sent to his presence two of our very good brothers, Bernard, of the title of St. Clement, and Roland, our chancellor, of the title of St. Mark, cardinal priests, he seems to have received them gladly when first they came into his presence. But on the following day, when they returned to him and our letter was read in his hearing, taking umbrage at a certain expression therein employed, namely, 'we have bestowed upon you the benefice (*beneficium*) of the imperial crown,' he blazed forth with such great anger that it was disgraceful to hear and would be painful to repeat the insults that he is said to have hurled at us and our legates, and to recall in how humiliating a fashion he obliged them to retire from his presence and with all speed from his land. And as they departed from his presence, he issued an edict that no one from your realm should approach the apostolic see, and is said to have set guards throughout all the bounds of that same realm who should forcibly detain those who desired to come to the apostolic see.

"Although we are somewhat disturbed by this act, yet at heart we draw very great consolation from the fact that he did not do this on your advice and that of the princes. Hence we are confident that by your counsel and persuasion his wrath may easily be calmed.

"Wherefore, brethren, inasmuch as your own interests, and those of all the churches—not our interest only—are clearly at stake in this matter, we admonish and exhort Your Love in the Lord to interpose yourselves as a wall before the house of the Lord, and strive to lead back our aforesaid son to the right way as soon as possible. See especially that he cause his chancellor Rainald and the count palatine, who had the presumption to spew forth great blasphemies against our aforesaid legates and your very holy mother, the Roman Church, to offer such apology and to do it so openly that, as the bitterness of their speech has offended the ears of many, so also their apology may tend to recall many to the right way. . . ."

Upon the receipt of this letter and an embassy to the same purport, the bishops of Germany took counsel and replied to the apostolic see in the following words:

"Although we know and are sure that neither wind nor storm can overthrow the Church of God, founded upon a firm rock, yet we, being weak and faint-hearted, are shaken and tremble whenever blows of this kind befall. Hence we are, of course, gravely disturbed and alarmed at these developments which seem likely to prove—unless God avert it—the source of great evil between Your Holiness and your most devoted son, our lord, the emperor. Indeed, in consequence of those words which were contained in your letter, which you sent by your messengers, those most prudent and honorable men, the Lord Bernard and the Lord Roland, the chancellor, venerable cardinal priests, our whole empire has been thrown into confusion. Neither the ears of the emperor nor those of the princes could endure to hear them. All have so stopped their ears that—saving Your Holiness' grace—we dare not and cannot uphold or approve in any way those words, by reason of their unfortunate ambiguity of meaning, because they were hitherto unknown and unheard of. We received and welcomed, however, with due reverence your letter, and have advised your son, our lord the emperor, as you ordered, and—thanks be to God!—have received from him the following reply, worthy of a Catholic prince, namely:

"'There are two things by which our realm should be governed, the sacred laws of the emperors, and the good customs of our predecessors and our fathers. The limits set by them on the Church we do not wish to overstep, nor can we; whatever is not in accord with them, we reject. We gladly accord to our father the reverence that is his due. The free crown of empire we ascribe solely to the divine beneficence (*beneficium*). We recognize first in the election the vote of the archbishop of Mainz, then those of the other princes, according of their rank; the anointing as king we recognize as the prerogative of the archbishop of Cologne; the final anointing, as emperor, indeed pertains to the supreme pontiff. "Whatsoever is more than these cometh of evil."

"'It is not to show disrespect for our most beloved and reverend father and consecrator that we obliged the cardinals to depart from our land. But we did not wish to permit them to proceed further, to the disgrace and shame of our empire, with their letters, written or blank. We have not closed the way in and out of Italy by edict, nor do we wish in any way to close it to those going to the Roman see as pilgrims or on their own necessary business, in reasonable fashion, with testimonials from their bishops and prelates. But we intend to resist those abuses by which all the churches of our realm have been burdened and weakened, and almost all the discipline of the cloisters killed and buried. In the chief city of the world God has, through the power of the empire, exalted the Church; in the chief city of the world the Church, not through the power of God, we believe, is now destroying the empire. It began with a picture, the picture became an inscription, the inscription seeks to become an authoritative utterance. We shall not endure it, we shall not submit to it; we shall lay down the crown before we consent to have the imperial crown and ourself thus degraded. Let the pictures be destroyed, let the inscriptions be withdrawn, that they may not remain as eternal memorials of enmity between the empire and the papacy.'

"These and other matters—for instance, concerning the agreement between the Ro[mans] and W[illiam] of Sicily, and other pacts made in Italy—which we do not venture to recount in detail, we heard from the lips of our lord the emperor. In the absence of the count palatine, who has already been sent ahead to make preparations for the expedition into Italy, we have heard nothing from the chancellor, who is still present here, save that he was of meek and peaceful bearing, except when he defended the ambassadors with all his might when their lives were threatened by those present, as everyone there could attest.

"As for the rest, we humbly ask and beseech Your Sanctity to pardon our weakness and, like a good shepherd, calm the high spirits of your son with a letter more conciliatory than that former one, that the Church of God may rejoice in tranquil devotion and that the empire may glory in its sublimity, with the mediation and aid of the 'Mediator between God and man, the man Christ Jesus.'"

• • •

Meanwhile the Roman bishop, being informed of the coming of the prince—for his legates, the above-mentioned Chancellor Rainald and Count Palatine Otto, had entered Italy long before—now changed his attitude for the better and sent ambassadors to calm Frederick's spirit, namely, Henry, cardinal priest of the title of Saints Nereus and Achilles, and Hyacinth, cardinal deacon of St. Mary-in-the-Greek-School, men of prudence in secular matters, and much better qualified for dealing with affairs of state than those previously sent.

• • •

They then produced a letter which was given to the venerable Bishop Otto of Freising to read and to interpret—a man who felt a peculiar grief at the controversy between the state and the Church. This is a copy of the letter:

"Since we assumed the care of the Church Universal by God's will and pleasure, we have been careful to do honor to Your Magnificence in all matters, that your love of us and veneration for the apostolic see might daily increase. When we heard that your feelings had been roused against us by certain people, we sent to you, to ascertain your will, two of our best and most distinguished brothers, the Cardinal Priest R[oland], the chancellor, of the title of St. Mark, and B[ernard], of the title of St. Clement, who had always been solicitous in the Roman Church for the honor of Your Majesty. Hence we learned with great astonishment that they were treated otherwise than behooved the imperial dignity. For your heart was stirred to anger, it is said, by the use of a certain word, namely *beneficium*. Yet this should not have vexed the heart of even one in lowly station, to say nothing of so great a man. For although this word *beneficium* is by some interpreted in a different significance than it has by derivation, it should nevertheless have been understood in the meaning which we ourselves put upon it, and which it is known to have possessed from the beginning. For this word is formed of *bonus* (good) and *factum* (deed), and among us *beneficium* means not a fief but a good deed. In this sense it is found in the entire body of Holy Scripture, wherein we are said to be ruled and supported *ex beneficio Dei,* not as by a fief *(feudum)* but as by His benediction and His 'good deed' *(bono facto).* And indeed Your Highness clearly recognizes that we placed the emblem of imperial dignity upon your head in so good and honorable a fashion that it merits recognition by all as a good deed. Hence when certain people have tried to twist that word and the following formula, namely, 'we have conferred upon you the imperial crown,' from its own proper meaning to another, they have done this not on the merits of the case, but of their own desire and at the instigation of those who by no means love the concord of Church and state. For by 'we have conferred' *(contulimus)* we meant nothing else than when we said before 'we have placed' *(imposuimus).* As for the report that you afterward ordered the turning back of ecclesiastical persons on due visitation to the sacrosanct Roman Church, if it be so, we believe that Your Discretion, O very dear son in Christ, must realize how unseemly an act that was. For if you harbored any bitterness toward us, it should have been intimated to us by your envoys and letters, and we would have taken care to safeguard your honor, as that of our very dear son. Now therefore, as we have, at the advice of our beloved son H[enry], duke of Bavaria and Saxony, sent into your presence two of our brothers, Henry, cardinal priest of the title of Saints Nereus and Achilles, and Hyacinth, cardinal deacon of St. Mary in Cosmedin, truly wise and estimable men, we urge and exhort Your Highness in the Lord that you receive them with honor and kindness. Know also that what is imparted to Your Magnificence by them on our behalf has proceeded from the sincerity of our heart. And therefore may Your Highness so strive to reach an agreement with these our sons, through the mediation of our aforesaid son, the duke, that there may remain no seed of discord between you and your mother, the Holy Roman Church."

When the letter had been read and set forth with favorable interpretation, the emperor was mollified, and becoming more gracious he indicated to the legates certain specific matters to be considered later which might lead to dispute unless properly corrected. When to this they made answer agreeable to the prince and in all respects satisfactory, and promised that the bishop of Rome would do nothing derogatory to the royal dignity, but would always preserve inviolate the honor and the just claims of empire, he guaranteed peace and friendship both to the supreme pontiff and to all the Roman clergy, and certified it for the absent by giving them also, through those who were present, a kiss in token of peace. So the ambassadors were gladdened and enriched with royal gifts, and set forth for the City.

57.   Canonistic Views on Imperial and Papal Power

By the end of the twelfth century the right relationship between papal and imperial power had become a subject of warm debate among the canonists of Bologna. Two opposing points of view were put forward by the eminent jurists Huguccio and Alanus. Both were commenting on Distinctio *96 c.6 of* Gratian's Decretum, *the most widely used canon law collection of the twelfth century.*

HUGUCCIO

After the coming of the Truth.   Up until the coming of Christ the imperial and pontifical rights were not separated, for the same man was emperor and pontiff, as at *Dist.* 21 c.1. But the offices and rights of the emperor and the pontiff were separated by Christ and some things, namely temporal affairs, were assigned to the emperor, others, namely spiritual affairs, to the pontiff, and this was done for the sake of preserving humility and avoiding pride. If the emperor or the pontiff held all offices he would easily grow proud but now since each needs the other and sees that he is not fully self-sufficient he is made humble. . . . Here it can clearly be gathered that each power, the apostolic and imperial, was instituted by God and that neither is derived from the other and that the emperor does not have the sword from the apostle. The argument is stated here and below in the same Distinction at c.8, c.10, c.11 and also at *Dist.* 93 c.24 and at C.3 q.4 c.45.

There is a contrary argument at *Dist.* 22 c.1, *Dist.* 63 c.33, *Dist.* 63 c.23, c.15 q.6 c.3. . . . All these contrary arguments seem to imply that the emperor receives the power of the sword and the imperial authority from the apostle and that the pope makes him emperor and can depose him. I believe however, that the emperor has the power of the sword and the imperial dignity from election by the princes and people, as at *Dist.* 93 c.24, for there was an emperor before there was a pope, an empire before a papacy. Again the words, "Behold, here are two swords" (Luke 22:38), were spoken to symbolize the fact that the two powers, namely the apostolic and imperial, are distinct and separate. If, therefore, it is anywhere stated or implied that the emperor has the power of the sword from the pope, I understand it as meaning the unction and confirmation which he has from the pope when he swears fidelity to him; for before this, although he is not called emperor, he is an emperor as regards dignity though not as regards unction, and before this he has the power of the sword and exercises it. When it is said that the pope can depose him I believe this to be true, but by the will and consent of the princes if he is convicted before them. Then I take it, in the last resort, if he has been convicted and admonished and will not desist or give satisfaction, he should be excommunicated and all should be removed from fealty to him as argued at C.15 q.6 c.4,5. If still he is not corrected then finally he is justly smitten with a sentence and rightly expelled by armed force, and another legitimately elected. But by whom is the sentence pronounced? By the lord pope before whom he was convicted or by his princes if the Roman pontiff has approved this.

ALANUS

This indeed is certain according to everyone, that the pope has jurisdiction over the emperor in spiritual matters so that he can bind and loose him . . . but, according to Huguccio, by no means in temporal matters though the pope can judge him in temporal matters and depose him by the wish of the princes who elect him according to customary law. According to Huguccio the emperor has the sword from God alone and not from the pope except as regards coronation and confirmation, and he has full imperial jurisdiction beforehand although he is not called emperor.

But in truth, and according to the Catholic faith, he is subject to the pope in spiritual matters and also receives his sword from him, for the right of both swords belongs to the pope. This is proved by the fact that the Lord had both swords on earth and used both as is mentioned here, and he established Peter as his vicar on earth and all Peter's successors. Therefore today Innocent has by right the material sword. If you deny this you are saying that Christ established a secular prince as his vicar in this regard. Again Peter said to the Lord, "Behold, here are two swords" (Luke 22:38), so the material sword too was with Peter. Again if the emperor was not subject to the pope in temporalities he could not sin against the church in temporalities. Again the church is one body and so it shall have only one head or it will be a monster.

This opinion is not invalidated by the fact that there were emperors before there were popes, because they were only *de facto* emperors and none except those who believed in the true God had a right to the sword; nor do infidel rulers have it nowadays. Likewise it is not invalidated by the fact that Constantine conferred temporal jurisdiction on Sylvester as is said at *Dist.* 63 c.30. [In a reference to the Donation of Constantine at *Dist.* 63 c.30 Alanus commented, "From his plenitude of right the pope could take away the City and other possessions even if the emperor was unwilling."]

The emperor then has the sword from the pope. The electors indeed confer it on him, not the pope, but every bishop has his bishopric from the pope and yet the pope does not confer it but rather canonical election of the clergy does. The pope therefore is the ordinary judge of the emperor in both temporal and spiritual affairs and can depose him, as at C.15 q.6 c.3. But can he depose him for any crime? I answer, rather for none, unless he is determined to persist in it, and even then perhaps not for any offence but only for those which harm the people, as for instance the continued discord of heresy. But could the pope keep the material sword for himself if he wished? I answer no, because the Lord divided the swords as is said here, and the church would be gravely disturbed by this.

What has been said of the emperor may be held true of any prince who has no superior lord. Each one has as much jurisdiction in his kingdom as the emperor has in the empire, for the division of kingdoms that has been introduced nowadays by the law of nations is approved by the pope although the ancient law of nations held that there should be one emperor in the world.

Huguccio and Alanus also discussed the possibility of deposing a pope who fell into heresy in their commentaries on Distinctio 40 c.6 *of the* Decretum.

HUGUCCIO

Behold, a pope can be condemned for heresy by his subjects! *Dist.* 21 c.7 above states the contrary. There it is said that Marcellinus was guilty of heresy but none the less his subjects did not condemn him. Some say that they did not wish to do so, but I say that they could not and should not have condemned him because he freely and humbly confessed his error, for the pope can be condemned for heresy only in the last resort when he contumaciously and persistently resists and strives to defend and uphold his error. . . . But behold, a pope invents a new heresy; some one wishes to prove that it is a heresy; the pope says it is not a heresy but the Catholic faith; is the proof against him to be accepted? I believe not. Again, he secretly adheres to a heresy already condemned. Some persons, however, know of this and wish to prove that the pope follows such a heresy. But he denies it. Ought they to be heard? I believe not; for the pope can be accused of heresy only in the last resort when there is agreement concerning the fact of heresy and the pope does not deny the fact and, being admonished, refuses to come to his senses but contumaciously defends his error. . . .

Can the pope be accused of simony or any other crime? Some say no, whether it is notorious or not, because we ought not to stipulate what the canon does not stipulate. They say that the reason for the difference—why he can be accused of heresy more readily than of any other crime—is that if a pope were a heretic he would not harm only himself but the whole world, especially since the simple and foolish would easily accept that heresy, not believing it to be a heresy. But if the pope commits simony or fornication or theft or anything of the sort he seems to harm only himself, for everyone knows that no one is permitted to steal or commit fornication or simony or anything of the sort. But I believe that it is the same in any notorious crime, that the pope can be accused and condemned if, being admonished, he is not willing to desist. What then? Behold, he steals publicly, he fornicates publicly, he keeps a concubine publicly, he has intercourse with her publicly in the church, near the altar or on it, and being admonished will not desist. Shall he not be accused? Shall he not be condemned? Is it not like heresy to scandalize the church in such a fashion? Moreover contumacy is the crime of idolatry and like to heresy, as at *Dist.* 91 c.9, whence a contumacious person is called an infidel as at *Dist.* 38 c.16. and so it is the same with any notorious crime as with heresy.

ALANUS

If he was a public usurer might he not be accused? He can be accused of any notorious crime according to some who accept "to sin in faith" in a broad sense as meaning to sin against the teaching of the faith, just as anyone committing mortal sin is said to deny Christ, as at C.11 q.3 c.83. But, according to this view, the privilege of the pope would amount to nothing. Therefore it is to be said that, since he has no superior judge, he cannot be judged against his will except for the crime of heresy, in which case it was so decreed because of the enormity of the crime and the common danger to the church. But can anyone lay down a law for the pope, when the pope is not bound by the canons and can change them? Perhaps it is so in the case of that crime because there, as a consequence of it, a question arises whether he really is pope; for it seems that if he is a heretic he is not the head of the church. If he is suspected of any other crime and some one wishes to accuse him, lest he bring scandal on the church, although he cannot be compelled, nevertheless, having been admonished, he ought to select a judge and go to trial under him, for although he is not bound by the laws nevertheless he ought to live according to them.

THE THIRTEENTH CENTURY

chapter
XVIII

The Zenith of Papal Power

58. Letters of Innocent III

The medieval papacy reached a zenith of power during the pontificate of Innocent III (1198–1216). The following excerpts from Innocent's letters illustrate his claims in the temporal sphere.

To the Nobles of Tuscany (1198)

Just as the founder of the universe established two great lights in the firmament of heaven, a greater one to preside over the day and a lesser to preside over the night, so too in the firmament of the universal church, which is signified by the word heaven, he instituted two great dignities, a greater one to preside over souls as if over day and a lesser one to preside over bodies as if over night. These are the pontifical authority and the royal power. Now just as the moon derives its light from the sun and is indeed lower than it in quantity and quality, in position and in power, so too the royal power derives the splendor of its dignity from the pontifical authority. . . .

To the Eastern Emperor Alexius (1201)

. . . To us in the person of blessed Peter the flock of Christ was committed when the Lord said, "Feed my sheep" (John 21:17), not making any distinction between these sheep and those in order to show that

From "Letters of Innocent III," in Brian Tierney, *The Crisis of Church and State, 1050–1300*, with selected documents, © 1964 (Englewood Cliffs, N.J.: Prentice-Hall, 1964), pp. 132–136. Reprinted by permission of Prentice-Hall, Inc., Englewood Cliffs, New Jersey.

anyone who fails to acknowledge Peter and his successors as pastors and teachers is outside his flock. We need hardly mention, since they are so well known, the words that Christ spoke to Peter and through Peter to his successors, "Whatsoever you bind upon earth, etc." (Matthew 16:19), excepting nothing when he said, "Whatsoever."

To the Princes of Germany (1202)

. . . We indeed by virtue of our office of apostolic service, owe justice to each man and, just as we do not want our justice to be usurped by others, so too we do not want to claim for ourselves the rights of the princes. We do indeed acknowledge, as we should, that the princes, to whom this belongs by right and ancient custom, have the right and power to elect a king who is afterwards to be promoted emperor; and especially so since this right and power came to them from the apostolic see which transferred the Roman empire from the Greeks to the Germans in the person of the great Charles. But the princes should acknowledge, and indeed they do acknowledge, that right and authority to examine the person elected as king, who is to be promoted to the imperial dignity, belong to us who anoint, consecrate and crown him; for it is regularly and generally observed that the examination of a person pertains to the one to whom the laying-on of hands belongs. If the princes elected as king a sacrilegious man or an excommunicate, a tyrant, a fool or a heretic, and that not just by a divided vote but unanimously, ought we to anoint, consecrate and crown such a man? Of course not. Therefore, replying to the objection of the princes, we maintain that our legate the bishop of Palestrina, our dearly beloved brother in Christ, did not act as either an elector . . . or as a judge when he approved King Otto and rejected Duke Philip. And so he in no way usurped the right of the princes or acted against it. Rather he exercised the office of one who declared that the king was personally worthy and the duke personally unworthy to obtain the imperial dignity, not considering so much the zeal of the electors as the merits of those elected. . . .

It is clear from law and precedent that, if the votes of the princes are divided in an election, we can favor one of the parties after due warning and a reasonable delay, especially after the unction, consecration and coronation are demanded of us, for it has often happened that both parties demanded them. For if the princes after due warning and delay cannot or will not agree, shall the apostolic see then lack an advocate and defender and be penalized for their fault? . . .

To the Bishops of France (1204)

. . . Let no one suppose that we wish to diminish or disturb the jurisdiction and power of the king when he ought not to impede or restrict our jurisdiction and power. Since we are insufficient to exercise all our own jurisdiction why should we want to usurp another's? But the Lord says in the Gospel, "If thy brother shall offend against thee, go, and rebuke him between thee and him alone. If he shall hear thee thou shalt gain thy brother. And if he will not hear thee, take with thee one or two more, that in the mouth of two or three witnesses every word may stand. And if he will not hear them, tell the church. And if he will not hear the church let him be to thee as the heathen and the publican" (Matthew 18:15); and the king of England is ready, so he asserts, to prove fully that the king of the French is offending against him and that he has proceeded according to the evangelical rule in rebuking him and, having achieved nothing, is at last telling it to the church. How then can we, who have been called to the rule of the universal church by divine providence, obey the divine command if we do not proceed as it lays down, unless perhaps [King Philip] shows sufficient reason to the contrary before us or our legate. For we do not intend to judge concerning a fief, judgement on which belongs to him — except when some special privilege or contrary custom detracts from the common law — but to decide concerning a sin, of which the judgement undoubtedly belongs to us, and we can and should exercise it against any-one. . . .

The emperor Theodosius decreed and Charles, ancestor of the present king, confirmed that "If anyone has a legal case . . . and chooses to take it before the bishop of the most holy see, without question and even if the other party objects, he is to be sent to the bishop's court with the statements of the litigants." This, however, we pass over in humility for we do not rely on human statutes but on divine law since our power is not from man but from God.

No man of sound mind is unaware that it pertains to our office to rebuke any Christian for any mortal sin and to coerce him with ecclesiastical penalties if he spurns our correction. That we can and should rebuke is evident from the pages of both the Old and New Testaments. . . . That we can and should coerce is evident from what the Lord said to the prophet who was among the priests of Anathoth, "Lo I have set thee over nations, and over kingdoms to root up and to pull down and to waste, and to destroy, and to build, and to plant" (Jeremias 1:10). No one doubts that all mortal sin must be rooted up and destroyed and pulled down. Moreover, when the Lord gave the keys of the kingdom of heaven to blessed Peter, he said, "Whatsoever thou shalt bind upon earth, it shall be bound also in heaven: and whatsoever thou shalt loose on earth it shall be loosed also in heaven" (Matthew 16:19). . . . But it may be said that kings are to be treated differently from others. We, however, know that it is written in divine law, "You shall judge the great as well as the little and there shall be no difference of persons" (*cf.* Deuteronomy 1:17). . . . Although we are empowered to proceed in this fashion against any criminal sin in order to recall the sinner from error to truth and from vice to virtue, this is especially so when it is a sin against peace, peace which is the bond of love. . . . Finally, when a treaty of peace was made between the kings and confirmed on both sides by oaths which, however, were not kept for the agreed period, can we not take cognizance of such a sworn oath, which certainly belongs to the judgement of the church, in order to re-establish the broken treaty of peace? . . .

To King John of England (1214)

The king of kings and lord of lords, Jesus Christ, a priest for ever after the order of Melchisedech, has so established the priesthood and kingship in the church that the kingship is priestly and the priesthood is royal, as Peter in his Epistle and Moses in the Law bear witness, and he has set over all one whom he appointed to be his vicar on earth so that, just as every knee on earth and in heaven and even under the earth is bowed to him, so all should obey his vicar and strive that there be one fold and one shepherd. The kings of the world so venerate this vicar for the sake of God that they do not regard themselves as reigning properly unless they take care to serve him devotedly. Prudently heeding this, beloved son, and mercifully inspired by him in whose hand are the hearts of kings and who sway them as he wishes, you have decreed that your person and your kingdom should be temporally subject to the one to whom you knew them to be spiritually subject, so that kingship and priesthood, like body and soul, should be united in the one person of the vicar of Christ to the great advantage and profit of both. He has deigned to bring this about who, being alpha and omega, related the end to the beginning and revealed the beginning in the end, so that those provinces which formerly had the holy Roman church as their proper teacher in spiritual matters now have her as their special lord in temporal affairs also. . . .

59.   The Fourth Lateran Council

Among Innocent's greatest achievements was his work for church reform at the Fourth Lateran Council (1215). The council promulgated a new statement of Christian faith directed against contemporary heresies and enacted a substantial body of reform legislation.

Innocent's Letter of Summons

To the archbishop, bishops, abbots, and priors of the province of Vienne:

From J. P. Migne, *Patrologia Latina*, CCXVI, cols. 823–825, translated by Brian Tierney, in Brian Tierney, Donald Kagan, and L. Pearce Williams, eds., *Great Issues in Western Civilization* (New York: Random House, 1967), Vol I, pp. 446–447; reprinted by permission of the publisher.

Many kinds of beasts strive to ruin the vineyard of the Lord and their attacks have so prevailed that in no small part of it thorns have grown up in place of vines. Furthermore — we state it with grief — the vines themselves, infected and corrupted in many ways, may bring forth bad fruit. We therefore invoke the witness of Him who is a faithful witness in Heaven that among all the desires of our heart there are two that we principally wish for in this world, that we may be able to bring about the recovery of the Holy Land and the reform of the universal church. . . . Accordingly, having held diligent and frequent consultations with our brothers and other prudent men, as the responsibility of such a great undertaking demanded, we have finally decided with their counsel that, in order to achieve these things and because they concern the common state of all the faithful, we shall convoke a general council to be celebrated solely for the profit of souls at an opportune time according to the ancient custom of the holy Fathers; in which council, to extirpate vice and implant virtues, to correct excesses and reform morals, to eliminate heresies and strengthen the faith . . . there may be established, to be inviolably observed by prelates and subjects both regular and secular, whatsoever shall be seen by the approval of the council to be expedient for the praise and glory of His name who is the healer and savior of our souls and for the profit and advantage of the Christian people. . . .

Believing then that this healthful intention comes from Him from Whom is every good gift and every perfect gift, we command you all by these apostolic letters to so prepare that in two and a half years from this twelve hundred and thirteenth year from the Incarnation of our Lord you may present yourselves in our sight. . . . Furthermore, O brother archbishops and bishops, you shall charge all chapters of churches, not only cathedral churches but others as well, to send provosts or deans or other suitable men to the council on their behalf, since various matters that especially concern the chapters of churches are to be treated in it. . . . No one shall plead as an excuse difficulties of the journey or obstacles of strife, which for the most part is beginning to cease (a good sign from God). The greater the dangers that threaten the stronger the remedies that should be applied. No one ever sailed through calm waters who always waited for the sea to stop throwing up waves.

[Similar letters were sent to prelates throughout Europe—B.T.]

Decrees of the Council

Canon I

Text. We firmly believe and openly confess that there is only

From *The Disciplinary Decrees of the General Council,* translated by H. J. Schroeder (St. Louis: B. Herder Book Co., 1937), pp. 237-239, 242-243, 246-247, 252-253, 256-260, 262, 267-268, 274; reprinted by permission of the publisher.

one true God, eternal and immense, omnipotent, unchangeable, incomprehensible, and ineffable, Father, Son, and Holy Ghost; three Persons indeed but one essense, substance, or nature absolutely simple; the Father (proceeding) from no one, but the Son from the Father only, and the Holy Ghost equally from both, always without beginning and end. The Father begetting, the Son begotten, and the Holy Ghost proceeding; consubstantial and coequal, co-omnipotent and coeternal, the one principle of the universe, Creator of all things invisible and visible, spiritual and corporeal, who from the beginning of time and by His omnipotent power made from nothing creatures both spiritual and corporeal, angelic, namely, and mundane, and then human, as it were, common, composed of spirit and body. The devil and the other demons were indeed created by God good by nature but they became bad through themselves; man, however, sinned at the suggestion of the devil. This Holy Trinity in its common essense undivided and in personal properties divided, through Moses, the holy prophets, and other servants gave to the human race at the most opportune intervals of time the doctrine of salvation.

And finally, Jesus Christ, the only begotten Son of God made flesh by the entire Trinity, conceived with the co-operation of the Holy Ghost of Mary ever Virgin, made true man, composed of a rational soul and human flesh, one Person in two natures, pointed out more clearly the way of life. Who according to His divinity is immortal and impassable, according to His humanity was made passable and mortal, suffered on the cross for the salvation of the human race, and being dead descended into hell, rose from the dead, and ascended into heaven. But He descended in soul, arose in flesh, and ascended equally in both; He will come at the end of the world to judge the living and the dead and will render to the reprobate and to the elect according to their works. Who all shall rise with their own bodies which they now have that they may receive according to their merits, whether good or bad, the latter eternal punishment with the devil, the former eternal glory with Christ.

There is one Universal Church of the faithful, outside of which there is absolutely no salvation. In which there is the same priest and sacrifice, Jesus Christ, whose body and blood are truly contained in the sacrament of the altar under the forms of bread and wine; the bread being changed *(transsubstantiatis)* by divine power into the body, and the wine into the blood, so that to realize the mystery of unity we may receive of Him what He has received of us. And this sacrament no one can effect except the priest who has been duly ordained in accordance with the keys of the Church, which Jesus Christ Himself gave to the Apostles and their successors.

But the sacrament of baptism, which by the invocation of each Person of the Trinity, namely of the Father, Son, and Holy Ghost, is effected in water, duly conferred on children and adults in the form prescribed by the Church by anyone whatsoever, leads to salvation. And should anyone after the reception of baptism have fallen into sin, by true repentance he can always be restored. Not only virgins and those practicing chastity, but also those united in marriage, through the right faith and through works pleasing to God, can merit eternal salvation.

Canon 3

Text. We excommunicate and anathematize every heresy that raises against the holy, orthodox and Catholic faith which we have above explained; condemning all heretics under whatever names they may be known, for while they have different faces, they are nevertheless bound to each other by their tails, since in all of them vanity is a common element. Those condemned, being handed over to the secular rulers or their bailiffs, let them be abandoned, to be punished with due justice, clerics being first degraded from their orders. As to the property of the condemned, if they are laymen, let it be confiscated; if clerics, let it be applied to the churches from which they received revenues. But those who are only suspected, due consideration being given to the nature of the suspicion and the character of the person, unless they prove their innocence by a proper defense, let them be anathematized and avoided by all until they have made suitable satisfaction; but if they have been under excommunication for one year, then let them be condemned as heretics. Secular authorities, whatever office they may hold, shall be admonished and induced and if necessary compelled by ecclesiastical censure, that as they wish to be esteemed and numbered among the faithful, so for the defense of the faith they ought publicly to take an oath that they will strive in good faith and to the best of their ability to exterminate in the territories subject to their jurisdiction all heretics pointed out by the Church; so that whenever anyone shall have assumed authority, whether spiritual or temporal, let him be bound to confirm this decree by oath. But if a temporal ruler, after having been requested and admonished by the Church, should neglect to cleanse his territory of this heretical foulness, let him be excommunicated by the metropolitan and the other bishops of the province. If he refuses to make satisfaction within a year, let the matter be made known to the supreme pontiff, that he may declare the ruler's vassals absolved from their allegiance and may offer the territory to be ruled by Catholics, who on the extermination of the heretics may possess it without hindrance and preserve it in the purity of faith; the right, however, of the chief ruler is to be respected so long as he offers no obstacle in this matter and permits freedom of action. The same law is to be observed in regard to those who have no chief rulers (that is, are independent). Catholics who have girded themselves with the cross for the extermination of the heretics, shall enjoy the indulgences and privileges granted to those who go in defense of the Holy Land. . . .

Canon 6

SUMMARY *Provincial synods for the correction of abuses and the enforcement of canonical enactments must be held annually. To ensure this, reliable persons are to be appointed who will investigate such things as need correction.*

Text.   In accordance with the ancient provisions of the holy Fathers, the metropolitans must not neglect to hold with their suffragans the annual provincial synods. In these they should be actuated with a genuine fear of God in correcting abuses and reforming morals, especially the morals of the clergy, familiarizing themselves anew with the canonical rules, particularly those that are enacted in this general council, that they may enforce their observance by imposing due punishment on transgressors. That this may be done more effectively, let them appoint in each and every diocese prudent and upright persons, who throughout the entire year shall informally and without any jurisdiction diligently investigate such things as need correction or reform and faithfully present them to the metropolitan, suffragans, and others in the following synod, so that they may give prudent consideration to these and other matters as circumstances demand; and in reference to those things that they decree, let them enforce observance, publishing the decisions in the episcopal synods to be held annually in each diocese. Whoever shall neglect to comply with this salutary statute, let him be suspended from his office and benefits till it shall please his superior to restore him.

Canon II

SUMMARY *In every cathedral church and other churches also that have sufficient means, a master is to be appointed to instruct* gratis *the clerics and poor students. The metropolitan church ought to have a theologian who shall teach the clergy whatever pertains to the* cura animarum *(i.e. care of souls).*

Text.   Since there are some who, on account of the lack of necessary means, are unable to acquire an education or to meet opportunities for perfecting themselves, the Third Lateran Council in a salutary decree provided that in every cathedral church a suitable benefice be assigned to a master who shall instruct *gratis* the clerics of that church and other poor students, by means of which benefice the material needs of the master might be relieved and to the students a way opened to knowledge. But, since in many churches this is not observed, we, confirming the aforesaid decree, add that, not only in every cathedral church but also in other churches where means are sufficient, a competent master be appointed by the prelate with his chapter, or elected by the greater and more discerning part of the chapter, who shall instruct *gratis* and to the best of his ability the clerics of those and other churches in the art of grammar and in other branches of knowledge. In addition to a master, let the metropolitan church have also a theologian, who shall instruct the priests and others in the Sacred Scriptures and in those things especially that pertain to the *cura animarum*. To each master let there be assigned by the chapter the revenue of one benefice, and to the theologian let as much be given by the metropolitan; not that they thereby become canons, but they shall enjoy the revenue only so long as they hold the office of instructor. If the metropolitan church cannot support two masters, then it shall provide for the theologian in the aforesaid manner, but for the one teaching grammar, let it see to it that a sufficiency is provided by another church of its city or diocese.

Canon 15

SUMMARY *Clerics, who after being warned do not abstain from drunkenness, shall be suspended from their office and benefice.*

Text. All clerics shall carefully abstain from drunkenness. Wherefore, let them accommodate the wine to themselves, and themselves to the wine. Nor shall anyone be encouraged to drink, for drunkenness banishes reason and incites to lust. We decree, therefore, that that abuse be absolutely abolished by which in some localities the drinkers bind themselves *suo modo* to an equal portion of drink and he in their judgment is the hero of the day who outdrinks the others. Should anyone be culpable in this matter, unless he heeds the warning of the superior and makes suitable satisfaction, let him be suspended from his benefice or office.

We forbid hunting and fowling to all clerics; wherefore, let them not presume to keep dogs and birds for these purposes.

Canon 16

SUMMARY *Clerics are not to engage in secular pursuits, attend unbecoming exhibitions, visit taverns, or play games of chance. Their clothing must be in keeping with their dignity.*

Text. Clerics shall not hold secular offices or engage in secular and, above all, dishonest pursuits. They shall not attend the performances of mimics and buffoons, or theatrical representations. They shall not visit taverns except in case of necessity, namely, when on a journey. They are forbidden to play games of chance or be present at them. They must have a becoming crown and tonsure and apply themselves diligently to the study of the divine offices and other useful subjects. Their garments must be worn clasped at the top and neither too short nor too long. They are not to use red or green garments or curiously sewed together gloves, or beak-shaped shoes or gilded bridles, saddles, pectoral ornaments (for horses), spurs, or anything else indicative of superfluity. At the divine office in the church they are not to wear cappas with long sleeves, and priests and dignitaries may not wear them elsewhere except in case of danger when circumstances should require a change of outer garments. Buckles may under no condition be worn, nor sashes having ornaments of gold or silver, nor rings, unless it be in keeping with the dignity of their office. All bishops must use in public and in the church outer garments made of linen, except those who are monks, in which case they must wear the habit of their order; in public they must not appear with open mantles, but these must be clasped either on the back of the neck or on the bosom.

Canon 18

SUMMARY *Clerics may neither pronounce nor execute a sentence of death. Nor may they act as judges in extreme criminal cases, or take part in matters connected with judicial tests and ordeals.*

Text.   No cleric may pronounce a sentence of death, or execute such a sentence, or be present at its execution. If anyone in consequence of this prohibition (*hujusmodi occasione statuti*) should presume to inflict damage on churches or injury on ecclesiastical persons, let him be restrained by ecclesiastical censure. Nor may any cleric write or dictate letters destined for the execution of such a sentence. Wherefore, in the chanceries of the princes let this matter be committed to laymen and not to clerics. Neither may a cleric act as judge in the case of the Rotarrii, archers, or other men of this kind devoted to the shedding of blood. No subdeacon, deacon, or priest shall practice that part of surgery involving burning and cutting. Neither shall anyone in judicial tests or ordeals by hot or cold water or hot iron bestow any blessing; the earlier prohibitions in regard to dueling remain in force.

Canon 21

SUMMARY *Everyone who has attained the age of reason is bound to confess his sins at least once a year to his own parish priest or with his permission to another, and to receive the Eucharist at least at Easter. A priest who reveals a sin confided to him in confession is to be deposed and relegated to a monastery for the remainder of his life.*

Text.   All the faithful of both sexes shall after they have reached the age of discretion faithfully confess all their sins at least once a year to their own (parish) priest and perform to the best of their ability the penance imposed, receiving reverently at least at Easter the sacrament of the Eucharist, unless perchance at the advice of their own priest they may for a good reason abstain for a time from its reception; otherwise they shall be cut off from the Church (excommunicated) during life and deprived of Christian burial in death. Wherefore, let this salutary decree be published frequently in the churches, that no one may find in the plea of ignorance a shadow of excuse. But if anyone for a good reason should wish to confess his sins to another priest, let him first seek and obtain permission from his own (parish) priest, since otherwise he (the other priest) cannot loose or bind him.

Let the priest be discreet and cautious that he may pour wine and oil into the wounds of the one injured after the manner of a skilful physician, carefully inquiring into the circumstances of the sinner and the sin, from the nature of which he may understand what kind of advice to give and what remedy to apply, making use of different experiments to heal the sick one. But let him exercise the greatest precaution that he does not in any degree by word, sign, or any other manner make known the sinner, but should he need more prudent counsel, let him seek it cautiously without any mention of the person. He who dares to reveal a sin confided to him in the tribunal of penance, we decree that he be not only deposed from the sacerdotal office but also relegated to a monastery of strict observance to do penance for the remainder of his life.

Canon 23

SUMMARY *If those to whom it pertains neglect to elect a bishop for a cathedral within three months, then this duty devolves upon the next immediate superior. If he neglects to do so within three months, he shall be punished.*

Text. That the ravenous wolf may not invade the Lord's flock that is without a pastor, that a widowed church may not suffer grave loss in its properties, that danger to souls may be averted, and that provision may be made for the security of the churches, we decree that a cathedral or regular church must not be without a bishop for more than three months. If within this time an election has not been held by those to whom it pertains, though there was no impediment, the electors lose their right of voting, and the right to appoint devolves upon the next immediate superior. Let the one upon whom this right to appoint devolves, having God before his eyes, not delay more than three months to provide canonically and with the advice of the chapter and other prudent men the widowed church with a suitable pastor, if he wishes to escape canonical punishment. This pastor is to be chosen from the widowed church itself, or from another in case a suitable one is not found therein.

Canon 27

SUMMARY *Incompetent persons must not be promoted to the priesthood or given the direction of souls.*

Text. Since the direction of souls is the art of arts, we strictly command that bishops, either themselves or through other qualified men, diligently prepare and instruct those to be elevated to the priesthood in the divine offices and in the proper administration of the sacraments of the Church. If in the future they presume to ordain ignorant and unformed men (a defect that can easily be discovered), we decree that both those ordaining and those ordained be subject to severe punishment. In the ordination of priests especially, it is better to have a few good ministers than many who are no good, for if the blind lead the blind both will fall into the pit (Matt. 15:14).

Canon 29

SUMMARY *Anyone having a benefice with the* cura animarum *annexed, if he accepts another, shall lose the first; and if he attempts to retain it, he shall lose the other also. After the reception of the second benefice, the first may be freely conferred on another. If he to whom that collation belongs should delay beyond six months, then it shall devolve on another and the former shall indemnify the church for the losses incurred during the vacancy.*

Text. With much foresight it was prohibited in the Lateran Council that no one should, contrary to the sacred canons, accept several ecclesiastical dignities or several parochial churches; otherwise the one receiving should lose what he received, and the one who bestowed be deprived of the right of collation. But since, on account of the boldness and avarice of some, the aforesaid statute has thus far produced little or no fruit, we, wishing to meet the situation more clearly and emphatically, declare in the present decree that whoever shall accept a benefice to which is annexed the *cura animarum* after having previously obtained such a benefice, shall *ipso jure* be deprived of this (the first one); and if perchance he should attempt to retain it, let him be deprived of the other one also. He to whom the collation of the first benefice belongs may freely confer it, after the incumbent has accepted a second, on anyone whom he may deem worthy; should he delay to do so beyond a period of six months, then in accordance with the decree of the Lateran Council, let not only its collation devolve on another, but also let him be compelled to indemnify the church in question from his own resources equal to the amount of the revenues drawn from it during its vacancy. The same we decree is to be observed in regard to dignities (*personatus*), adding, that no one may presume to have several dignities in the same church, even though they have not the *cura animarum* annexed. Only in the case of eminent and learned persons who are to be honored with major benefices, can the Apostolic See, if need be, grant a dispensation.

Canon 42

SUMMARY *No cleric may so extend his jurisdiction as to become detrimental to secular justice.*

Text. As desirous as we are that laymen do not usurp the rights of clerics, we are no less desirous that clerics abstain from arrogating to themselves the rights of laymen. Wherefore we forbid all clerics so to extend in the future their jurisdiction under the pretext of ecclesiastical liberty as to prove detrimental to secular justice; but let them be content with the laws and customs thus far approved, that the things that are Caesar's may be rendered to Caesar, and those that are God's may by a just division be rendered to God.

60.   The Church and the Jews

The centralization of ecclesiastical government in the thirteenth century was accompanied by increased pressures on people outside the church. Several canons of the Fourth Lateran Council imposed restrictive measures on Jews which tended to segregate them from the social life of the Christian community.

Canon 68

In some provinces a difference in dress distinguishes the Jews or Saracens from the Christians, but in certain others such a confusion has grown up that they cannot be distinguished by any difference. Thus it happens at times that through error Christians have relations with the women of Jews or Saracens, and Jews and Saracens with Christian women. Therefore, that they may not, under pretext of error of this sort, excuse themselves in the future for the excesses of such prohibited intercourse, we decree that such Jews and Saracens of both sexes in every Christian province and at all times shall be marked off in the eyes of the public from other peoples through the character of their dress. Particularly, since it may be read in the writings of Moses [Numbers 15:37–41], that this very law has been enjoined upon them.

Moreover, during the last three days before Easter and especially on Good Friday, they shall not go forth in public at all, for the reason that some of them on these very days, as we hear, do not blush to go forth better dressed and are not afraid to mock the Christians who maintain the memory of the most holy Passion by wearing signs of mourning.

This, however, we forbid most severely, that any one should presume at all to break forth in insult to the Redeemer. And since we ought not to ignore any insult to Him who blotted out our disgraceful

From Jacob R. Marcus, *The Jew in the Medieval World* (New York: Atheneum, 1972), pp. 138–139, 152–154. Reprinted through the courtesy of Jewish Publications Society of America.

deeds, we command that such impudent fellows be checked by the secular princes by imposing them proper punishment so that they shall not at all presume to blaspheme Him who was crucified for us.

Although much church legislation concerning the Jews was hostile in tone, the medieval popes would never countenance the charge of ritual murder which often led to fanatical outbursts of anti-Jewish violence. The following letter of Pope Gregory X (1271–1276) incorporates material from earlier letters of Innocent III (1198–1216) and Innocent IV (1243–1254).

Gregory, bishop, servant of the servants of God, extends greetings and the apostolic benediction to the beloved sons in Christ, the faithful Christians, to those here now and to those in the future. Even as it is not allowed to the Jews in their assemblies presumptuously to undertake for themselves more than that which is permitted them by law, even so they ought not to suffer any disadvantage in those [privileges] which have been granted them. Although they prefer to persist in their stubbornness rather than to recognize the words of their prophets and the mysteries of the Scriptures, and thus to arrive at a knowledge of Christian faith and salvation; nevertheless, inasmuch as they have made an appeal for our protection and help, we therefore admit their petition and offer them the shield of our protection through the clemency of Christian piety. In so doing we follow in the footsteps of our predecessors of blessed memory, the popes of Rome—Calixtus, Eugene, Alexander, Clement, Celestine, Innocent, and Honorius.

We decree moreover that no Christian shall compel them or any one of their group to come to baptism unwillingly. But if any one of them shall take refuge of his own accord with Christians, because of conviction, then, after his intention will have been manifest, he shall be made a Christian without any intrigue. For, indeed, that person who is known to have come to Christian baptism not freely, but unwillingly, is not believed to possess the Christian faith.

Moreover no Christian shall presume to seize, imprison, wound, torture, mutilate, kill, or inflict violence on them; furthermore no one shall presume, except by judicial action of the authorities of the country, to change the good customs in the land where they live for the purpose of taking their money or goods from them or from others.

In addition, no one shall disturb them in any way during the celebration of their festivals, whether by day or by night, with clubs or stones or anything else. Also no one shall exact any compulsory service of them unless it be that which they have been accustomed to render in previous times.

Inasmuch as the Jews are not able to bear witness against the Christians, we decree furthermore that the testimony of Christians against Jews shall not be valid unless there is among these Christians some Jew who is there for the purpose of offering testimony.

Since it happens occasionally that some Christians lose their Christian children, the Jews are accused by their enemies of secretly carrying off and killing these same Christian children and of making sacrifices of the heart and blood of these very children. It happens, too, that the parents of these children or some other Christian enemies of these Jews, secretly hide these very children in order that they may be able to injure these Jews, and in order that they may be able to extort from them a certain amount of money by redeeming them from their straits.

And most falsely do these Christians claim that the Jews have secretly and furtively carried away these children and killed them, and that the Jews offer sacrifice from the heart and blood of these children, since their law in this matter precisely and expressly forbids Jews to sacrifice, eat, or drink the blood, or to eat the flesh of animals having claws. This has been demonstrated many times at our court by Jews converted to the Christian faith: nevertheless very many Jews are often seized and detained unjustly because of this.

We decree, therefore, that Christians need not be obeyed against Jews in a case or situation of this type, and we order that Jews seized under such a silly pretext be freed from imprisonment, and that they shall not be arrested henceforth on such a miserable pretext, unless — which we do not believe — they be caught in the commission of the crime. We decree that no Christian shall stir up anything new against them, but that they should be maintained in that status and position in which they were in the time of our predeccessors, from antiquity till now.

chapter
XIX

Heretics and Friars

---

61. *Peter Waldo and the Waldensians*

Although papal power reached a high point under Innocent III the age saw new movements of criticism directed against the organized church. The conversion of Peter Waldo, founder of the Waldensian sect, was described in an anonymous chronicle of the early thirteenth century.

And during the same year, that is the 1173d since the Lord's Incarnation, there was at Lyons in France a certain citizen, Waldo by name, who had made himself much money by wicked usury. One Sunday, when he had joined a crowd which he saw gathered around a troubadour, he was smitten by his words, and, taking him to his house, he took care to hear him at length. The passage he was reciting was how the holy Alexis died a blessed death in his father's house. When morning had come the prudent citizen hurried to the schools of theology to seek counsel for his soul, and when he was taught many ways of going to God, he asked the master what way was more certain and more perfect than all others. The master answered him with this text: "If thou wilt be perfect, go and sell all that thou hast," etc.

Then Waldo went to his wife and gave her the choice of keeping his personal property or his real estate, namely, what he had in ponds, groves and fields, houses, rents, vineyards, mills, and fishing rights. She was displeased at having to make this choice, but she kept the real estate. From his personal property he made restitution to those whom he had treated unjustly; a great part of it he gave to his two little daughters,

From J. H. Robinson, ed., *Reading in European History* (Boston: Ginn, 1904), Vol. I, pp. 380-381.

who, without their mother's knowledge, he placed in the convent of Font Evrard; but the greatest part of his money he spent for the poor. A very great famine was then oppressing France and Germany. The prudent citizen, Waldo, gave bread, with vegetables and meat, to every one who came to him for three days in every week from Pentecost to the feast of St. Peter's bonds.

At the Assumption of the blessed Virgin, casting some money among the village poor, he cried, "No man can serve two masters, God and mammon." Then his fellow-citizens ran up, thinking he had lost his mind. But going to a higher place, he said: "My fellow-citizens and friends, I am not insane, as you think, but I am avenging myself on my enemies, who made me a slave, so that I was always more careful of money than of God, and served the creature rather than the Creator. I know that many will blame me that I act thus openly. But I do it both on my own account and on yours; on my own, so that those who see me henceforth possessing any money may say that I am mad, and on yours, that you may learn to place hope in God and not in riches."

On the next day, coming from the church, he asked a certain citizen, once his comrade, to give him something to eat, for God's sake. His friend, leading him to his house, said, "I will give you whatever you need as long as I live." When this came to the ears of his wife, she was not a little troubled, and as though she had lost her mind, she ran to the archbishop of the city and implored him not to let her husband beg bread from any one but her. This moved all present to tears.

[Waldo was accordingly conducted into the presence of the bishop.] And the woman, seizing her husband by the coat, said, "Is it not better, husband, that I should redeem my sins by giving you alms than that strangers should to so?" And from that time he was not allowed to take food from any one in that city except from his wife.

The charges most commonly brought against Peter Waldo's followers (the Waldensians) complained of their attitudes toward the sacraments of the church and toward the wealth and privileges of the clergy.

First, They say that the Romish Church, is not the Church of Jesus Christ, but a church of malignants and that it apostatized under Sylvester, when the poison of temporalities was infused into the church. And they say, that they are the church of Christ, because they observe both in word, and deed, the doctrine of Christ, of the Gospel, and of the Apostles.

2. Their second error is that all vices and sins are in the church, and that they alone live righteously.

From Reinerius Saccho, "Of the Sects of Modern Heretics" (1254), in S. R. Maitland, trans., *History of the Albigenses and Waldenses* (London: C. J. G. and F. Rivington, 1832), pp. 407–413.

3. That scarcely anyone in the church, but themselves, preserves the evangelical doctrine.

4. That they are the true poor in spirit, and suffer persecution for righteousness and faith.

5. That they are the Church of Jesus Christ.

6. That the Church of Rome is the Harlot in the Apocalypse, on account of its superfluous decoration which the Eastern Church does not regard.

7. That they despise all the statutes of the Church, because they are heavy and numerous.

8. That the Pope is the head of all errors.

9. That the Prelates are Scribes; and the Monks, Pharisees.

10. That the Pope and all Bishops, are homicides on account of wars.

11. That we are not to obey Prelates; but only God.

12. That no one is greater than another in the church. Matt. 23. "All of you are brethren."

13. That no one ought to bow the knee before a priest. Rev. ii. where the Angel says to John "See thou do it not."

14. That tithes are not to be given, because first fruits were not given to the church.

15. That the clergy ought not to have possessions; Deut. xviii. "The Priests and all the tribe of Levi, shall not have part and inheritance with the people of Israel, because they eat the sacrifices, and they shall receive nothing else."

16. That the clergy, and monks, ought not to have Prebends.

17. That the Bishops and Abbots ought not to have royal rights.

18. That the land, and the people, are not to be divided into parts.

19. That it is a bad thing to found and endow churches and monasteries.

20. That wills are not to be made in favor of Churches—also, that no one ought to be a tenant of the church—also, they condemn all the clergy for idleness, saying that they ought to work with their hands as the Apostles did—also, they reprobate titles of dignity such as Pope, Bishops, &c.—also, that no one is to be forced into belief—also, that they make no account of all ecclesiastical offices—also, that they care nothing for ecclesiastical privileges—also, they despise the immunity of the Church and of ecclesiastical persons and things—also, they condemn Councils, Synods, and Assemblies—also, they say that all parochial rights are invention—also, they say that monastic rules are the traditions of the Pharisees.

Secondly, they condemn all the Sacraments of the Church; in the first place, as to baptism, they say that the Catechism is nothing—also, that the ablution which is given to infants profits nothing. . . .

Also, they condemn the sacrament of Marriage, saying that married persons sin mortally if they come together without the hope of offspring

—also, they disregard compaternity—also, they despise the degrees of affinity, carnal and spiritual, and the impediments of Orders, and of public decency, and of ecclesiastical prohibitions—also, they say that a woman after child-bearing does not require benediction, or introduction—also, they say that the church has erred in prohibiting the marriage of the Clergy, while even those of the East marry—also, they say that the continent do not sin in kisses and embraces.

The sacrament of Unction, they reprobate, because it is only given to the rich; and because several priests are required for it—also, they say that the sacrament of Orders is nothing—also, they say that every good layman is a priest, as the Apostles were laymen—also, that the prayer of an evil priest does not profit—also, they deride the clerical tonsure—also, that Latin prayer does not profit the vulgar—also, they make it a matter of ridicule that illegitimate persons and wicked sinners are raised to eminence in the church—also, they say that every layman, and even woman ought to preach, I. Cor. xiv. "I would that ye spake in tongues, that the church might receive edification"—also, whatever is preached which cannot be proved by the text of Scripture they consider as fabulous. . . .

. . . also, they say that the doctrine of Christ and the Apostles is sufficient for salvation without the statutes of the church—that the tradition of the church is the tradition of the Pharisees; and that there is more made of the transgression of a human tradition than of a divine law. Matt. xv. "Why do ye transgress the commands of God by reason of your traditions?" Also, they reject the mystical sense in the holy Scriptures, principally as it regards the sayings and doings delivered in the Church by tradition; as that the cock upon the steeple signifies a doctor.

62. Accusations Against the Albigensians

Often we know of the beliefs of heretical sects mainly through the accounts of their orthodox opponents, who may have distorted them. The following account of the Albigensians of Provence is from an early thirteenth-century source.

First it is to be known that the heretics held that there are two Creators; viz. one of invisible things, whom they called the benevolent God, and another of visible things, whom they named the malevolent

From Raynaldus, "Annales," in S. R. Maitland, trans., *History of the Albigenses and Waldense's* (London: C. J. G. and F. Rivington, 1832), pp. 392-394.

God. The New Testament they attributed to the benevolent God; but
the Old Testament to the malevolent God, and rejected it altogether,
except certain authorities which are inserted in the New Testament
from the Old; which, out of reverence to the New Testament, they esteemed worthy of reception. They charged the author of the Old Testament with falsehood, because the Creator said, "In the day that ye
eat of the tree of the knowledge of good and evil ye shall die;" nor (as
they say) after eating did they die; when, in fact, after the eating the
forbidden fruit they were subjected to the misery of death. They also
call him a homicide, as well because he burned up Sodom and Gomor-
rha, and destroyed the world by the waters of the deluge, as because
he overwhelmed Pharaoh, and the Egyptians, in the sea. They affirmed also, that all the fathers of the Old Testament were damned;
that John the Baptist was one of the greater demons. They said also, in
their secret doctrine, (*in secreto suo*) that that Christ who was born in
the visible, and terrestrial Bethlehem, and crucified in Jerusalem, was
a bad man, and that Mary Magdalene was his concubine; and that she
was the woman taken in adultery, of whom we read in the gospel. For
the good Christ, as they said, never ate, nor drank, nor took upon him
true flesh, nor ever was in this world, except spiritually in the body of
Paul. . . .

They said that almost all the Church of Rome was a den of thieves;
and that it was the harlot of which we read in the Apocalypse. They so
far annulled the sacraments of the Church, as publicly to teach that
the water of holy Baptism was just the same as river water, and that
the Host of the most holy body of Christ did not differ from common
bread; instilling into the ears of the simple this blasphemy, that the
body of Christ, even though it had been as great as the Alps, would
have been long ago consumed, and annihilated by those who had eaten
of it. Confirmation and Confession, they considered as altogether vain
and frivolous. They preached that Holy Matrimony was meretricious,
and that none could be saved in it, if they should beget children. De-
nying also the Resurrection of the flesh, they invented some unheard
of notions, saying, that our souls are those of angelic spirits who, being
cast down from heaven by the apostacy of pride, left their glorified
bodies in the air; and that these souls themselves, after successively in-
habiting seven terrene bodies, of one sort or another, having at length
fulfilled their penance, return to those deserted bodies.

It is also to be known that some among the heretics were called
"perfect" or "good men;" others "believers" of the heretics. Those who
were called perfect, wore a black dress, falsely pretended to chastity,
abhorred the eating of flesh, eggs and cheese, wished to appear not
liars, when they were continually telling lies, chiefly respecting God.
They said also that they ought not on any account to swear.

Those were called *believers* of the heretics, who lived after the manner of the world, and who though they did not attain so far as to imi-

tate the life of the perfect, nevertheless hoped to be saved in their faith; and though they differed as to their mode of life, they were one with them in belief and unbelief. Those who were called believers of the heretics were given to usury, rapine, homicide, lust, perjury and every vice; and they, in fact, sinned with more security, and less restraint, because they believed that without restitution, without confession and penance, they should be saved, if only, when on the point of death, they could say a *Pater noster,* and received imposition of hands from the teachers.

As to the *perfect* heretics however they had a magistracy whom they called Deacons and Bishops, without the imposition of whose hands, at the time of his death, none of the believers thought that he could be saved; but if they laid their hands upon any dying man, however wicked, if he could only say a *Pater noster,* they considered him to be saved, that without any satisfaction, and without any other aid, he immediately took wing to heaven.

63. St. Francis of Assisi

The Testament of St. Francis

St. Francis of Assisi (1182–1226) established a way of life within the medieval church that attracted many men who might have drifted into heretical groups. His ideals were most clearly expressed in his "Testament" written shortly before his death.

The Lord gave to me, Brother Francis, thus to begin to do penance; for when I was in sin it seemed to me very bitter to see lepers, and the Lord Himself led me amongst them and I showed mercy to them. And when I left them, that which had seemed to me bitter was changed for me into sweetness of body and soul. And afterwards I remained a little and I left the world. And the Lord gave me so much faith in churches and that I would simply pray and say thus: "We adore Thee Lord Jesus Christ here and in all Thy churches which are in the whole world, and we bless Thee because by Thy holy cross Thou hast redeemed the world."

After that the Lord gave me, and gives me, so much faith in priests who live according to the form of the holy Roman Church, on account of their order, that if they should persecute me, I would have recourse to them. And if I had as much wisdom as Solomon had, and if I should

From *The Writings of Saint Francis of Assisi,* Paschal Robinson, trans. (Philadelphia: Dolphin Press, 1906), pp. 81–86, 152–153.

find poor priests of this world, I would not preach against their will in the parishes in which they live. And I desire to fear, love, and honor them and all others as my masters; and I do not wish to consider sin in them, for in them I see the Son of God and they are my masters. And I do this because in this world, I see nothing corporally of the most high Son of God himself except His most holy Body and Blood, which they receive and they alone administer to others. And I will that these most holy mysteries be honored and revered above all things and that they be placed in precious places. Wheresoever I find His most holy Names and written words in unseemly places, I wish to collect them, and I ask that they may be collected and put in a becoming place. And we ought to honor and venerate all theologians and those who minister to us the most holy Divine Words as those who minister to us spirit and life.

And when the Lord gave me some brothers, no one showed me what I ought to do, but the Most High Himself revealed to me that I should live according to the form of the holy Gospel. And I caused it to be written in few words and simply, and the Lord Pope confirmed it for me. And those who came to take this life upon themselves gave to the poor all that they might have and they were content with one tunic, patched within and without, by those who wished, with a cord and breeches, and we wished for no more.

We clerics said the Office like other clerics; the laics said the *Paternoster,* and we remained in the churches willingly enough. And we were simple and subject to all. And I worked with my hands and I wish to work and I wish firmly that all the other brothers should work at some labor which is compatible with honesty. Let those who know not [how to work] learn, not through desire to receive the price of labor but for the sake of example and to repel idleness. And when the price of labor is not given to us, let us have recourse to the table of the Lord, begging alms from door to door.

The Lord revealed to me this saluation, that we should say: "The Lord give thee peace." Let the brothers take care not to receive on any account churches, poor dwelling-places, and all other things that are constructed for them, unless they are as is becoming the holy poverty which we have promised in the Rule, always dwelling there as strangers and pilgrims.

I strictly enjoin by obedience on all the brothers that, wherever they may be, they should not dare, either themselves or by means of some interposed person, to ask any letter in the Roman curia either for a church or for any other place, nor under pretext of preaching, nor on account of their bodily persecution; but, wherever they are not received let them flee to another land to do penance, with the blessing of God. And I wish to obey the minister general of this brotherhood strictly and the guardian whom it may please him to give me. And I wish to be so captive in his hands that I cannot go or act beyond his obedience and his will because he is my master. And although I am simple and infirm, I desire withal always to have a cleric who will perform the office with me as it is contained in the Rule.

And let all the other brothers be found to obey their guardian and to perform the office according to the Rule. And those who may be found not performing the office according to the Rule and wishing to change it in some way, or who are not Catholics, let all the brothers wherever they may be, if they find one of these, be bound by obedience to present him to the custos who is nearest to the place where they have found him. And the custos shall be strictly bound, by obedience, to guard him strongly day and night as a prisoner so that he cannot be snatched from his hands until he shall personally place him in the hands of his ministers. And the minister shall be firmly bound by obedience to send him by such brothers as shall watch him day and night like a prisoner until they shall present him to the Lord of Ostia, who is master protector, and corrector of this brotherhood.

And let not the brothers say: This is another Rule; for this is a remembrance, a warning, and an exhortation and my Testament which I, little Brother Francis, make for you, my blessed brothers, in order that we may observe in a more Catholic way the Rule which we have promised to the Lord. And let the minister general and all the other ministers and custodes be bound by obedience not to add to these words or to take from them. And let them always have this writing with them beside the Rule. And in all the Chapters they hold, when they read the Rule let them read these words also. And I strictly enjoin on all my brothers, clerics and laics, by obedience, not to put glosses on the Rule or on these words saying: Thus they ought to be understood; but as the Lord has given me to speak and to write the Rule and these words simply and purely, so shall you understand them simply and purely and with holy operation observe them until the end.

And whoever shall observe these things may he be filled in heaven with the blessing of the Most High Father and may he be filled on earth with blessing of His Beloved Son together with the Holy Ghost, the Paraclete, and all the Powers of heaven and all the saints. And I, Brother Francis, your little one and servant, in so far as I am able, I confirm to you within and without this most holy blessing. Amen.

Unlike the Albigensians, who believed that all material creation was evil, Francis saw all created things as good and beautiful because God had made them so. The original Italian of the following verses is ambiguous. It is not clear whether Francis was praising God for the beauty of his creatures or praising God through the creatures, that is calling on all creation to praise God. Perhaps he meant to convey both meanings.

The Canticle of the Sun

Altissimu, omnipotente, bon Signore,
tue so' le laude, la gloria, l'honore
et omne benedictione.

Most high, omnipotent, good Lord,
Praise, glory and honor and benediction
  all, are Thine.
To Thee alone do they belong, most High,
And there is no man fit to mention Thee.

Praise be to Thee, my Lord, with all Thy crea-
  tures,
Especially to my worshipful brother sun,
The which lights up the day, and through him
  dost Thou brightness give;
And beautiful is he and radiant with splendor
  great;
Of Thee, most High, signification gives.

Praised be my Lord, for sister moon and for the
  stars,
In heaven Thou has formed them clear and
  precious and fair.
Praised be my Lord for brother wind
And for the air and clouds and fair and every
  kind of weather,
By the which Thou givest to Thy creatures
  nourishment.
Praised be my Lord for sister water,
The which is greatly helpful and humble and
  precious and pure.

Praised be my Lord for brother fire,
By the which Thou lightest up the dark.
And fair is he and gay and mighty and strong.

Praised be my Lord for our sister, mother earth,
The which sustains and keeps us
And brings forth diverse fruits with grass and
  flowers bright.

Praised be my Lord for those who for Thy love
  forgive
And weakness bear and tribulation.
Blessed those who shall in peace endure,
For by Thee, most High, shall they be crowned.

Praised be my Lord for our sister, the bodily
  death,
From the which no living man can flee.
Woe to them who die in mortal sin;

Blessed those who shall find themselves in Thy
    most holy will,
For the second death shall do them no ill.

Praise ye and bless ye my Lord, and give Him
    thanks,
And be subject unto Him with great humility.

chapter

XX

The French Monarchy

64. *Joinville's Account of St. Louis*

Louis IX of France has been called the "ideal feudal king." The following ac-
count of his personality is by John de Joinville, a knight who served at
Louis' court and accompanied the king on a Crusade in 1248.

Dedication and Prologue

To his good Lord Louis, son of the King of France, by the grace of
God, King of Navarre, Count Palatine of Champagne and Brie, John,
Lord of Joinville, his seneschal in Champagne, sends greeting, love
and honour, and his ready service.

I must tell you, my dear Lord, that my Lady the Queen, your mother,
who was a dear friend to me—God grant her His kind mercy—was
most earnest in asking me to have a book written of the holy sayings
and good deeds of our King Saint Louis. I gave her my promise to do
so, and now by the help of God the book is finished. . . .

. . . From the beginning of his reign to the end of his life no layman
of our time spent his whole life in so saintly a manner. I was not with
him when he died, but Count Peter of Alençon, his son, who was my
dear friend, was there, and he told me of the fine end he made; you
may read of this in the last part of my book.

I cannot but think that it was an injustice to him not to include him
in the roll of the martyrs, when you consider the great hardships he suffered as a pilgrim and Crusader during the six years that I served with

From *The Life of St. Louis* by John of Joinville, translated by Rene Hague from the
text edited by Natalis De Wailly. Copyright 1955, Sheed & Ward, Inc., New York.

him; in particular because it was even to the Cross that he followed Our Lord—for if God died on the Cross, so did St. Louis; for when he died at Tunis it was the Cross of the Crusade that he bore.

My second book will tell you of his great deeds of knighthood and of his high courage. These were such that four times I saw him risk death that he might save his people from harm. Of this you may read later.

St. Louis' Devotion to His People

The first occasion on which he risked death was when we arrived off Damietta. All his Council advised him, I heard, to stay in his ship until he saw how his knights fared in landing.

This advice they gave him because if he landed with the knights and his people were killed and he with them the whole enterprise would be lost; but if he stayed on board his ship he could himself undertake a new expedition to take Egypt. But he would not listen to any of them; he leapt fully armed into the water, his shield around his neck, his spear in his hand, and he was among the first to land.

The second occasion on which he risked death was this: when he was leaving Mansura for Damietta his Council urged him, so I was told, to go to Damietta by galley. And this advice they gave him, it was said, because if things were to fall out badly for his people he might still be able himself to free them from captivity.

There was another special reason: the poor condition of his body. He suffered from several diseases; he had a double tertian fever and a severe dysentery, and the "camp fever," which attacked his mouth and legs. Even so, he would not listen to anyone. He said that he would never abandon his people, but would meet whatever end was to be theirs. That evening his dysentery made it necessary for him to have the ends of his drawers cut away, and he fainted several times from the camp fever; of this, too, you may read later.

The third occasion on which he ran the risk of death was when he stayed for four years in the Holy Land, after his brothers had left. We were then in great danger of death, for while the King was stationed at Acre he had hardly one man of arms in his command for every thirty that the people of Acre had when the town was captured.

The only reason I know for the Turk's failing to come and take us in the town was God's love for the King. He put fear into the hearts of our enemies that they might be afraid to come and attack us. Such is the meaning of the words, "If you fear God, all things that see you will hold you in fear." Again, it was against the advice of his Council that he stayed in Acre, as you may read later. He risked his own life for the safety of the people of the Holy Land, who would have been lost had he not remained.

The fourth occasion on which he risked his life was when we were coming back from overseas and were off the island of Cyprus. Our ship struck with such force that the bottom carried away three fathoms of the keel on which it was built.

The King then sent for fourteen of the master mariners, some from our own ship and some from other ships that were in company with him, and asked them what was best for him to do. They all advised him —and this you may read of later—to move into another ship; they could not see how his ship could stand the force of the waves, for the bolts which held the timbers were all strained. As an example of the danger which the ship was running, they pointed out to the King that when we were on our journey overseas a vessel in similar case had been lost; I saw myself, at the Count of Joigny's, the woman and child who were the only survivors.

This was the King's answer: "Sirs, I can see that if I leave this ship she will be abandoned, and I can also see that there are more than eight hundred person in her. Every man's life is as dear to him as mine is to me, and no one accordingly will dare to stay in the ship; they will all stay in Cyprus. For that reason I shall not, please God, endanger the many lives that she carries. I shall stay in the ship to save my people."

The Virtues of St. Louis

St. Louis loved God with his whole heart and it was on Him that he modelled his actions. This could be seen in that, as God died for the love of His people, so did the King more than once put his own body in danger of death for the love he bore his people; and this although, had he wished it, he might well have been excused. Of this I will tell you more later.

The great love that he had for his people was shown by what he said, when he lay very sick at Fontainebleau, to his eldest son, my Lord Louis. "Dear son," he said, "I pray you to win the love of the people of your Kingdom. In truth, I would rather that a Scotsman came from Scotland and governed them, so long as his rule was good and fair, than that you should be seen by the world to govern it ill." The holy King so loved truth that not even to the Saracens would he break his word when he had once an agreement with them, as I shall tell you later.

In eating he was so temperate that never once in my life did I hear him order any dish for his table, as many rich men do. He was content to eat what his cook prepared for him and what was set before him. In his speech he was restrained. Never in my life did I hear him speak ill of any man, nor name the devil—whose name is much heard in the Kingdom now, a thing which I think can hardly be pleasing to God.

He mixed his wine with water, measuring the water according to the amount that he saw the wine could stand. Once in Cyprus he asked me why I put no water in my wine. I told him that the doctors were responsible for this; they told me that I had a large head and a cold stomach and that it was impossible for me to get drunk. The King told me that they were deluding me, for if I did not learn to water my wine in my youth and tried to do so when I was old, I should be attacked by gout and diseases of the stomach, so that I should never enjoy my health; and if I drank my wine neat when I was an old man I should be drunk every evening; and it was a mighty ugly thing for a good man to get drunk.

Daily Life of St. Louis

He so arranged the business of governing his country that every day he heard the hours of the Office sung, and a Requiem Mass without chant, and then a sung Mass of the day or the feast, if there was one. Every day after dinner he rested on his bed, and when he had slept and rested he said the Office of the Dead privately in his room with one of his chaplains, before hearing Vespers. In the evening he heard Compline.

St. Louis' Justice

Often in the summer he went after Mass to the wood of Vincennes and sat down with his back against an oak tree, and made us sit all around him. Everyone who had an affair to settle could come and speak to him without the interference of any usher or other official. The King would speak himself and ask, "Is there any one here who has a case to settle?" All those who had would then stand up and he would say, "Quiet, all of you, and your cases shall be dealt with in turn." Then he would call my Lord Peter of Fontaines and my Lord Geoffrey of Villette and say to one of them, "Now give me your judgment in this case."

When those who spoke for him or for the other party said anything which he saw needed correction he corrected it himself. Once in the summer I saw him as he went to the gardens in Paris to give judgment for his people. He wore a tunic of natural wool, a sleeveless surcoat of cotton, and a black satin cloak around his shoulders; he wore no cap, but his hair was well combed, and on his head he wore a hat of white peacocks' feathers. He had carpets spread so that we could sit about him, and all who had business with him would stand around. Then he settled their claims as I have just told you he used to do in the wood of Vincennes.

St. Louis and the Claims of the Clergy

Another occasion on which I saw him was at Paris. It was when a message came to him from all the French prelates that they wished to speak with him. The King went to the palace to hear what they had to say: Bishop Guy of Auxerre was there, the son of my Lord William of Mello. As spokesman for the whole hierarchy, he addressed the King as follows: "Sir, the lords here present, archbishops and bishops, have bidden me warn you that in your hands Christendom, of which you should be the guardian, is being destroyed." When the King heard this accusation, he crossed himself, and asked how that might be.

"Sir," he answered, "it is because men have now so little regard for excommunication that they are prepared to die without obtaining absolution, and refuse to give the Church the satisfaction she demands. These lords accordingly require you, for the love of God and in execution of your duty, to give an order to your provosts and bailiffs that all who have been under sentence of excommunication for a year and a day must be forced by seizure of their goods to obtain absolution.

The King's answer was that he would gladly give such orders in all cases where certain proof of guilt were given to him. The Bishop said that they could by no means consent to this condition, since they refused to acknowledge the King's jurisdiction in their cases. The King told him that he would not change his mind, for it would be unreasonable and an offence against God to force people to seek absolution when it was the clergy who were wronging them.

"I can give you an example of this," he said, "in the Count of Brittany. For seven years, while he was excommunicated, he fought the prelates of Brittany at law; and finally he won from the Pope a judgment against them all. Had I in the first year forced the Count of Britany to obtain absolution I should have sinned towards God and towards him." The prelates had to be satisfied with this; and afterwards I never heard of such a claim being put forward again.

St. Louis and the Spirit of Justice

When the King made peace with the King of England, he did so against the wish of his Council. They said to him, "Sir, we think that you are throwing away the territory which you are ceding to the King of England; he has no rights over it, for his father forfeited it by judgment." The King's answer was that while he well knew that the King of England had no right to it, there was yet a good reason why he should give it to him. "We have married sisters, and our children are first cousins. It is fitting, therefore, that there should be peace between us. Moreover from the peace I am making with the King of England I derive the great honour of having him as my vassal, which he was not before."

The King's respect for the spirit of the law may be seen in the case of my Lord Renaud of Trie. He brought the Saint a document which said that the King had given the county of Dammartin in Gouelle to the heirs of the then lately deceased Countess of Boulogne. The seal of the letter was broken, so that all that remained was the lower half of the legs in the King's figure and the stool on which his feet rested. The King showed it to all of us who were in Council with him and asked us to help him to come to a decision.

We were unanimous that he was under no obligation to give effect to the document. The King then asked John Sarrasin, his chamberlain, to give him another letter which he had asked him to fetch. When he had it in his hand he said to us, "My Lords, this is the seal which I used before I went overseas; you can see quite clearly from this seal that the broken impression fits the complete seal. I cannot, then, in good conscience withhold the said county." Then he called my Lord Renaud of Trie and told him that he made the county over to him.

St. Louis' Charity

From his childhood the King was very compassionate to the poor and suffering. It was always the custom, wherever he went, every day for six score poor persons to be fed in his house with bread and wine and meat or fish. In Lent and Advent a larger number were fed; and it sometimes happened that the King served them himself and set their meat before them, carving it for them, and when they left giving them money with his own hand.

In particular, on the high vigils of solemn feasts, he served all this food to the poor before he ate or drank himself. Moreover, every day at dinner and supper he had with him old and decrepit men to whom he gave the same food as he ate himself, and after they had fed they took with them a sum of money.

In addition to all this, the King daily gave countless generous alms, to poor religious, to poor hospitals, to poor sick people, to other poor convents, to poor gentlemen and gentlewomen and girls, to fallen women, to poor widows and women in childbed, and to poor minstrels who from old age or sickness were unable to work or follow their trade. So we may well say that he was happier than Titus, the Emperor of Rome, of whom the old books tell us that he was greatly cast down and grieved on any day when he had done not act of charity. . . .

Some of his household grumbled at his giving such generous alms and spending so much on them. He answered, "I would rather my extravagance should be in almsgiving for the love of God than in the pomp and vain glory of this world." In spite, however, of the King's great expenditure in almsgiving, his daily household expenses were none the less very high. He was liberal and generous at the Parliaments and meetings of barons and knights, and entertained them at his court with greater courtesy and prodigality than had been seen for a long time at the courts of his predecessors.

chapter XXI

The Holy Roman Empire

---

65. Frederick II and Germany

*The greatest emperor of the thirteenth century was the formidable and bril-
liant Frederick II (1215–1250). In order to secure a free hand in Italy he vir-
tually abandoned Germany to the rule of the princes. The following grant
of privileges was made in 1231.*

Statute in Favor of the Princes

In the name of the holy and undivided Trinity, Frederick II, by divine
mercy emperor of the Romans, Augustus, king of Jerusalem, king of
Sicily.

· · ·

1. No new castles or cities shall be erected by us or by anyone else to
the prejudice of the princes.

2. New markets shall not be allowed to interfere with the interests
of former ones.

3. No one shall be compelled to attend any market against his will.

4. Travellers shall not be compelled to leave the old highways, unless they desire to do so.

5. We will not exercise jurisdiction within the ban-mile of our
cities.

6. Each prince shall possess and exercise in peace according to the
customs of the land the liberties, jurisdiction, and authority over
counties and hundreds which are in his own possession or are held as
fiefs from him.

From O. J. Thatcher and E. H. McNeal, trans., *A Source Book for Mediaeval History*
(New York: Charles Scribner's, 1905), pp. 238-240.

7. Centgrafs shall receive their office from the prince or from the person who holds the land as a fief.

8. The location of the hundred court shall not be changed without the consent of the lord.

9. No nobleman shall be amenable to the hundred court.

10. The citizens who are known as *phalburgii* [*i.e.,* persons or corporations existing outside the city, but possessing political rights within it] shall be expelled from the cities.

11. Payments of wine, money, grain, and other rents, which free peasants have formerly agreed to pay [to the emperor], are hereby remitted, and shall not be collected henceforth.

12. The serfs of princes, nobles, ministerials, and churches shall not be admitted to our cities.

13. Lands and fiefs of princes, nobles, ministerials, and churches, which have been seized by our cities, shall be restored and shall never again be taken.

14. The right of the princes to furnish safe-conduct within the lands they hold as fiefs from us shall not be infringed by us or by anyone else.

15. Inhabitants of our cities shall not be compelled by our judges to restore any possessions which they may have received from others before they moved there.

16. Notorious, condemned, and proscribed persons shall not be admitted to our cities; if they have been, they shall be driven out.

17. We will never cause any money to be coined in the land of any of the princes which shall be injurious to his coinage.

18. The jurisdiction of our cities shall not extend beyond their boundaries, unless we possess special jurisdiction in the region.

19. In our cities the plaintiff shall bring suit in the court of the accused.

20. Lands or property which are held as fiefs shall not be pawned without the consent of the lord from whom they are held.

21. No one shall be compelled to aid in the fortifying of cities unless he is legally bound to render that service.

22. Inhabitants of our cities who hold lands outside shall pay to their lords or advocates the regular dues and services, and they shall not be burdened with unjust exactions.

23. If serfs, freemen subject to advocates, or vassals of any lord, shall dwell within any of our cities, they shall not be prevented by our officials from going to their lords.

66.   *Frederick II and the Papacy*

Frederick's Italian policies led to a long series of conflicts with the papacy that culminated with the emperor's excommunication and deposition by Pope Innocent IV in 1245. The following papal bull deposing Frederick was promulgated in a general council held at Lyons.

Bishop Innocent, servant of God, to the present holy Council for the eternal record of the matter.

Having been exalted to the summit of the Apostolic dignity, although unworthy of such a favor from the Divine Majesty, we have to take care of all Christians with a vigilant and diligent solicitude, discern their merits through the eye of intimate consideration and weigh them carefully on the scales of our deliberation; so that we elevate with adequate favors those whom the strength of a just examination shows worthy and afflict with due penalties the guilty ones, weighing always the merits and rewards impartially and recompensing each one for the quality of his deeds with a just amount of punishment or grace. . . .

[Frederick] has committed four very grave offences, which can not be covered up by any subterfuge (we say nothing for the moment about his other crimes); he has abjured God on many occasions; he has wantonly broken the peace which had been re-established between the Church and the Empire; he has also committed sacrilege by causing to be imprisoned the Cardinals of the holy Roman Church and the prelates and clerics, regular and secular, of other churches, coming to the Council which our predecessor had summoned; he is also accused of heresy not by doubtful and flimsy but by formidable and clear proofs.

. . . Also after after he had joined himself in a detestable friendship to the Saracens, he sent messengers and presents to them on several occasions and received them from the Saracens in return with honor and joy; he embraced their customs, observing them notoriously in his daily life, for he did not even blush to appoint as guardians for his wives (descendants from royal stock) eunuchs. What is more abominable still is that once, when he was in the countries beyond the sea, he made a treaty or rather a conspiracy with the Sultan and allowed the name of Mahomet to be publicly proclaimed day and night in the Temple of the Lord. And lately, as it is said, he caused the messengers of the Sultan of Babylon (after the same Sultan had inflicted personally and through his subordinates very grave and inestimable injuries upon the

From Innocent IV, in S. Z. Ehler and J. B. Morrall, eds. and trans., *Church and State Through the Centuries* (Westminster, Md.: Newman Press, 1954), pp. 79–86, reprinted by permission of the publisher. Frederick II, in Brian Tierney, *The Crisis of Church and State, 1050–1300,* with selected documents, © 1964 (Englewood Cliffs, N.J.: Prentice-Hall, 1964), pp. 145–146; reprinted by permission of Prentice-Hall, Inc., Englewood Cliffs, New Jersey.

Holy Land and its Christian inhabitants) to be honorably received and magnificently entertained in the kingdom of Sicily, with praises for the prestige of the same Sultan.

We therefore, who are the vicar, though unworthy, of Jesus Christ on earth and to whom it was said in the person of blessed Peter the Apostle: "Whatever thou shalt bind on earth," etc., show and declare an account of the above-mentioned shameful crimes and of many others, having held careful consultation with our brethren and the holy Council, that the aforesaid prince—who has rendered himself so unworthy of all the honor and dignity of the Empire and the kingdom and who, because of his wickedness, has been rejected by God from acting as king or Emperor—is bound by his sins and cast out and deprived of all honor and dignity by God, to which we add our sentence of deprivation also. We absolve for ever all who owe him allegiance in virtue of an oath of fealty from any oath of this kind; and we strictly forbid by Apostolic authority that any one should obey him or look upon him henceforth as king or Emperor, and we decree that whoever shall in the future afford him advice, help or goodwill as if he were Emperor or king, shall fall "ipso facto" under the binding force of excommunication. But let those in the same Empire whose duty it is to look to the election of an Emperor, elect a successor freely. We shall make it our business to provide for the aforesaid kingdom of Sicily as seems best to us with the advice of our brethren.

Frederick replied to his deposition with this letter of defiance addressed to the princes of Europe.

What is implied by our maltreatment is made plain by the presumption of Pope Innocent IV for, having summoned a council—a general council he calls it—he has dared to pronounce a sentence of deposition against us who were neither summoned nor proved guilty of any deceit or wickedness, which sentence he could not enact without grievous prejudice to all kings. You and all kings of particular regions have everything to fear from the effrontery of such a prince of priests when he sets out to depose us who have been divinely honored by the imperial diadem and solemnly elected by the princes with the approval of the whole church at a time when faith and religion were flourishing among the clergy, us who also govern in splendor other noble kingdoms; and this when it is no concern of his to inflict any punishment on us for temporal injuries even if the cases were proved according to law. In truth we are not the first nor shall we be the last that this abuse of priestly power harasses and strives to cast down from the heights; but this indeed you also do when you obey these men who feign holiness, whose ambition hopes that "the whole Jordan will flow into their mouth" (*cf.* Job 40:18). O if your simple credulity would care to turn itself "from the leaven of the Scribes and Pharisees which is hypocrisy" (Luke 12:1) according to the words of the Savior, how many foul deeds of that court you would be able to execrate, which honor and shame forbid us to relate. The copious revenues with which they are enriched by the impoverishment of many kingdoms, as you yourself know, make them rage like madmen. Christians and pilgrims beg in your land so that Patarene heretics may eat in ours. You are closing up your houses there to build the towns of your enemies here. These poor followers of Christ are supported and enriched by your tithes and alms, but by what compensating benefit, or what expression of gratitude even do they show themselves beholden to you? The more generously you stretch out a hand to these needy ones the more greedily they snatch not only the hand but the arm, trapping you in their snare like a little bird that is the more firmly entangled the more it struggles to escape.

We have concerned ourselves to write these things to you for the present, though not adequately expressing our intentions. We have decided to omit other matters and to convey them to you more secretly; namely the purpose for which the lavishness of these greedy men expends the riches of the poor; what we have found out concerning the election of an emperor if peace is not established at least superficially between us and the church, which peace we intend to establish through eminent mediators; what dispositions we intend to make concerning all the kingdoms in general and each in particular; what has been arranged concerning the islands of the ocean; how that court is plotting against all princes with words and deeds which could not be concealed from us who have friends and subjects there, although clandestinely; with what stratagems and armies trained for war we hope in this coming spring to oppress all those who now oppress us, even though the whole world should set itself against us.

But whatever our faithful subjects, the bearers of this letter, relate to you you may believe with certainty and hold as firmly as if St. Peter had sworn to it. Do not suppose on account of what we ask of you that the magnanimity of our majesty has been in any way bowed down by the sentence of deposition launched against us, for we have a clean conscience and so God is with us. We call him to witness that it was always our intention to persuade the clergy of every degree that they should continue to the end as they were in the early days of the church living an apostolic life and imitating the Lord's humility, and that it was our intention especially to reduce those of highest rank to this condition. Those clergy [of former days] used to see angels and were resplendent with miracles: they used to heal the sick, raise the dead and subject kings and princes to themselves by holiness, not by arms. But these, drunk with the pleasures of the world and devoted to them, set aside God, and all true religion is choked by their surfeit of riches and power. Hence, to deprive such men of the baneful wealth that burdens them to their own damnation is a work of charity. You and all princes, united with us, ought to be as diligent as you can in achieving this end so that, laying aside all superfluities and content with modest possessions, they may serve the God whom all things serve.

67. A Contemporary View of the Emperor

The following account of Frederick II is from the Chronicle of Salimbene, *a thirteenth-century Italian Franciscan, as translated and paraphrased by G. G. Coulton.*

To Salimbene, as to Dante, Frederick was a man of heroic proportions in his very sins. "Of faith in God he had none; he was crafty, wily, avaricious, lustful, malicious, wrathful; and yet a gallant man at times, when he would show his kindness or courtesy; full of solace, jocund, delightful, fertile in devices. He knew to read, write, and sing, to make songs and music. He was a comely man, and well-formed, but of middle stature. I have seen him, and once I loved him, for on my behalf he wrote to Bro. Elias, Minister-General of the Friars Minor, to send me back to my father. Moreover, he knew to speak with many and varied tongues, and, to be brief, if he had been rightly Catholic, and had loved God and His Church, he would have had few emperors his equals in the world." [Salimbene] goes on to enumerate several specimens of the Emperor's "curiosities" or "excesses," though for sheer weariness he will not tell them all. Frederick cut off a notary's thumb who had spelt his name *Fredericus* instead of *Fridericus*. Like Psammetichus in Herodotus, he made linguistic experiments on the vile bodies of hapless infants, "bidding foster-mothers and nurses to suckle and bathe and wash the children, but in no wise to prattle or speak with them; for he would have learnt whether they would speak the Hebrew language (which had been the first), or Greek, or Latin, or Arabic, or perchance the tongue of their parents of whom they had been born. But he laboured in vain, for the children could not live without clappings of the hands, and gestures, and gladness of countenance, and blandishments." Again, "when he saw the Holy Land, (which God had so oft-times commended as a land flowing with milk and honey and most excellent above all lands,) it pleased him not, and he said that if the God of the Jews had seen *his* land of Terra di Lavoro, Calabria, Sicily, and Apulia, then He would not so have commended the land which He promised to the Jews." Again, he compelled "Nicholas the Fish," whom his mother's curse had condemned to an amphibious life, to dive and fetch his golden cup a second time from the very bottom of Charybdis: in which repeated attempt the poor man knew that he must perish. Fifthly, "he enclosed a living man in a cask that he might die there, wishing thereby to show that the soul perished utterly, as if he might say the word of Isaiah 'Let us eat and drink, for

From G. G. Coulton, *St. Francis to Dante* (London: David Nutt, 1906), pp. 242-243.

to-morrow we die.' For he was an Epicurean; wherefore, partly of himself and partly through his wise men, he sought out all that he could find in Holy Scripture which might make for the proof that there was no other life after death, as for instance 'Thou shalt destroy them, and not build them up': and again 'Their sepulchres shall be their houses for ever.' Sixthly, he fed two men most excellently at dinner, one of whom he sent forthwith to sleep, and the other to hunt; and that same evening he caused them to be disembowelled in his presence, wishing to know which had digested the better: and it was judged by the physicians in favour of him who had slept. Seventhly and lastly, being one day in his palace, he asked Michael Scot the astrologer how far he was from the sky, and Michael having answered as it seemed to him, the Emperor took him to other parts of his kingdom as if for a journey of pleasure, and kept him there several months, bidding meanwhile his architects and carpenters secretly to lower the whole of his palace hall. Many days afterwards, standing in that same palace with Michael, he asked of him, as if by the way, whether he were indeed so far from the sky as he had before said. Whereupon he made his calculations, and made answer that certainly either the sky had been raised or the earth lowered; and then the Emperor knew that he spake truth." Yet Salimbene is careful to note that Frederick's cruelties might justly be excused by the multitude of his open and secret enemies, and that he had a saving sense of humour. "He was wont at times to make mocking harangues before his court in his own palace, speaking for example after the fashion of the Cremonese ambassadors," at whose tediousness and outward flourishes our good friar laughs again later on. "Moreover, he would suffer patiently the scoffings, and mockings and revilings of jesters, and often feign that he heard not. For one day, after the destruction of Victoria by the men of Parma, he smote his hand on the hump of a certain jester, saying 'My Lord Dallio, when shall this box be opened?' to whom the other answered, ''Tis odds if it be ever opened now, for I lost the key in Victoria.' The Emperor, hearing how this jester recalled his own sorrow and shame, groaned and said, with the Psalmist, 'I was troubled, and I spoke not.' If any had spoken such a jest against Ezzelino da Romano, he would without doubt have let him be blinded or hanged. . . ."

chapter XXII

Constitutionalism in England

---

68. The Jury: Assize of Novel Disseisin and Assize Utrum

The English common law grew out of a series of royal writs providing for jury trial in civil suits. Two of the earliest such writs, from the late twelfth century, are given below.

Assize of Novel Disseisin

The king to the sheriff, greeting. Complaint has been made to me by N. that R. has unlawfully and without judgment disseised him of his free tenement in ———— since my last crossing to Normandy; and so I command you, if the aforesaid N. will give you security for prosecuting his claim, to have restored to that tenement the chattels taken from it and [to let] the said tenement with its chattels remain in peace until ————. And in the meantime you shall have twelve free and lawful men of the neighbourhood view that land, and you shall have their names written down. And summon them through good summoners to be before me or my justices, prepared to make recognition concerning it. And place under gage and good pledges the aforesaid R., or his bailiff if he himself cannot be found, to be there in order to hear that recognition. And you are to have there the summoners and this writ.

From *Sources of English Constitutional History,* translated by C. Stephenson and F. G. Marcham: Assize of *Novel Disseisin* and Assize of *Utrum* (New York: Harper and Brothers, 1937), p. 83; Copyright 1937, 1965 by Harper and Row, Publishers, Incorporated; reprinted by permission of the publishers.

Assize Utrum

The king to the sheriff, greeting. Summon through good summoners twelve free and lawful men from the neighbourhood of ———, to be before me or my justices on ———, prepared to recognize by oath whether the one hide of land, which N., parson of the church in that vill, claims against R. in that vill as free alms of his said church, is lay fee of the said R. or church fee. And in the meantime let them view that land and have their names written down. And summon through good summoners the aforesaid R., who holds that land, to be there in order to hear recognition. And you are to have there the summoners and this writ.

69.   *Magna Carta*

Magna Carta (1215) is perhaps the most famous constitutional document in English history. It was described by a contemporary as a "treaty of peace" between the king and his barons.

John, by the grace of God, king of England, lord of Ireland, duke of Normandy and Aquitaine, count of Anjou, to the archbishops, bishops, abbots, earls, barons, justiciars, foresters, sheriffs, reeves, servants, and all bailiffs and his faithful people greeting.

1. In the first place we have granted to God, and by this our present charter confirmed, for us and our heirs forever, that the English church shall be free, and shall hold its rights entire and its liberties uninjured; and we will that it thus be observed; which is shown by this, that the freedom of elections, which is considered to be most important and especially necessary to the English church, we, of our pure and spontaneous will, granted, and by our charter confirmed, before the contest between us and our barons had arisen; and obtained a confirmation and which we will shall be observed in good faith by our heirs forever.

We have granted moreover to all free men of our kingdom for us and our heirs forever all the liberties written below, to be had and holden by themselves and their heirs from us and our heirs.

2. If any of our earls or barons, or others holding from us in chief by military service shall have died, and when he has died his heir shall be of full age and owe relief, he shall have his inheritance by the ancient relief; that is to say, the heir or heirs of an earl for the whole barony of an earl a hundred pounds; the heir or heirs of a baron for a

From "Magna Carta," in E. P. Cheyney, trans., *University of Pennsylvania Translations and Reprints* (Philadelphia: University of Pennsylvania, 1897), Vol. I, No. 6, pp. 6-16.

whole barony a hundred pounds; the heir or heirs of a knight, for a whole knight's fee, a hundred shillings at most; and who owes less let him give less according to the ancient custom of fiefs.

3. If moreover the heir of any one of such shall be under age, and shall be in wardship, when he comes of age he shall have his inheritance without relief and without a fine.

4. The custodian of the land of such a minor heir shall not take from the land of the heir any except reasonable products, reasonable customary payments, and reasonable services, and this without destruction or waste of men or of property; and if we shall have committed the custody of the land of any such a one to the sheriff or to any other who is to be responsible to us for its proceeds, and that man shall have caused destruction or waste from his custody we will recover damages from him, and the land shall be committed to two legal and discreet men of that fief, who shall be responsible for its proceeds to us or to him to whom we have assigned them; and if we shall have given or sold to any one the custody of any such land, and he has caused destruction or waste there, he shall lose that custody, and it shall be handed over to two legal and discreet men of that fief who shall be in like manner responsible to us as is said above.

5. The custodian moreover, so long as he shall have the custody of the land, must keep up the houses, parks, warrens, fish ponds, mills, and other things pertaining to the land, from the proceeds of the land itself; and he must return to the heir, when he has come to full age, all his land, furnished with ploughs and implements of husbandry according as the time of wainage requires and as the proceeds of the land are able reasonably to sustain.

6. Heirs shall be married without disparity, so nevertheless that before the marriage is contracted, it shall be announced to the relatives by blood of the heir himself.

7. A widow, after the death of her husband, shall have her marriage portion and her inheritance immediately and without obstruction, nor shall she give anything for her dowry or for her marriage portion, or for her inheritance which inheritance her husband and she held on the day of the death of her husband; and she may remain in the house of her husband for forty days after his death, within which time her dowry shall be assigned to her.

8. No widow shall be compelled to marry so long as she prefers to live without a husband, provided she gives security that she will not marry without our consent, if she holds from us, or without the consent of her lord from whom she holds, if she holds from another.

• • •

11. And if any one dies leaving a debt owing to the Jews, his wife shall have her dowry, and shall pay nothing of that debt; and if there remain minor children of the dead man, necessaries shall be provided for them corresponding to the holding of the dead man; and from the

remainder shall be paid the debt, the service of the lords being retained. In the same way debts are to be treated which are owed to others than the Jews.

12. No scutage or aid shall be imposed in our kingdom except by the common council of our kingdom, except for the ransoming of our body, for the making of our oldest son a knight, and for once marrying our oldest daughter, and for these purposes it shall be only a reasonable aid; in the same way it shall be done concerning the aids of the city of London.

13. And the city of London shall have all its ancient liberties and free customs, as well by land as by water. Moreover, we will and grant that all other cities and boroughs and villages and ports shall have all their liberties and free customs.

14. And for holding a common council of the kingdoms concerning the assessment of an aid otherwise than in the three cases mentioned above, or concerning the assessment of a scutage we shall cause to be summoned the archbishops, bishops, abbots, earls, and greater barons by our letters under seal; and besides we shall cause to be summoned generally, by our sheriffs and bailiffs all those who hold from us in chief, for a certain day, that is at the end of forty days at least, and for a certain place; and in all the letters of that summons, we will express the cause of the summons, and when the summons has thus been given the business shall proceed on the appointed day, on the advice of those who shall be present, even if not all of those who were summoned have come.

15. We will not grant to any one, moreover, that he shall take an aid from his men, except for ransoming his body, for making his oldest son a knight, and for once marrying his oldest daughter; and for these purposes only a reasonable aid shall be taken.

16. No one shall be compelled to perform any greater service for a knight's fee, or for any other free tenement than is owed from it.

17. The common pleas shall not follow our court, but shall be held in some certain place.

18. The recognitions of *novel disseisin, mort d'ancestor,* and *darrein presentment* shall be held only in their own counties and in this manner: we, or if we are outside of the kingdom our principal justiciar, will send two justiciars through each county four times a year, who with four knight of each county, elected by the county, shall hold in the county and on the day and in the place of the county court, the aforesaid assizes of the county.

19. And if the aforesaid assizes cannot be held within the day of the county court, a sufficient number of knights and free-holders shall remain from those who were present at the county court on that day to give the judgments, according as the business is more or less.

20. A free man shall not be fined for a small offence, except in proportion to the measure of the offence; and for a great offence he shall

be fined in proportion to the magnitude of the offence, saving his freehold; and a merchant in the same way, saving his merchandise; and the villain shall be fined in the same way, saving his wainage, if he shall be at our mercy; and none of the above fines shall be imposed except by the oaths of honest men of the neighborhood.

21. Earls and barons shall only be fined by their peers, and only in proportion to their offence.

• • •

28. No constable or other bailiff of ours shall take anyone's grain or other chattels, without immediately paying for them in money, unless he is able to obtain a postponement at the good-will of the seller.

• • •

39. No free man shall be taken or imprisoned or dispossessed, or outlawed, or banished, or in any way destroyed, nor will we go upon him, nor send upon him, except by the legal judgment of his peers or by the law of the land.

40. To no one will we sell, to no one will we deny, or delay right or justice.

41. All merchants shall be safe and secure in going out from England and coming into England and in remaining and going through England, as well by land as by water, for buying and selling, free from all evil tolls, by the ancient and rightful customs, except in time of war, and if they are of a land at war with us; and if such are found in our land at the beginning of war, they shall be attached without injury to their bodies or goods, until it shall be known from us or from our principal justiciar in what way the merchants of our land are treated who shall be then found in the country which is at war with us; and if ours are safe there, the others shall be safe in our land.

• • •

52. If anyone shall have been dispossessed or removed by us without legal judgment of his peers, from his lands, castles, franchises, or his right we will restore them to him immediately; and if contention arises about this, then it shall be done according to the judgment of the twenty-five barons, of whom mention is made below concerning the security of the peace.

• • •

60. Moreover, all those customs and franchises mentioned above which we have conceded in our kingdom, and which are to be fulfilled, as far as pertains to us, in respect to our men; all men of our kingdom as well clergy as laymen, shall observe as far as pertains to them, in respect to their men.

61. Since, moreover, for the sake of God, and for the improvement of our kingdom, and for the better quieting of the hostility sprung up lately between us and our barons, we have made all these concessions; wishing them to enjoy these in a complete and firm stability forever, we make and concede to them the security described below; that is to

say, that they shall elect twenty-five barons of the kingdom, whom they will, who ought with all their power to observe, hold, and cause to be observed, the peace and liberties which we have conceded to them, and by this our present charter confirmed to them; in this manner, that if we or our justiciar, or our bailiffs, or any one of our servants shall have done wrong in any way toward any one, or shall have transgressed any of the articles of peace or security; and the wrong shall have been shown to four barons of the aforesaid twenty-five barons, let those four barons come to us or to our justiciar, if we are out of the kingdom, laying before us the transgression, and let them ask that we cause that transgression to be corrected without delay. And if we shall not have corrected the transgression or, if we shall be out of the kingdom, if our justiciar shall not have corrected it within a period of forty days, counting from the time in which it has been shown to us or to our justiciar, if we are out of the kingdom; the aforesaid four barons shall refer the matter to the remainder of the twenty-five barons, and let these twenty-five barons with the whole community of the country distress and injure us in every way they can; that is to say by the seizure of our castles, lands, possessions, and in such other ways as they can until it shall have been corrected according to their judgment, saving our person and that of our queen, and those of our children; and when the correction has been made, let them devote themselves to us as they did before. And let whoever in the country wishes take an oath that in all the above-mentioned measures he will obey the orders of the aforesaid twenty-five barons, and that he will injure us as far as he is able with them, and we give permission to swear publicly and freely to each one who wishes to swear, and no one will we ever forbid to swear. All those, moreover, in the country who of themselves and their own will are unwilling to take an oath to the twenty-five barons as to distressing and injuring us along with them, we will compel to take the oath by our mandate, as before said. And if any one of the twenty-five barons shall have died or departed from the land or shall in any other way be prevented from taking the above-mentioned action, let the remainder of the aforesaid twenty-five barons choose another in his place, according to their judgment, who shall take an oath in the same way as the others. In all those things, moreover, which are committed to those five and twenty barons to carry out, if perhaps the twenty-five are present, and some disagreement arises among them about something, or if any of them when they have been summoned are not willing or are not able to be present, let that be considered valid and firm which the greater part of those who are present arrange or command, just as if the whole twenty-five had agreed in this; and let the aforesaid twenty-five swear that they will observe faithfully all the things which are said above, and with all their ability cause them to be observed. And we will obtain nothing from anyone, either by ourselves or by another by which any of these concessions and liberties shall be revoked or diminished; and if any such thing shall have been obtained, let it be invalid and void, and we will never use it by ourselves or by another.

70. *The Parliament of Edward I*

Parliament began to assume an important role in English government under Edward I (1272–1307). The writs of summons to the Parliament of 1295 provide evidence concerning the nature and functions of the assembly.

Summons of a Bishop to Parliament (1295)

The King to the venerable father in Christ Robert, by the same grace archbishop of Canterbury, primate of all England, greeting. As a most just law, established by the careful providence of sacred princes, exhorts and decrees that what affects all, by all should be approved, so also, very evidently should common danger be met by means provided in common. You know sufficiently well, and it is now, as we believe, divulged through all regions of the world, how the king of France fraudulently and craftily deprives us of our land of Gascony, by withholding it unjustly from us. Now, however, not satisfied with the before-mentioned fraud and injustice, having gathered together for the conquest of our kingdom a very great fleet, and an abounding multitude of warriors, with which he has made a hostile attack on our kingdom and the inhabitants of the same kingdom, he now proposes to destroy the English language altogether from the earth, if his power should correspond to the detestable proposition of the contemplated injustice, which God forbid. Because, therefore, darts seen beforehand do less injury, and your interest especially, as that of the rest of the citizens of the same realm, is concerned in this affair, we command you, strictly enjoining you in the fidelity and love in which you are bound to us, that on the Lord's day next after the feast of St. Martin, in the approaching winter, you be present in person at Westminster; citing beforehand the dean and chapter of your church, the archdeacons and all the clergy of your diocese, causing the same dean and archdeacons in their own persons, and the said chapter by one suitable proctor, and the said clergy by two, to be present along with you, having full and sufficient power from the same chapter and clergy, to consider,

From summonses in E. P. Cheyney, trans., *University of Pennsylvania Translations and Reprints* (Philadelphia: University of Pennsylvania, 1897), Vol. I, No. 6, pp. 33–35. From *Sources of English Constitutional History*, translated by C. Stephenson and F. G. Marcham: Confirmation of the Charters (New York: Harper and Brothers, 1937), p. 164; Copyright 1937, 1965 by Harper and Row, Publishers, Incorporated; reprinted by permission of the publishers.

ordain and provide, along with us and with the rest of the prelates and principal men and other inhabitants of our kingdom, how the dangers and threatened evils of this kind are to be met. Witness the king at Wangham, the thirtieth day of September.

Identical summonses were sent out to the two archbishops and eighteen bishops, and, with the omission of the last paragraph, to seventy abbots.

Summons of a Baron to Parliament (1295)

The king to his beloved and faithful relative, Edmund, Earl of Cornwall, greeting. Because we wish to have a consultation and meeting with you and with the rest of the principal men of our kingdom, as to provision for remedies against the dangers which in these days are threatening our whole kingdom; we command you, strictly enjoining you in the fidelity and love in which you are bound to us, that on the Lord's day next after the feast of St. Martin, in the approaching winter, you be present in person at Westminster, for considering, ordaining and doing along with us and with the prelates, and the rest of the principal men and other inhabitants of our kingdom, as may be necessary for meeting dangers of this kind.

Witness the king at Canterbury, the first of October.

Similar summonses were sent to seven earls and forty-one barons.

Summons of Representatives of Shires and Towns to Parliament (1295)

The king to the sheriff of Northamptonshire. Since we intend to have a consultation and meeting with the earls, barons and other principal men of our kingdom with regard to providing remedies against the dangers which are in these days threatening the same kingdom; and on that account have commanded them to be with us on the Lord's day next after the feast of St. Martin in the approaching winter, at Westminster, to consider, ordain, and do as may be necessary for the avoidance of these dangers; we strictly require you to to cause two knights from the aforesaid county, two citizens from each city in the same county, and two burgesses from each borough, of those who are especially discreet and capable of laboring, to be elected without delay, and to cause them to come to us at the aforesaid said time and place.

Moreover, the said knights are to have full and sufficient power for themselves and for the community of the aforesaid county, and the said citizens and burgesses for themselves and the communities of the aforesaid cities and boroughs separately, then and there for doing what shall then be ordained according to the common counsel in the premises; so that the aforesaid business shall not remain unfinished in any way for defect of this power. And you shall have there the names of the knights, citizens and burgesses and this writ.

Witness the king at Canterbury on the third day of October.

Identical summonses were sent to the sheriffs of each county. At a Parliament held in 1297 Edward I was obliged to reissue Magna Carta and to reaffirm the principle of consent to taxation.

Confirmation of the Charters (1297)

Edward, by the grace of God king of England, lord of Ireland, and duke of Aquitaine, to all who may see or hear these present letters, greeting. Know that, for the honour of God and of Holy Church and for the benefit of our entire kingdom, we have granted for ourself and for our heirs that the Great Charter of Liberties and the Charter of the Forest, which were drawn up by the common assent of the whole kingdom in the time of King Henry, our father, are to be observed without impairment in all their particulars.

And whereas some people of our kingdom are fearful that the aids and taxes (*mises*), which by their liberality and good will they have heretofore paid to us for the sake of our wars and other needs, shall, despite the nature of the grants, be turned into a servile obligation for them and their heirs because these [payments] may at a future time be found in the rolls, and likewise the prises that in our name have been taken throughout the kingdom by our ministers: [therefore] we have granted, for us and our heirs, that, on account of anything that has been done or that can be found from a roll or in some other way, we will not make into a precedent for the future any such aids, taxes, or prises. And for us and our heirs we have also granted to the archbishops, bishops, abbots, priors, and other folk of Holy Church, and to the earls and barons and the whole community of the land, that on no account will we henceforth take from our kingdom such aids, taxes, and prises, except by the common assent of the whole kingdom and for the common benefit of the same kingdom, saving the ancient aids and prises due and accustomed.

And whereas the greater part of the community all feel themselves gravely oppressed by the maltote on wool — that is to say, 40s. from each sack of wool — and have besought us to relieve them [of the charge], at their prayer we have fully relieved them, granting that henceforth we will take neither this nor any other [custom] without their common assent and good will, saving to us and our heirs the custom on wool, wool-fells, and hides previously granted by the community of the kingdom aforesaid.

71.   *Coronation Oath of Edward II*

The coronation oath sworn by King Edward II in 1308 contained a new clause (the last one), which apparently granted to the community of the realm a right to participate in future legislation.

"Sire, will you grant and keep and by your oath confirm to the people of England the laws and customs given to them by the previous just and god-fearing kings, your ancestors, and especially the laws, customs, and liberties granted to the clergy and people by the glorious king, the sainted Edward, your predecessor?" "I grant and promise them."

"Sire, will you in all your judgments, so far as in you lies, preserve to God and Holy Church, and to the people and clergy, entire peace and concord before God?" "I will preserve them."

"Sire, will you, so far as in you lies, cause justice to be rendered rightly, impartially, and wisely, in compassion and in truth?" "I will do so."

"Sire, do you grant to be held and observed the just laws and customs that the community of your realm shall determine, and will you, so far as in you lies, defend and strengthen them to the honour of God?" "I grant and promise them."

From *Sources of English Constitutional History,* translated by C. Stephenson and F. G. Marcham: Edward II, Coronation Oath (New York: Harper and Brothers, 1937), p. 192; Copyright 1937, 1965 by Harper and Row, Publishers, Incorporated; reprinted by permission of the publishers.

XXIII

Rural Life

---

72. The Manor House and Manor: Peasant Obligations

This description of a thirteenth-century manor house was recorded in a document made for the Chapter of St. Paul's Cathedral, to whom the house belonged when it was granted to Robert Le Moyne, in 1265.

The Manor House at Chingford, Essex

He received also a sufficient and handsome hall well ceiled with oak. On the western side is a worthy bed, on the ground, a stone chimney, a wardrobe and a certain other small chamber; at the eastern end is a pantry and a buttery. Between the hall and the chapel is a sideroom. There is a decent chapel covered with tiles, a portable altar, and a small cross. In the hall are four tables on trestles. There are likewise a good kitchen well covered with tiles, with a furnace and ovens, one large, the other small, for cakes, two tables, and alongside the kitchen a small house for baking. Also a new granary covered with oak shingles, and a building in which the dairy is contained, though it is divided. Likewise a chamber suited for clergymen and a necessary chamber. Also a hen-house. These are within the inner gate.

Likewise outside of that gate are an old house for the servants, a good stable, long and divided, and to the east of the principal building, beyond the smaller stable, a solar for the use of the servants. Also a building in which is contained a bed; also two barns, one for wheat

From J. H. Robinson, trans., *University of Pennsylvania Translations and Reprints* (Philadelphia: University of Pennsylvania, 1897), Vol. III, No. 5, pp. 31, 3-4, 4-8.

and one for oats. These buildings are enclosed with a moat, a wall, and a hedge. Also beyond the middle gate is a good barn, and a stable of cows and another for oxen, these old and ruinous. Also beyond the outer gate is a pigstye.

The most extensive survey of the resources of English manors was compiled in William the Conqueror's Domesday Book *(1086). The following excerpt illustrates the kind of information that was collected from thousands of English villages.*

A Domesday Manor: Hecham, Essex

Peter de Valence holds in domain Hecham, which Haldane a freeman held in the time of King Edward, as a manor, and as 5 hides. There have always been 2 ploughs in the demesne, 4 ploughs of the men. At that time there were 8 villeins, now 10; then there were 2 bordars, now 3; at both times 4 *servi,* woods for 300 swine, 18 acres of meadow. Then there were 2 fish ponds and a half, now there are none. At that time there was 1 ox, now there are 15 cattle and 1 small horse and 18 swine and 2 hives of bees. At that time it was worth 60s., now 4£. 10s. When he received this manor he found only 1 ox and 1 planted acre. Of those 5 hides spoken of above, one was held in the time of King Edward by 2 freemen, and was added to this manor in the time of King William. It was worth in the time of King Edward 10s., now 22s., and William holds this from Peter de Valence.

A description of the manor of Alwalton, Huntingdonshire, was recorded in the Hundred Rolls *of the year 1279. It included details of the peasants' obligations to the lord.*

The abbot of Peterborough holds the manor of Alwalton and vill from the lord king directly; which manor and vill with its appurtenances the lord Edward, formerly king of England gave to the said abbot and convent of that place in free, pure, and perpetual alms. And the court of the said manor with its garden contains one half an acre. And to the whole of the said vill Alwalton belong 5 hides and a half and 1 virgate of land and a half; of which each hide contains 5 virgates of land and each virgate contains 25 acres. Of these hides the said abbot has in demesne 1 hide and a half of land and half a virgate, which contain as above. Likewise he has there 8 acres of meadow. Also he has there separable pasture which contains 1 acre. Likewise he has there three water mills. Likewise he has there a common fish pond with a fish-weir on the bank of the Nene, which begins at Wildlake and extends to the mill of Newton and contains in length 2 leagues. Likewise he has there a ferry with a boat.

Free tenants. Thomas le Boteler holds a messuage with a court yard which contains 1 rood, and 3 acres of land, by charter, paying thence yearly to the said abbot 14s.

Likewise the rector of the church of Alwalton holds 1 virgate of land with its appurtenances, with which the said church was anciently endowed. Likewise the said rector has a holding the tenant of which holds 1 rood of ground by paying to the said rector yearly 12d.

And the abbot of Peterboro is patron of the church.

Villeins. Hugh Miller holds 1 virgate of land in villenage by paying thence to the said abbot 3s. 1d. Likewise the same Hugh works through the whole year except 1 week at Christmas, 1 week at Easter, and 1 at Whitsuntide, that is in each week 3 days, each with 1 man, and in autumn each day with 2 men, performing the said works at the will of the said abbot as in plowing and other work. Likewise he gives 1 bushel of wheat for benseed and 18 sheaves of oats for fodder-corn. Likewise he gives 3 hens and 1 cock yearly and 5 eggs at Easter. Likewise he does carrying to Peterborough and to Jakele and no where else, at the will of the said abbot. Likewise if he sells a brood mare in his court yard for 10s. or more, he shall give to the said abbot 4d., and if for less he shall give nothing to the aforesaid. He gives also merchet and heriot, and is tallaged at the feast of St. Michael, at the will of the said abbot. There are also there 17 other villeins, viz. John of Ganesoupe, Robert son of Walter, Ralph son of the reeve, Emma ate Pertre, William son of Reginald, Thomas son of Gunnilda, Eda widow of Ralph, Ralph Reeve, William Reeve, William son of William Reeve, Thomas Flegg, Henry Abbott, William Hereward, Serle son of William Reeve, Walter Palmer, William Abbot, Henry Serle; each of whom holds 1 virgate of land in villenage, paying and doing in all things, each for himself, to the said abbot yearly just as the said Hugh Miller. There are also 5 other villeins, viz. Simon Mariot, Robert of Hastone, Thomas Smith, John Mustard, and William Carter, each of whom holds half a virgate of land by paying and doing in all things half of the whole service which Hugh Miller pays and does.

Cotters. Henry, son of the miller, holds a cottage with a croft which contains 1 rood, paying thence yearly to the said abbot 2s. Likewise he works for 3 days in carrying hay and in other works at the will of the said abbot, each day with 1 man and in autumn 1 day in cutting grain with 1 man.

Likewise Ralph Miller holds a cottage with a croft which contains a rood, paying to the said abbot 2s.; and he works just as the said Henry.

Likewise William Arnold holds a cottage with a croft which contains half a rood, paying to the abbot 2d.; and he works just as the said Henry.

Likewise Hugh Day holds a cottage with a croft which contains 1 rood, paying to the abbot 8d.; and he works just as the said Henry.

Likewise Sara, widow of Matthew Miller, holds a cottage and a croft which contains half a rood, paying to the said abbot 4d.; and she works just as the said Henry.

Likewise Sara, widow of William Miller, holds a cottage and a croft which contains half a rood, paying to the abbot 4d,; and she works just as the said Henry.

Likewise William Kendale holds a cottage and a croft which contains 1 rood, paying to the abbot 8d.; and he works just as the said Henry.

Likewise Agnes the widow holds a cottage with a croft which contains 1 rood, paying thence yearly 12d.; and she works just as the said Henry.

Likewise Geoffrey Note holds a cottage and croft which contains half a rood; paying yearly 8d.; and he works just as the said Henry.

Likewise Beatrice the widow holds a cottage and croft which contains half a rood, paying to the abbot 8d.; and she works just as the said Henry.

Likewise Henry of Aylingtone holds a cottage with a croft which contains half a rood, and 1 acre of land, paying to the abbot 2s. 8d.; and he works just as the said Henry.

Likewise Benedict Atelane holds a cottage with a croft which contains a half rood, paying to the abbot 8d.; and he works just as the said Henry.

Likewise Geoffrey Baker holds a toft and croft, and it contains half a rood, paying to the abbot 4d.; and he works just as the said Henry.

Likewise Robert Prenk holds a cottage with a croft which contains half a rood, paying to the said abbot 4d.; and he works just as the said Henry.

Likewise Roger Doket holds a cottage with a croft which contains half a rood, paying to the abbot 4d.; and he works just as the said Henry.

Likewise Geoffrey Drake holds a cottage with a croft and which contains half a rood, paying to the abbot 4d.; and he works just as the said Henry.

Likewise Sara the widow holds a cottage with a croft which contains a rood, and a half acre of land, paying to the abbot 8d.; and she works just as the said Henry.

Likewise William Drake holds a cottage with a croft which contains half a rood, paying to the abbot 6d.; and he works just as the said Henry.

There are there also 6 other cotters, viz. William Drake Jr., Amycia the widow, Alice the widow, Robert son of Eda, Willam Pepper, William Coleman, each of whom holds a cottage with a croft which contains half a rood, paying and doing in all things, each for himself, just as the said William Drake.

Likewise William Russel holds a cottage with a croft which contains half a rood, paying to the abbot 8d.; and he works in all things just as the said Henry Miller.

There are moreover there 5 other cotters, viz. Walter Pestel, Ralph Shepherd, Henry Abbot, Matilda Tut, Jordan Mustard, each of whom holds a cottage with a croft which contains half a rood, paying thence and doing in all things to the said abbot just as the said William Russel.

Likewise Beatrice of Hampton holds a cottage and croft which contains 1 rood, paying to the abbot 12d.; and she works in all things just as the said Henry.

Likewise Hugh Miller holds 3 acres of land paying to the abbot 42d.

Likewise Thomas, son of Richard, holds a cottage with a croft which contains half a rood, and 3 acres of land, paying to the abbot 4s. and he works just as the said Henry.

Likewise Ralph Reeve holds a cottage with a croft which contains 1 rood, and 1 acre of land, paying to the abbot 2s.; and he works just as the said Henry.

Likewise each of the said cottages, except the widows, gives yearly after Christmas a penny which is called head-penny.

73. The Manorial Court

The following cases, from the year 1246 to 1249, are typical of those heard in manorial courts.

John Sperling complains that Richard of Newmere on the Sunday next before S. Bartholomew's day last past with his cattle, horses, and pigs wrongfully destroyed the corn on his [John's] land to his damage to the extent of one thrave of wheat, and to his dishonour to the extent of two shillings; and of this he produces suit. And Richard comes and defends all of it. Therefore let him go to the law six handed. His pledges, Simon Combe and Hugh Frith.

Hugh Free in mercy for his beast caught in the lord's garden. Pledges, Walter Hill and William Slipper. Fine 6d.

[The] twelve jurors say that Hugh Cross has right in the bank and hedge about which there was a dispute between him and William White. Therefore let him hold in peace and let William be distrained for his many trespasses. (Afterwards he made fine for 12d.)

Roger Pleader is at his law against Nicholas Croke [to prove] that neither he [Roger] nor his killed [Nicholas's] peacock. Pledges, Ringer and Jordan. Afterwards he made his law and therefore is quit.

From the whole township of Little Ogbourne, except seven, for not coming to wash the lord's sheep, 6s. 8d.

Gilbert Richard's son gives 5s. for license to marry a wife. Pledge, Seaman. Term [for payment,] the Purification.

William Jordan in mercy for bad ploughing on the lord's land. Pledge, Arthur. Fine, 6d.

From F. W. Maitland, ed., "Select Pleas in Manorial Courts," in G. G. Coulton, ed., *Social Life in Britain from the Conquest to the Reformation* (London: Cambridge University Press, 1918), pp. 306–308; reprinted by permission of the publisher.

The parson of the Church is in mercy for his cow caught in the lord's meadow. Pledges, Thomas Ymer and William Coke.

From Martin Shepherd 6*d*. for the wound that he gave Pekin.

Ragenhilda of Bec gives 2*s*. for having married without licence. Pledge, William of Primer.

Walter Hull gives 13*s*. 4*d*. for licence to dwell on the land of the Prior of Harmondsworth so long as he shall live and as a condition finds pledges, to wit, William Slipper, John Bisuthe, Gilbert Bisuthe, Hugh Tree, William Johnson, John Hulle, who undertake that the said Walter shall do to the lord all the services and customs which he would do if he dwelt on the lord's land, and that his heriot shall be secured to the lord in case he dies there [i.e. at Harmondsworth].

The Court presented that William Noah's son is the born bondman of the lord and a fugitive and dwells at Dodford. Therefore he must be sought. They say also that William Askil, John Parsons and Godfrey Green have furtively carried off four geese from the vill of Horepoll.

It was presented that Robert Carter's son by night invaded the house of Peter Burgess and in felony threw stones at his door so that the said Peter raised the hue. Therefore let the said Robert be committed to prison. Afterwards he made fine with 2*s*.

All the ploughmen of Great Ogbourne are convicted by the oath of twelve men . . . because by reason of their default [the land] of the lord was ill-ploughed whereby the lord is damaged to the amount of 9*s*. . . . And Walter Reaper is in mercy for concealing [i.e. not giving information as to] the said bad ploughing. Afterwards he made fine with the lord with 1 mark.

74.   *Manumission of a Villein*

During the thirteenth century many serfs received their freedom. The act of manumission, however commonly specified heavy services that the peasant still owed to his lord, as in this example, dated 1278, from the records of the abbey of Peterborough.

To all the faithful of Christ to whom the present writing shall come, Richard by the divine permission abbot of Peterborough and the Convent of the same place, eternal greeting in the Lord. Let all know that we have manumitted and liberated from all yoke of servitude William, the son of Richard of Wythington whom previously we have held as our born bondman, with his whole progeny and all his chattels, so that

From J. H. Robinson, trans., *University of Pennsylvania Translations and Reprints* (Philadelphia: University of Pennsylvania, 1897), Vol. III, No. 5, pp. 31-32.

neither we nor our successors shall be able to require or exact any right or claim in the said William, his progeny, or his chattel. But the same William with his whole progeny and all his chattels will remain free and quit and without disturbance, exaction, or any claim on the part of us or our successors by reason of any servitude, forever. We will moreover and concede that he and his heirs shall hold the messuages, land, rents, and meadows in Wythington which his ancestors held from us and our predecessors, by giving and performing the fine which is called merchet for giving his daughter in marriage, and tallage from year to year according to our will, — that he shall have and hold these for the future from us and our successors freely, quietly, peacefully, and hereditarily, by paying thence to us and our successors yearly 40s. sterling, at the four terms of the year, namely; at St. John the Baptist's day, 10s., at Michaelmas, 10s., At Christmas, 10s., and at Easter, 10s., for all service, exaction, custom, and secular demand; saving to us nevertheless attendance at our court of Castre every three weeks, wardship and relief, and outside service of our lord the king, when they shall happen. And if it shall happen that the said William or his heirs shall die at any time without an heir, the said messuage, land, rents, and meadows with their appurtenances shall return fully and completely to us and our successors. Nor will it be allowed to the said William or his heirs the said messuages, land, rents, meadows, or any part of them to give, sell, alienate, mortgage, or in any way encumber by which the said messuage, land, rents, and meadows should not return to us and our successors in the form declared above. But if this should occur later their deed shall be declared null and what is thus alienated shall come to us and our successors. In testimony of which duplicate seals are appended to this writing, formed as a chirograph, for the sake of greater security. These being witnesses, etc. Given at Borough for the love of lord Robert of good memory, once abbot, our predecessor and maternal uncle of the said William, and at the instance of the good man brother Hugh of Mutton, relative of the said abbot Robert; A.D. 1278, on the eve of Pentecost.

chapter
XXIV

The World of Thought

75.   *University Regulations*

Universities grew into existence when groups of masters and students formed themselves into organized corporations with the right to control courses of study and determine conditions for the award of degrees.

The following decree of Pope Gregory IX (1231) marks an important stage in the rise of the University of Paris.

Statutes of Gregory IX for the University of Paris in 1231

Gregory, the bishop, servant of the servants of God, to his beloved sons, all the masters and students of Paris—greeting and apostolic benediction.

Paris, the mother of sciences, like another Cariath Sepher, a city of letters, stands forth illustrious, great indeed, but concerning herself she causes greater things to be desired, full of favor for the teachers and students. . . .

. . . Wherefore, since we have diligently investigated the questions referred to us concerning a dissension which, through the instigation of the devil, has arisen there and greatly disturbed the university, we have decided, by the advice of our brethren, that these should be set at rest rather by precautionary measures, than by a judicial sentence.

Therefore, concerning the condition of the students and schools, we have decided that the following should be observed: each chancellor,

From Statutes of Gregory IX, in D. C. Munro, trans., *University of Pennsylvania Translations and Reprints* (Philadelphia: University of Pennsylvania, 1897), Vol. II, No. 3, pp. 7-11.

appointed hereafter at Paris, at the time of his installation, in the presence of the bishop, or at the command of the latter in the chapter at Paris—two masters of the students having been summoned for this purpose and present in behalf of the university—shall swear that, in good faith, according to his conscience, he will not receive as professors of theology and canon law any but suitable men, at a suitable place and time, according to the condition of the city and the honor and glory of those branches of learning; and he will reject all who are unworthy without respect to persons or nations. Before licensing anyone, during three months, dating from the time when the license is requested, the chancellor shall make diligent inquiries of all the masters of theology present in the city, and of all other honest and learned men through whom the truth can be ascertained, concerning the life, knowledge, capacity, purpose, prospects and other qualities needful in such persons; and after the inquiries, in good faith and according to his conscience, he shall grant or deny the license to the candidate, as shall seem fitting and expedient. The masters of theology and canon law, when they begin to lecture, shall take a public oath that they will give true testimony on the above points. The chancellor shall also swear, that, he will in no way reveal the advice of the masters, to their injury; the liberty and privileges being maintained in their full vigor for the canons at Paris, as they were in the beginning. Moreover, the chancellor shall promise to examine in good faith the masters in medicine and arts and in the other branches, to admit only the worthy and to reject the unworthy.

In other matters, because confusion easily creeps in where there is no order, we grant to you the right of making constitutions and ordinances regulating the manner and time of lectures and disputations, the costume to be worn, the burial of the dead; and also concerning the bachelors, who are to lecture and at what hours, and on what they are to lecture; and concerning the prices of the lodgings or the interdiction of the same; and concerning a fit punishment for those who violate your constitutions or ordinances, by exclusion from your society. And if, perchance, the assessment of the lodgings is taken from you, or anything else is lacking, or an injury or outrageous damage, such as death or the mutilation of a limb, is inflicted on one of you; unless through a suitable admonition satisfaction is rendered within fifteen days, you may suspend your lectures until you have received full satisfaction. And if it happens that any one of you is unlawfully imprisoned, unless the injury ceases on a remonstrance from you, you may, if you judge it expedient, suspend your lectures immediately.

We command, moreover, that the bishop of Paris shall so chastise the excesses of the guilty, that the honor of the students shall be preserved and evil deeds shall not remain unpunished. But in no way shall the innocent be seized on account of the guilty; nay rather, if a probable suspicion arises against anyone, he shall be detained honorably and on giving suitable bail he shall be freed, without any exactions from the jailors. But if, perchance, such a crime has been committed that imprisonment is necessary, the bishop shall detain the criminal in his prison. The chancellor is forbidden to keep him in his prison. We also forbid holding a student for a debt contracted by another, since this is interdicted by canonical and legitimate sanctions. Neither the bishop, nor his official, nor the chancellor shall exact a pecuniary penalty for removing an excommunication or any other censures of any kind. Nor shall the chancellor demand from the masters who are licensed an oath, or obedience, or any pledge; nor shall he receive any emolument or promise for granting a license, but be content with the above-mentioned oath.

Also, the vacation in summer is not to exceed one month, and the bachelors, if they wish, can continue their lectures in vacation time. Moreover, we prohibit more expressly the students from carrying weapons in the city, and the university from protecting those who disturb the peace and study. And those who call themselves students but do not frequent the schools, or acknowledge any master, are in no way to enjoy the liberties of the students.

Moreover, we order that the masters in arts shall always read one lecture on Priscian, and one book after the other in the regular courses. Those books on natural philosophy which for a certain reason were prohibited in a provincial council, are not to be used at Paris until they have been examined and purged of all suspicion of error. The masters and students in theology shall strive to exercise themselves laudably in the branch which they profess; they shall not show themselves philosophers, but they shall strive to become God's learned. And they shall not speak in the language of the people, confounding the sacred language with the profane. In the schools they shall dispute only on such questions as can be determined by theological books and the writings of the holy fathers.

• • •

It is not lawful for any man whatever to infringe this deed of our provision, constitution, concession, prohibition and inhibition or to act contrary to it, from rash presumption. If anyone, however, should dare to attempt this, let him know that he incurs the wrath of almighty God and of the blessed Peter and Paul, his apostles.

Given at the Lateran, on the Ides of April [April 13,] in the fifth year of our pontificate.

The syllabus drawn up by the Arts Faculty of the University of Paris in 1255 indicates the extraordinary influx of new Aristotelian learning during the preceding half century.

Lynn Thorndike, trans., *University Records and Life in the Middle Ages* (New York: Columbia University Press, 1944), pp. 64-66, 80-81, 66-67; Copyright 1944 by Columbia University Press; reprinted by permission of the publisher.

Courses in Arts, Paris (1255)

In the year of the Lord 1254. Let all know that we, all and each, masters of arts by our common assent, no one contradicting, because of the new and incalculable peril which threatens in our faculty—some masters hurrying to finish their lectures sooner than the length and difficulty of the text permits, for which reason both masters in lecturing and scholars in hearing make less progress—worrying over the ruin of our faculty and wishing to provide for our status, have decreed and ordained for the common utility and the reparation of our university to the honor of God and the church universal that all the single masters of our faculty in the future shall be required to finish the texts which they shall have begun on the feast of St. Remy [October 1] at the times below noted, not before.

The Old Logic, namely the book of Porphyry, the *Praedicamenta, Periarmeniae, Divisions* and *Topics* of Boethius, except the fourth, on the feast of the Annunication of the blessed Virgin [March 25] or the last day for lectures preceding. *Priscian minor* and *major, Topics* and *Elenchi, Prior* and *Posterior Analytics* they must finish in the said or equal time. The *Ethics* through four books in twelve weeks, if they are read with another text; if *per se,* not with another, in half that time. Three short texts, namely *Sex principia, Barbarismus,* Priscian on accent, if read together and nothing else with them, in six weeks. The *Physics* of Aristotle, *Metaphysics,* and *De animalibus* on the feast of St. John the Baptist [June 24]; *De celo et mundo,* first book of *Meterology* with the fourth, on Ascension day [a movable feast, forty days after Easter, usually in May]; *De anima,* if read with the books on nature, on the feast of the Ascension, if with the logical texts, on the feast of the Annunciation of the blessed Virgin; *De generatione* on the feast of the Chair of St. Peter [February 25]; *De causis* in seven weeks; *De sensu et sensato* in six weeks; *De sompno et vigilia* in five weeks; *De plantis* in five weeks; *De memoria et reminiscentia* in two weeks; *De differentia spiritus et animae* in two weeks; *De morte et vita* in one week. Moreover, if masters begin to read the said books at another time than the feast of St. Remy, they shall allow as much time for lecturing on them as is indicated above. Moreover, each of the said texts, if read by itself, not with another text, can be finished in half the time of lecturing assigned above. It will not be permitted anyone to finish the said texts in less time, but anyone may take the time. Moreover, if anyone reads some portion of a text, so that he does not wish, or is unable, to complete the whole of it, he shall read that portion in a corresponding amount of time.

. . . These things, moreover, we have decreed and ordained to be observed inviolate. Let no one, therefore, infringe this page of our ordinance or rashly go against it. But should anyone presume to attempt this, let him know that he will incur the wrath of the whole university and suspension of lectures for a year. In testimony and support of which thing we have decreed that the present letter be sealed with the seals of the four nations by their consent. Given in the year 1254 on the Friday before Palm Sunday.

The dangers of Aristotelian studies are suggested by the following decree. The errors condemned were mainly those of the Averroists, who followed the Arab commentator on Aristotle, Averroes.

Thirteen Errors Condemned by Stephen, Bishop of Paris (1270)

These are the errors condemned and excommunicated with all who taught or asserted them knowingly by Stephen, bishop of Paris, in the year of the Lord 1270, the Wednesday after the feast of the blessed Nicholas in the winter [December 10, St. Nicholas day being December 6].

The first article is: That the intellect of all men is one and the same in number.

2. That this is false or inappropriate: Man understands.

3. That the will of man wills or chooses from necessity.

4. That all things which are done here below depend upon the necessity of the celestial bodies.

5. That the world is eternal.

6. That there never was a first man.

7. That the soul, which is the form of man as a human being, is corrupted when the body is corrupted.

8. That the soul separated after death does not suffer from corporal fire.

9. That free will is a passive power, not active; and that it is moved necessarily by appetite.

10. That God does not know things in particular.

11. That God does not know other things than Himself.

12. That human actions are not ruled by divine Providence.

13. That God cannot give immortality or incorruptibility to a corruptible or mortal thing.

The manner of lecturing in medieval universities was described by Odofredus, introducing his course on the Corpus Juris Civilis *at Bologna (ca. 1250).*

If you please, I will begin the *Old Digest* on the eighth day or thereabouts after the feast of St. Michael and I will finish it entire with all ordinary and extraordinary, Providence permitting, in the middle of August or thereabouts. The *Code* I will always begin within about a fortnight of the feast of St. Michael [September 29] and I will finish it with all ordinary and extraordinary, Providence permitting, on the first of August or thereabouts. The extraordinary lectures used not to be given by the doctors. And so all scholars including the unskilled and novices will be able to make good progress with me, for they will hear their text as a whole, nor will anything be left out, as was once done in this region, indeed was the usual practice. For I shall teach the unskilled, and novices but also the advanced students. For the unskilled will be able to make satisfactory progress in the position of the case and exposition of the letter; the advanced students can become more erudite in the subtleties of questions and contrarieties. I shall also read all the glosses, which was not done before my time. . . .

For it is my purpose to teach you faithfully and in a kindly manner, in which instruction the following order has customarily been observed by the ancient and modern doctors and particularly by my master, which method I shall retain. First, I shall give you the summaries of each title before I come to the text. Second, I shall put forth well and distinctly and in the best terms I can the purport of each law. Third, I shall read the text in order to correct it. Fourth, I shall briefly restate the meaning. Fifth, I shall solve conflicts, adding general matters (which are commonly called *brocardica*) and subtle and useful distinctions and questions with the solutions, so far as divine Providence shall assist me. And if any law is deserving of a review by reason of its fame or difficulty, I shall reserve it for an afternoon review.

76. *Student Life*

Medieval universities, like modern ones, knew good students, bad students, and, worst of all, non-students.

A Good Student

The model student described below became a bishop and was canonized as St. Richard of Chichester.

Richard therefore hastily left both [his father's] lands and the lady [who had been chosen as his wife], and all his friends, and betook himself to the University of Oxford and then to that of Paris, where he learned logic. Such was his love of learning, that he cared little or nothing for food or raiment. For, as he was wont to relate, he and two companions who lodged in the same chamber had only their tunics,

From "Acta Sanctorum," in G. G. Coulton, ed., *Social Life in Britain from the Conquest to the Reformation* (London: Cambridge University Press, 1918), p. 61; reprinted by permission of the publisher.

and one gown between them, and each of them a miserable pallet. When one, therefore, went out with the gown to hear a lecture, the other sat in their room, and so they went forth alternately; and bread with a little wine and pottage sufficed for their food. For their poverty never suffered them to eat flesh or fish, save on the Sunday or on some solemn holy day or in presence of companions or friends; yet he hath oftentimes told me how, in all his days, he had never after led so pleasant and delectable a life.

Bad Students

Alvarus Pelagius (ca. 1275–1349) wrote the following account of student vices. He was a Franciscan friar who castigated all the faults of his age in a rambling work called The Plaint of the Church.

1. Sometimes they wish to be above their masters, impugning their statements more with a certain wrong-headedness than with reason. . . .

2. Those wish to become masters who were not legitimate disciples. . . .

3. They attend classes but make no effort to learn anything. . . . Such are limbs of Satan rather than of Christ. . . . And these persons who go to a university but do not study cannot with clear consciences enjoy the privilege of the fruits of benefices in a university. . . . And if they receive such, they are held to restitution because they receive them fraudulently, as the tenor of the canon cited makes evident.

4. They frequently learn what they would better ignore . . . such things as forbidden sciences, amatory discourses, and superstitions.

5. On obscure points they depend upon their own judgment, passing over scripture and canonical science of which they are ignorant. And so they become masters of error. For they are ashamed to ask of others what they themselves don't know, which is stupid pride. . . .

6. They defraud their masters of their due salaries, although they are able to pay. Wherefore they are legally bound to make restitution, because, says Gregory XII, query 2, One serving ecclesiastical utilities ought to rejoice in ecclesiastical remuneration.

7. They have among themselves evil and disgraceful societies, associating together for ill. And while in residence they sometimes are guilty of vices, against which their masters ought to provide and take action so far as they can. . . .

8. They are disobedient to the masters and rectors of the universi-

From Alvarus Pelagius, "De Planctu Ecclesiae," in Lynn Thorndike, trans., *University Records and Life in the Middle Ages* (New York: Columbia University Press, 1944), pp. 173–174; Copyright 1944 by Columbia University Press; reprinted by permission of the publisher.

ties and sometimes transgress the statutes which they have sworn to observe. And sometimes they contend against and resist the officials, for which they should be subjected to blows or rods, a method of coercion admissible against clerics by masters of liberal arts and by their parents. . . .

9. On feast days they don't go to church to hear divine service and sermons and above all the full mass which all Christians are supposed to attend (*de conse, di.i. missas*), but gad about town with their fellows or attend lectures or write up their notes at home. Or, if they go to church, it is not for worship but to see the girls or swap stories.

10. They foment rows and form parties and tickets in electing the rector or securing the appointment of professors, not following the interests of the student body as a whole but their own affections, sometimes to this intent alluring with gifts and flattering attentions for their own masters, and sometimes drawing scholars away from other teachers and persuading them to come to theirs, and not for the best interest of the scholars. . . .

11. If they are clergymen with parishes, when they go off to universities, they do not leave good and sufficient vicars in their churches to care diligently for the souls of their parishioners. . . . Or they hear lectures in fields forbidden to them, such as the law.

12. The expense money which they have from their parents or churches they spend in taverns, conviviality, games and other superfluities, and so they return home empty, without knowledge, conscience, or money. Against whom may be quoted that observation of Jerome, "It is praiseworthy, not to have seen Jerusalem, but to have lived well." So, not to have studied at Paris or Bologna, but to have done so diligently merits praise.

13. They contract debts and sometimes withdraw from the university without paying them, on which acccount they are excommunicated and do not care, but they may not be absolved. . . .

Non-students

Seeing that the peace of this kindly [*almae*] University is seen to be frequently broken by divers persons who, under pretence of being scholars, wait and lurk within the University and its precincts, but outside the Halls and under tutelage of no Principal—men known by the abominable name of "Chamberdeacons," who sleep all day and by night haunt the taverns and brothels for occasions of robbery and manslaughter—therefore it is decreed by the said University that all and every scholar do dwell in that Hall or College wherein his common contributions are

From "Statute of Oxford University," in G. G. Coulton, ed., *Social Life in Britain from the Conquest to the Reformation* (London: Cambridge University Press, 1918), p. 64; reprinted by permission of the publisher.

registered, or in Halls thereunto annexed, which share with the aforesaid in commons or battels, under pain of imprisonment for the first offence. If, moreover, having been once admonished by the Chancellor or his Commissary, or by Proctors, they neglect the transfer themselves to those abodes aforesaid, then let them be banished and cut off from the University, as rotten members thereof, within eight days.

77.   Philosophy and Science: Thomas Aquinas, Bonaventura, John Buridan, Nicholas Oresme

Thomas Aquinas: Summa Theologiae

Thomas Aquinas (1225–1274) is commonly regarded as the greatest of medieval philosophers. The following excerpts from his Summa Theologiae *are intended to illustrate both his manner of argument and some of his characteristic conclusions.*

Part One

QUESTION 1: THE NATURE AND DOMAIN OF SACRED DOCTRINE

First Article: whether, besides the philosophical disciplines, any further doctrine is required? *We proceed thus to the First Article:—*

Objection 1.   It seems that, besides the philosophical disciplines, we have no need of any further doctrine. For man should not seek to know what is above reason: *Seek not the things that are too high for thee (Ecclus.* iii. 22). But whatever is not above reason is sufficiently considered in the philosophical disciplines. Therefore any other doctrine besides the philosophical disciplines is superfluous.

Objection 2.   Further, doctrine can be concerned only with being, for nothing can be known, save the true, which is convertible with being. But everything that is, is considered in the philosophical disciplines —even God Himself; so that there is a part of philosophy called theology, or the divine science, as is clear from Aristotle. Therefore, besides the philosophical disciplines, there is no need of any further doctrine.

On the contrary, It is written (2 *Tim.* iii. 16): *All Scripture inspired*

From Thomas Aquinas, "Summa Theologiae," in *Basic Writings of Saint Thomas Aquinas,* A. C. Pegis, trans. (New York: Random House, 1945), Vol. I, pp. 5-6, 21-24; Vol. II, pp. 773-775, 794-795; reprinted by permission of Random House and Burns & Oates Ltd.

of God is profitable to teach, to reprove, to correct, to instruct in justice. Now Scripture, inspired of God, is not a part of the philosophical disciplines discovered by human reason. Therefore it is useful that besides the philosophical disciplines there should be another science — *i.e.,* inspired by God.

I answer that, It was necessary for man's salvation that there should be a doctrine revealed by God, besides the philosophical disciplines investigated by human reason. First, because man is directed to God as to an end that surpasses the grasp of his reason: *The eye hath not seen, O God, besides Thee, what things Thou has prepared for them that wait for Thee (Isa.* lxiv. 4). But the end must first be known by men who are to direct their intentions and actions to the end. Hence it was necessary for the salvation of man that certain truths which exceed human reason should be made known to him by divine revelation. Even as regards those truths about God which human reason can investigate, it was necessary that man be taught by a divine revelation. For the truth about God, such as reason can know it, would only be known by a few, and that after a long time; and with the admixture of many errors; whereas man's whole salvation, which is in God, depends upon the knowledge of this truth. Therefore, in order that the salvation of men might be brought about more fitly and more surely, it was necessary that they be taught divine truths by divine revelation. It was therefore necessary that, besides the philosophical disciplines investigated by reason, there should be a sacred doctrine by way of revelation.

Reply Obj. 1. Although those things which are beyond man's knowledge may not be sought for by man through his reason, nevertheless, what is revealed by God must be accepted through faith. Hence the sacred text continues, *For many things are shown to thee above the understanding of man (Ecclus.* iii. 25). And in such things sacred doctrine consists.

Reply Obj. 2. Sciences are diversified according to the diverse nature of their knowable objects. For the astronomer and the physicist both prove the same conclusion — that the earth, for instance, is round: the astronomer by means of mathematics (*i.e.,* abstracting from matter), but the physicist by means of matter itself. Hence there is no reason why those things which are treated by the philosophical disciplines, so far as they can be known by the light of natural reason, may not also be treated by another science so far as they are known by the light of the divine revelation. Hence the theology included in sacred doctrine differs in genus from that theology which is part of philosophy.

QUESTION 2: THE EXISTENCE OF GOD

Third Article: whether God exists? *We proceed thus to the Third Article:* —

Objection 1. It seems that God does not exist; because if one of two contraries be infinite, the other would be altogether destroyed.

But the name *God* means that He is infinite goodness. If, therefore, God existed, there would be no evil discoverable; but there is evil in the world. Therefore God does not exist.

Obj. 2.   Further it is superfluous to suppose that what can be accounted for by a few principles has been produced by many. But it seems that everything we see in the world can be accounted for by other principles, supposing God did not exist. For all natural things can be reduced to one principle, which is nature; and all voluntary things can be reduced to one principle, which is human reason, or will. Therefore there is no need to suppose God's existence.

On the contrary, It is said in the person of God: *I am Who am* (*Exod.* iii. 14).

I answer that, The existence of God can be proved in five ways.

The first and more manifest way is the argument from motion. It is certain, and evident to our senses, that in the world some things are in motion. Now whatever is moved is moved by another, for nothing can be moved except it is in potentiality to that towards which is it moved; whereas a thing moves inasmuch as it is in act. For motion is nothing else than the reduction of something from potentiality to actuality. But nothing can be reduced from potentiality to actuality, except by something in a state of actuality. Thus that which is actually hot, as fire, makes wood, which is potentially hot, to be actually hot, and thereby moves and changes it. Now it is not possible that the same thing should be at once in actuality and potentiality in the same respect, but only in different respects. For what is actually hot cannot simultaneously be potentially hot; but it is simultaneously potentially cold. It is therefore impossible that in the same respect and in the same way a thing should be both mover and moved, *i.e.,* that it should move itself. Therefore, whatever is moved must be moved by another. If that by which it is moved be itself moved, then this also must needs be moved by another, and that by another again. But this cannot go on to infinity, because then there would be no first mover, and, consequently, no other mover, seeing that subsequent movers move only inasmuch as they are moved by the first mover; as the staff moves only because it is moved by the hand. Therefore it is necessary to arrive at a first mover, moved by no other; and this everyone understands to be God.

The second way is from the nature of efficient cause. In the world of sensible things we find there is an order of efficient causes. There is no case known (neither is it, indeed, possible) in which a thing is found to be the efficient cause of itself; for so it would be prior to itself, which is impossible. Now in efficient causes it is not possible to go on to infinity, because in all efficient causes following in order, the first is the cause of the intermediate cause and the intermediate is the cause of the ultimate cause, whether the intermediate cause be several, or one only. Now to take away the cause is to take away the effect. Therefore, if there be no first cause among efficient causes, there will be no ultimate, nor any intermediate, cause. But if in efficient causes it is possible to go on to infinity, there will be no first efficient cause, neither will there be an ultimate effect, nor any intermediate efficient causes; all of which is plainly false. Therefore it is necessary to admit a first efficient cause, to which everyone gives the name of God.

The third way is taken from possibility and necessity, and runs thus. We find in nature things that are possible to be and not be, since they are found to be generated, and to be corrupted, and consequently, it is possible for them to be and not to be. But it is impossible for these always to exist, for that which can not-be at some time is not. Therefore, if anything can not-be, then at one time there was nothing in existence. Now if this were true, even now there would be nothing in existence, because that which does not exist begins to exist only through something already existing. Therefore, if at one time nothing was in existence, it would have been impossible for anything to have begun to exist; and thus even now nothing would be in existence—which is absurd. Therefore, not all beings are merely possible, but there must exist something the existence of which is necessary. But every necessary thing either has its necessity caused by another, or not. Now it is impossible to go to infinity in necessary things which have their necessity caused by another, as has been already proved in regard to efficient causes. Therefore we cannot but admit the existence of some being having of itself its own necessity, and not receiving it from another, but rather causing in others their necessity. This all men speak of as God.

The fourth way is taken from the gradation to be found in things. Among beings there are some more and some less good, true, noble, and the like. But *more* and *less* are predicated of different things according as they resemble in their different ways something which is the maximum, as a thing is said to be hotter according as it more nearly resembles that which is hottest; so that there is something which is truest, something best, something noblest, and, consequently, something which is most being, for those things that are greatest in truth are greatest in being, as it is written in *Metaph.* ii. Now the maximum in any genus is the cause of all in that genus, as fire, which is the maximum of heat, is the cause of all hot things, as is said in the same book. Therefore there must also be something which is to all beings the cause of their being, goodness, and every other perfection; and this we call God.

The fifth way is taken from the governance of the world. We see that things which lack knowledge, such as natural bodies, act for an end, and this is evident from their acting always, or nearly always, in the same way, so as to obtain the best result. Hence it is plain that they achieve their end, not fortuitously, but designedly. Now whatever lacks knowledge cannot move towards an end, unless it be directed by some being endowed with knowledge and intelligence; as the arrow is directed by the archer. Therefore some intelligent being exists by whom all natural things are directed to their end; and this being we call God.

Reply Obj. 1.   As Augustine says: *Since God is the highest good, He would not allow any evil to exist in His works, unless His omnipotence and goodness were such as to bring good even out of evil.* This is part of the infinite goodness of God, that He should allow evil to exist, and out of it produce good.

Reply Obj. 2.   Since nature works for a determinate end under the direction of a higher agent, whatever is done by nature must be traced back to God as to its first cause. So likewise whatever is done voluntarily must be traced back to some higher cause other than human reason and will, since these can change and fail; for all things that are changeable and capable of defect must be traced back to an immovable and self-necessary first principle, as has been shown.

Part Two (1)

QUESTION 94: THE NATURAL LAW

Second Article: whether the natural law contains several precepts, or only one? . . .

. . . The first principle in the practical reason is one founded on the nature of good, viz., that *good is that which all things seek after.* Hence this is the first precept of law, that *good is to be done and promoted, and evil is to be avoided.* All other precepts of the natural law are based upon this; so that all the things which the practical reason naturally apprehends as man's good belong to the precepts of the natural law under the form of things to be done or avoided.

Since, however, good has the nature of an end, and evil, the nature of the contrary, hence it is that all those things to which man has a natural inclination are naturally apprehended by reason as being good, and consequently as objects of pursuit, and their contraries as evil, and objects of avoidance. Therefore, the order of the precepts of the natural law is according to the order of natural inclinations. For there is in man, first of all, an inclination to good in accordance with the nature which he has in common with all substances, inasmuch, namely, as every substance seeks the preservation of its own being, according to its nature; and by reason of this inclination, whatever is a means of preserving human life, and of warding off its obstacles, belongs to the natural law. Secondly, there is in man an inclination to things that pertain to him more specially, according to that nature which he has in common with other animals; and in virtue of this inclination, those things are said to belong to the natural law *which nature has taught to all animals,* such as sexual intercourse, the education of offspring and so forth. Thirdly, there is in man an inclination to good according to the nature of his reason, which nature is proper to him. Thus man has a natural inclination to know the truth about God, and to live in society; and in this respect, whatever pertains to this inclination belongs to the natural law: *e.g.*, to shun ignorance, to avoid offending those among whom one has to live, and other such things regarding the above inclination.

· · ·

QUESTION 96: ON THE POWER OF HUMAN LAW

Fourth Article: whether human law binds a man in conscience? . . .

. . . Laws framed by man are either just or unjust. If they be just, they have the power of binding in conscience from the eternal law whence they are derived, according to *Prov.* viii. 15: *By Me kings reign, and lawgivers decree just things.* Now laws are said to be just, both from the end (when, namely, they are ordained to the common good), from their author (that is to say, when the law that is made does not exceed the power of the lawgiver), and from their form (when, namely, burdens are laid on the subjects according to an equality of proportion and with a view to the common good). For, since one man is a part of the community, each man, in all that he is and has, belongs to the community; just as a part, in all that it is, belongs to the whole. So, too, nature inflicts a loss on the part in order to save the whole; so that for this reason such laws as these, which impose proportionate burdens, are just and binding in conscience, and are legal laws.

On the other hand, laws may be unjust in two ways: first, by being contrary to human good, through being opposed to the things mentioned above:—either in respect of the end, as when an authority imposes on his subjects burdensome laws, conducive, not to the common good, but rather to his own cupidity or vainglory; or in respect of the author, as when a man makes a law that goes beyond the power committed to him; or in respect of the form, as when burdens are imposed unequally on the community, although with a view to the common good. Such are acts of violence rather than laws, because, as Augustine says, *a law that is not just seems to be no law at all.* Therefore, such laws do not bind in conscience, except perhaps in order to avoid scandal or disturbance, for which cause a man should even yield his right according to *Matt.* v. 40, 41: *If a man . . . take away thy coat, let go thy cloak also unto him; and whosoever will force thee one mile, go with him another two.*

Secondly, laws may be unjust through being opposed to the divine good. Such are the laws of tyrants inducing to idolatry, or to anything else contrary to the divine law. Laws of this kind must in no way be observed, because, as is stated in *Acts* v. 29, *we ought to obey God rather than men.*

· · ·

Bonaventura: Of the Stages in the Ascent to God and of His Reflection in His Traces in the Universe

The philosophy of Bonaventura (1217–1274) was less coolly rationalistic than that of Thomas Aquinas. Bonaventura thought that to know God a man had to live a life of prayer and virtue. The mind of such a man could ascend from a knowledge of creation to a knowledge of the Creator. But this was not achieved merely by abstract argumentation. Rather the mind of a believer would be divinely illumined so that he could intuitively recognize the "traces" of God in created things.

Blessed is the man whose help is from Thee. In his heart he hath disposed to ascend by steps, in the vale of tears, in the place which he hath set [Ps., 83, 6]. Since beatitude is nothing else than the fruition of the highest good, and the highest good is above us, none can be made blessed unless he ascend above himself, not by the ascent of his body but by that of his heart. But we cannot be raised above ourselves except by a higher power raising us up. For howsoever the interior steps are disposed, nothing is accomplished unless it is accompanied by divine aid. Divine help, however, comes to those who seek it from their hearts humbly and devoutly; and this means to sigh for it in this vale of tears, aided only by fervent prayer. Thus prayer is the mother and source of ascent (*sursum-actionis*) in God. Therefore Dionysius, in his book, *Mystical Theology* [ch. 1, 1], wishing to instruct us in mental elevation, prefaces his work by prayer. Therefore let us pray and say to the Lord our God, "Conduct me, O Lord, in Thy way, and I will walk in Thy truth; let my heart rejoice that it may fear Thy name" [Ps., 85, 11].

By praying thus one is enlightened about the knowledge of the stages in the ascension to God. For since, relative to our life on earth, the world is itself a ladder for ascending to God, we find here certain traces [of His hand], certain images, some corporeal, some spiritual, some temporal, some aeviternal; consequently some outside us, some inside. That we may arrive at an understanding of the First Principle, which is most spiritual and eternal above us, we ought to proceed through the traces which are corporeal and temporal and outside us; and this is to be led into the way of God. We ought next to enter into our minds, which are the eternal image of God, spiritual and internal; and this is to walk in the truth of God. We ought finally to pass over into that which is eternal, most spiritual, and above us, looking to the First Principle; and this is to rejoice in the knowledge of God and in the reverence of His majesty. . . .

Now at the Creation, man was made fit for the repose of contempla-

From Saint Bonaventura, *The Mind's Road to God*, translated by George Boas, copyright © 1953 by The Liberal Arts Press, Inc., reprinted by permission of The Bobbs-Merrill Company, Inc.

tion, and therefore God placed him in a paradise of delight [Gen., 2, 16]. But turning himself away from the true light to mutable goods, he was bent over by his own sin, and the whole human race by original sin, which doubly infected human nature, ignorance infecting man's mind and concupiscence his flesh. Hence man, blinded and bent, sits in the shadows and does not see the light of heaven unless grace with justice succor him from concupiscence, and knowledge with wisdom against ignorance. All of which is done through Jesus Christ, Who of God is made unto us wisdom and justice and sanctification and redemption [I Cor., 1, 30]. He is the virtue and wisdom of God, the Word incarnate, the author of grace and truth—that is, He has infused the grace of charity, which, since it is from a pure heart and good conscience and unfeigned faith, rectifies the whole soul in the threefold way mentioned above. He has taught the knowledge of the truth according to the triple mode of theology—that is, the symbolic, the literal, and the mystical—so that by the symbolic we may make proper use of sensible things, by the literal we may properly use the intelligible, and by the mystical we may be carried aloft to supermental levels.

Therefore he who wishes to ascend to God must, avoiding sin, which deforms nature, exercise the above-mentioned natural powers for regenerating grace, and do this through prayer. He must strive toward purifying justice, and this in intercourse; toward the illumination of knowledge, and this in meditation; toward the perfection of wisdom, and this in contemplation. Now just as no one comes to wisdom save through grace, justice, and knowledge, so none comes to contemplation save through penetrating mediation, holy conversation and devout prayer. Just as grace is the foundation of the will's rectitude and of the enlightenment of clear and penetrating reason, so, first, we must pray; secondly, we must live holily; thirdly, we must strive toward the reflection of truth and, by our striving, mount step by step until we come to the high mountain where we shall see the God of gods in Sion [Ps., 83, 8].

Since, then, we must mount Jacob's ladder before descending it, let us place the first rung of the ascension in the depths, putting the whole sensible world before us as a mirror, by which ladder we shall mount up to God, the Supreme Creator, that we may be true Hebrews crossing from Egypt to the land promised to our fathers; let us be Christians crossing with Christ from this world over to the Father [John, 13, 1]; let us also be lovers of wisdom, which calls to us and says, "Come over to me, all ye that desire me, and be filled with my fruits" [Ecclesiasticus, 24, 26]. For by the greatness of the beauty and of the creature, the Creator of them may be seen [Wisdom, 13, 5].

This consideration, however, is extended according to the sevenfold condition of creatures, which is a sevenfold testimony to the divine power, wisdom, and goodness, as one considers the origin, magnitude, multitude, beauty, plenitude, operation, and order of all things. For the *origin* of things, according to their creation, distinction, and beauty, in the work of the six days indicates the divine power producing all things from nothing, wisdom distinguishing all things clearly, and goodness adorning all things generously. *Magnitude* of things, either according to the measure of their length, width, and depth, or according to the excellence of power spreading itself in length, breadth, and depth, as appears in the diffusion of light, or again according to the efficacy of its inner, continuous, and diffused operation, as appears in the operation of fire—magnitude, I say, indicates manifestly the immensity of the power, wisdom, and goodness of the triune God, Who exists unlimited in all things through His power, presence, and essence. *Multitude* of things, according to the diversity of genus, species, and individuality, in substance, form, or figure, and efficacy beyond all human estimation, clearly indicates and shows the immensity of the aforesaid traits in God. *Beauty* of things, according to the variety of light, figure, and color in bodies simple and mixed and even composite, as in the celestial bodies, minerals, stones and metals, plants and animals, obviously proclaims the three mentioned traits. *Plenitude* of things—according to which matter is full of forms because of the seminal reasons; form is full of power because of its activity; power is full of effects because of its efficiency—declares the same manifestly. *Operation,* multiplex inasmuch as it is natural, artificial, and moral, by its very variety shows the immensity of that power, art, and goodness which indeed are in all things the cause of their being, the principle of their intelligibility, and the order of their living. *Order,* by reason of duration, situation, and influence, as prior and posterior, upper and lower, nobler and less noble, indicates clearly in the book of creation the primacy, sublimity, and dignity of the First Principle in relation to its infinite power. The order of the divine laws, precepts, and judgments in the Book of Scripture indicates the immensity of His wisdom. The order of the divine sacraments, rewards, and punishments in the body of the Church indicates the immensity of His goodness. Hence order leads us most obviously into the first and highest, most powerful, wisest, and best.

He, therefore, who is not illumined by such great splendor of created things is blind; he who is not awakened by such great clamor is deaf; he who does not praise God because of all these effects is dumb; he who does not note the First Principle from such great signs is foolish. Open your eyes therefore, prick up your spiritual ears, open your lips, and apply your heart, that you may see your God in all creatures, may hear Him, praise Him, love and adore Him, magnify and honor Him, lest the whole world rise against you. For on this account the whole world will fight against the unwise [Prov., 5, 21]; but to the wise will there be matter for pride, who with the Prophet can say, "Thou hast given me, O Lord, a delight in Thy doings: and in the works of Thy hands I shall rejoice [Ps., 91, 5]. . . . How great are Thy works, O lord; Thou hast made all things in wisdom; the earth is filled with Thy riches" [Ps., 103, 24].

John Buridan: Questions on the Four Books on the Heavens and the World of Aristotle

Fourteenth-century thinkers made important advances in considering problems of physical science. The following discussion of the rotation of the earth was written by John Buridan (ca. 1290–ca. 1360). The problem he considered was an ancient one. It is noteworthy that Buridan did not approach it merely by citing authorities. Rather he used rational arguments based on observations of natural phenomena. (The medieval phrase "to save the appearances" meant to frame a hypothesis that would account for all the relevant observations.)

1. BOOK II, QUESTION 22. It is sought consequently whether the earth always is at rest in the center of the universe. . . .

This question is difficult. For in the first place there is a significant doubt as to whether the earth is directly in the middle of the universe so that its center coincides with the center of the universe. Furthermore, there is a strong doubt as to whether it is not sometimes moved rectilinearly as a whole, since we do not doubt that often many of its parts are moved, for this is apparent to us through our senses. There is also another difficult doubt as to whether the following conclusion of Aristotle is sound, namely, if the heaven is by necessity to be moved circularly forever, then it is necessary that the earth be at rest forever in the middle. There is also a fourth doubt whether, in positing that the earth is moved circularly around its own center and about its own poles, all the phenomena that are apparent to us can be saved (*possent salvari omnia nobis apparentia*). Concerning this last doubt let us now speak.

2. It should be known that many people have held as probable that it is not contradictory to appearances for the earth to be moved circularly in the aforesaid manner, and that on any given natural day it makes a complete rotation from west to east by returning again to the west — that is, if some part of the earth were designated [as the part to observe]. Then it is necessary to posit that the stellar sphere would be at rest, and then night and day would take place through such a motion of the earth, so that that motion of the earth would be a diurnal motion (*motus diurnus*). The following is an example of this [kind of thing]: If anyone is moved in a ship and he imagines that he is at rest, then, should he see another ship which is truly at rest, it will appear to him that the other ship is moved. This is so because his eye would be completely in the same relationship to the other ship regardless of whether his own ship is at rest and the other moved, or the contrary situation prevailed. And so we also posit that the sphere of the sun is

From M. Clagett, *The Science of Mechanics in the Middle Ages* (Madison: The University of Wisconsin Press; © 1959 by The Board of Regents of The University of Wisconsin System), pp. 594–596; 602–603.

everywhere at rest and the earth in carrying us would be rotated. Since, however, we imagine that we are at rest, just as the man located on the ship which is moving swiftly does not perceive his own motion nor the motion of the ship, then it is certain that the sun would appear to us to rise and then to set, just as it does when it is moved and we are at rest.

3. It is true, however, that if the stellar sphere is at rest, it is necessary to concede generally that the spheres of the planets are moving, since otherwise the planets would not change their positions relative to each other and to the fixed stars. And, therefore, this opinion imagines that any of the spheres of the planets moved evidently like the earth from west to east, but since the earth has a lesser circle, hence it makes its rotation (*circulatio*) in less time. Consequently, the moon makes its rotation in less time than the sun. And this is universally true, so that the earth completes its rotation in a natural day, the moon in a month, and the sun in a year, etc.

4. It is undoubtedly true that, if the situation were just as this position posits, all the celestial phenomena would appear to us just as they now appear. We should know likewise that those persons wishing to sustain this opinion, perhaps for reason of disputation, posit for it certain persuasions. . . . The third persuasion is this: To celestial bodies ought to be attributed to nobler conditions, and to the highest sphere, the noblest. But it is nobler and more perfect to be at rest than to be moved. Therefore, the highest sphere ought to be at rest. . . .

The last persuasion is this: Just as it is better to save the appearances through fewer causes than through many, if this is possible, so it is better to save [them] by an easier way than by one more difficult. Now it is easier to move a small thing than a large one. Hence it is better to say that the earth, which is very small, is moved most swiftly and the highest sphere is at rest than to say the opposite.

5. But still this opinion is not to be followed. In the first place because it is against the authority of Aristotle and of all the astronomers (*astrologi*). But these people respond that *authority does not demonstrate,* and that it suffices astronomers that they posit a method by which appearances are saved, whether or not it is so in actuality. Appearances can be saved in either way; hence they posit the method which is more pleasing to them.

6. Others argue [against the theory of the earth's diurnal rotation] by many appearances (*apparentiis*). One of these is that the stars sensibly appear to us to be moved from the east to the west. But they solve this [by saying] that it would appear the same if the stars were at rest and the earth were moved from west to east.

7. Another appearance is this: If anyone were moving very swiftly on horseback, he would feel the air resisting him. Therefore, similarly, with the very swift motion of the earth in motion, we ought to feel the air noticeably resisting us. But these [supporters of the opinion] re-

spond that the earth, the water, and the air in the lower region are moved simultaneously with diurnal motion. Consequently there is no air resisting us.

8. Another appearance is this: Since local motion heats, and therefore since we and the earth are moved so swiftly, we should be made hot. But these [supporters] respond that motion does not produce heat except by the friction (*confricatio*), rubbing, or separation of bodies. These [causes] would not be applicable there, since the air, water, and earth would be moved together.

9. But the last appearance which Aristotle notes is more demonstrative in the question at hand. This is that an arrow projected from a bow directly upward falls again in the same spot of the earth from which it was projected. This would not be so if the earth were moved with such velocity. Rather before the arrow falls, the part of the earth from which the arrow was projected would be a league's distance away. But still the supporters would respond that it happens so because the air, moved with the earth, carries the arrow, although the arrow appears to us to be moved simply in a straight line motion because it is being carried along with us. Therefore, we do not perceive that motion by which it is carried with the air. But this evasion is not sufficient because the violent impetus of the arrow in ascending would resist the lateral motion of the air so that it would not be moved as much as the air. This is similar to the occasion when the air is moved by a high wind. For then an arrow projected upward is not moved as much laterally as the wind is moved, although it would be moved somewhat. . . .

Nicholas Oresme: On the Book of the Heavens and the World of Aristotle

A few years later Nicholas Oresme (ca. 1320–1382) suggested a solution for the last of the difficulties raised by Buridan.

To the third experience, which seems more effective, i.e., the experience concerning the arrow or stone projected upward etc., one would say that the arrow is trajected upwards and [simultaneously] with this trajection it is moved eastward very swiftly with the air through which it passes and with all the mass of the lower part of the universe mentioned above, it all being moved with a diurnal movement. For this reason the arrow returns to the place on the earth from which it left. This appears possible by analogy: If a person were on a ship moving toward the east very swiftly without his being aware of the movement, and he drew his hand downward, describing a straight line against the mast of the ship, it would seem to him that his hand was moved with rectilinear movement only. According to this opinion [of the diurnal rotation of the earth], it seems to us in the same way that the arrow descends or ascends in a straight line. . . .

. . . In support of this [position, consider the following]: If a man in that ship were going westward less swiftly than the ship was going eastward, it would seem to him that he was approaching the east, when actually he would be moving toward the west. Similarly, in the case put forth above, all the movements would seem to be as if the earth were at rest.

Also, in order to make clear the response to the third experience, I wish to add a natural example verified by Aristotle to the artificial example already given. It posits in the upper region of the air a portion of pure fire called *a*. This latter is of such a degree of lightness that it mounts to its highest possible point *b* near the concave surface of the heavens. I say that just as with the arrow in the case posited above, there would result in this case [of the fire] that the movement of *a* is composed of rectilinear movement, and, in part, of circular movement, because the region of the air and the sphere of fire through which *a* passes are moved, according to Aristotle, with circular movement. Thus if it were not so moved, *a* would ascend rectilinearly in the path *ab*, but because *b* is meanwhile moved to point *c* by the circular daily movement, it is apparent that *a* is composed of a rectilinear and a circular movement. So also would be the movement of the arrow, as was said. Such composition or mixture of movements was spoken of in the third chapter of the first book [of the *De caelo*]. . . . I conclude then that one could not by any experience whatsoever demonstrate that the heavens and not the earth are moved with diurnal movement.

THE LATE MIDDLE AGES

The Papacy and Its Critics

78. Boniface VIII: Clericis Laicos and Unam Sanctam

The claims of the medieval papacy in the temporal sphere reached a high-water mark in two bulls of Pope Boniface VIII (1294–1303).

The Decree Clericis Laicos (1296)

Boniface Bishop, servant of the servants of God, for the perpetual record of the matter. That laymen have been very hostile to the clergy antiquity relates; and it is clearly proved by the experiences of the present time. For not content with what is their own the laity strive for what is forbidden and loose the reins for things unlawful. Nor do they prudently realize that power over clerks or ecclesiastical persons or goods is forbidden them: they impose heavy burdens on the prelates of the churches and ecclesiastical persons regular and secular, and tax them, and impose collections: they exact and demand from the same the half, tithe, or twentieth, or any other portion or proportion of their revenues or goods; and in many ways they try to bring them into slavery, and subject them to their authority. And, we regret to say, some prelates of the churches and ecclesiastical persons, fearing where there should be no fear, seeking a temporary peace, fearing more to offend the temporal majesty than the eternal, acquiesce in such abuses, not so much rashly as improvidently, without obtaining authority or

From "Clericis Laicos," in *Documents of the Christian Church,* edited by H. Bettenson, published by the Oxford University Press (2nd ed.; London: Oxford University Press, 1963), pp. 157-159; reprinted by permission of the publisher.

license from the Apostolic See. We therefore, desirous of preventing such wicked actions, decree, with apostolic authority and on the advice of our brethren, that any prelates and ecclesiastical persons, religious or secular, of whatsoever orders, condition or standing, who shall pay or promise or agree to pay to lay persons collections or taxes for the tithe, twentieth, or hundredth of their own rents, or goods, or those of the churches, or any other portion, proportion, or quantity of the same rents, or goods, at their own estimate or at the actual value, under the name of aid, loan, relief, subsidy, or gift, or by any other title, manner, or pretext demanded, without the authority of the same see:

And also whatsoever emperors, kings, or princes, dukes, earls, or barons, powers, captains, or officials, or rectors, by whatsoever names they are called, of cities, castles, or any places whatsoever, wheresoever situate, and all others of whatsoever rank, eminence or state, who shall impose, exact, or receive the things aforesaid, or arrest, seize, or presume to take possession of things anywhere deposited in holy buildings, or to command them to be arrested, seized, or taken, or receive them when taken, seized, or arrested, and also all who knowingly give aid, counsel, or support, openly or secretly, in the things aforesaid, by this same should incur sentence of excommunication. Universities, too, which may have been to blame in these matters, we subject to ecclesiastical interdict.

The prelates and ecclesiastical persons above mentioned we strictly command, in virtue of their obedience, and on pain of deposition, that they in no wise acquiesce in such things without express leave of the said see, and that they pay nothing under pretext of any obligation, promise, and acknowledgment whatsoever, made in the past, or in existence before this time, and before such constitution, prohibition, or order come to their notice, and that the seculars aforesaid do not in any wise receive it; and if the clergy do pay, or the laymen receive, let them fall under sentence of excommunication by the very deed.

Moreover, let no one be absolved from the aforesaid sentences of excommunications and interdict, save at the moment of death, without authority and special leave of the Apostolic See, since it is part of our intention that such a terrible abuse of secular powers should not be carried on under any pretense whatever, any privileges whatsoever notwithstanding, in whatsoever tenors, forms or modes, or arrangement of words, conceded to emperors, kings and the others aforesaid; and we will that aid be given by no one, and by no persons in any respect in contravention of these provisions.

Let it then be lawful to none at all to infringe this page of our constitution, prohibition, or order, or to gainsay it by any rash attempt; and if anyone presume to attempt this, let him know that he will incur the indignation of Almighty God, and of his blessed apostles Peter and Paul.

The Decree Unam Sanctam *(1302)*

That there is one holy, Catholic and apostolic church we are bound to believe and to hold, our faith urging us, and this we do firmly believe and simply confess; and that outside this church there is no salvation or remission of sins, as her spouse proclaims in the Canticles, "One is my dove, my perfect one. She is the only one of her mother, the chosen of her that bore her" (Canticles 6:8); which represents one mystical body whose head is Christ, while the head of Christ is God. In this church there is one Lord, one faith, one baptism. At the time of the Flood there was one ark, symbolizing the one church. It was finished in one cubit and had one helmsman and captain, namely Noah, and we read that all things on earth outside of it were destroyed. This church we venerate and this alone, the Lord saying through his prophet, "Deliver, O God, my soul from the sword, my only one from the power of the dog" (Psalm 21:21). He prayed for the soul, that is himself, the head, and at the same time for the body, which he called the one church on account of the promised unity of faith, sacraments and charity of the church. This is that seamless garment of the Lord which was not cut but fell by lot. Therefore there is one body and one head of this one and only church, not two heads as though it were a monster, namely Christ and Christ's vicar, Peter and Peter's successor, for the Lord said to this Peter, "Feed my sheep" (John 21:17). He said "My sheep" in general, not these or those, whence he is understood to have committed them all to Peter. Hence, if the Greeks or any others say that they were not committed to Peter and his successors, they necessarily admit that they are not of Christ's flock, for the Lord says in John that there is one sheepfold and one shepherd.

We are taught by the words of the Gospel that in this church and in her power there are two swords, a spiritual one and a temporal one. For when the apostles said "Here are two swords" (Luke 22:38), meaning in the church since it was the apostles who spoke, the Lord did not reply that it was too many but enough. Certainly anyone who denies that the temporal sword is in the power of Peter has not paid heed to the words of the Lord when he said, "Put up thy sword into its sheath" (Matthew 26:52). Both then are in the power of the church, the material sword and the spiritual. But the one is exercised for the church, the other by the church, the one by the hand of the priest, the other by the hand of kings and soldiers, though at the will and sufferance of the priest. One sword ought to be under the other and the temporal authority subject to the spiritual power. For, while the apostle says, "There is no power but from God and those that are are ordained of

"Unam Sanctam," in Brian Tierney, *The Crisis of Church and State, 1050–1300,* with selected documents, © 1964 (Englewood Cliffs, N.J.: Prentice-Hall, 1964), pp. 188–189. Reprinted by permission of Prentice-Hall, Inc., Englewood Cliffs, New Jersey.

God" (Romans 13:1), they would not be ordained unless one sword was under the other and, being inferior, was led by the other to the highest things. For, according to the blessed Dionysius, it is the law of divinity for the lowest to be led to the highest through intermediaries. In the order of the universe all things are not kept in order in the same fashion and immediately but the lowest are ordered by the intermediate and inferiors by superiors. But that the spiritual power excels any earthly one in dignity and nobility we ought the more openly to confess in proportion as spiritual things excel temporal ones. Moreover we clearly perceive this from the giving of tithes, from benediction and sanctification, from the acceptance of this power and from the very government of things. For, the truth bearing witness, the spiritual power has to institute the earthly power and to judge it if it has not been good. So is verified the prophecy of Jeremias [1:10] concerning the church and the power of the church, "Lo, I have set thee this day over the nations and over kingdoms" etc.

Therefore, if the earthly power errs, it shall be judged by the spiritual power, if a lesser spiritual power errs it shall be judged by its superior, but if the supreme spiritual power errs it can be judged only by God not by man, as the apostle witnesses, "The spiritual man judgeth all things and he himself is judged of no man" (1 Corinthians 2:15). Although this authority was given to a man and is exercised by a man it is not human but rather divine, being given to Peter at God's mouth, and confirmed to him and to his successors in him, the rock whom the Lord acknowledged when he said to Peter himself "Whatsoever thou shalt bind" etc. (Matthew 16:19). Whoever therefore resists this power so ordained by God resists the ordinance of God unless, like the Manicheans, he imagines that there are two beginnings, which we judge to be false and heretical, as Moses witnesses, for not "in the beginnings" but "in the beginning" God created heaven and earth (Genesis 1:1). Therefore we declare, state, define and pronounce that it is altogether necessary to salvation for every human creature to be subject to the Roman Pontiff.

79. *Four Secularist Philosophers: John of Paris, William of Ockham, Marsiglio of Padua, and John Wycliff*

The claims of the fourteenth-century papacy stimulated a substantial body of writing in defense of the autonomous secular state. The French Dominican John of Paris adopted a position of moderate dualism in discussing the issue. His Tractatus de Potestate Regia et Papali *was written in 1302–1303.*

. . . As regards the power of ecclesiastical pontiffs, the truth occupies a middle ground between two errors. The error of the Waldensians was to deny to the successors of the apostles, that is the pope and the prelates of the church, any rightful lordship over temporal things and to maintain that it is illicit for them to have any temporal riches. Hence they say that the church of God and the successors of the apostles and true prelates of the church lasted only until the time of Sylvester and that, when the church received the emperor Constantine's donation, the Roman church had its beginning and, according to them, this is not at present the church of God. Rather, they say, the church of God has ceased to exist except in so far as it is continued or restored in themselves. . . . The other error is that of Herod who, when he heard that Christ was born, believed him to be an earthly king. From this seems to be derived the opinion of certain moderns who, in rejecting the first error, go so far in the opposite direction as to assert that the lord pope, since he stands in place of Christ, has dominion over the temporal goods of princes and barons and jurisdiction and cognizance concerning them. . . .

First it should be known that kingship, properly understood, can be defined as the rule of one man over a perfect multitude so ordered as to promote the public good. . . . Such a government is based on natural law and the law of nations. For, since man is naturally a civil or political creature as is said in Book I of the *Politics*—and the Philosopher

From John of Paris, "Tractatus de Potestate Regia et Papali," in Brian Tierney, *The Crisis of Church and State, 1050–1300,* with selected documents, © 1964 (Englewood Cliffs, N.J.: Prentice-Hall, 1964), pp. 206–210; reprinted by permission of Prentice-Hall, Inc., Englewood Cliffs, New Jersey. William of Ockham, "Dialogue," in *Medieval Political Ideas,* E. Lewis, trans. (New York: Alfred A. Knopf, 1954), Vol. II, pp. 399–400; reprinted by permission of Alfred A. Knopf and Routledge & Kegan Paul Ltd. Marsiglio of Padua, "Defensor Pacis," in A. Gewirth, *The Defender of the Peace* (New York: Columbia University Press, 1956), Vol. II, pp. 426–431; Copyright 1951 Columbia University Press; reprinted by permission of the publisher. John Wycliff, in *Documents of the Christian Church,* edited by H. Bettenson, published by the Oxford University Press (2nd ed.; London: Oxford University Press, 1963), pp. 243–244; reprinted by permission of the publisher.

proves this from food, clothing and defense in which a solitary man is not self-sufficient as also from speech which is addressed to another, these things being necessary only for men — it is essential for a man to live in a multitude and in such a multitude as is self-sufficient for life. The community of a household or village is not of this sort, but the community of a city or kingdom is, for in a household or village there is not found everything necessary for food, clothing and defense through a whole life as there is in a city or kingdom. But every multitude scatters and disintegrates as each man pursues his own ends unless it is ordered to the common good by some one man who has charge of this common good. . . .

Next it must be borne in mind that man is not ordered only to such a good as can be acquired by nature, which is to live virtuously, but is further ordered to a supernatural end which is eternal life, and the whole multitude of men living virtuously is ordered to this. Therefore it is necessary that there be some one man to direct the multitude to this end. If indeed this end could be attained by the power of human nature, it would necessarily pertain to the office of the human king to direct men to this end, for we call a human king him to whom is committed the highest duty of government in human affairs. But since man does not come to eternal life by human power but by divine . . . this kind of rule pertains to a king who is not only man but also God, namely Jesus Christ . . . and because Christ was to withdraw his corporal presence from the church it was necessary for him to institute others as ministers who would administer the sacraments to men, and these are called priests. . . . Hence priesthood may be defined in this fashion. Priesthood is a spiritual power of administering sacraments to the faithful conferred by Christ on ministers of the church. . . .

The royal power both existed and was exercised before the papal, and there were kings in France before there were Christians. Therefore neither the royal power nor its exercise is from the pope but from God and from the people who elect a king by choosing either a person or a royal house. . . . It would seem that the power of inferior pontiffs and ministers is derived from the pope more than the royal power, for ecclesiastical prelates are more immediately dependent on the pope than secular princes. But the power of prelates is not from God through the pope but immediately from God and from the people who elect or consent. . . .

. . . Although a form of government in which one man simply rules according to virtue is better than any other simple government, as the Philosopher proves in Book III of the *Politics,* nevertheless if it is mixed with aristocracy and democracy it is better than a simple form in that, in a mixed constitution, all have some part of the government. Through this the peace of the people is maintained and all of them love such a government and preserve it. . . .

From the foregoing material it is easy to see which is first in dignity, the kingship or the priesthood. . . . A kingdom is ordered to this end, that an assembled multitude may live virtuously, as has been said, and it is further ordered to a higher end which is the enjoyment of God; and responsibility for this end belongs to Christ, whose ministers and vicars are the priests. Therefore the priestly power is of greater dignity than the secular and this is commonly conceded. See *Dist.* 96 c.10, "As gold is more precious than lead so the priestly order is higher than the royal power." And in the *Decretales* 1.33.6 it is said that as the sun excels the moon so spiritualities excel temporalities. And Hugh of St. Victor in his *De Sacramentis,* Book II, Part II, c.4 declares, "In proportion as the spiritual life is of greater dignity than the earthly and the spirit than the body, so the spiritual power excels the secular or earthly power in honor and dignity." And likewise Bernard to Pope Eugenius, Book I, "Which seems to you the greater dignity, the power of forgiving sins or of dividing estates? But there is no comparison." It is as if he would say, "The spiritual power is greater; therefore it excels in dignity."

But if the priest is greater in himself than the prince and is greater in dignity, it does not follow that he is greater in all respects. For the lesser secular power is not related to the greater spiritual power as having its origin from it or being derived from it as the power of a proconsul is related to that of the emperor, which is greater in all respects since the power of the former is derived from the latter. The relationship is rather like that of a head of a household to a general of armies, since one is not derived from the other but both from a superior power. And so the secular power is greater than the spiritual in some things, namely in temporal affairs, and in such affairs it is not subject to the spiritual power in any way because it does not have its origin from it but rather both have their origin immediately from the one supreme power, namely the divine. Accordingly the inferior power is not subject to the superior in all things but only in those where the supreme power has subordinated it to the greater. A teacher of literature or an instructor in morals directs the members of a household to a nobler end, namely the knowledge of truth, than a doctor who is concerned with a lower end, namely the health of bodies, but who would say therefore the doctor should be subjected to the teacher in preparing his medicines? For this is not fitting, since the head of the household who established both in his house did not subordinate the lesser to the greater in this respect. Therefore the priest is greater than the prince in spiritual affairs and, on the other hand, the prince is greater in temporal affairs. . . .

Concerning the ecclesiastical power of censure or correction it should be known that, directly, it is only spiritual, for it can impose no penalty in the external court but a spiritual one, except conditionally and incidentally. For though the ecclesiastical judge has to lead men back to God and draw them away from sin and correct them, he has to do this only in the way laid down for him by God, which is to say by cutting them off from the sacraments and from the company of the faithful and by similar measures which are proper to ecclesiastical censure. I said "conditionally" in reference to one who is willing to repent and accept a pecuniary penalty, for the ecclesiastical judge cannot impose any corporal or pecuniary penalty for a crime as a secular judge can, except only on one who is willing to accept it. . . . I said "incidentally" because if a prince was a heretic and incorrigible and contemptuous of ecclesiastical censures, the pope might so move the people that he would be deprived of his secular dignity and deposed by the people. The pope might do this in the case of an ecclesiastical crime, of which cognizance belonged to him, by excommunicating all who obeyed such a man as a lord, and thus the people would depose him, and the pope "incidentally." So too, if the pope on the other hand behaved criminally and brought scandal on the church and was incorrigible, the prince might indirectly excommunicate him and "incidentally" bring about his deposition by warning him personally or through the cardinals. And if the pope were unwilling to yield the emperor might so move the people as to compel him to resign or be deposed by the people, for the emperor could, by taking securities or imposing corporal penalties, prevent each and everyone from obeying him or serving him as pope. So each can act toward the other, for both pope and emperor have jurisdiction universally and everywhere, but the one has spiritual jurisdiction, the other temporal.

As for the argument that corporeal beings are ruled by spiritual beings and depend on them as on a cause, I answer that an argument so constructed fails on many grounds. Firstly because it assumes that royal power is corporeal and not spiritual and that it has charge of bodies and not of souls which is false, as is said above, since it is ordained, not for any common good of the citizens whatsoever, but for that which consists in living according to virtue. Accordingly the Philosopher says in the *Ethics* that the intention of a legislator is to make men good and to lead them to virtue, and in the *Politics* that a legislator is more estimable than a doctor since the legislator has charge of souls, the doctor of bodies.

William of Ockham (1299–1350) defended the independence of the empire against the claims of the papacy and also questioned the power of the pope even in the ecclesiastical sphere. The following excerpts are from his Dialogus.

TEACHER: They say that in this case any catholic who knows that the pope is a notorious heretic, or hears it publicly discussed that the pope is a notorious heretic, ought to be ready to assemble for a general council if it is expedient, and anyone, in so far as befits his rank, ought to exhort other catholics to assemble for a general council. However, this primarily concerns prelates and those learned in divine law. Secondarily, it concerns kings and princes and other public powers. In the third place, however, it concerns all catholics, men and women. Thus even catholic women, if they know the pope to be a heretic and the electors negligent in regard to the election of a supreme pontiff, ought, if it is expedient, to urge catholics to convene in a general council for the ordaining of the church; nay, more, even the women themselves ought to attend, if they can further the common good thereby.

PUPIL: This assertion amazes me. For it seems to contain three absurdities: first, that a general council ought to be called without the authorization of the pope; second, that kings and princes and other laymen ought to assemble for a general council; third, that women can and should take part in a general council. For it is clearly proved by the sacred canons that the first is absurd. For, as is maintained throughout di. 17 [of the *Decretum*], a general council cannot be convened without the authority of the supreme pontiff. For Pope Pelagius says [c.5]: "We are instructed again and again, by many papal and canonic and ecclesiastical rules, that councils may not be held without the licence of the Roman pontiff. . . ."

TEACHER: That a general council can be convened without the authority of the pope seems to be proved by several arguments. The first is as follows: a particular council can lawfully be convened without the authority of the pope to judge concerning the same true pope. Therefore, all the more, a general council can be convened to judge concerning a heretical pseudo-pope without his authority. The premise of this argument seems to be proved by two manifest examples. The first is that of the bishops who convened to inquire about the deed and idolatry of the blessed Marcellinus; their assembly was a particular council, convened without the authority of this same Pope Marcellinus. The second is that of the assembly which convened to judge and depose Pope John XXII; this assembly was only a particular and not a general council. All the more, therefore, a general council could be formed to judge concerning a heretical pope detected in notorious heresy.

PUPIL: This argument seems clearly to prove that a general council could be assembled without the authority of a false, heretical pope; but it does not prove that one could be convened without the authority of a true pope. Whence it also seems that if the pope is a heretic, a catholic pope ought to be elected before the general council is summoned.

TEACHER: It appears to some thinkers that the argument just given patently shows that a general council can be convoked without the authority of any pope whatever, true or false. For if it is lawful to hold a particular council without the authority of the pope for the purpose of inquiring or judging about a true pope, it is much more lawful to hold a general council during the vacancy of the apostolic see, without the authority of a pope, for the due coercion of a pseudo-pope, especially if the pseudo-pope cannot otherwise be coerced. The former is lawful, as is proved by the two examples; therefore the latter ought also to be considered lawful.

The second argument is as follows: every people and every community and every body which can make law for itself without the consent or authority of anyone else can without the authority of anyone else elect certain persons to represent the whole community or body. But all the faithful are one body, as Paul says in Romans 12:[5], "We, being many, are one body in Christ"; and they are one people and one community. Therefore they can elect certain persons to represent the whole body. Moreover, if men so elected come together at one time, they constitute a general council, since a general council seems to be nothing else than an assembly of certain men who represent the whole of Christendom. Therefore, a general council can be convened without the authority of anyone whatever who is not a catholic and a believer, and, consequently, without the authority of a heretical pope.

Marsiglio of Padua (d. 1343) wrote the most thorough-going medieval defense of the secular state in his Defensor Pacis *(1324). He ended his work with the following statement of conclusions. It should be noted that, in Marsiglio's book, the term "legislator" always means "the whole body of citizens or the weightier part thereof." Similarly, the term "faithful legislator" refers to the whole body of Christians.*

Of the conclusions to be inferred, we shall place this one first:

1. For the attainment of eternal beatitude it is necessary to believe in the truth of only the divine or canonic Scripture, together with its necessary consequences and the interpretations of it made by the common council of the believers, if these have been duly propounded to the person concerned.

2. Doubtful sentences of divine law, especially on those matters which are called articles of the Christian faith, as well as on other matters belief in which is necessary for salvation, must be defined only by the general council of the believers, or by the weightier multitude or part thereof; no partial group or individual person, of whatever status, has the authority to make such definitions.

3. The evangelic Scripture does not command that anyone be compelled by temporal pain or punishment to observe the commands of divine law.

4. For eternal salvation it is necessary to observe only the commands of the evangelic law, and their necessary consequences, and the dictates of right reason as to what should be done and not done; but not all the commands of the Old Law. . . .

6. Only the whole body of citizens, or the weightier part thereof, is the human legislator.

7. The decretals or decrees of the Roman or any other pontiffs, col-

lectively or distributively, made without the grant of the human legislator, bind no one to temporal pain or punishment.

8. Human laws can be dispensed with only by the human legislator or by someone else actiñg by its authority.

9. An elective ruler, or any other official, is dependent only upon election by the body having the authority therefor, and needs no other confirmation or approval.

10. The election of any elective ruler or other official, especially it such office carries coercive force, depends upon the expressed will of the legislator alone.

11. The supreme government in a city or state must be only one in number. . . .

14. A bishop or priest, as such, has no rulership or coercive jurisdiction over any clergyman or layman, even if the latter be a heretic.

15. Only the ruler by authority of the legislator has coercive jurisdiction over the person and property of every individual mortal person, of whatever status, and of every group of laymen or clergymen.

16. No bishop or priest or group of them is allowed to excommunicate anyone without authorization by the faithful legislator.

17. All bishops are of equal authority immediately through Christ, nor can it be proved by divine law that there is any superiority or subjection among them in spiritual or in temporal affairs.

18. By divine authority, accompanied by the consent or concession of the faithful human legislator, the other bishops, collectively or distributively, can excommunicate the Roman bishop and exercise other authority over him, just as conversely. . . .

21. It pertains only to the faithful legislator to exercise coercive judgment with regard to candidates for church orders and their qualifications, and no priest or bishop is allowed to promote anyone to these orders without a ·thorization by this legislator. . . .

25. No licence for the public teaching or practice of any art or discipline can be bestowed by any bishop, collectively or distributively, as such; but this pertains only to the legislator, at least the faithful one, or to the ruler by its authority. . . .

27. Ecclesiastic temporal goods which remain over and above the needs of priests and other gospel ministers and of the helpless poor, and which are not needed for divine worship, can lawfully, in accordance with divine law, be used in whole or in part by the legislator for the common or public welfare or defense.

28. All temporal goods which have been set aside for religious purposes or for deeds of mercy, such as legacies bequeathed for overseas crossing to resist the infidels, or for the redemption of captives, or for the support of the helpless poor, and for other similar purposes, are to be distributed only by the ruler in accordance with the designation of the legislator and the intention of the donor.

29. Only the faithful legislator has the authority to grant exemption

to any group or religious body, and to approve or institute such exemption.

30. Only the ruler in accordance with the designation of the human legislator has the authority to exercise coercive judgment over all heretics, criminals, and other persons subject to temporal pain or punishment; to inflict on them penalties in person, to exact penalties in property, and to dispose of these latter penalties.

31. No one who is subject and obligated to someone else by lawful oath can be released by any bishop or priest without reasonable cause, which cause is to be judged by the faithful legislator by a judgment in the third sense; and the opposite of this is contrary to sound doctrine.

32. Only the general council of all the faithful has the authority to designate a bishop or any metropolitan church highest of all, and to deprive or depose them from such position.

33. Only the faithful legislator, or the ruler by its authority in communities of believers may assemble through coercive power a general or partial council of priests, bishops, and other believers; and if a council is assembled in a different way, then decisions made therein have no force or validity, and no one is obliged under temporal or spiritual guilt or punishment to observe such decisions.

34. Fasts and prohibitions of food must be imposed only by the authority of the general council of believers, or of the faithful legislator; if divine law does not prohibit the practice of mechanical arts or the teaching of disciplines on any day, then these can be forbidden only by the aforesaid council or legislator; and only the faithful legislator or the ruler by its authority can enforce the observance of such prohibitions by temporal pain or punishment.

35. The canonization and worship of anyone as a saint must be established and ordained only by the general council.

36. Only the general council of believers has the authority to make decrees forbidding bishops, priests, and other temple ministers to have wives, as well as other ordinances with regard to church practice; and such decrees may be dispensed with only by that group or person to whom the authority for this has been given by the aforesaid council.

37. From the coercive jurisdiction granted to a bishop or priest a litigant may always appeal to the legislator or to the ruler by its authority.

38. A person who is to maintain the evangelical perfection of supreme poverty can have no chattels in his power without the firm intention of selling them as soon as possible and giving the price received to the poor; of no thing, movable or immovable, can he have the ownership or power, that is, with the intention of having claim to that thing before a coercive judge from anyone who seizes or wishes to seize it.

39. Communities and individuals are obliged by divine law to contribute, so far as they can, the food and clothing which are needed, at least on each successive day, by the bishops and others who minister

the gospel to them; but they are not obliged to give tithes or anything else over and above the needs of the aforesaid ministers.

40. The faithful legislator, or the ruler by its authority in a province subject to it, can compel bishops and other gospel ministers, who have been provided with sufficient food and clothing, to perform the divine functions and to minister the ecclesiastic sacraments.

41. Appointments of the Roman bishop and of any other ecclesiastic or temple ministers in accordance with divine law to separable ecclesiastic offices, as well as suspensions and removals therefrom because of delict, must be effected only by the faithful legislator, or the ruler by its authority, or the general council of the believers.

42. We might infer many other useful conclusions which necessarily follow from the first two discourses; but let us be content with those deduced above, because they afford a ready and sufficient entering wedge for cutting away the afore-mentioned pestilence and its cause, and also for the sake of brevity.

John Wycliff (1324–1384) combined an attack on the popes' temporal claims with more formal theological heresies. The following propositions attributed to him were condemned in 1382 at a council held in London.

1. That the material substance of bread and the material substance of wine remain in the Sacrament of the altar.

2. That the accidents of bread do not remain without a subject (substance) in the said Sacrament.

3. That Christ is not in the Sacrament essentially and really, in his own corporeal presence.

4. That if a bishop or priest be in mortal sin he does not ordain, consecrate or baptize.

5. That it is not laid down in the Gospel that Christ ordained the Mass.

6. That God ought to obey the devil.

7. That if a man be duly penitent any outward confession is superfluous and useless.

• • •

10. That it is contrary to Holy Scripture that ecclesiastics should have possessions.

• • •

14. That any deacon or priest may preach the word of God apart from the authority of the Apostolic See or a Catholic bishop.

15. That no one is civil lord, or prelate, or bishop, while he is in mortal sin.

16. That temporal lords can at their will take away temporal goods from the church, when those who hold them are sinful (habitually sinful, not sinning in one act only).

17. That the people can at their own will correct sinful lords.

18. That tithes are mere alms, and that parishioners can withdraw them at their will because of the misdeeds of their curates.

• • •

20. That he who gives alms to friars is by that fact excommunicate.

21. That any one who enters a private religion [i.e. religious house], either of those having property or of mendicants, is rendered more inapt and unfit for the performance of the commands of God.

22. That holy men have sinned in founding private religions.

23. That the religious who live in private religions are not of the Christian religion.

24. That friars are bound to gain their livelihood by the labour of their hands, and not by begging.

80.   Dante on Papal Avarice

Dante (1265–1321), the greatest poet of his age, condemned several contemporary popes for avarice and simony (the selling of spiritual offices). He put them in the third "bowge" (pit) of Hell.

O Simon Magus! O disciples of his!
  Miserable pimps and hucksters, that have sold
  The things of God, troth-plight to righteousness,

Into adultery for silver and gold;
  For you the trump must sound now — you are come
  To the bag: the third bowge has you in its hold. . . .

I saw the gulley, both its banks and ground,
  Thickset with holes, all of the selfsame size,
  Pierced through the livid stone; and each was round, . . .

From each hole's mouth stuck out a sinner's feet
  And legs up to the calf; but all the main
  Part of the body was hid within the pit.

The soles of them were all on fire, whence pain
  Made their joints quiver and thrash with such strong throes,
  They'd have snapped withies and hempen ropes in twain. . .

"O thou, whoever thou art[1], unhappy shade,
  Heels over head thus planted like a stake,
  Speak if thou canst." This opening I essayed,

From Dante, *The Divine Comedy: I, Hell,* Dorothy L. Sayers, trans. (Harmondsworth: Penguin Books, 1955), pp. 188–191. Reprinted by permission.

[1]*whoever thou art:* The shade is Nicholas III, Pope 1277–80.

And stood there like the friar who leans to take
   Confession from the treacherous murderer
   Quick-buried, who calls him back for respite's sake.

He cried aloud: "Already standing there?
   Art standing there already, Boniface?[2]
   Why then, the writ has lied[3] by many a year.

What! so soon sated with the gilded brass
   That nerved thee to betray and then to rape
   The Fairest among Women that ever was?"[4]

Then I became like those who stand agape,
   Hearing remarks which seem to make no sense
   Blank of retort for what seems jeer and jape.

But Virgil now broke in: "Tell him at once:
   'I am not who thou think'st, I am not he'";
   So I made answer in obedience.

At this the soul wrenched his feet furiously,
   Almost to spraining; then he sighed, and wept,
   Saying: "Why then, what dost thou ask of me?

Art so concerned to know my name, thou'st leapt
   These barriers just for that? Then truly know
   That the Great Mantle[5] once my shoulders wrapped.

Son of the Bear was I,[6] and thirsted so
   To advance the ursine litter that I pouched
   Coin up above, and pouched myself below.

Dragged down beneath my head lie others couched,
   My predecessors who simonised before,
   Now in the deep rock-fissures cowering crouched.

I too shall fall down thither and make one more
   When he shall come to stand here in my stead
   Whom my first sudden question took thee for.

But already have I been planted in this bed
   Longer with baked feet and thus topsy-turvy
   Than he shall stand flame-footed on his head;

---

   [2]*Boniface:* The shade thinks he is being addressed by Pope Boniface VIII. There appears to have been only one hole allotted to popes, each of whom remained with his burning feet protruding till his successor arrived to thrust him down lower and take his place.

   [3]*the writ has lied:* Nicholas, like the other damned souls, can foresee the distant future, and, knowing that Boniface is not due to die till 1303, is amazed to find him (as he supposes) there already.

   [4]*the Fairest among Women:* i.e. the Church, the Bride of God, identified with the "Spouse of Lebanon" (*Song of Songs,* i. 8, etc.).

   [5]*the Great Mantle:* i.e. the Papal Mantle.

   [6]*son of the Bear:* Nicholas was one of the Orsini family — *orsa* is the Italian for "bear" — hence the pun on the "ursine" litter.

For after him from the west comes one to serve ye
  With uglier acts, a lawless Shepherd indeed,[7]
  Who'll cover us both – fit end for soul so scurvy;

He'll be another Jason,[8] as we read
  The tale in Maccabees; as that controlled
  His king, so this shall bend France like a reed."

I know not whether I was here too bold,
  But in this strain my answer flowed out free:
  "Nay, tell me now how great a treasure of gold

Our Lord required of Peter, ere that He
  Committed the great Keys into his hand;
  Certes He nothing asked save 'Follow Me.'

Nor Peter nor the others made demand
  Of silver or gold when, in the lost soul's room,
  They chose Matthias to complete their band.

Then bide thou there; thou hast deserved thy doom;
  Do thou keep well those riches foully gained[9]
  That against Charles made thee so venturesome.

And were it not that I am still constrained
  By veneration for the most high Keys
  Thou barest in glad life, I had not refrained

My tongue from yet more grievous words than these;
  Your avarice saddens the world, trampling on worth,
  Exalting the workers of iniquities. . . .

You deify silver and gold; how are you sundered
  In any fashion from the idolator,
  Save that he serves one god and you an hundred?

Ah, Constantine![10] what ills were gendered there –
  No, not from thy conversion, but the dower
  The first rich Pope received from thee as heir!"

---

[7]*a lawless Shepherd:* Pope Clement V, who came from Gascony (the West). Nicholas will hold
the uppermost place for twenty-three years (1280–1303), but Boniface only for eleven (from his
death in 1303 to that of Clement in 1314).

[8]*Jason:* See 2 *Maccabees* iv. 7 *sqq.* He bribed Antiochus Epiphanes to make him High Priest
and to connive at pagan practices; similarly Clement V will rise to the papacy by the influence of
Philip the Fair of France.

[9]*those riches foully gained:* Having been thwarted in his ambitious scheme to marry his niece
to Charles of Anjou, king of Sicily, Nicholas joined a conspiracy against Charles, which eventually resulted in the notorious massacre known as the Sicilian Vespers.

[10]*Constantine:* The allusion is to the so-called "Donation of Constantine", by which the first
Christian Emperor was alleged to have transferred to the Papal See his temporal sovereignty over
Italy.

chapter
XXVI

Fourteenth-Century Calamities

The fourteenth century has been called a "calamitous" age. Certainly the people of that time had to endure more than their share of disasters.

81. The Famine of 1315

The famine of 1315 was widespread throughout Europe. The effects in England were described by a contemporary chronicler.

In the year of our Lord 1315, apart from the other hardships with which England was afflicted, hunger grew in the land. . . . Meat and eggs began to run out, capons and fowl could hardly be found, animals died of pest, swine could not be fed because of the excessive price of fodder. A quarter of wheat or beans or peas sold for twenty shillings,[1] barley for a mark, oats for ten shillings. A quarter of salt was commonly sold for thirty-five shillings, which in former times was quite unheard of. The land was so oppressed with want that when the king came to St. Albans on the feast of St. Laurence [August 10] it was hardly possible to find bread on sale to supply his immediate household. . . .

The dearth began in the month of May and lasted until the feast of the nativity of the Virgin [September 8]. The summer rains were so heavy that grain could not ripen. It could hardly be gathered and used to bake bread down to the said feast day unless it was first put in vessels to dry. Around the end of autumn the dearth was mitigated in part, but toward Christmas it became as bad as before. Bread did not have its usual nourishing power and strength because the grain was not nourished by the warmth of summer sunshine. Hence those who ate it, even in large quantities, were hungry again after a little while.

---

[1] In 1313 a quarter of wheat sold for five shillings.

From Johannes de Trokelowe, *Annales,* H. T. Riley, ed., Rolls Series, No. 28, vol. 3 (London, 1866), pp. 92–95. Translated by Brian Tierney.

There can be no doubt that the poor wasted away when even the rich were constantly hungry. . . .

Considering and understanding these past miseries and those that were still to come, we can see how the prophecy of Jeremiah is fulfilled in the English people: "If I go forth into the fields, behold those slain with the sword, and if I enter into the city behold them that are consumed with famine" (Jeremiah 14.18). Going "forth into the fields" when we call to mind the ruin of our people in Scotland and Gascony, Wales and Ireland . . . Entering the city we consider "them that are consumed with famine" when we see the poor and needy, crushed with hunger, lying stiff and dead in the wards and streets. . . .

Four pennies worth of coarse bread was not enough to feed a common man for one day. The usual kinds of meat, suitable for eating, were too scarce; horse meat was precious; plump dogs were stolen. And, according to many reports, men and women in many places secretly ate their own children. . . .

82.   The Black Death

The greatest disaster of the age, the Black Death, was described by Giovanni Boccaccio (1313–1375).

I say, then, that the years of the beatific incarnation of the Son of God had reached the tale of one thousand three hundred and forty-eight, when in the illustrious city of Florence, the fairest of all the cities of Italy, there made its appearance that deadly pestilence, which, whether disseminated by the influence of the celestial bodies, or sent upon us mortals by God in His just wrath by way of retribution for our iniquities, had had its origin some years before in the East, whence, after destroying an innumerable multitude of living beings, it had propagated itself without respite from place to place, and so, calamitously, had spread into the West.

In Florence, despite all that human wisdom and forethought could devise to avert it, as the cleansing of the city from many impurities by officials appointed for the purpose, the refusal of entrance to all sick folk, and the adoption of many precautions for the preservation of health; despite also humble supplications addressed to God, and often repeated both in public procession and otherwise, by the devout; towards the beginning of the spring of the said year the doleful effects of the pestilence began to be horribly apparent by symptoms that shewed as if miraculous.

From Boccaccio, *The Decameron,* J. M. Rigg, trans. (London: Navarre Society, 1921), Vol. I, pp. 5–11.

Not such were they as in the East, where an issue of blood from the nose was a manifest sign of inevitable death; but in men and women alike it first betrayed itself by the emergence of certain tumours in the groin or the armpits, some of which grew as large as a common apple, others as an egg, some more, some less, which the common folk called gavoccioli. From the two said parts of the body this deadly gavocciolo soon began to propagate and spread itself in all directions indifferently; after which the form of the malady began to change, black spots or livid making their appearance in many cases on the arm or the thigh or elsewhere, now few and large, now minute and numerous. And as the gavocciolo had been and still was an infallible token of approaching death, such also were these spots on whomsoever they shewed themselves. Which maladies seemed to set entirely at naught both the art of the physician and the virtues of physic; indeed, whether it was that the disorder was of a nature to defy such treatment, or that the physicians were at fault — besides the qualified there was now a multitude both of men and of women who practised without having received the slightest tincture of medical science — and, being in ignorance of its source, failed to apply the proper remedies; in either case, not merely were those that recovered few, but almost all within three days from the appearance of the said symptoms, sooner or later, died, and in most cases without any fever or other attendant malady.

Moreover, the virulence of the pest was the greater by reason that intercourse was apt to convey it from the sick to the whole, just as fire devours things dry or greasy when they are brought close to it. Nay, the evil went yet further, for not merely by speech or association with the sick was the malady communicated to the healthy with consequent peril of common death; but any that touched the clothes of the sick or aught else that had been touched, or used by them, seemed thereby to contract the disease.

So marvellous sounds that which I have now to relate, that, had not many, and I among them, observed it with their own eyes, I had hardly dared to credit it, much less to set it down in writing, though I had had it from the lips of a credible witness.

I say, then, that such was the energy of the contagion of the said pestilence, that it was not merely propagated from man to man, but, what is much more startling, it was frequently observed, that things which had belonged to one sick or dead of the disease, if touched by some other living creature, not of the human species, were the occasion, not merely of sickening, but of an almost instantaneous death. Whereof my own eyes (as I said a little before) had cognisance, one day among others, by the following experience. The rags of a poor man who had died of the disease being strewn about the open street, two hogs came thither, and after, as is their wont, no little trifling with their snouts, took the rags between their teeth and tossed them to and fro about their chaps; whereupon, almost immediately, they gave a few turns, and fell down dead, as if by poison, upon the rags which in an evil hour they had disturbed.

In which circumstances, not to speak of many others of a similar or even graver complexion, divers apprehensions and imaginations were engendered in the minds of such as were left alive, inclining almost all of them to the same harsh resolution, to wit, to shun and abhor all contact with the sick and all that belonged to them, thinking thereby to make each his own health secure. Among whom there were those who thought that to live temperately and avoid all excess would count for much as a preservative against seizures of this kind. Wherefore they banded together, and dissociating themselves from all others, formed communities in houses where there were no sick, and lived a separate and secluded life, which they regulated with the utmost care, avoiding every kind of luxury, but eating and drinking very moderately of the most delicate viands and the finest wines, holding converse with none but one another, lest tidings of sickness or death should reach them, and diverting their minds with music and such other delights as they could devise. Others, the bias of whose minds was in the opposite direction, maintained, that to drink freely, frequent places of public resort, and take their pleasure with song and revel, sparing to satisfy no appetite, and to laugh and mock at no event, was the sovereign remedy for so great an evil: and that which they affirmed they also put in practice, so far as they were able, resorting day and night, now to this tavern, now to that, drinking with an entire disregard of rule or measure, and by preference making the houses of others, as it were, their inns, if they but saw in them aught that was particularly to their taste or liking; which they were readily able to do, because the owners, seeing death imminent, had become as reckless of their property as of their lives; so that most of the houses were open to all comers, and no distinction was observed between the stranger who presented himself and the rightful lord. Thus, adhering ever to their inhuman determination to shun the sick, as far as possible, they ordered their life. In this extremity of our city's suffering and tribulation the venerable authority of laws, human and divine, was abased and all but totally dissolved, for lack of those who should have administered and enforced them, most of whom, like the rest of the citizens, were either dead or sick, or so hard bested for servants that they were unable to execute any office; whereby every man was free to do what was right in his own eyes.

Not a few there were who belonged to neither of the two said parties, but kept a middle course between them, neither laying the same restraint upon their diet as the former, nor allowing themselves the same license in drinking and other dissipations as the latter, but living with a degree of freedom sufficient to satisfy their appetites, and not as recluses. They therefore walked abroad, carrying in their hands flowers or fragrant herbs or divers sorts of spices, which they frequently raised to their noses, deeming it an excellent thing thus to comfort the brain with such perfumes, because the air seemed to be everywhere laden and reeking with the stench emitted by the dead and the dying, and the odours of drugs.

Some again, the most sound, perhaps, in judgment, as they were also the most harsh in temper, of all, affirmed that there was no medicine for the disease superior or equal in efficacy to flight; following which prescription a multitude of men and women, negligent of all but themselves, deserted their city, their houses, their estates, their kinsfolk, their goods, and went into voluntary exile, or migrated to the country parts, as if God in visiting men with this pestilence in requital of their iniquities would not pursue them with His wrath wherever they might be, but intended the destruction of such alone as remained within the circuit of the walls of the city; or deeming, perchance, that it was now time for all to flee from it, and that its last hour was come.

Of the adherents of these divers opinions not all died, neither did all escape; but rather there were, of each sort and in every place, many that sickened, and by those who retained their health were treated after the example which they themselves, while whole, had set, being everywhere left to languish in almost total neglect. Tedious were it to recount, how citizen avoided citizen, how among neighbours was scarce found any that shewed fellow-feeling for another, how kinsfolk held aloof, and never met, or but rarely; enough that this sore affliction entered so deep into the minds of men and women, that in the horror thereof brother was forsaken by brother, nephew by uncle, brother by sister, and oftentimes husband by wife; nay, what is more, and scarcely to be believed, fathers and mothers were found to abandon their own children, untended, unvisited, to their fate, as if they had been strangers. Wherefore the sick of both sexes, whose number could not be estimated, were left without resource but in the charity of friends (and few such there were), or the interest of servants, who were hardly to be had at high rates and on unseemly terms, and being, moreover, one and all, men and women of gross understanding, and for the most part unused to such offices, concerned themselves no further than to supply the immediate and expressed wants of the sick, and to watch them die; in which service they themselves not seldom perished with their gains. In consequence of which dearth of servants and dereliction of the sick by neighbours, kinsfolk and friends, it came to pass—a thing, perhaps, never before heard of—that no woman, however dainty, fair or well-born she might be, shrank, when stricken with the disease, from the ministrations of a man, no matter whether he were young or no, or scrupled to expose to him every part of her body, with no more shame than if he had been a woman, submitting of necessity to that which her malady required; wherefrom, perchance, there resulted in after time some loss of modesty in such as recovered. Besides which many succumbed, who with proper attendance, would, perhaps, have escaped death; so that, what with the virulence of the plague and the lack of due tendance of the sick, the multitude of the deaths, that daily and nightly took place in the city, was such that those who heard the tale—not to say witnessed the fact—were struck dumb with amazement. Whereby, practices contrary to the former habits of the citizens could hardly fail to grow up among the survivors.

It had been, as to-day it still is, the custom for the women that were neighbours and of kin to the deceased to gather in his house with the women that were most closely connected with him, to wail with them in common, while on the other hand his male kinsfolk and neighbours, with not a few of the other citizens, and a due proportion of the clergy according to his quality, assembled without, in front of the house, to receive the corpse; and so the dead man was borne on the shoulders of his peers, with funeral pomp of taper and dirge, to the church selected by him before his death. Which rites, as the pestilence waxed in fury, were either in whole or in great part disused, and gave way to others of a novel order. For not only did no crowd of women surround the bed of the dying, but many passed from this life unregarded, and few indeed were they to whom were accorded the lamentations and bitter tears of sorrowing relations; nay, for the most part, their place was taken by the laugh, the jest, the festal gathering; observances which the women, domestic piety in large measure set aside, had adopted with very great advantage to their health. Few also there were whose bodies were attended to the church by more than ten or twelve of their neighbours, and those not the honourable and respected citizens; but a sort of corpse-carriers drawn from the baser ranks, who called themselves becchini and performed such offices for hire, would shoulder the bier, and with hurried steps carry it, not to the church of the dead man's choice, but to that which was nearest at hand, with four or six priests in front and a candle or two, or, perhaps, none; nor did the priests distress themselves with too long and solemn an office, but with the aid of the becchini hastily consigned the corpse to the first tomb which they found untenanted. The condition of the lower, and, perhaps, in great measure of the middle ranks, of the people shewed even worse and more deplorable; for, deluded by hope or constrained by poverty, they stayed in their quarters, in their houses, where they sickened by thousands a day, and, being without service or help of any kind, were, so to speak, irredeemably devoted to the death which overtook them. Many died daily or nightly in the public streets; of many others, who died at home, the departure was hardly observed by their neighbours, until the stench of their putrefying bodies carried the tidings; and what with their corpses and the corpses of others who died on every hand the whole place was a sepulchre.

It was the common practice of most of the neighbours, moved no less by fear of contamination by the putrefying bodies than by charity towards the deceased, to drag the corpses out of the houses with their own hands, aided, perhaps, by a porter, if a porter was to be had, and to lay them in front of the doors, where any one who made the round might have seen, especially in the morning, more of them than he could count; afterwards they would have biers brought up, or, in default, planks, whereon they laid them. Nor was it once or twice only that one and the same bier carried two or three corpses at once; but quite a considerable number of such cases occurred, one bier sufficing for husband and wife, two or three brothers, father and son, and so forth. And times without number it happened, that, as two priests, bearing the cross, were on their way to perform the last office for some one, three or four biers were brought up by the porters in rear of them, so that, whereas the priests supposed that they had but one corpse to bury, they discovered that there were six or eight, or sometimes more. Nor, for all their number, were their obsequies honoured by either tears or lights or crowds of mourners; rather, it was come to this, that a dead man was then of no more account than a dead goat would be to-day.

83.   The Hundred Years' War

The Hundred Years' War between France and England (1337–1453) was fought with a strange mixture of chivalry and savagery. Both aspects are evident in these excerpts from Froissart's Chronicle. *The first describes the battle of Crecy (1346).*

The Englishmen, who were in three battles lying on the ground to rest them, as soon as they saw the Frenchmen approach, they rose upon their feet fair and easily without any haste and arranged their battles. The first, which was the prince's battle, the archers there stood in manner of a herse and the men of arms in the bottom of the battle. The earl of Northampton and the earl of Arundel with the second battle were on a wing in good order, ready to comfort the prince's battle, if need were.

The lords and knights of France came not to the assembly together in good order, for some came before and some came after in such haste and evil order, that one of them did trouble another. When the French king saw the Englishmen, his blood changed, and [he] said to his marshals: "Make the Genoways go on before and begin the battle in the name of God and Saint Denis." There were of the Genoways crossbows about a fifteen thousand, but they were so weary of going afoot that day a six leagues armed with their crossbows, that they said to their constables: "We be not well ordered to fight this day, for we be not in the case to do any great deed of arms: we have more need of

From G. C. Macauly, ed., *The Chronicles of Froissart,* Lord Berners, trans. (London: Macmillan and Co., 1904), pp. 104–105.

rest." These words came to the earl of Alençon, who said: "A man is well at ease to be charged with such a sort of rascals, to be faint and fail now at most need." Also the same season there fell a great rain and a clipse with a terrible thunder, and before the rain there came flying over both battles a great number of crows for fear of the tempest coming. Then anon the air began to wax clear, and the sun to shine fair and bright, the which was right in the Frenchmen's eyes and on the Englishmen's backs. When the Genoways were assembled together and began to approach, they made a great [shout] and cry to abash the Englishmen, but they stood still and stirred not for all that: then the Genoways again the second time made another leap and a fell cry, and stept forward a little, and the Englishmen removed not one foot: thirdly, again they lept and cried, and went forth till they came within shot; then they shot fiercely with their cross-bows. Then the English archers stept forth one pace and let fly their arrows so wholly [together] and so thick, that it seemed snow. When the Genoways felt the arrows piercing through heads, arms and breasts, many of them cast down their cross-bows and did cut their strings and returned discomfited. When the French king saw them fly away, he said: "Slay these rascals, for they shall let and trouble us without reason." Then ye should have seen the men at arms dash in among them and killed a great number of them: and ever still the Englishmen shot whereas they saw thickest press; the sharp arrows ran into the men of arms and into their horses, and many fell, horse and men, among the Genoways, and when they were down, they could not relieve again, the press was so thick that one overthrew another. And also among the Englishmen there were certain rascals that went afoot with great knives, and they went in among the men of arms, and slew and murdered many as they lay on the ground, both earls, barons, knights, and squires, whereof the king of England was after displeased, for he had rather they had been taken prisoners.

The valiant king of Bohemia called Charles of Luxembourg, son to the noble emperor Henry of Luxembourg, for all that he was nigh blind, when he understood the order of the battle, he said to them about him: "Where is the lord Charles my son?" His men said: "Sir, we cannot tell; we think he be fighting." Then he said: "Sirs, ye are my men, my companions and friends in this journey: I require you bring me so far forward, that I may strike one stroke with my sword." They said they would do his commandment, and to the intent that they should not lose him in the press, they tied all their reins of their bridles each to other and set the king before to accomplish his desire, and so they went on their enemies. The lord Charles of Bohemia his son, who wrote himself king of Almaine and bare the arms, he came in good order to the battle; but when he saw that the matter went awry on their party, he departed, I cannot tell you which way. The king his father was so far forward that he strake a stroke with his sword, yea and more than four, and fought valiantly and so did his company; and they adventured themselves so forward, that they were there all slain; and the next day they were found in the place about the king, and all their horses tied each to other.

• • •

[The contingent led by the king's son, the Black Prince, was hard-pressed in the fighting.] Then the second battle of the Englishmen came to succour the prince's battle, the which was time, for they had as then much ado and they with the prince sent a messenger to the king, who was on a little windmill hill. Then the knight said to the king: "Sir, the earl of Warwick and the earl of Oxford, sir Raynold Cobham and other, such as be about the prince your son, are fiercely fought withal and are sore handled; wherefore they desire you that you and your battle will come and aid them; for if the Frenchmen increase, as they doubt they will, your son and they shall have much ado." Then the king said: "Is my son dead or hurt or on the earth felled?" "No, sir," quoth the knight, "but he is hardly matched; wherefore he hath need of your aid." "Well," said the king, "return to him and to them that sent you hither, and say to them that they send no more to me for any adventure that falleth, as long as my son is alive: and also say to them that they suffer him this day to win his spurs; for if God be pleased, I will this journey be his and the honour thereof, and to them that be about him."

In 1356 the English won another great victory at Poitiers and captured the French king.

Oftentimes the adventures of amours and of war are more fortunate and marvellous than any man can think or wish. Truly this battle, the which was near to Poitiers in the fields of Beauvoir and Maupertuis, was right great and perilous, and many deeds of arms there was done the which all came not to knowledge. The fighters on both sides endured much pain: king John with his own hands did that day marvels in arms: he had an axe in his hands wherewith he defended himself and fought in the breaking of the press. Near to the king there was taken the earl of Tancarville, sir Jaques of Bourbon earl of Ponthieu, and the lord John of Artois earl of Eu, and a little above that under the banner of the captal of Buch was taken sir Charles of Artois and divers other knights and squires. The chase endured to the gates of Poitiers: there were many slain and beaten down, horse and man, for they of Poitiers closed their gates and would suffer none to enter; wherefore in the street before the gate was horrible murder, men hurt and beaten down. . . .

Then there was a great press to take the king, and such as knew him

From G. C Macauly, ed., *The Chronicles of Froissart,* Lord Berners, trans. (London: Macmillan and Co., 1904), pp. 128–131.

cried, "Sir, yield you, or else ye are but dead." There was a knight of
Saint-Omer's, retained in wages with the king of England, called sir
Denis Morbeke, who had served the Englishmen five year before, because in his youth he had forfeited the realm of France for a murder
that he did at Saint-Omer's. It happened so well for him, that he was
next to the king when they were about to take him: he stept forth into
the press, and by strength of his body and arms he came to the French
king and said in good French, "Sir, yield you." The king beheld the
knight and said: "To whom shall I yield me? Where is my cousin the
prince of Wales? If I might see him, I would speak with him." Denis
answered and said: "Sir, he is not here; but yield you to me and I shall
bring you to him." "Who be you?" quoth the king. "Sir," he, "I am
Denis of Morbeke, a knight of Artois; but I serve the king of England
because I am banished the realm of France and I have forfeited all
that I had there." Then the king gave him his right gauntlet, saying "I
yield me to you." There was a great press about the king, for every
man enforced him to say, "I have taken him," so that the king could
not go forward with his young son the lord Philip with him because of
the press.

• • •

[The Black Prince sent two lords to search for the French king.]
These two lords took their horses and departed from the prince and
rode up a hill to look about them: then they perceived a flock of men
of arms coming together right wearily: there was the French king afoot
in great peril, for Englishmen and Gascons were his masters; they had
taken him from sir Denis Morbeke perforce, and such as were most of
force said, "I have taken him"; "Nay," quoth another, "I have taken
him"; so they strave which should have him. Then the French king, to
eschew that peril, said: "Sirs, strive not: lead men courteously, and my
son, to my cousin the prince, and strive not for my taking, for I am so
great a lord to make you all rich." The king's words somewhat appeased
them; howbeit ever as they went they made riot and brawled for the
taking of the king. When the two foresaid lords saw and heard that
noise and strife among them they came to them and said: "Sirs, what
is the matter that ye strive for?" "Sirs," said one of them, "it is for the
French king, who is here taken prisoner, and there be more than ten
knights and squires that challengeth the taking of him and of his son."
Then the two lords entered into the press and caused every man to
draw aback, and commanded them in the prince's name on pain of
their heads to make no more noise nor to approach the king no nearer,
without they were commanded. Then every man gave room to the
lords, and they alighted and did their reverence to the king, and so
brought him and his son in peace and rest to the prince of Wales.

• • •

The same day of the battle at night the prince made a supper in his
lodging to the French king and to the most part of the great lords that

were prisoners. The prince made the king and his son, the lord James of Bourbon, the lord John d'Artois, the earl of Tancarville, the earl of Estampes, the earl of Dammartin, the earl of Joinville and the lord of Partenay to sit all at one board, and other lords, knights and squires at other tables; and always the prince served before the king as humbly as he could, and would not sit at the king's board for any desire that the king could make, but he said he was not sufficient to sit at the table with so great a prince as the king was. But then he said to the king, "Sir, for God's sake make none evil nor heavy cheer, though God this day did not consent to follow your will; for, sir, surely the king my father shall bear you as much honour and amity as he may do, and shall accord with you so reasonably that ye shall ever be friends together after. And, sir, methink ye ought to rejoice, though the journey be not as ye would have had it, for this day ye have won the high renown of prowess and have passed this day in valiantness all other of your party. Sir, I say not this to mock you, for all that be on our party, that saw every man's deeds, are plainly accorded by true sentence to give you the prize and chaplet." Therewith the Frenchmen began to murmur and said among themselves how the prince had spoken nobly, and that by all estimation he should prove a noble man, if God send him life and to persevere in such good fortune.

While King John was a prisoner in London, a savage peasant rebellion broke out in France.

Anon after the deliverance of the king of Navarre there began a marvellous tribulation in the realm of France, as in Beauvoisin, in Brie, on the river of Marne, in Laonnois, and about Soissons. For certain people of the common villages, without any head or ruler, assembled together in Beauvoisin. In the beginning they passed not a hundred in number they said how the noblemen of the realm of France, knights and squires, shamed the realm, and that it should be a great wealth to destroy them all: and each of them said it was true, and said all with one voice: "Shame have he that doth not his power to destroy all the gentlemen of the realm!"

Thus they gathered together without any other counsel, and without any armour saving with staves and knives, and so went to the house of a knight dwelling thereby, and brake up his house and slew the knight and the lady and all his children great and small and brent his house. And they they went to another castle, and took the knight thereof and bound him fast to a stake, and then violated his wife and his daughter before his face and then slew the lady and his daughter and all his other children, and then slew the knight by great torment

From G. C. Macauly, ed., *The Chronicles of Froissart*, Lord Berners, trans. (London: Macmillan and Co., 1904), pp. 136-137.

and brent and beat down the castle. And so they did to divers other castles and good houses; and they multiplied so that they were a six thousand, and ever as they went forward they increased, for such like as they were fell ever to them, so that every gentleman fled from them and took their wives and children with them, and fled ten or twenty leagues off to be in surety, and left their house void and their goods therein.

These mischievous people thus assembled without captain or armour robbed, brent and slew all gentlemen that they could lay hands on, and forced and ravished ladies and damosels, and did such shameful deeds that no human creature ought to think on any such, and he that did most mischief was most praised with them and greatest master. I dare not write the horrible deeds that they did to ladies and damosels; among other they slew a knight and after did put him on a broach and roasted him at the fire in the sight of the lady his wife and his children; and after the lady had been enforced and ravished with a ten or twelve, they made her perforce to eat of her husband and after made her to die an evil death and all her children. They made among them a king, one of Clermont in Beauvoisin: they chose him that was the most ungraciousest of all other and they called him king Jaques Goodman, and so thereby they were called companions of the Jaquery. They destroyed and brent in the country of Beauvoisin about Corbie, and Amiens and Montdidier more than threescore good houses and strong castles. In like manner these unhappy people were in Brie and Artois, so that all the ladies, knights and squires of that country were fain to fly away to Meaux in Brie, as well the duchess of Normandy and the duchess of Orleans as divers other ladies and damosels, or else they had been violated and after murdered. Also there were a certain of the same ungracious people between Paris and Noyon and between Paris and Soissons, and all about in the land of Coucy, in the county of Valois, in the bishopric of Laon, Nyon and Soissons. There were brent and destroyed more than a hundred castles and good houses of knights and squires in that country.

English invaders continued to ravage France in the 1370s.

About the space of a month or more was the prince of Wales before the city of Limoges, and there was neither assault nor scrimmish, but daily they mined. And they within knew well how they were mined, and made a countermine thereagainst to have destroyed the English miners; but they failed of their mine. And when the prince's miners saw how the countermine against them failed, they said to the prince: "Sir, whensoever it shall please you we shall cause a part of the wall to

From G. C. Macauly, ed., *The Chronicles of Froissart,* Lord Berners, trans. (London: Macmillan and Co., 1904), p. 201.

fall into the dikes, whereby ye shall enter into the city at your ease without any danger." Which words pleased greatly the prince, and said: " I will that to-morrow betimes ye shew forth and execute your work." Then the miners set fire into their mine, and so the next morning, as the prince had ordained, there fell down a great pane of the wall and filled the dikes, whereof the Englishmen were glad and were ready armed in the field to enter into the town. The foot-men might well enter at their ease, and so they did and ran to the gate and beat down the fortifying and barriers, for there was no defence against them: it was done so suddenly that they of the town were not ware thereof.

Then the prince, the duke of Lancaster, the earl of Cambridge, the earl of Pembroke, sir Guichard d'Angle and all the other with their companies entered into the city, and all other foot-men, ready apparelled to do evil, and to pill and rob the city, and to slay men, women and children, for so it was commanded them to do. It was great pity to see the men, women and children that kneeled down on their knees before the prince for mercy; but he was so inflamed with ire, that he took no heed to them, so that none was heared, but all put to death, as they were met withal, and such as were nothing culpable. There was no pity take of the poor people, who wrought never no manner of treason, yet they bought it dearer than the great personages, such as had done the evil and trespass. There was not so hard a heart within the city of Limoges, an if he had any remembrance of God, but that wept piteously for the great mischief that they saw before their eyen: for more than three thousand men, women and children were slain and beheaded that day, God have mercy on their souls, for I trow they were martyrs.

XXVII

Aspects of Late Medieval Government

In the later Middle Ages complex problems arose concerning the authority of rulers and the rights of subjects. The documents in this section illustrate developments in government in Germany, England, and France.

84. Germany: The Golden Bull of Charles IV

The constitutional structure of imperial Germany was defined in the Golden Bull of 1356. The historian Lord Bryce wrote that this document "codified anarchy and called it a constitution."

Chapter I: Escort and Safe-conduct for the Electors

1. We decree and determine by this imperial edict that, whenever the electoral princes are summoned according to the ancient and praiseworthy custom to meet and elect a king of the Romans and future emperor, each of them shall be bound to furnish on demand an escort and safe-conduct to his fellow electors or their representatives, within his own lands and as much farther as he can, for the journey to and from the city where the election is to be held. Any electoral prince who refuses to furnish escort and safe-conduct shall be liable to the penalties for perjury and to the loss of his electoral vote for that occasion.

• • •

16. When the news of the death of the king of the Romans has been received at Mainz, within one month from the date of receiving it the archbishop of Mainz shall send notices of the death and of the approaching election to all the electoral princes. But if the archbishop neglects or refuses to send such notices, the electoral princes are commanded on their fidelity to assemble on their own motion and without

From "The Golden Bull of Charles IV," in O. J. Thatcher and E. H. McNeal, trans., *A Source Book for Mediaeval History* (New York: Charles Scribner's, 1905), pp. 284-298.

summons at the city of Frankfort within three months from the death of the emperor, for the purpose of electing a king of the Romans and future emperor.

Chapter II: The Election of the King of the Romans

1. (Mass shall be celebrated on the day after the arrival of electors. The archbishop of Mainz administers this oath, which the other electors repeat:)

2. "I, archbishop of Mainz, archchancellor of the empire for Germany, electoral prince, swear on the holy gospels here before me, and by the faith which I owe to God and to the holy Roman empire, that with the aid of God, and according to my best judgment and knowledge, I will cast my vote; in this election of the king of the Romans and future emperor, for a person fitted to rule the Christian people. I will give my voice and vote freely, uninfluenced by any agreement, price, bribe, promise, or anything of the sort, by whatever name it may be called. So help me God and all the saints."

3. After the electors have taken this oath, they shall proceed to the election, and shall not depart from Frankfort until the majority have elected a king of the Romans and future emperor, to be ruler of the world and of the Christian people. If they have not come to a decision within thirty days from the day on which they took the above oath, after that they shall live upon bread and water and shall not leave the city until the election has been decided.

4. Such an election shall be as valid as if all the princes had agreed unanimously and without difference upon a candidate. If any one of the princes or his representatives has been hindered or delayed for a time, but arrives before the election is over, he shall be admitted and shall take part in the election at the stage which had been reached at the time of his arrival. According to the ancient and approved custom, the king of the Romans elect, immediately afer his election and before he takes up any other business of the empire, shall confirm and approve by sealed letters for each and all of the electoral princes, concessions, ancient customs, and dignities, and whatever else the princes held and possessed from the empire at the time of the election; and he shall renew the confirmation and approval when he becomes emperor. The original confirmation shall be made by him as king, and the renewal as emperor. It is his duty to do this graciously and in good faith, and not to hinder the princes in the exercise of their rights.

5. In the case where three of the electors vote for a fourth electoral prince, his vote shall have the same value as that of the others to make a majority and decide the election.

Chapter IX: Mines of Gold, Silver, and Other Metals

We decree, by this present law, that our successors, the kings of Bohemia, and all the electoral princes, ecclesiastical and secular, shall hold and possess with full rights, all mines of gold, silver, tin, copper, iron, lead, or other metals, and all salt works, both those already discovered and those which shall be discovered in the future, situated within their lands, domains, and dependencies. They shall also have authority to tax Jews, the right to collect tolls already in force, and all other rights which they or their predecessors have possessed to the present day.

Chapter X: Coinage

1. We also decree that our successors, the future kings of Bohemia, shall possess and exercise in peace the rights of coinage of gold and silver, in all parts of their dominions and of the lands belonging to their subjects, in such form and manner as they may determine; a right which is known to have belonged to our predecessors, the former kings of Bohemia.

2. We also grant to the future kings of Bohemia forever the right to buy, purchase, or receive as gift or in payment, any lands, castles, possessions, or goods from any princes, magnates, counts, or other persons; such lands and property to remain, however, in their former legal status and to pay the customary dues and services to the empire

3. We extend this right by the present law to all the electoral princes, ecclesiastical and secular, and to their legal heirs, under the same conditions and form.

Chapter XI: The Immunities of the Princes

1. We decree also that no count, baron, noble, vassal, burggrave, knight, client, citizen, burgher, or other subject of the churches of Cologne, Mainz, or Trier, of whatever status, condition, or rank, shall be cited, haled, or summoned to any authority before any tribunal outside of the territories, boundaries, and limits of these churches and their dependencies, or before any judge, except the archbishops and their judges. . . . We refuse to hear appeals based upon the authority of others over the subjects of these princes; if these princes are accused by their subjects of injustice, appeal shall lie to the imperial diet, and shall be heard there and nowhere else. . . .

2. We extend this right by the present law to the secular electoral princes, the count palatine of the Rhine, the duke of Saxony, and the margrave of Brandenburg, and to their heirs, successors, and subjects forever.

Chapter XII: Assemblies of the Princes

. . . It has been decided in the general diet held at Nürnburg with the electoral princes, ecclesiastical and secular, and other princes and magnates, by their advice and with their consent, that in the future, the electoral princes shall meet every year in some city of the empire four weeks after Easter; this year they are to meet at that date in the imperial city of Metz; on that occasion, and on every meeting thereafter, the place of assembling for the following year shall be fixed by us with the advice and consent of the princes. This ordinance shall remain in force as long as it shall be pleasing to us and to the princes; and as long as it is in effect, we shall furnish the princes with safe-conduct for that assembly, going, staying, and returning. . . .

Chapter XVII: Renunciation of Allegiance

If any person renounces his allegiance or alliance without due notice and in a place where he does not have his residence, even if he thinks he has just grounds, we declare that he shall not have the right to inflict injury or violence upon those from whom he has in this manner withdrawn. And since fraud and deceit cannot constitute legal defence, we hereby declare that renunciation of this sort from the society or association of any lord or person shall not be valid, and may not be used as pretext for making war, unless the renunciation has been announced to those who are concerned personally or publicly in the place where they have their regular residence, three full days before, and the notification can be proved by good witnesses. Whoever shall make war on another without making renunciation in this form, shall be branded with infamy, just as if he had never made any renunciation, and he shall be punished as a traitor by all judges. We forbid and condemn also all unjust wars and strife, all unjust burning, wasting, and rapine, all unusual and unjust tolls and exactions for safe-conduct, under penalties fixed by the laws of the empire.

85. England: The Deposition of Richard II

King Richard II of England was accused of trying to establish an arbitrary, despotic government. In 1399 he was deposed and replaced by his cousin, Henry of Lancaster. This account of the proceedings is from the Rolls of Parliament.

Here follow the record and process of the renunciation by King Richard II after the Conquest, and of the acceptance of the same renuncia-

From *Sources of English Constitutional History,* translated by C. Stephenson and F. G. Marcham (New York: Harper and Brothers, 1937), pp. 251-254; Copyright 1937, 1965 by Harper and Row, Publishers, Incorporated; reprinted by permission of the publishers.

tion; likewise of the deposition of the same King Richard. . . . On the next day, however . . . , in the great hall at Westminter, honourably prepared for the holding of parliament, in the presence of the said archbishops of Canterbury and York, of the duke of Lancaster, of other dukes and lords both spiritual and temporal whose names are inscribed below, and of the people of the said kingdom then and there assembled in a very great multitude for the sake of [witnessing] the deeds of parliament, while the aforesaid duke of Lancaster occupied the place due and accustomed to his estate and while the royal throne, solemnly prepared with cloth of gold, stood vacant in the absence of any presiding officer whatsoever, the aforesaid archbishop of York . . . had the said cession and renunciation read by another, first in Latin and then in English. And immediately it was asked of the estates and the people then and there present . . . whether for their own interest and for the benefit of the kingdom, they wished to accept the same renunciation and cession. And the same estates and people, considering, for the reasons specified by the king himself in his aforesaid renunciation and cession, that to do so would be highly expedient, all singly and in common with the people unanimously and with one accord accepted such renunciation and cession. After this acceptance, however, it was then publicly set forth that, besides the renunciation and cession accepted as aforesaid, it would in many ways be expedient and advantageous for the said kingdom if, in order to obviate all scruple and evil suspicion, the many crimes and defaults frequently committed by the said king in connection with the bad government of his kingdom — on account of which, as he himself had asserted in the cession made by him, he merited deposition — should be written down in the form of articles, to be publicly read and declared to the people. And so a large part of those articles was then publicly read, of all which articles the tenor is as follows. . . .

Item, in the parliament recently held at Shrewsbury the same king, proposing to oppress his people, subtly procured and caused it to be granted that, by the counsel of all the estates of his realm, the power of parliament to decide certain petitions, which had been presented in the same parliament but on which no progress had as yet been made, should devolve upon certain persons. By colour of which concession the persons thus deputed proceeded with other matters of common concern to that parliament — and this at the will of the king and in derogation of the estate of parliament, to the great damage of the entire kingdom, and [by way of setting] a pernicious example. And in order that [these persons] might seem to have a certain colour of authority for such deeds, the king had the rolls of parliament deleted and changed to suit himself and contrary to the terms of the aforesaid concession. . . .

Item, when the king of England was able, without oppressing his people, to live honourably from the issues of his kingdom and from the patrimony belonging to his crown, since the kingdom was not burdened with the expense of wars, the same king, while truces between the kingdom of England and his adversaries continued during almost his entire reign, not only gave the greater part of his said patrimony to unworthy persons, but also, on that account, threw such burdens of taxation on his subjects in nearly every year of his reign that he widely and outrageously oppressed his people, to the impoverishment of his kingdom. And the income thus obtained was not used for the benefi. and advantage of the kingdom of England, but was prodigally dissipated for the sake of his own ostentation, pomp, and vainglory. And great sums of money were owed in his kingdom for the victuals of his household and other purchases of his, although, more than any of his progenitors, he enjoyed an abundance of treasure and riches. Item, the same king, refusing to keep and defend the just laws and customs of his kingdom, but [wishing] at his own arbitrary will to do whatever appealed to his desires, sometimes — and very often when the laws of the kingdom had been declared and explained to him by his justices and others of his council, and when, according to those laws, he was to administer justice to those seeking it — expressly said, with an austere and determined countenance, that his laws were in his own mouth or, occasionally, in his own breast; and that he alone could establish and change the laws of his realm. And he, seduced by that opinion, would not permit justice to be done to many of his lieges, but by threats and intimidation compelled many to abstain from the pursuit of common justice. . . .

Item, although, according to the statutes and custom of his realm, his people in all the counties of the kingdom ought, on the summoning of every parliament, to be free to elect and depute knights on behalf of such counties to attend parliament, explain their grievances, and in that connection sue for remedies as may seem best to them; nevertheless, the aforesaid king, in order that he might be able the more freely to carry out his own headstrong will, very often sent mandates to his sheriffs that they should cause certain persons, nominated as knights of the shires by the king himself, to come to his parliaments. And these knights, since they favoured the same king, he was able to induce — as he very often did, sometimes by divers threats and intimidation and sometimes by rewards — to support matters prejudicial to the kingdom and extremely burdensome to the people, especially the grant to the same king of a subsidy on wool for the term of his life and another subsidy for a number of years, to the excessive oppression of his people. . . .

Item, although the lands, tenements, goods, and chattels of every freeman, according to the laws of the realm accustomed throughout all times past, ought not to be seized unless they have been [lawfully] forfeited, nevertheless the said king, proposing and determining to undo such laws, in the presence of very many lords and of other men from the commonalty cf the realm, often said and affirmed that the life of every one of his lieges, together with the lands, tenements, goods, and chattels of such men, was subject to his own pleasure, apart from any [lawful] forfeiture — which is wholly contrary to the laws and customs of his kingdom aforesaid.

Item, although it is established and ordained that no freeman shall be seized, etc., or in any way destroyed, and that the king will neither go against him nor send against him, except by the lawful judgment of his peers, or by the law of the land; nevertheless, by the will, mandate, and order of the said king, very many of his lieges, maliciously accused of having publicly or secretly said something that might lead to the slander, shame, or humiliation of the said king's person, were seized and imprisoned and taken to a military court before the constable and marshal of England. . . . Wherefore, since the aforesaid king wilfully contravened such statute of his realm, it is not to be doubted that he thereby committed perjury. . . .

And since it seemed to all these estates, thereupon interrogated singly and in common, that those statements of his crimes and defaults were notoriously sufficient for deposing the same king, considering also his own confession with regard to his incompetence and other matters contained in the said renunciation and cession which had been openly published, all the estates aforesaid unanimously agreed that the deposition of the said king was abundantly justified in order to secure the greater safety and tranquillity of the people and the good of the kingdom. . . .

And immediately, as it appeared from the foregoing [actions] and their result that the kingship of England, together with its appurtenances, was vacant, the aforesaid Henry, duke of Lancaster, rising from his place and standing so erect that he could be well seen by all the people, humbly signing himself on the brow and breast with the symbol of the Cross and first invoking Christ by name, laid claim to the said kingship of England, thus declared vacant, together with the crown and all its members and appurtenances; [and this he did] in his mother tongue by the form of words following: —

"In the name of Fadir, Son, and Holy Gost, I, Henry of Lancaster chalenge this rewme of Yngland and the corone with all the membres and the appurtenances, als I that am disendit be right lyne of the blode comyng fro the gude lorde Kyng Henry Therde, and thorghe that ryght that God of his grace hath sent me, with the helpe of my kyn and of my frendes, to recover it — the whiche rewme was in poynt to be undone for defaut of governance and undoyng of the gode lawes."

After which declaration and claim the lords both spiritual and temporal, and all the estates there present, were asked singly and in common what they thought of that declaration and claim; and the same estates, together with all the people, unanimously agreed without difficulty or delay that the aforesaid duke should reign over them. And immediately . . . the aforesaid archbishop, taking the said King

Henry by the right hand, led him to the royal throne aforesaid. And after the said king, kneeling before the said throne, had made a short prayer, the same archbishop of Canterbury, with the assistance of the aforesaid archbishop of York, placed the said king and caused him to sit on the aforesaid royal throne, while the people in their excessive joy loudly applauded. And then the said archbishop of Canterbury, when silence had with difficulty been obtained, on account of the joy of all the bystanders, preached a brief sermon, speaking in these words. . . . And when this sermon had been ended, the said Lord King Henry, in order to put at rest the minds of his subjects, in the same place publicly spoke the following words: —

"Sires, I thank God and yowe, spiritual and temporal and all the astates of the lond, and do yowe to wyte it is noght my will that no man thynk that be waye of conquest I wold disherit any man of his heritage, franches, or other ryghtes that hym aght to have, no put hym out of that that he has and has had by the gude laws and customs of the rewme—except thos persons that has ben agan the gude purpose and the commune profyt of the rewme."

86.   *France: Jeanne d'Arc and Divine Right Monarchy*

The English invasions of France led to a rallying of support for the French monarchy and a strong reinsistence on the old doctrine of the divine right of kings. This letter of Jeanne d'Arc to the English, written in 1429, typifies the new mood of the French people.

JHESUS MARIA

King of England, and you Duke of Bedford, calling yourself regent of France, you William Pole, Count of Suffolk John Talbot, and you Thomas Lord Scales, calling yourselves lieutenants of the said Duke of Bedford, do right in the King of Heaven's sight. Surrender to *The Maid* sent hither by God the King of Heaven, the keys of all the good towns you have taken and laid waste in France. She comes in God's name to establish the Blood Royal, ready to make peace if you agree to abandon France and repay what you have taken. And you, archers, comrades in arms, gentles and others, who are before the town of Orleans, retire in God's name to your own country. If you do not, expect to hear tidings from *The Maid* who will shortly come upon you to your very great hurt. And to you, King of England, if you do not thus,

From W. P. Barrett, trans., *The Trial of Jeanne d'Arc* (London: George Routledge, 1931), pp. 165-166, 54-57; reprinted by permission of the publisher.

I am a chieftain of war, and whenever I meet your followers in France, I will drive them out; if they will not obey, I will put them all to death. I am sent here in God's name, the King of Heaven, to drive you body for body out of all France. If they obey, I will show them mercy. Do not think otherwise; you will not withhold the kingdom of France from God, the King of Kings, Blessed Mary's Son. The King Charles, the true inheritor, will possess it, for God wills it, and has revealed it to him through *The Maid,* and he will enter Paris with a good company. If you do not believe these tidings from God and *The Maid,* wherever we find you we shall strike you and make a greater tumult than France has heard for a thousand years. Know well that the King of Heaven will send a greater force to *The Maid* and her good people than you in all your assaults can overcome: and by blows shall the favour of the God of Heaven be seen. You Duke of Bedford, *The Maid* prays and beseeches not to bring yourself to destruction. If you obey her, you may join her company, where the French shall do the fairest deed ever done for Christendom. Answer, if you desire peace in the city of Orleans; if not, bethink you of your great hurt soon. Written this Tuesday of Holy Week.

At her trial Jeanne d'Arc repeatedly stated that she knew Charles VII was the true king of France through divine inspiration. The following excerpt is from the record of her trial.

. . Afterwards she declared that at the age of thirteen she had a voice from God to help her and guide her. And the first time she was much afraid. And this voice came towards noon, in summer, in her father's garden: and the said Jeanne had [not] fasted on the preceding day. She heard the voice on her right, in the direction of the church; and she seldom heard it without a light. This light came from the same side as the voice, and generally there was a great light. When she came to France she often heard the voice.

Asked how she could see the light of which she spoke, since it was at the side, she made no reply, and went on to other things. She said that if she was in a wood she easily heard the voices come to her. It seemed to her a worthy voice, and she believed it was sent from God; when she heard the voice a third time she knew that it was the voice of an angel. She said also that this voice always protected her well and that she understood it well.

Asked what instruction this voice gave her for the salvation of her soul: she said it taught her to be good and to go to church often; and it told her that she must come to France. And, Jeanne added, Beaupère would not learn from her, this time, in what form that voice appeared to her. She further said that this voice told her once or twice a week that she should leave and come to France, and that her father knew nothing of her leaving. She said that the voice told her to come, and she could no longer stay where she was; and the voice told her again that she should raise the siege of the city of Orleans. She said moreover that the voice told her that she, Jeanne, should go to Robert de Baudricourt, in the town of Vaucouleurs of which he was captain, and he would provide an escort for her. And the said Jeanne answered that she was a poor maid, knowing nothing of riding or fighting. She said she went to an uncle of hers, and told him she wanted to stay with him for some time; and she stayed there for about eight days. And she told her uncle she must go to the said town of Vaucouleurs, and so her uncle took her

Then she said that when she reached Vaucouleurs she easily recognized Robert de Baudricourt, although she had never seen him before; and she knew him through her voice, for the voice had told her it was he. And the said Jeanne told Robert she must come to France. The said Robert twice refused to hear her and repulsed her; the third time he listened to her and gave her an escort. And the voice had told her that it would be so.

Then she declared that the duke of Lorraine ordered that she should be taken to him; and she went to him and told him she wished to go to France. And the duke questioned her about the recovery of his health; but she said she knew nothing about that; and she spoke to him little concerning her journey. She told the duke nevertheless to send his son and some men to escort her to France, and she would pray to God for his health. She visited him with a safe conduct and returned to the town of Vaucouleurs.

She declared that, on her departure from Vaucouleurs, she wore the habit of a man, and carried a sword which Robert de Baudricourt had given her, but no other arms; and accompanied by a knight, a squire, and four servants, she reached the town of Saint Urbain, where she slept in an abbey.

She said that on her journey she passed through Auxerre, and she heard Mass in the principal church there; and from that time she frequently heard her voices, including the one already mentioned.

Required to say by what advice she took to man's dress, she several times refused to answer. Finally she answered that she charged no one with that; and several times she answered variously.

She said that Robert de Baudricourt had sworn those who accompanied her to conduct her well and safely. "Go," said Robert to Jeanne, as she departed, "Go, and come what may."

Jeanne said furthermore that she knows very well that God loves the duke of Orleans; and so she had more revelations concerning him than any man alive, except him whom she calls her king. She said also that it was altogether necessary to change her women's clothes for men's. She believed that her counsel said well.

She said that she sent to the English at Orleans letters telling them to depart, as shown in the copy of the letters which had been read to her in this town of Rouen, except two or three words in the copy: for example, where in this copy it read *Surrender to the Maid* it should read *Surrender to the King*. There are also these words, *body for body* and *chieftain of war,* which were not in the original letters.

After this the said Jeanne told that she went without hindrance to him whom she calls her king. And when she had arrived at Ste. Catherine de Fierbois, then she sent first to Chinon, where he who she calls her king was. She reached Chinon towards noon and lodged at an inn; and after dinner she went to him whom she calls king, who was at the castle. She said that when she entered her king's room she recognized him among many others by the counsel of her voice, which revealed him to her. She told him she wanted to make war on the English.

Asked whether, when the voice showed her her king, there was no light, she answered: "Pass on to the next question." Asked if she saw no angel above the king, she answered: "Spare me that, Continue." She said also that before the king put her to work he had several apparitions and beautiful revelations.

Asked what revelations and apparitions the king had, she answered: "I will not tell you. It is not now the time to tell you; but send to the king and he will tell you."

chapter
XXVIII

Conciliarism in the Church

---

87. The Doctrine of Conciliar Supremacy

The Council of Constance met in 1414 to seek a way of ending the papal schism that had begun in 1378. In 1415 the council enacted the decree Haec sancta *which affirmed the supreme authority of General Councils in the government of the church*

This holy synod of Constance, constituting a general council, lawfully assembled to bring about the end of the present Schism and the union and reformation of the Church of God in head and members, to the praise of Almighty God in the Holy Spirit, in order that it may achieve more readily, safely, amply, and freely the union and reformation of the Church of God, does hereby ordain, ratify, enact, decree, and declare the following:

First, it declares that being lawfully assembled in the Holy Spirit, constituting a general council and representing the Catholic Church Militant, it has its power directly from Christ, and that all persons of whatever rank or dignity, even a Pope, are bound to obey it in matters relating to faith and the end of the Schism and the general reformation of the Church of God in head and members.

Further, it declares that any person of whatever position, rank, or dignity, even a Pope, who contumaciously refuses to obey the man-

From "Cardinal Fillastre's Diary of the Council of Constance," in L. R. Loomis, trans., *The Council of Constance* (New York: Columbia University Press, 1961), pp. 229, 246–247; Copyright 1961 Columbia University Press; reprinted by permission of the publisher.

dates, statutes, ordinance, or regulations enacted or to be enacted by this holy synod, or by any other general council lawfully assembled, relating to the matters aforesaid or to other matters involved with them, shall, unless he repents, be subject to condign penalty and duly punished, with recourse, if necessary, to other aids of the law   . [April 6, 1415]

The council proceeded to exercise the authority it had claimed for itself by deposing John XXIII of the "Pisan line" of popes.

Accordingly, on Wednesday, May 29, anno Domini 1415, the vigil of the feast of the Holy Eucharist, the Council held a session, with the King present and the Cardinal of Ostia presiding, and pronounced the sentence of deposition of the Pope. It was read by the Bishop of Arras, who has a loud, deep voice. The tenor of it was as follows:

"The sacrosanct general synod of Constance, representing the Catholic Church . . . decrees, enacts, and ordains that if the Apostolic See should for any reason become vacant, no steps whatever shall be taken at the beginning of the vacancy to elect a future supreme pontiff without the decision and consent of this sacred general Council. If any such steps are taken, they shall be *ipso facto,* by authority of the said Council, null and void. . . .

"Further, the said holy synod decrees, enacts, and ordains, for the good of the union of the Church of God, that lord Baldassarre Cossa, Pedro de Luna, and Angelo Corario, known of late by their obediences as John XXIII, Benedict XIIII, and Gregory XII, shall never be reelected to the papacy.

"In the name of the Holy and Indivisible Trinity, Father, Son, and Holy Spirit. Amen. The sacrosanct general synod of Constance, lawfully assembled in the Holy Spirit invoking the name of Christ and keeping God only before its eyes, has noted the articles formulated and presented in the case against the lord Pope John XXIII, the proofs of the same and his own voluntary submission, as also the entire procedure in the case, and after mature deliberation pronounces, decrees, and declares this definitive sentence, which it now issues in writing.

"The clandestine departure of the said lord Pope John XXIII from this city of Constance and the sacred general Council, at a suspicious hour of night, in unsuitable disguise, was and is unwarrantable, a notorious scandal to the Church of God and the Council, a disturbing obstacle to the peace and union of the Church, an aid to prolonging the schism and a violation of the vow, promise, and oath sworn by the same lord Pope John to God and the Church and this sacred Council. The same lord Pope John was and is a notorious simoniac, a notorious waster of the property and rights of the Roman and other churches and of many other pious institutions, and an evil administrator and dispenser of the spiritual and temporal treasures of the Church. By his detestable and dishonorable life and character he has notoriously scandalized the Church of God and Christian people, both before his elevation to the papacy and since, down to the present. On all these counts he has been and is in himself a notorious scandal to the Church of God and Christian people. In spite of due and charitable warnings, repeated on many occasions, he has persisted obstinately in his wicked course and proved himself notoriously incorrigible.

"Therefore, for these and other crimes, set forth and related in the proceedings of the case against him, he deserves to be unseated, removed, and deposed from the papacy and all administration, spiritual and temporal, as unworthy, unprofitable, and dangerous. And the said holy synod hereby unseats, removes, and deposes him, declaring all and every Christian of whatever rank, dignity, or condition released from obedience, fealty, and obligation to him, and forbidding all the faithful of Christ, now that he is herewith deposed from the papacy, from receiving him henceforth as pope or calling him pope or adhering to him as pope or paying him any obedience. . . . Other penalties that by canonical rules should be inflicted for his crimes and excesses the Council reserves to be pronounced and inflicted at its discretion, as strict justice or considerations of mercy may dictate."

88.   *Reform and Reaction*

After removing all three rival popes the Council of Constance turned to the task of reforming the church. The decree Frequens *laid down that this work was to be carried on in a series of future councils.*

I. The frequent holding of general councils is the best method of cultivating the field of the Lord, for they root out the briars, thorns, and thistles of heresies, errors, and schisms, correct abuses, make crooked things straight, and prepare the Lord's vineyard for fruitfulness and rich fertility. Neglect of general councils sows the seeds of these evils and encourages their growth. This truth is borne in upon us as we recall times past and survey the present.

Therefore by perpetual edict we affirm, enact, decree, and ordain that henceforth general councils shall be held as follows: the first within the five years immediately following the end of the present council, the second within seven years from the end of the council next after this, and subsequently every ten years forever, in places which

From "Cardinal Fillastre's Diary of the Council of Constance," in L. R. Loomis, trans., *The Council of Constance* (New York: Columbia University Press, 1961), pp. 407–409, 418; Copyright 1961 Columbia University Press; reprinted by permission of the publisher.

the supreme pontiff a month before the close of the previous council, with the council's approval and consent, shall name or failing him, the council itself shall appoint and designate. Thus there will always be a certain continuity. Either a council will be in session or one will be expected at the end of a fixed period. This period the supreme pontiff, on the advice of his brethren, the cardinals of the Holy Roman Church, may shorten in case of emergency but on no account prolong. Nor may he change the place set for the meeting of the approaching council, except for reasons of obvious necessity.

In case of an emergency, such as siege, war, pestilence, or something similar, when it seems imperative to change the place, then the supreme pontiff, with the signed consent of his said brethren or two thirds of them, may substitute another place near the spot first selected, convenient and inside the same nation, unless the same or a similar calamity affects the whole nation. In that event he may call the council at some near and convenient place inside another nation. The prelates and others who are habitually summoned to a council shall be required to attend just as if that place had been the one fixed upon from the beginning. Any change of place or shortening of period must be legally and formally published and announced by the supreme pontiff a year before the date set for the council, so that members can assemble to hold it at the time he appoints.

II. But if — which Heaven forbid — there should happen to arise a new schism in the future, so that two or more men claim to be supreme pontiffs, from the day when the two or more publicly assume the papal insignia or undertake administration of the office, *ipso jure,* the date of any council then pending, if it be more than a year distant, shall be moved nearer, to within the coming year. And all prelates and others who are bound to attend the council shall assemble even with out a summons, under the penalties set by law and others to be imposed by the council. The emperor also and other kings and princes are henceforward exhorted, by the bowels of mercy of our Lord Jesus Christ, to come either in person or through formal envoys, to help extinguish the general conflagration. . . . [October 9, 1417]

The Council of Constance also specified certain areas where immediate reforms were needed.

The holy synod of Constance enacts and decrees that the future supreme pontiff, soon by God's grace to be appointed, shall, in concert with this sacred Council or deputies to be chosen by the separate nations, before this sacred Council is dissolved, reform the Church in head and Roman Curia to meet the needs of justice and good government in the Church as regards the points comprised in the articles already presented by the nations to the reform commissioners, as follows:

First, number, qualifications and nationality of the lords cardinals

Item, reservations by the Apostolic See.

Item, annates, common and lesser services.

Item, appointments to benefices and expectatives.

Item, cases that must or must not be brought before the Roman Curia.

Item, appeals to the Roman Curia.

Item, offices of chancery and penitentiary.

Item, exemptions and incorporations granted during the Schism.

Item, commendams.

Item, confirmations of elections.

Item, revenues during vacancy.

gainst the alienation of property belonging to the Roman and other Churches.

Item, reasons and methods for correcting or deposing a pope.

Item, abolition of simony.

Item, dispensations.

Item, revenues for pope and cardinals.

Item, indulgences.

Item, tithes.

With this provision, that when the nations have chosen their deputies as aforesaid, the rest may with the Pope's permission return in freedom to their homes. . . . [October 30, 1417]

The Conciliarists were unable to carry through the program of reform they had planned. In 1459, after the failure of their movement, Pope Pius II (1458–1464) condemned as "erroneous and detestable" one of the central theses of the Conciliarists—the right of appeal from pope to general council.

The Decree Excecrabilis

The execrable and hitherto unknown abuse has grown up in our day, that certain persons, imbued with the spirit of rebellion, and not from a desire to secure a better judgment, but to escape the punishment of some offence which they have committed, presume to appeal from the pope to a future council, in spite of the fact that the pope is the vicar of Jesus Christ and to him, in the person of St. Peter, the following was said: "Feed my sheep" [John 21:16] and "Whatsoever thou shalt bind on earth shall be bound in heaven" [Matt. 16:18]. Wishing therefore to expel this pestiferous poison from the church of Christ and to care for the salvation of the flock entrusted to us, and to remove every cause of offence from the fold of our Saviour, with the advice and consent of our brothers, the cardinals of the holy Roman church, and of all the prelates, and of those who have been trained in the canon and civil law, who are at our court, and with our own sure knowledge, we condemn all such appeals and prohibit them as erroneous and detestable.

"Excecrabilis," in O. J. Thatcher and E. H. McNeal, trans., *A Source Book for Mediaeval History* (New York: Charles Scribner's, 1905), p. 332.

chapter
XXIX

Late Medieval People

89. Piers Plowman: Peasant Daily Fare

Langland's typical fourteenth-century peasant, Piers Plowman, had a scanty diet—except at harvest time.

"I have no penny," quoth Piers, "Pullets for to buy
Nor neither geese nor piglets, but two green [new] cheeses,
A few curds and cream and an oaten cake
And two loaves of beans and bran to bake for my little ones.
And besides I say by my soul I have no salt bacon,
Nor no little eggs, by Christ, collops for to make.
But I have parsley and leeks and many cabbages,
And besides a cow and a calf and a cart mare
To draw afield my dung the while the drought lasteth.
And by this livelihood we must live till lammas time [August].
And by that I hope to have harvest in my croft.
And then may I prepare the dinner as I dearly like.
All the poor people those peascods fatten.
Beans and baked apples they brought in their laps.
Shalots and chervils and ripe cherries many
And proffered pears these present. . . .
Then poor folk for fear fed hunger eagerly
With great leeks and peas. . . .
By then it came near harvest, New corn came to market.
Then were folk glad and fed hunger with the best,

From William Langland, "Piers Plowman," in W. O. Hassall, ed., *How they Lived* (Oxford: Basil Blackwell, 1962), pp. 148-149.

With good ale as Glutton taught and got hunger to sleep.
And when wasters wouldn't work but wander about
Nor no beggar eat bread that beans within were
But two sorts of fine white or else of clean wheat
Nor no halfpenny ale in nowise drink,
But of the best and the brownest that in town is to sell,
Labourers that have no land to live on, only their hands,
Deigned not to dine each day on herbs not fresh gathered,
Have no penny-ale given them, nor no piece of bacon,
But if it be fresh flesh or fish, fired or baked,
And that warm or hot to avoid chilling their bellies."

90.   In Praise of Merchants

An Italian merchant wrote this account of his calling in 1458.

The dignity and office of merchants is great and exalted in many respects, and most particularly in four. First, with respect to the common weal. For the advancement of public welfare is a very honorable [purpose], as Cicero states, and one ought [to be willing] even to die [for it]. . . . The advancement, the comfort, and the health of republics to a large extent proceed from merchants; we are always speaking, of course, not of plebeian and vulgar merchants but of the glorious merchant of whom we treat [and who is] lauded in this work of ours. And with respect to mercantile business and activity [we may say] this: Through trade, that ornament and advancement [of republics], sterile countries are provided with food and supplies and also enjoy many strange things which are imported from places where [other] commodities are lacking. [Merchants] also bring about an abundance of money, jewels, gold, silver, and all kinds of metals. They bring about an abundance of gilds of various crafts. Hence, cities and countries are driven to cultivate the land, to enlarge the herds, and to exploit the incomes and rents. And [merchants] through their activity enable the poor to live; through their initiative in tax farming they promote the activity of administrators; through their exports and imports of merchandise they cause the customs and excises of the lords and republics to expand, and consequently they enlarge the public and common treasury.

Secondly, I exalt the dignity and office of merchants with respect to the useful and honorable management of their private properties and

From R. S. Lopez and I. W. Raymond, *Medieval Trade in the Mediterranean World.* Records of Civilization, LII. (New York: Columbia University Press, 1955), pp. 416–418. Reprinted by permission.

goods. As a matter of fact, a sparing, temperate, solid, and upright merchant increases and augments his wealth. This is why we observe that merchants abound in movable and immovable property, in the wealth of their homes and furniture, in the ornaments and clothing of their families, in the dowering of their sons and daughters, and consequently in the continuous improvement of their condition through intermarriage with ever higher [families]. . . .

Third, the dignity of merchants is to be esteemed and appreciated with respect to association, both private and public. Private [association] means at home, where [the merchant] associates with an honorable family in continuous and virtuous activity. For you have to consider that where silver, gold, money, and other things of similar value are handled, there is no room for rogues, retainers, henchmen of all sorts, partisans, thieves, runaways, and gamblers such as are wont to live at the courts of princes, magnates, and lords. . . . Outside their homes, merchants associate with artisans, gentlemen, lords, princes and prelates of every rank, all of whom flock [to see] the merchants since they always need them. And very frequently great scholars come to visit merchants in their homes. . . . For no professional [man] understands or has ever understood the monarchies of this world and the states in regard to management of money—upon which all human states depend—as does a good and learned merchant. . . .

We have left for the fourth [place] the dignity of merchants with respect to [good] faith. . . . Neither kings nor princes nor any [other] rank of men enjoy as much reputation or credit as a good merchant. Hence, a merchant's [reputation and credit] serve him readily for cash, while those of others do not: and if they [i.e. the credit and reputation of others] are given in payment, they carry a much higher interest [charge than the merchants']. And whereas a simple and plain receipt of a merchant is valid even without witnesses, the rulers and any other people are not believed without an instrument and strong cautions. Hence, and for the reasons [already] given, merchants ought to take pride in their outstanding dignity.

91.   Ideal Marriage

This description of an ideal wife—from a husband's point of view—was written by an old merchant of Paris for his young wife.

Fair sister, if you have another husband after me, know that you should think much of his comfort, for after a woman has lost her first

From "Le Menagier de Paris," Eileen Power, trans., in *Medieval People* (London: Methuen and Co., 1963), pp. 105-107. Reprinted by permission.

husband she commonly finds it difficult to find another according to her estate, and she remains lonely and disconsolate for a long time; and more so still, if she lose the second. Wherefore cherish the person of your husband carefully, and, I pray you, keep him in clean linen, for 'tis your business. And because the care of outside affairs lieth with men, so must a husband take heed, and go and come and journey hither and thither, in rain and wind, in snow and hail, now drenched, now dry, now sweating, now shivering, ill-fed, ill-lodged, ill-warmed, ill-bedded; and nothing harms him, because he is upheld by the hope that he has of his wife's care of him on his return, and of the ease, the joys and the pleasures which she will do to him, or cause to be done to him in her presence; to have his shoes removed before a good fire, his feet washed and to have fresh shoes and stockings, to be given good food and drink, to be well served and well looked after, well bedded in white sheets and night-caps, well covered with good furs, and assuaged with other joys and amusements, privities, loves, and secrets, concerning which I am silent; and on the next day fresh shirts and garments. Certes, fair sister, such service maketh a man love and desire to return to his home and to see his goodwife and to be distant with other women.

And therefore I counsel you to make such cheer to your husband at all his comings and goings and to persevere therein; and also to be peaceable with him and remember the rustic proverb, which saith that there be three things which drive the goodman from home, to wit, a dripping roof, a smoking chimney and a scolding woman. Wherefore, fair sister, I pray you that in order to keep yourself in love and good favour with your husband you be unto him gentle, amiable and debonair.

Do unto him what the good simple women of our country say has been done unto their sons, when the lads have set their love elsewhere and their mothers cannot wean them from it. It is certain that when fathers and mothers be dead, and stepfathers and stepmothers argue with their stepsons, and scold them and repulse them, and take not thought for their sleeping, nor for their food and drink, their hose and their shirts and all their other needs and affairs, and the same children find elsewhere a good home and good counsel from some other woman, who receives them and takes thought to warm them with some poor gruel with her and to give them a bed and keep them tidy, mending their hosen, breeches, shirts, and other garments, then those lads cleave to her and desire to be with her, and to sleep warm between her breasts, and are altogether estranged from their mothers and fathers, who before took no heed of them, and now want to get them back and have them again. But it may not be, for these children hold more dear the company of strangers, who think and care for them, than that of their kinsfolk, who have no care of them. Then the parents lament and weep and say that these same women have bewitched their children and that they are spellbound and cannot leave, but are never easy save when they are with their enchantresses. But whatever may be said of it, it is not witchcraft, but it by reason of the love, the care, the intimacies, joys and pleasures, which these women do in all ways unto the lads, and on my soul there is no other enchantment. . . .

Wherefore, dear sister, I pray you thus to bewitch and bewitch again your husband, and beware of dripping roof and smoking fire, and scold him not, but be unto him gentle and amiable and peaceable. Be careful that in winter he has good fire without smoke, and let him rest well and be well covered between your breasts and thus bewitch him. . . . And thus you shall preserve and guard him from all discomforts and give him all the ease that you can, and serve him and cause him to be well served in your house; and you shall look to him for outside things, for if he be a good man he will take even more care and trouble over them than you wish, and by doing as I have said, you will make him always miss you and have his heart with you and with your loving service, and he will shun all other houses, all other women, all other services and households; all will be naught to him save you alone, if you think of him as aforesaid. . . . And so on the road, husbands will think of their wives, and no trouble will be a burden to them for the hope and love they will have of their wives, whom they will long to see, even as poor hermits, penitents and fasting monks long to see the face of Christ Jesus; and husbands served thus will never desire to abide elsewhere or in other company but will withhold, withdraw and abstain themselves there-from; all the rest will seem to them but a bed of stones compared with their homes.

92.   *Chaucer's People*

The richest pageant of late medieval people is presented in Chaucer's description of his Canterbury pilgrims.

Whan that Aprille with his shoures sote
The droght of Marche hath perced to the rote

When the sweet showers of April fall and shoot
Down through the drought of March to pierce
    the root,
Bathing every vein in liquid power
From which there springs the engendering of the flower,
When also Zephyrus with his sweet breath
Exhales an air in every grove and heath
Upon the tender shoots, and the young sun
His half-course in the sign of the *Ram* has run,

From Chaucer, *The Canterbury Tales,* N. Coghill, trans. (Baltimore, Md.: Penguin Books, 1952), pp. 25–33, 38–39.

And the small fowl are making melody
That sleep away the night with open eye
(So nature pricks them and their heart engages)
Then people long to go on pilgrimages
And palmers long to seek the stranger strands
Of far-off saints, hallowed in sundry lands,
And specially, from every shire's end
In England, down to Canterbury they wend
To seek the holy blissful martyr, quick
In giving help to them when they were sick.
  It happened in that season that one day
In Southwark, at *The Tabard,* as I lay
Ready to go on pilgrimage and start
For Canterbury, most devout at heart,
At night there came into that hostelry
Some nine and twenty in a company
Of sundry folk happening then to fall
In fellowship, and they were pilgrims all
That towards Canterbury meant to ride.
The rooms and stables of the inn were wide,
They made us easy, all was of the best.
And shortly, when the sun had gone to rest,
By speaking to them all upon the trip
I was admitted to their fellowship
And promised to rise early and take the way
To Canterbury, as you heard me say.
  But none the less, while I have time and space,
Before my story takes a further pace,
It seems a reasonable thing to say
What their condition was, the full array
Of each of them, as it appeared to me.
According to profession and degree,
And what apparel they were riding in;
And at a Knight I therefore will begin.
  There was a *Knight,* a most distinguished man,
Who from the day on which he first began
To ride abroad had followed chivalry,
Truth, honor, greatness of heart and courtesy.
He had done nobly in his sovereign's war
And ridden into battle, no man more,
As well in christian as in heathen places,
And ever honored for his noble graces.
  He saw the town of Alexandria fall;
Often, at feasts, the highest place of all
Among the nations fell to him in Prussia.
In Lithuania he had fought, and Russia,

No christian man so often, of his rank.
And he was in Granada when they sank
The town of Algeciras, also in
North Africa, right through Benamarin:
And in Armenia he had been as well
And fought when Ayas and Attalia fell,
For all along the Mediterranean coast
He had embarked with many a noble host.
In fifteen mortal battles he had been
And jousted for our faith at Tramissene
Thrice in the lists, and always killed his man.
This same distinguished knight had led the van
Once with the Bey of Balat, doing work
For him against another heathen Turk;
He was of sovereign value in all eyes.
And though so much distinguished, he was wise
And in his bearing modest as a maid.
He never yet a boorish thing had said
In all his life to any, come what might;
He was a true, a perfect gentle-knight.

Speaking of his appearance, he possessed
Fine horses, but he was not gaily dressed.
He wore a fustian tunic stained and dark
With smudges where his armor had left mark;
Just home from service, he had joined our ranks
To do his pilgrimage and render thanks.

He had his son with him, a fine young *Squire,*
A lover and cadet, a lad of fire
With curly locks, as if they had been pressed.
He was some twenty years of age, I guessed.
In stature he was of a moderate length,
With wonderful agility and strength.
He'd seen some service with the cavalry
In Flanders and Artois and Picardy
And had done valiantly in little space
Of time, in hope to win his lady's grace.
He was embroidered like a meadow bright
And full of freshest flowers, red and white.

Singing he was, or fluting all the day;
He was as fresh as is the month of May.
Short was his gown, the sleeves were long and wide;
He knew the way to sit a horse and ride.
He could make songs and poems and recite,
Knew how to joust and dance, to draw and write.
He loved so hotly that till dawn grew pale
He slept as little as a nightingale.

Courteous he was, lowly and serviceable.
And carved to serve his father at the table
   There was a *Yeoman* with him at his side,
No other servant; so he chose to ride.
This Yeoman wore a coat and hood of green,
And peacock-feathered arrows, bright and keen
And neatly sheathed, hung at his belt the while
—For he could dress his gear in yeoman style,
His arrows never drooped their feathers low—
And in his hand he bore a mighty bow.
His head was like a nut, his face was brown.
He knew the whole of woodcraft up and down.
A saucy brace was on his arm to ward
It from the bow-string, and a shield and sword
Hung at one side, and at the other slipped
A jaunty dirk, spear-sharp and well-equipped.
A medal of St. Christopher he wore
Of shining silver on his breast, and bore
A hunting-horn, well slung and burnished clean,
That dangled from a baldrick of bright green.
He was a proper forester I guess.
   There also was a *Nun,* a Prioress;
Simple her way of smiling was and coy.
Her greatest oath was only 'By St Loy!!'
And she was known as Madam Eglantyne.
And well she sang a service, with a fine
Intoning through her nose, as was most seemly,
And she spoke daintily in French, extremely,
After the school of Stratford-atte-Bowe;
French in the Paris style she did not know.
At meat her manners were well taught withal;
No morsel from her lips did she let fall,
Nor dipped her fingers in the sauce too deep;
But she could carry a morsel up and keep
The smallest drop from falling on her breast.
For courtliness she had a special zest.
And she would wipe her upper lip so clean
That not a trace of grease was to be seen
Upon the cup when she had drunk; to eat,
She reached a hand sedately for the meat.
She certainly was very entertaining,
Pleasant and friendly in her ways, and straining
To counterfeit a courtly kind of grace,
A stately bearing fitting to her place,
And to seem dignified in all her dealings.
As for her sympathies and tender feelings,

She was so charitably solicitous
She use to weep if she saw a mouse
Caught in a trap, if it were dead or bleeding.
And she had little dogs she would be feeding
With roasted flesh, or milk, or fine white bread.
Sorely she wept if one of them were dead
Or someone took a stick and made it smart;
She was all sentiment and tender heart.
Her veil was gathered in a seemly way,
Her nose was elegant, her eyes glass-gray;
Her mouth was very small, but soft and red,
And certainly she had a well-shaped head,
Almost a span across the brows, I own;
She was indeed by no means undergrown.
Her cloak, I noticed, had a graceful charm.
She wore a coral trinket on her arm,
A set of beads, the gaudies tricked in green,
Whence hung a golden brooch of brighest sheen
On which there first was graven a crowned A,
and lower, *Amor vincit omnia.*
    Another *Nun,* the chaplain at her cell,
Was riding with her, and *three Priests* as well.
    There was a *Monk,* a leader of the fashions;
Inspecting farms and hunting were his passions,
A manly man, to be an Abbot able,
Many the dainty horses in his stable;
His bridle, when he rode, a man might hear
Jingling in a whistling wind as clear,
Aye, and as loud as does the chapel bell
Where my lord Monk was Prior of the cell.
The Rule of good St Benet or St Maur
As old and strict he tended to ignore;
He let go by the things of yesterday
And followed the new world's more spacious way.
He did not rate that text at a plucked hen
Which says that hunters are not holy men
And that a monk uncloistered is a mere
Fish out of water, flapping on the pier,
That is to say a monk out of his cloister.
That was a text he held not worth an oyster;
And I said I agreed with his opinion;
What! Study until reason lost dominion
Poring on books in cloisters? Must he toil
As Austin bade and till the very soil?
Was he to leave the world upon the shelf?
Let Austin have his labor to himself.

This Monk was therefore a good man to horse;
Greyhounds he had, as swift as birds, to course.
Hunting a hare or riding at a fence
Was all his fun, he spared for no expense.
I saw his sleeves were garnished at the hand
With fine gray fur, the finest in the land,
And where his hood was fastened at his chin
He had a wrought-gold cunningly fashioned pin,
Into a lover's knot it seemed to pass.
His head was bald and shone as any glass,
So did his face, as if it had been greased.
He was a fat and personable priest;
His bright eyes rolled, they never seemed to settle,
And glittered like the flames beneath a kettle;
Supple his boots, his horse in fine condition.
He was a prelate fit for exhibition,
He was not pale like a tormented soul.
He liked a fat swan best, and roasted whole.
His palfrey was as brown as is a berry.
    There was a *Friar,* a wanton one and merry,
A Limiter, a very festive fellow.
In all Four Orders there was none so mellow
As he in flattery and dalliant speech.
He'd fixed up many a marriage, giving each
Of his young women what he could afford her.
He was a noble pillar to his Order.
Highly beloved and intimate was he
With Country folk wherever he might be,
And worthy city women with possessions;
For he was qualified to hear confessions;
Or so he said, with more than priestly scope;
He had a special license from the Pope.
Sweetly he heard his penitents at shrift
With pleasant absolution, for a gift.
He was an easy man in penance-giving
Where he could hope to make a decent living;
It's a sure sign whenever gifts are given
To a poor Order that a man's well shriven,
And should he give enough he knew in verity
The penitent repented in sincerity.
For many a fellow is so hard of heart
He cannot weep, for all his inward smart.
Therefore instead of weeping and of prayer
One should give silver for a poor Friar's care.
He kept his tippet stuffed with pins for curls,
And pocket-knives to give to pretty girls.

And certainly his voice was gay and sturdy,
For he sang well and played the hurdy-gurdy.
At sing-songs he was champion of the hour.
His neck was whiter than a lily-flower
But strong enough to butt a bruiser down.
He knew the taverns well in every town
And every innkeeper and barmaid too
Better than lepers, beggars and that crew,
For in so eminent a man as he
It was not fitting with the dignity
Of his position dealing with such scum.
It isn't decent, nothing good can come
Of having truck with slum-and-gutter dwellers,
But only with the rich and victual-sellers.
But anywhere a profit might accrue
Courteous he was and lowly of service too.
Natural gifts like his were hard to match.
He was the finest beggar of his batch,
And, for his begging-district, payed a rent;
His brethren did no poaching where he went.
For though a widow mightn't have a shoe,
So pleasant was his holy how-d' ye-do
He got his farthing from her just the same
Before he left, and so his income came
To more than he laid out. And how he romped,
Just like a puppy! He was ever prompt
To arbitrate disputes on settling days
(For a small fee) in many helpful ways,
Not then appearing as your cloistered scholar
With threadbare habit hardly worth a dollar,
But much more a like a Doctor or a Pope.
Of double-worsted was the semi-cope
Upon his shoulders, and the swelling fold
About him, like a bell about its mold
When it is casting, rounded out his dress.
He lisped a little out of wantonness
To make his English sweet upon his tongue.
When he played his harp, or having sung,
His eyes would twinkle in his head as bright
As any star upon a frosty night.
This worthy's name was Hubert, it appeared.
  There was a *Merchant* with a forking beard
And motley dress; high on his horse he sat,
Upon his head a Flemish beaver hat
And on his feet daintily buckled boots.
He told of his opinions and pursuits

In solemn tones, and how he never lost.
The sea should be kept free at any cost
(He thought) upon the Harwich-Holland ranges.
He was expert at dabbling in exchanges.
This estimable Merchant so had set
His wits to work, none knew he was in debt,
He was so stately in negotiation,
Loan, bargain and commercial obligation.
He was an excellent fellow all the same;
To tell the truth I do not know his name.

    There was an *Oxford Cleric* too, a student,
Long given to Logic, longer than was prudent;
The horse he had was leaner than a rake,
And he was not too fat, I undertake,
But had a hollow look, a sober air;
The thread upon his overcoat was bare.
He had found no preferment in the church
And he was too unworldly to make search.
He thought far more of having by his bed
His twenty books all bound in black and red,
Of Aristotle and philosophy
Than of gay music, fiddles or finery.
Though a philosopher, as I have told,
He had not found the stone for making gold.
Whatever money from his friends he took
He spent on learning or another book
And prayed for them most earnestly, returning
Thanks to them thus for paying for his learning.
His only care was study, and indeed
He never spoke a word more than was need,
Formal at that, respectful in the extreme,
Short, to the point, and lofty in his theme.
The thought of moral virture filled his speech
And he would gladly learn, and gladly teach.

• • •

    A holy-minded man of good renown
There was, and poor, the *Parson* to a town,
Yet he was rich in holy thought and work.
He also was a learned man, a clerk,
Who truly knew Christ's gospel and would preach it
Devoutly to parishioners, and teach it.
Benign and wonderfully diligent,
And patient when adversity was sent
(For so he proved in great adversity)
He much disliked extorting tithe or fee,
Nay rather he preferred beyond a doubt

Giving to poor parishioners round about
From his own goods and Easter offerings.
He found sufficiency in little things.
Wide was his parish, with houses far asunder,
Yet he neglected not in rain or thunder,
In sickness or in grief, to pay a call
On the remotest whether great or small
Upon his feet, and in his hand a stave.
This noble example to his sheep he gave,
First following the word before he taught it,
And it was from the gospel he had caught it
This little proverb he would add thereto
That if gold rust, what then will iron do?
For if a priest be foul in whom we trust
No wonder that a common man should rust;
And shame it is to see—let priests take stock—
A shitten shepherd and a snowy flock.
The true example that a priest should give
Is one of cleanness, how the sheep should live.
He did not set his benefice to hire
And leave his sheep encumbered in the mire
Or run to London to earn easy bread
By singing masses for the wealthy dead,
Or find some Brotherhood and get enrolled.
He stayed at home and watched over his fold
So that no wolf should make the sheep miscarry.
He was a shepherd and no mercenary.
Holy and virtuous he was, but then
Never contemptuous of sinful men,
Never disdainful, never too proud or fine,
But was discreet in teaching and benign.
His business was to show a fair behavior
And draw men thus to Heaven and their Saviour,
Unless indeed a man were obstinate;
And such, whether of high or low estate,
He put to sharp rebuke to say the least.
   I think there never was a better priest.
He sought no pomp or glory in his dealings,
No scrupulosity had spiced his feelings.
Christ and His Twelve Apostles and their lore
He taught, but followed it himself before.

chapter
XXX

Epilogue

---

93. François Villon: Laughter and Tears

The poems of François Villon (ca. 1431–after 1463) illustrate the sharply contradictory moods that seem characteristic of late medieval culture.

Ballade of the Concourse of Blois

Je meurs de seuf auprès de la fontaine

I die of thirst where fountains play,
With chattering teeth, like fire I burn;
In my own land I'm far away;
I shiver near a heated urn;
Nude as a grub, dressed to a turn,
I laugh through tears, despondent, wait;
Take comfort in my hopeless state;
Enjoy myself, and yet am grieved;
Am strong, and lack both strength and weight,
At once rebuffed and well received.

I'm only sure when there is doubt;
I find obscure what's evident;
When I should act: I stand about;
I keep my wits through accident;
I win, and yet am indigent;

From François Villon, *I Laugh Through Tears*, G. P. Cuttino, trans. (New York: Philosophical Library, 1955), pp. 40–41; reprinted by permission of the publisher.

Good Night's my usual morning quip;
Flat on my back, I fear I'll slip;
With plenty of all, of all relieved:
I'm no man's heir, but wait my ship;
At once rebuffed and well received.

With need of little, how I strain
For goods whose price I cannot pay;
Who soothes me adds but to my pain,
And tells the truth but to betray;
He is my friend who fain would say
The swan is of the raven's band;
He hurts me most who lends a hand;
Alike are truth and lies believed;
I know, but do not understand,
At once rebuffed and well received.

ENVOY
Now may it please my clement Prince,
I know more than my wits evince:
Subject to every law conceived.
My wish? The pawn I've pledged long since,
At once rebuffed and well received.

Ballade for Fat Margot

Se j'aime et sers la belle de bon hait
M'en devez vous tenir a vil ne sot?

If I love and serve my lovely lady willingly,
should you therefore think me vile and stupid?

She has all the charms a man could want.
For love her of her I gird on sword and shield;
when people come I run and grab a pot
to go get wine, as quietly as possible;
I serve them water, cheese, bread and fruit.
If they pay me well, I say, "That's good,
and please come back whenever you're in rut,
to this brothel where we ply our trade."

But then bad feelings start to fly
when she comes home without a cent;
I cannot stand her, and feel a deathly hatred

Villon, "Ballade for Fat Margot," in *The Complete Works of François Villon,* edited and translated by Anthony Bonner, p. 107; Copyright © 1960 by Bantam Books, Inc.; all rights reserved.

for her. I grab her dress, her belt and slip,
and swear I'll make them do in place of cash.
Hands on hips, she shouts, "You Antichrist!",
and swears on Jesus' death that I
will not. So then I snatch some club
and with it write a message on her nose,
in this brothel were we ply our trade.

Then we make up in bed, and she, more bloated
than a poisonous dung-hill beetle, farts
and laughs and claps me on the head,
says I'm cute and whacks my thigh.
Then, both drunk, we sleep like logs.
When we awake, her belly starts to quiver
and she mounts me, to spare love's fruit;
I groan, squashed beneath her weight —
this lechery of hers will ruin me,
in this brothel where we ply our trade.

Through wind, hail or frost my living's made.
I am a lecher, and she's a lecher with me.
Which one of us is better? We're both alike:
the one as worthy as the other. Bad rat, bad cat.
We both love filth, and filth pursues us;
we flee from honor, honor flees from us,
in this brothel where we ply our trade.

Ballade to Our Lady
WRITTEN FOR HIS MOTHER

Dame du ciel, regente terrienne,
Emperiere des infernaux palus. . . .

Lady of Heaven and earth, and therewithal
   Crowned Empress of the nether clefts of Hell, —

I, thy poor Christian, on thy name do call,
   Commending me to thee, with thee to dwell,
   Albeit in nought I be commendable.
But all mine undeserving may not mar
Such mercies as thy sovereign mercies are;
   Without the which (as true words testify)
No soul can reach thy Heaven so fair and far.
   Even in this faith I choose to live and die.

From Villon, "Ballade to Our Lady," Dante Gabriel Rossetti, trans., in *Poems* (Boston: Roberts Brothers, 1870), pp. 178–179.

Unto thy Son say thou that I am His,
   And to me graceless make Him gracious.
Sad Mary of Egypt lacked not of that bliss,
   Nor yet the sorrowful clerk Theophilus,
   Whose bitter sins were set aside even thus
Though to the Fiend his bounden service was.
Oh help me, lest in vain for me should pass
   (Sweet Virgin that shalt have no loss thereby!)
The blessed Host and sacring of the Mass
   Even in this faith I choose to live and die.

A pitiful poor woman, shrunk and old,
   I am, and nothing learn'd in letter-lore.
Within my parish-cloister I behold
   A painted Heaven where harps and lutes adore,
   And eke an Hell whose damned folk seethe full sore:
One bringeth fear, the other joy to me.
That joy, great Goddess, make thou mine to be,—
   Thou of whom all must ask it even as I;
And that which faith desires, that let it see.
   For in this faith I choose to live and die.

O excellent Virgin Princess! thou didst bear
   King Jesus, the most excellent comforter,
Who even of this our weakness craved a share
   And for our sake stooped to us from on high,
Offering to death His young life sweet and fair.
Such as He is, Our Lord, I Him declare,
   And in this faith I choose to live and die.

Epitaph in the Form of a Ballade

Frères humains qui après nous vivez,
N'ayez les coeurs contre nous endurcis . . .

Men, brother men, that after us yet live,
   Let not your hearts too hard against us be;
For if some pity of us poor men ye give,
   The sooner God shall take of you pity
   Here are we five or six strung up, you see,
And here the flesh that all too well we fed
Bit by bit eaten and rotten, rent and shred,
   And we the bones grow dust and ash withal;

From Villon, "Epitaph in the Form of a Ballade," Algernon Charles Swinburne trans. in *Poems and Ballads*. Second Series (London: Chatto and Windus, 1891), pp 222-224.

Let no man laugh at us discomforted,
　But pray to God that he forgive us all.

If we call on you, brothers, to forgive,
　Ye should not hold our prayer in scorn, though we
Were slain by law; ye know that all alive
　Have not wit always to walk righteously;
Make therefore intercession heartily
With him that of a virgin's womb was bred,
That his grace be not as a dry well-head
　For us, nor let hell's thunder on us fall;
We are dead, let no man harry or vex us dead,
　But pray to God that he forgive us all.

The rain has washed and laundered us all five,
　And the sun dried and blackened; yea, perdie,
Ravens and pies with beaks that rend and rive
　Have dug our eyes out, and plucked off for fee
　Our beards and eyebrows; never we are free,
Not once, to rest; but here and there still sped,
Driven at its wild will by the wind's change led,
　More pecked of birds than fruits on garden-wall;
Men, for God's love, let no gibe here be said,
　But pray to God that he forgive us all.

Prince Jesus, that of all art lord and head,
Keep us, that hell be not our bitter bed;
　We have nought to do in such a master's hall.
Be not ye therefore of our fellowhead,
　But pray to God that he forgive us all.

About the Author

After serving in the Royal Air Force, Brian Tierney received his B.A. and Ph.D. from Cambridge University. He has taught at Catholic University, Washington, D.C., and at Cornell, where he is now Bryce and Edith M. Bowmar Professor in Humanistic Studies. He has been the recipient of Guggenheim Fellowships and of fellowships from the American Council of Learned Societies and the National Endowment for the Humanities. Professor Tierney has been awarded the honorary degrees of Doctor of Theology by Uppsala University, Sweden, and Doctor of Humane Letters by Catholic University. A specialist in medieval church history, he has published many articles and several books, among them *Foundations of the Conciliar Theory*; *Medieval Poor Law*; and *Origins of Papal Infallibility, 1150–1350*. He is coeditor with Donald Kagan and L. Pearce Williams of *Great Issues in Western Civilization*. His most recent work is *Religion, Law, and the Growth of Constitutional Thought, 1150–1650*.

A NOTE ON THE TYPE

The text of this book has been set on an Editwriter 7500 in a typeface called "Baskerville." The face is a facsimile reproduction of types cast from molds made for John Baskerville (1706–75) from his designs. John Baskerville's original face was one of the forerunners of the type-style known as "modern face" to printers — a "modern" of the period A.D. 1800.